THE
INSTITUTIONAL
INVESTOR

SERIES IN FINANCE

Corporate Restructuring
and
Executive Compensation

The Institutional Investor Series in Finance

Corporate Restructuring and Executive Compensation

EDITED BY

Joel M. Stern
G. Bennett Stewart III
and Donald H. Chew, Jr.

Ballinger Publishing Company

Cambridge, Massachusetts
A Subsidiary of Harper & Row, Publishers, Inc.

International Standard Book Number: 0-88730-374-9

Library of Congress Catalog Card Number: 88-29207

Printed in the United States of America

Library of Congress Cataloging-in-Publication Data

Corporate restructuring and executive compensation / edited by
    Joel M. Stern, G. Bennett Stewart III, and Donald H. Chew, Jr.
        p.   cm. — (The Institutional investor series in finance)
    Includes bibliographies and index.
    ISBN 0-088730-374-9
    1. Corporate reorganizations—United States. 1. Executives—
Salaries, etc.—United States. 3. Consolidation and merger of
corporations—United States. I. Stern, Joel M. II. Stewart, G.
Bennett. III. Chew, Donald H. IV. Series.
HD2746.5.C674 1989
658.1'6—dc19   88-29207
                                                            CIP

Contents

List of Figures

Chapter 17

Chapter 19

Chapter 21

List of Tables

Contributing Authors

Louis J. Brindisi, Jr., American Compensation Systems Inc.
Robert F. Bruner, University of Virginia
Andrew H. Chen, Southern Methodist University
Donald H. Chew, Jr., Stern Stewart & Co.
Harry DeAngelo, University of Michigan
Linda DeAngelo, University of Michigan
Peter Dodd, University of New South Wales
Carl Ferenbach, Berkshire Partners
David M. Glassman, Stern Stewart & Co.
Gailen L. Hite, Columbia University
Clifford G. Holderness, University of Rochester
Michael C. Jensen, Harvard Business School
John W. Kensinger, University of Texas at Austin
Robert T. Kleiman, Babson College
Richard A. Lambert, Northwestern University
David F. Larcker, University of Pennsylvania
Scott C. Linn, University of Iowa
John D. Martin, University of Texas at Austin
James E. Owers, University of Massachusetts
Kevin J. Perry, Baring America Asset Management Co.
Edward M. Rice, University of Washington
Michael S. Rozeff, University of Iowa
Katherine Schipper, University of Chicago
Dennis P. Sheehan, Purdue University
Abbie Smith, University of Chicago
Joel M. Stern, Stern Stewart & Co.
G. Bennett Stewart III, Stern Stewart & Co.
Robert A. Taggart, Jr., Boston University
J. Randall Woolridge, Pennsylvania State University

Introduction:
The Role of Management Incentives in Corporate Restructuring

Donald H. Chew, Jr.
Stern Stewart & Co.

In the 1980s we have seen an unprecedented wave of transactions that, for want of a better name, we are calling "reverse mergers." The increasing number and size of corporate divestitures, spin-offs, split-ups, buybacks, ESOPs, partial public offerings, limited partnerships, and leveraged buyouts—all of which have been yoked together under the name of "corporate restructuring"—are bringing about striking changes in the product mix and organizational structure of American corporations. Casual observation, together with considerable academic research, suggests that the stock market is strongly endorsing such changes. And if the market is right, we may well be witnessing a new phase in the evolution of the public corporation into a more efficient vehicle for building stockholder wealth. The market's endorsement of this widespread restructuring also suggests that some forms of corporate organization—most notably, the large conglomerate—are now under serious challenge from increasingly activist investors, and are perhaps even in the earliest stages of obsolescence.

Corporate restructuring is primarily a movement of large (or at least mature) companies, whose core businesses are generating large amounts of operating cash flow while offering few promising investment opportunities. The principal problem faced by the management of such companies has been what to do with excess capital. In the past, especially in the 1970s and early 1980s, the typical management response was either to continue to make large-scale investment in declining core businesses or, if prospects became too grim, to diversify through acquisition into new businesses.

The restructuring movement of the 1980s can be seen largely as a response to the failure of these older solutions to the problem of too much corporate capital chasing too few good investment opportunities. In place of indiscriminate reinvestment and baseless diversification, the current restructuring wave has substituted the unprecedented use of corporate leverage to focus management's attention on its core businesses through (1) dramatic recapitalizations of no- or slow-growth businesses (through LBOs, ESOPs, limited partnerships, or large stock buybacks); (2) highly leveraged consolidating acquisitions in industries with excess capacity; and (3) sales or spin-offs of unrelated businesses. The pressure to produce operating cash flow exerted by large amounts of debt, combined with greater concentrations of equity ownership by management, is leading to dramatic improvements in managerial accountability and incentives—and, as a result, in the competitive strength of U.S. corporations.

Strong pressures from capital markets, including of course the actions of "corporate raiders," are also bringing about new organizational alternatives to the public corporation: leveraged buyouts, ESOPs, royalty trusts, and limited partnerships of all varieties (R&D, manufacturing, marketing). What these relatively new organizational forms have in common is their restriction of management's principal role to the supervision of operations; in all of these new forms, investors effectively retain control of strategic decisions to reinvest operating cash flow.

The rising popularity of these new organizational forms means that the once dominant model of the large public corporation as a self-financing, self-perpetuating portfolio of businesses at different points in the growth cycle (a model promoted by the Boston Consulting Group and others) is now giving way to the idea of self-sustaining and, in some cases, self-liquidating ventures—in effect, the triumph of project finance. Such new forms, at any rate, are expected to provide increasingly activist institutional investors and portfolio managers with much greater say in strategic business decisions now entrusted to corporate management.

While this general market pressure to return excess capital to investors is causing many Fortune 500 companies to shrink, much of the relased capital is finding its way into small, start-up ventures and medium-sized growth companies. This massive recycling of capital from the moribund to the vital can be seen as part of a general "downsizing process," in which many traditional corporate functions are now being performed as parts of smaller, independent firms and tax-advantaged partnerships. Corporate America has become the site, in effect, of an ongoing market test weighing the conventional benefits of scale economies and access to public capital markets against what increasingly appear to be the inefficiencies of large, especially conglomerate, organizations.

The extraordinary number and size of divestitures, for example, suggests a rolling back of the conglomerate merger wave of the 1960s and 1970s. Once popular corporate diversification programs are being reconsidered generally and, in many cases, completely reversed. The primary consequence of such diversification, it now seems clear, has been to provide management with greater job security and control over corporate resources—largely at the expense of its stockholders. With the rise of junk bonds and large leveraged takeovers, the sheer size of conglomerates is proving much less a deterrent to acquirers, who are realizing large profits from taking over and then simply dismantling them. At the same time, in response to these new developments in capital markets, the emphasis of strategic planning has fallen increasingly on sharpening corporate "focus" by identifying a company's strengths or comparative advantages, and by eliminating those businesses that do not offer a good strategic "fit."

Such a shift in strategic thinking has thus by no means put an end to merger activity. In fact, there has also been a large merger wave in the 1980s. But, with the exception of a few very large, highly publicized, diversifying takeovers, which have been uniformly received with unmistakable market disapproval (the Eastman Kodak purchase of Sterling Drug is the most recent notable example), the majority of acquisitions appear to have been prompted by some prospect of real business synergies. With the relaxation of anti-trust enforcement by the Reagan administration, there have also been a large number of consolidating takeovers in industries with excess capacity, such as oil and gas, mining, packaging, forest products, broadcasting, and financial services. And, besides consolidating "horizontal" acquisitions, we are also seeing takeovers by very aggressive individual investors known as "raiders" (although they might, with more propriety, be described as stockholder benefactors) whose primary purpose is often to dismember inefficient conglomerates. The case of Beatrice Foods is perhaps the most dramatic example.

The growing number of divestitures points, then, to a general corporate trend toward more streamlined, decentralized, entrepreneurial organizations. Perhaps more direct evidence of the expected benefits from this movement, however, is the recent popularity of spin-offs and split-ups of unrelated businesses into largely autonomous, self-trading units. Such transactions, which simply divide a corporation into a number of separate firms with no change in stockholders' proportional ownership, suggest that a

> new kind of arithmetic has come into play. Whereas corporate management once seemed to behave as if $2 + 2$ were equal to 5, especially during the conglomerate heyday of the 60s, the wave of reverse mergers seems based on the counter proposition that $5 - 1$ is 5. And . . . the market's consistently positive response to such deals seems to be providing broad confirmation of this 'new math.'[1]

Many observers have argued that spin-offs and partial public offerings (also known as "partial spin-offs") increase stock values by enabling analysts properly to evaluate divisions buried within a conglomerate structure. However, as argued by Professors Katherine Schipper and Abbie Smith of the University of Chicago,

> In a sophisticated market, with its incentives to identify undervalued companies, there are enough analysts adept at untangling consolidated financial statements

---

1. See Chapter 4 of this book, "The Restructuring of Corporate America: An Overview," by Gailen L. Hite and James E. Owers.

to ensure that conglomerates will trade at fair value. We shouldn't expect diversified companies to sell consistently below a value which reflects the sum of the values of their component businesses *simply* because the market is incapable of understanding them.

There may indeed by a systematic investor preference for "pure plays." But such a preference, we suspect, reflects less the inability of analysts to comprehend conglomerates than the market's skepticism about the quality of management decision-making, controls and incentives in large, sprawling organizations. . . . If there are management inefficiencies that result from the conglomerate form *per se*, then the market may assign systematically higher prices to the parts when separated rather than combined.[2]

As the authors go on to say, the market's consistently positive response to the announcements of spin-offs—and to partial spin-offs (public offerings of subsidiaries) as well—is more likely to be based on expected improvements in managerial accountability and incentives from separating unrelated business units than on market incomprehension. Both spin-offs and partial public offerings are likely to achieve dramatic improvements in managerial incentives by providing operating management with greater autonomy, market recognition, and financial rewards (including stock options tied to the profitability of their own business) than was possible within a conglomerate structure.

I. Agency Cost Theory: The Consequences of Separating Ownership from Control

Perhaps the most remarkable development in recent years, however, is the growing number and size of companies going private through leveraged buyouts. Management's willingness to pay 50 percent premiums and more to buy out the public equity of multibillion dollar corporations raises two important questions: What are the expected benefits to going private? Further, what do such management buyouts suggest about the efficiency of the public corporation as a form of business organization?

Recent advances in finance theory—most notably, Michael Jensen and William Meckling's formulation of "agency cost" theory—have drawn attention to the potential loss in value of public corporations caused by the divergence of interest between management and its stockholders. Most finance scholars, including Jensen and Meckling, began by arguing that the agency costs of separating ownership from control could not be very great for several reasons: competition from international product and factor markets and the existence of a market for executive labor should all serve to limit the natural tendency of corporate managements to pursue their own interests at the expense of their stockholders, and management incentive compensation plans are presumably designed to mitigate this potential conflict of interest.

---

2. See Chapter 9 of this book, "The Corporate Spin-Off Phenomenon," by Katherine Schipper and Abbie Smith.

If all of these fail to join managerial and stockholder interests, then a vigorously operating takeover market (or, in academic parlance, the "market for corporate control") should prevent self-serving managers from entrenching themselves at the expense of their stockholders.

But the recent proliferation of leveraged buyouts seems to be saying quite clearly that the agency costs of outside equity ownership—and thus the benefits from uniting managerial and investor interests by eliminating outside stockholders—are far greater than finance scholars once suspected. The popularity of going private no doubt reflects, in large part, the significant tax and regulatory burden imposed on the public corporation. But it also strongly suggests that management committees of public corporations could be doing far more to strengthen management incentives to perform—or that the political and legal impediments to adopting more effective management compensation schemes in public corporations are very great. For, besides providing significant stock ownership for a number of key managers, leveraged buyouts often strengthen managerial incentives by designing compensation agreements that tie management bonuses more closely to increases in a company's profitability (often measured in terms of cash flow rather than accounting earnings).

Greater leverage, and the resulting tax benefits, play a major role in the success story of LBOs. But the use of large amounts of debt may have a more important function: namely, it provides the means of achieving the desired concentration of ownership among a small group of equity participants, and this concentration of ownership makes the LBO a superior alternative to the public corporation (at least for companies that do not require access to capital markets in the near term). The LBO substitutes intensive monitoring of management by sophisticated leveraged buyout specialists for the considerably less vigilant attentions of a diffuse body of stockholders in the public corporation.

The success of the LBO begs the question: What of our public companies? Are there means of incorporating the incentives benefits of LBOs *within* the existing form of the public corporation?

Besides the spin-offs and partial initial public offerings (IPOs) mentioned earlier, the corporate restructuring movement has also produced two relatively new variants of the LBO structure that have been accommodated within the structure of the public corporation: (1) the large leveraged recapitalization (known as the "leveraged cash-out") and (2) the leveraged equity purchase plan. Leveraged cashouts (or "public LBOs" as they are sometimes called) are remarkable recapitalizations in which mangement borrows a sum larger than the book value of the firm and pays it out as a special dividend (typically about equal to its current stock price) only to outside stockholders, thus significantly increasing its own proportional equity ownership. In leveraged equity purchase plans (as designed and introduced by Michael Dingman of the Henley Group), operating management purchases a significant fraction (generally 10 percent) of its company's stock. This purchase is financed by borrowings (typically 90 percent of the purchase price) from the company itself. Both of these innovations combine leverage and managerial equity ownership to produce dramatic improvements in operating results. In so doing, they have restored declining corporate enterprises ("Dingman's dogs" was the name given the collection of companies in the Henley Group) to profitability and held out the promise of renewal for mature public companies.

II. About This Book

Corporate Restructuring and Executive Compensation is a collection of twenty-one articles, all of which were published previously in either the *Midland Corporate Finance Journal* (which came to an end in 1987) or the new *Continental Bank Journal of Applied Corporate Finance*. The aim of the *Continental Bank Journal* is to translate outstanding academic research in finance into a form accessible to practicing corporate executives. As such, the chapters in this book reflect our efforts to achieve an ideal balance between theoretical rigor and applicability, analytical precision and compact clarity.

The twenty-one chapters have been organized into three separate sections, which form a natural and, to us, inevitable progression that starts with a brief review of recent developments in the takeover market, dwells at length on corporate restructuring transactions, and then closes with a look at the current state of executive compensation in the public corporation (and how it may be contributing significantly to the current restructuring wave).

Part I: An Overview of The Market for Corporate Control

The first section features two ambitious surveys by Professors Michael Jensen and Peter Dodd, both of which demonstrate the benefits of a well- and freely-functioning takeover market to stockholders and the economy at large. As both chapters suggest, however, corporate takeovers are generating intense controversy, and mounting managerial and political resistance are impairing the efficient operation of this market. Moreover, as Dodd suggests, a disturbing percentage of takeovers in the late 1970s and early 1980s have resulted in significant market losses for acquiring companies' stockholders (especially in the case of large acquirers of unrelated businesses), thus reinforcing the rationale for dismantling conglomerates.

Jensen's chapter uses his relatively new "Free Cash Flow" theory of takeovers to produce a remarkably ambitious and coherent explanation of the current restructuring wave. His argument leads to conclusions like the following:

1. Mergers in a wide range of mature or shrinking industries—most notably oil and gas, but also forest products, minerals, tobacco, broadcasting, food processing, and financial services—are reducing waste and curbing unprofitable reinvestment, thereby creating stockholder value and promoting the national economic interest;

2. The use of large amounts of debt to finance acquisitions, leveraged buyouts, and large stock buybacks is increasing corporate efficiency;

3. Junk bonds, besides providing a valuable investment alternative to conventional lending for S&Ls, hold out the promise of much larger stockholder gains by removing size as a deterrent to takeover;

4. The stock market, contrary to the frequent claims of management and the financial press, is quite capable of taking the long view in assessing corporate performance, even though management often does not (which is also the thesis of an entire chapter in this book);

5. The capital markets are bringing about the dismemberment of inefficient conglomerates through takeovers, divestitures, spin-offs, and LBOs;

6. Golden parachutes, when properly structured, are unifying management and stockholder interests;

7. The practice of greenmail should, and can quite easily, be prevented by corporate boards; and

8. Court decisions to uphold poison pills, as well as Unocal's exclusionary self-tender, threaten to undermine the contractual agreement that is at the heart of the corporate form of organization.

The third and final chapter in the introductory section presents the findings of what, to our knowledge, is the first and only systematic attempt to measure the stockholder consequences of corporate raiders. In this study, Professors Cliff Holderness and Dennis Sheehan examine the effects of the actions of well-known raiders (including Carl Icahn, Victor Posner, Irwin Jacobs, Carl Lindner, and David Murdock) on the stock market performance of raided companies. Unlike most academic event studies, this one examines market movements not only at the time of initial announcements of raiders' acquired interests but also over a two-year period thereafter.

Part II: Corporate Restructuring

The second section of the book consists of thirteen chapters devoted largely to the corporate motives and stockholder consequences of a variety of specific restructuring transactions. These chapters concentrate exclusively on (1) divestitures (or "sell-offs"), (2) spin-offs, (3) partial public offerings (or "equity carve-outs"), (4) management buyouts, (5) ESOPs, (6) leveraged cash-outs, and (7) limited partnerships. Radical improvements in managerial focus, accountability, and incentives, as suggested throughout this introduction, are seen as playing a critical—if not indeed the leading—role in all of these transactions.

Also included in the second section is a provocative overview of the restructuring movement, entitled "Royalty Trusts, Master Partnerships, and Other Organizational Means of 'Unfirming' the Firm." In this chapter, Professors John Martin and John Kensinger push Jensen's Free Cash Flow theory, with interesting effect, to its reductio ad absurdum: the rise of new organizational alternatives such as LBOs and limited partnerships culminating in the end of the public corporation as the dominant form of American business.

Part III: Executive Compensation

In response to this threat to the durability of the public corporation from the rift between ownership and control, the third and final section of the book is devoted to the search for more effective ways of unifying management and stockholder interests *while preserving* the form of the public corporation. The section consists of five chapters on incentive compensation contributed by two leading academics in the compensation field, a prominent compensation and strategy consultant, and two principals of a corporate finance and restructuring firm.

The first chapter in this section is a general review of the current state of academic research on management compensation by Professors David Larcker and Richard Lambert. Some of the findings of this research seem merely to confirm the obvious—for example, the observation that executive decisions are influenced by provisions in their compensation plans. Others, however, are less accessible to simple intuition. For example, the market responds negatively, on average, to unexpected deaths of CEOs (except in those cases where CEOs are also founders, where the response is positive), suggesting that the majority of CEOs of public companies are worth significantly more to their companies than they are paid. (And, in fact, Michael Jensen has argued, in a paper soon to be published by the *Harvard Business Review*, that American corporate executives are "systematically and seriously underpaid" relative to their counterparts in private organizations such as law and investment banking firms.) Also noteworthy, managers of companies with dispersed stock ownership are much more likely to undertake conglomerate mergers than those with concentrated equity ownership.

In the chapter that follows the initial survey, "Managerial Incentives in Mergers and Their Effect on Shareholder Wealth," David Larcker elaborates on this last point and presents evidence that the predominance in acquiring companies of short-term, EPS-oriented compensation plans may be responsible for the significant number of mergers—especially in the 1970s—that were unfavorably received by the market (and that are thus presumably a major cause of the current restructuring movement).

In the third chapter, Louis Brindisi, formerly head of Booz Allen's compensation consulting practice, reports a growing disparity between executive pay and corporate performance caused, in large part, by a focus on EPS growth as the primary gauge of corporate performance. Throughout the 1970s, Brindisi maintains, many companies reported steady increases in EPS, while their stock prices remained flat or even fell. According to the results of a 1983 Booz Allen study, inflation-adjusted ROE does a much better job of explaining stock market performance, and it accordingly provides a more reliable measure of corporate performance.

A more radical departure from current corporate performance is proposed by Bennett Stewart, a partner of Stern Stewart & Co., a corporate finance advisory firm specializing in corporate valuation and restructuring. In "Performance Measurement and Management Incentive Compensation," Stewart offers an extended critique of accounting-based performance measures. In their stead, he proposes a measure of cash flow rates of return on total corporate investment—a measure that converts conventional accounting income into estimates of operating cash flow. What further distinguishes Stewart's proposal from traditional, accounting-based criteria is his suggestion that, for highly cyclical industries, performance standards should be adjusted, *after the fact*, for general economic and industry-wide conditions, thereby shielding management (at least *operating* management) from uncontrollable risks.

In the final chapter, "The Motives and Methods of Corporate Restructuring," Stewart and his colleague David Glassman offer an entertaining as well as edifying series of corporate case studies demonstrating how new restructuring techniques (especially ESOPs, leveraged cash-outs, and leveraged equity purchase plans) are dramatically strengthening management incentives to serve stockholders within the form of the public corporation.

In closing, the corporate restructuring movement of the 1980s can be seen as part of an ongoing process of innovation in organizational form. And like other forms of technological progress, such structural innovation is providing American corporations—even those in apparently stagnant industries—with the promise of renewal. The more tangible benefits of this process are more competitive U.S. corporations, higher employment on net (although some industries must clearly shrink), better motivated and compensated management, wealthier stockholders (who accordingly can be expected to become more inclined to save and invest), and a stronger economy overall. These are among the already realized as well as the expected fruits of corporate restructuring, both in the 1980s and beyond.

PART I

An Overview of the Market for Corporate Control

1

The Takeover Controversy:
Analysis and Evidence*

Michael C. Jensen
Harvard Business School

I. Introduction

The market for corporate control is fundamentally changing the corporate land-scape. Transactions in this market in 1985 were at a record level of $180 billion, 47 percent above the $122 billion in 1984. The purchase prices in 36 of the 3,000 deals exceeded a billion dollars in 1985, compared with 18 in 1984.[1] These trans-actions involve takeovers, mergers, and leveraged buyouts. Closely associated are corporate restructurings involving divestitures, spinoffs, and large stock repurchases for cash and debt.

The changes associated with these control transactions are causing considerable controversy. Some argue that takeovers are damaging to the morale and productivity of organizations and therefore damaging to the economy. Others argue that takeovers represent productive entrepreneurial activity that improves the control and manage-ment of assets and helps move assets to more productive uses.

The controversy has been accompanied by strong pressure on regulators and legislatures to enact restrictions that would curb activity in the market for corporate control. In the spring of 1985 there were over 20 bills under consideration in Con-gress that proposed new restrictions on takeovers. Within the past several years

*This article is a somewhat shortened version of Michael C. Jensen's "The Takeover Controversy: Analysis and Evidence," which appears in the volume *Takeovers and Contests for Corporate Control* (Oxford University Press, 1987), edited by John Coffee, Louis Lowenstein, and Susan Rose-Ackerman. It is printed here with permission.
1. W.T. Grimm, *Mergerstat Review* (1985).

the legislatures of New York, New Jersey, Maryland, Pennsylvania, Connecticut, Illinois, Kentucky, and Michigan have passed antitakeover laws. The Federal Reserve Board entered the fray early in 1986 when it issued its controversial new interpretation of margin rules that restricts the use of debt in takeovers.

Through dozens of studies, leading financial economists have accumulated considerable evidence and knowledge about the effects of the takeover market. Since most of the results of the work completed prior to 1984 are well summarized elsewhere,[2] I focus here on current aspects of the controversy and on new results. In a nutshell, the previous work tells us the following:

- Takeovers benefit target shareholders—premiums in hostile offers historically exceed 30 percent on average, and in recent times have averaged about 50 percent.
- Acquiring-firm shareholders on average earn about 4 percent in hostile takeovers and roughly zero in mergers.
- Takeovers do not waste credit or resources; they generate substantial gains— historically 8.4 percent of the total value of both companies. Recently the gains seem to have been even larger.
- Actions by managers that eliminate or prevent offers or mergers are most suspect as harmful to shareholders.
- Golden parachutes for top-level managers do not, on average, harm shareholders.
- The activities of takeover specialists such as Icahn, Posner, Steinberg, and Pickens, on average, benefit shareholders.[3]
- Takeover gains do not come from the creation of monopoly power.

This paper analyzes the controversy surrounding takeovers and provides both theory and evidence to explain the central phenomena at issue. The paper is organized as follows. Section 2 contains basic background analysis of the forces operating in the market for corporate control—analysis which provides an understanding of the conflicts and issues surrounding takeovers and the effects of activities in this market. Section 3 discusses the conflict between managers and shareholders over the payout of free cash flow and how takeovers represent both a symptom and a resolution of the conflict. Sections 4, 5, and 6 discuss the relatively new phenomena of, respectively, junk-bond financing, the use of golden parachutes, and the practice of greenmail. Section 7 analyzes the problems the Delaware court is having in dealing with the conflicts that arise over control issues and its confused application of the business judgment rule to these cases.

---

2. A detailed summary of this evidence is available in Michael C. Jensen and Richard S. Ruback, "The Market for Corporate Control: The Scientific Evidence," *Journal of Financial Economics* 11 (April, 1983); and in Michael C. Jensen, "Takeovers: Folklore and Science," *Harvard Business Review* (November/December, 1984). See also Paul J. Halpern, "Empirical Estimates of the Amount and Distribution of Gains to Companies in Mergers," *Journal of Business*, V, 46, No. 4 (October, 1973) pp. 554–575.

3. Clifford G. Holderness and Dennis P. Sheehan, "Raiders or Saviors? The Evidence on Six Controversial Investors," *Journal of Financial Economics* 14 (December, 1985); and Wayne H. Mikkelson and Richard S. Ruback, "An Empirical Analysis of the Interfirm Equity Investment Process," *Journal of Financial Economics* 14 (December, 1985).

The following topics are discussed:

- The reasons for takeovers and mergers in the petroleum industry and why they increase efficiency and thereby promote the national interest.
- The role of debt in bonding management's promises to pay out future cash flows, to reduce costs, and to reduce investments in low-return projects.
- The role of high-yield debt (junk bonds) in helping to eliminate mere size as a takeover deterrent.
- The effects of takeovers on the equity markets and claims that managers are pressured to behave myopically.
- The effects of antitakeover measures such as poison pills.
- The misunderstandings of the important role that "golden parachutes" play in reducing the conflicts of interests associated with takeovers and the valuable function they serve in alleviating some of the costs and uncertainty facing managers.
- The damaging effects of the Delaware court decision in Unocal vs. Mesa that allowed Unocal to make a self-tender offer that excluded its largest shareholder (reverse greenmail).
- The problems the courts are facing in applying the model of the corporation subsumed under the traditional business judgment rule to the conflicts of interest involved in corporate control controversies.

II. The Market for Corporate Control—Background

The Benefits of Takeovers

The market for corporate control is creating large benefits for shareholders and for the economy as a whole. The corporate control market generates these gains by loosening control over vast amounts of resources and enabling them to move more quickly to their highest-valued use. This is a healthy market in operation, on both the takeover side and the divestiture side.

Gains to Target Firms.   Total benefits created by the control market have been huge, as reflected in gains of $40 billion to stockholders of acquired firms in 260 tender offers alone in the period from January 1981 through May 1985.[4] This figure does not include the gains from other control transactions such as mergers, leveraged buyouts, or divestitures. Nor does it include the gains from reorganizations such as those of Phillips, Unocal and others that have been motivated by takeover attempts. (The Phillips, Unocal and ARCO reorganizations created gains of an additional $6.6 billion.) One study estimates the total premiums received by shareholders of target firms to have been approximately $75 billion in $239 billion of merger and acquisition deals in 1984 and 1985.[5]

---

4. As estimated by the Office of the Chief Economist of the SEC and provided to the author in private communication.

5. John D. Paulus, "Corporate Restructuring, 'Junk,' and Leverage: Too Much or Too Little?" (Morgan Stanley, February 1986).

Gains to Bidding Firms. The evidence on the returns to bidding firms is mixed. The data indicate that prior to 1980 shareholders of bidding firms earned on average about zero in mergers (which tend to be voluntary) and about 4 percent of their equity value in tender offers (which tend to be hostile).[6] These differences in returns are associated with the form of payment rather than the form of the offer (tender offers tend to be for cash and mergers lend to be for stock).[7]

Although there are measurement problems that make it difficult to estimate the returns to bidders as precisely as the returns to targets,[8] it appears the bargaining power of target managers, coupled with competition among potential acquirers, grants much of the acquisition benefits to selling shareholders. In addition, federal and state regulation of tender offers appears to have strengthened the hand of target firms; premiums received by target-firm shareholders increased substantially after introduction of such regulation.[9]

III. Causes of Current Takeover Activity

The current high level of takeover activity seems to be caused by a number of factors:

- the relaxation of restrictions on mergers imposed by the antitrust laws;
- the withdrawal of resources from industries that are growing more slowly or that must shrink;
- deregulation in the financial services, oil and gas, transportation, and broadcasting markets that is bringing about a major restructuring of those industries;
- and improvements in takeover technology, including a larger supply of increasingly sophisticated legal and financial advisers, and improvements in financing technology (for example, the strip financing commonly used in leveraged buyouts and the original issuance of high-yield non-investment-grade bonds).

Each of these factors has contributed to the increase in total takeover and reorganization activity in recent times. Moreover, the first three factors (antitrust relaxation, exit, and deregulation) are generally consistent with data showing the intensity of takeover activity by industry. For example, the value of merger and acquisition

---

6. See Jensen and Ruback [1983, Tables 1 and 2], cited earlier in note 2.

7. See Yen-Sheng Huang and Ralph A. Walkling, "Differences in Residuals Associated with Acquisition Announcements: Payment, Acquisition Form, and Resistance Effects" (Manuscript, Georgia Institute of Technology and Ohio State University, November, 1985).

8. See B. Espen Eckbo, "Do Acquiring Firms Gain From Merger?" (unpublished manuscript, University of British Columbia, June, 1985). Eckbo concludes that the zero returns to U.S. bidding firms is due to difficulties in measuring the gains to bidding firms when the bidder is substantially larger than the target firm. In his sample the average Canadian bidder was approximately the same size as the average target while the average U.S. bidder is approximately 8 times the size of the average Canadian target. See also Jensen and Ruback [1983, pp. 18ff], cited earlier in note 2.

9. See Gregg Jarrell and Michael Bradley, "The Economic Effects of Federal and State Regulation of Cash Tender Offers," *Journal of Law and Economics* 23 (1980), pp. 371–407.

Table 1. Intensity of Industry Takeover Activity: 1981–1984.[a]

Industry Classification of Seller	Percent of Total Takeover Activity[b]	Percent of Total Corporate Market Value[c]
Oil and gas	26.3	13.5
Banking and finance	8.8	6.4
Insurance	5.9	2.9
Food processing	4.6	4.4
Mining and minerals	4.4	1.5
Conglomerate	4.4	3.2
Retail	3.6	5.2
Transportation	2.4	2.7
Leisure and entertainment	2.3	.9
Broadcasting	2.3	.7
Other	39.4	58.5

a. Intensity of industry takeover activity as measured by the value of merger and acquisition transactions in the period 1981–84 (as a percent of total takeover transactions for which valuation data are publicly reported) compared to industry size (as measured by the fraction of overall corporate market value).

b. Source: W.T. Grimm, *Mergerstat Review* (1984), p. 41.

c. As of 12/31/84. Total value is measured as the sum of the market value of common equity for 4.305 companies, including 1,501 companies on the NYSE, 724 companies on the ASE, plus 2,080 companies in the Over-The-Counter market. Source: *The Media General Financial Weekly*, (December 31, 1984), p. 17.

transactions by industry in the period 1981–84 (see Table 1) indicates that acquisition activity was highest in oil and gas, followed by banking and finance, insurance, food processing, and mining and minerals. For comparison purposes, the last column of the table presents data on industry size measured as a fraction of the total value of all firms. All but two of the industries, retail and transportation, represent a larger fraction of total takeover activity than their representation in the economy as a whole.

Many areas of the U.S. economy have been experiencing slowing growth and, in some cases, even retrenchment—a phenomenon that has many causes, including substantially increased competition from foreign firms. This has increased takeover activity because takeovers play an important role in facilitating exit from an industry or activity. Major changes in energy markets have required a radical restructuring of and retrenchment in that industry; and, as discussed in detail below, takeovers have played an important role in accomplishing these changes. Deregulation of the financial service market is consistent with the high ranking in Table 1 of banking and finance and insurance. Deregulation has also been important in the transportation and broadcasting industries. Mining and minerals has been subject to many of the same forces affecting the energy industry, including the changes in the value of the dollar.

Takeovers Provide Competition for Top-level Management Jobs

The market for corporate control is best viewed as a major component of the managerial labor market. It is the arena in which different management teams compete for the rights to manage corporate resources.[10] Understanding this is crucial to understanding much of the rhetoric about the effects of hostile takeovers.

Managers formerly protected from competition for their jobs by antitrust constraints that prevented takeover of the nation's largest corporations are now facing a more demanding environment and a more uncertain future.

The development of innovative financing vehicles, such as high-yield, non-investment-grade bonds ("junk" bonds), has removed size as a significant impediment to competition in this market. Although they have not been widely used in takeovers yet, these new financing techniques permit small firms to obtain resources for acquisition of much larger firms by issuing claims on the value of the venture (that is, the target firm's assets) just as in any other corporate investment activity. It is not surprising that many executives of large corporations would like relief from this new competition for their jobs, but restricting the corporate control market is not the efficient way to handle the problems caused by the increased uncertainty in their contracting environment.

Takeovers Provide External Control

The internal control mechanisms of corporations, which operate through the board of directors, generally work well. On occasion, however, they break down. One important source of protection for investors in these situations is the takeover market. Other management teams that recognize an opportunity to reorganize or redeploy an organization's assets and thereby create new value can bid for the control rights in the takeover market. To be successful, such bids must be at a premium over current market value. This gives investors an opportunity to realize part of the gains from reorganization and redeployment of the assets.

The Market for Corporate Control Is an Agent for Change

Takeovers generally occur because changing technology or market conditions require a major restructuring of corporate assets. In some cases takeovers occur because incumbent managers are incompetent. When the internal processes for change in large corporations are too slow, costly and clumsy to bring about the required restructuring or management change in an efficient way, the capital markets are doing so through the operation of the market for corporate control. In this sense, the capital markets have been responsible for bringing about substantial changes in corporate strategy in recent times.

Managers often have difficulty abandoning strategies they have spent years devising and implementing, even when those strategies no longer contribute to the organization's survival. Such changes often require abandonment of major projects,

---

10. See Jensen and Ruback [1983], cited earlier in note 2.

relocation of facilities, changes in managerial assignments, and closure or sale of facilities or divisions. It is easier for new top-level managers with no ties with current employees or communities to make such changes. Moreover, normal organizational resistance to change commonly lessens significantly early in the reign of new top-level managers. For example, the premium Carl Icahn was able to offer for TWA, and his victory over Texas Air in the battle for control of TWA, were made possible in part by the willingness of the TWA unions to negotiate favorable contract concessions with Icahn—concessions that TWA itself was unable to attain prior to the takeover conflict. Such organizational factors that make change easier for newcomers, coupled with a fresh view of the business, can be a major advantage to new managers after a takeover. On the other hand, lack of detailed knowledge about the firm also poses risks for new managers and increases the likelihood of mistakes.

Takeovers are particularly important in bringing about efficiencies when exit from an activity is required. The oil industry is a good example. Changing market conditions mandate a major restructuring of the petroleum industry, and none of this is the fault of management. Management, however, must adjust to the new energy environment and recognize that many old practices and strategies are no longer viable. It is particularly hard for many managers to deal with the fact that some firms in the oil industry have to go out of business. This is cheaper to accomplish through merger and the orderly liquidation of marginal assets of the combined firms than by a slow, agonizing death in a competitive struggle in an industry with overcapacity. The end of the latter process often comes in the bankruptcy courts, with high losses and unnecessary destruction of valuable parts of organizations that could be used productively by others.

In short, the external takeover market serves as a court of last resort that plays an important role in (1) creating organizational change, (2) motivating the efficient use of resources, and (3) protecting shareholders when the corporation's internal controls and board-level control mechanisms are slow, clumsy, or defunct.

Divestitures Are the Subject of Much Erroneous Criticism

If assets are to move to their most highly valued use, acquirers must be able to sell off assets to those who can use them more productively. Therefore, divestitures are a critical element in the functioning of the corporate control market, and it is thus important to avoid inhibiting them. Indeed, over 1200 divestitures occurred in 1985, a record level.[11] Labeling divestitures with emotional terms such as "bust-ups" is not a substitute for analysis or evidence.

Moreover, it is important to recognize that divested plants and assets do not disappear; they are reallocated. Sometimes they continue to be used in similar ways in the same industry, and in other cases they are used in very different ways and in different industries. But in all cases, they are moving to uses that their new owners believe are more productive. This process is beneficial to society.

---

11. W.T. Grimm, *Mergerstat Review* (1985).

Finally, it is useful to recognize that the takeover and divestiture market provides a private market constraint against bigness for its own sake. The potential gains available to those who correctly perceive that a firm can be purchased for less than the value realizable from the sale of its components provide incentives for entrepreneurs to search out these opportunities and to capitalize on them by reorganizing such firms into smaller entities.

The mere possibility of such takeovers also motivates managers to avoid putting together uneconomic conglomerates and to break up existing ones. This is now happening. Recently it has appeared that many firms' defenses against takeovers have led to actions similar to those proposed by potential acquirers. Examples are the reorganizations occurring in the oil industry, the sale of "crown jewels," and divestitures brought on by the desire to liquidate large debts incurred to buy back stock or to make other payments to stockholders. Unfortunately, the basic economic sense of these transactions is often lost in a blur of emotional rhetoric and controversy.

The sale of a firm's crown jewels, for example, benefits shareholders when the price obtained for the division is greater than the present value of the future cash flows to the current owner. A takeover bid motivated by the desire to obtain such an underused division can stimulate current managers to reexamine the economics of the firm's current structure and to sell one or more of its divisions to a third party who is willing to pay even more than the initial offerer. Brunswick's sale of its Sherwood Medical Division to American Home Products after a takeover bid by Whittaker (apparently motivated by a desire to acquire Sherwood) is an example of such a transaction. The total value to Brunswick shareholders of the price received for selling Sherwood to American Home Products plus the remaining value of Brunswick without Sherwood (the proceeds from the sale of Sherwood were distributed directly to Brunswick's shareholders) was greater than Whittaker's offer for the entire company.[12]

Managers May Behave Myopically But Markets Do Not

It has been argued that growing institutional equity holdings and the fear of takeover cause managers to behave myopically and therefore to sacrifice long-term benefits to increase short-term profits. The arguments tend to confuse two separate issues: 1) whether *managers* are shortsighted and make decisions that undervalue future cash flows while overvaluing current cash flows (myopic managers) and 2) whether *security markets* are shortsighted and undervalue future cash flows while overvaluing near-term cash flows (myopic markets).

There is little formal evidence on the myopic managers issue, but I believe this phenomenon does occur. Sometimes it occurs when managers hold little stock in their companies and are compensated in ways that motivate them to take actions

---

12. See the analysis in Jensen [1984, p. 119], cited in note 2.

that increase accounting earnings rather than the value of the firm. It also occurs when managears make mistakes because they do not understand the forces that determine stock values.

There is much evidence inconsistent with the myopic markets view and none that supports it:

- Even casual observation of the equity markets reveals that the market values more than current earnings. It values growth as well. The mere fact that price/earnings ratios differ widely among securities indicates the market is valuing something other than current earnings. Indeed, the essence of a growth stock is one that has large investment projects yielding few short-term cash flows but high future earnings and cash flows.
- The continuing marketability of new issues for start-up companies with little record of current earnings—the Genentechs of the world—is also inconsistent with the notion that the market does not value future earnings.
- A recent study provides evidence that (except in the oil industry) stock prices respond positively to announcements of increased investment expenditures, and negatively to reduced expenditures.[13] This evidence is inconsistent with the notion that the equity market is myopic.
- The vast evidence on efficient markets indicating that current stock prices appropriately incorporate all currently available public information is also inconsistent with the myopic markets hypothesis. Although the evidence is not literally 100 percent in support of the efficient market hypothesis, there is no better documented proposition in any of the social sciences.[14]

    The evidence indicates, for example, that the market appropriately interprets the implications of corporate accounting changes that increase reported profits but cause no change in corporate cash flows.[15]

    Additional evidence is provided by the 30 percent increase in ARCO's stock price that occurred when it announced its major restructuring in 1985. This price increase is inconsistent with the notion that the market values only short-term earnings. Even though ARCO simultaneously revealed that it would have to take a $1.2 billion write-off as a result of the restructuring, the market still responded positively.

---

13. John J. McConnell and Chris J. Muscarella, "Corporate Capital Expenditure Decisions and the Market Value of the Firm," *Journal of Financial Economics* 14, No. 3 (1985).

14. For an introduction to the literature and empirical evidence on the theory of efficient markets, see E. Elton and M. Gruber, *Modern Portfolio Theory and Investment Analysis*, (New York: Wiley, 1984), Chapter 15, p. 375ff and the 167 studies referenced in the bibliography.

15. Examples are switches from accelerated to straight-line depreciation techniques and adoption of the flow-through method for reporting investment tax credits. Here the evidence indicates that "security prices increase around the date when a firm first announces earnings inflated by an accounting change. The effect appears to be temporary, and, certainly by the subsequent quarterly report, the price has resumed a level appropriate to the true economic status of the firm." See R. Kaplan and R. Roll, "Investor Evaluation of Accounting Information: Some Empirical Evidence," *Journal of Business*, (April, 1972), 225–257.

- Recent versions of the myopic markets hypothesis emphasize increasing institutional holdings and the pressures institutional investors face to show high returns on a quarter-to-quarter basis. It is argued that these pressures on institutions are a major cause of pressures on corporations to generate high current earnings on a quarter-to-quarter basis. The institutional pressures are said to lead to increased takeovers of firms (because institutions are not loyal shareholders) and to decreased research and development expenditures. It is argued that because R&D expenditures reduce current earnings, firms making them are therefore more likely to be taken over, and that reductions in R&D are leading to a fundamental weakening of the corporate sector of the economy.

A recent study of 324 firms by the Office of the Chief Economist of the SEC finds substantial evidence that is inconsistent with this version of the myopic markets argument.[16] The evidence indicates the following:

- increased institutional stock holdings are not associated with increased takeovers of firms;
- increased institutional holdings are not associated with decreases in research and development expenditures;
- firms with high research and development expenditures are not more vulnerable to takeovers;
- stock prices respond positively to announcements of increases in research and development expenditures.

Those who make the argument that takeovers are reducing R&D spending also have to come to grips with the aggregate data on such spending, which is inconsistent with the argument. Total spending on R&D in 1984, a year of record acquisition activity, increased by 14 percent according to *Business Week's* annual survey of 820 companies. (The sample companies account for 95 percent of total private-sector R&D expenditures.) This represented "the biggest gain since R&D spending began a steady climb in the late 1970s."[17] All industries in the survey increased R&D spending with the exception of steel. Moreover, R&D spending increased from 2 percent of sales, where it had been for five years, to 2.9 percent.

An Alternative Hypothesis

There is an alternative hypothesis that explains the current situation, including the criticisms of management, quite well.

Suppose that some managers are simply mistaken—that is, their strategies are wrong—and that the financial markets are telling them they are wrong. If they don't change, their stock prices will remain low. If the managers are indeed wrong, it is desirable for the stockholders and for the economy to remove them to make way for a change in strategy and more efficient use of the resources.

---

16. Office of the Chief Economist, Securities and Exchange Commission, "Institutional Ownership, Tender Offers, and Long-Term Investments," April 19, 1985.

17. "R&D Scoreboard: Reagan & Foreign Rivalry Light a Fire Under Spending," *Business Week* (July 8, 1985), p. 86ff.

IV. Free Cash Flow Theory of Takeovers[18]

More than a dozen separate forces drive takeover activity, including such factors as deregulation, synergies, economies of scale and scope, taxes, managerial incompetence, and increasing globalization of U.S. markets.[19] One major cause of takeover activity are the agency costs associated with conflicts between managers and shareholders over the payout of corporate free cash flow. Though this has received relatively little attention, it has played an important role in acquisitions over the last decade.

Managers are the agent of shareholders, and because both parties are self-interested, there are serious conflicts between them over the choice of the best corporate strategy. Agency costs are the total costs that arise in such cooperative arrangements. They consist of the costs of monitoring managerial behavior (such as the costs of producing audited financial statements and devising and implementing compensation plans that reward managers for actions that increase investors' wealth) and the inevitable costs that are incurred because the conflicts of interest can never be resolved perfectly. Sometimes these costs can be large and, when they are, takeovers can reduce them.

Free Cash Flow and the Conflict Between Managers and Shareholders

Free cash flow is cash flow in excess of that required to fund all projects that have positive net values when discounted at the relevant cost of capital. Such free cash flow must be paid out to shareholders if the firm is to be efficient and to maximize value for shareholders.

Payment of cash to shareholders reduces the resources under managers' control, thereby reducing managers' power, and potentially subjecting them to the monitoring by the capital markets that occurs when a firm must obtain new capital. Financing projects internally avoids this monitoring and the possibility that funds will be unavailable or available only at high explicit prices.

Managers have incentives to expand their firms beyond the size that maximizes shareholder wealth.[20] Growth increases managers' power by increasing the resources

---

18. This discussion is based on my article, "Agency Costs of Free Cash Flow, Corporate Finance and Takeovers," in *American Economic Review*, (May, 1986).

19. Richard Roll discusses a number of these forces in "Empirical Evidence on Takeover Activity and Shareholder Wealth," (presented at the Conference on Takeovers and Contests for Corporate Control, Columbia University, November, 1985).

20. See Gordon Donaldson, *Managing Corporate Wealth*, (Praeger: 1984). Donaldson, in a detailed study of 12 large Fortune 500 firms, concludes that managers of these firms were not driven by maximization of the value of the firm, but rather by the maximization of "corporate wealth." He defines corporate wealth as "*the aggregate purchasing power available to management for strategic purposes during any given planning period. . . .* this wealth consists of the stocks and flows of cash and cash equivalents (primarily credit) that management can use at its discretion to implement decisions involving the control of goods and services." (p. 3, emphasis in original) "In practical terms it is cash, credit, and other corporate purchasing power by which management commands goods and services." (p. 22).

under their control. In addition, changes in management compensation are positively related to growth.[21] The tendency of firms to reward middle managers through promotion rather than year-to-year bonuses also creates an organizational bias toward growth to supply the new positions that such promotion-based reward systems require.[22]

The tendency for managers to overinvest resources is limited by competition in the product and factor markets, which tends to drive prices toward minimum average cost in an activity. Managers must therefore motivate their organizations to be more efficient to improve the probability of survival. Product and factor market disciplinary forces are often weaker in new activities, however, and in activities that involve substantial economic rents or quasi-rents.[23] In these cases, monitoring by the firm's internal control system and the market for corporate control are more important. Activities yielding substantial economic rents or quasi-rents are the types of activities that generate large amounts of free cash flow.

Conflicts of interest between shareholders and managers over payout policies are especially severe when the organization generates substantial free cash flow. The problem is how to motivate managers to disgorge the cash rather than invest it at below the cost of capital or waste it through organizational inefficiencies.

Some finance scholars have argued that financial flexibility (unused debt capacity and internally generated funds) is desirable when a firm's managers have better information about the firm than outside investors.[24] Their arguments assume that managers act in the best interest of shareholders. The arguments offered here imply that such flexibility has costs: financial flexibility in the form of free cash flow, large cash balances, and unused borrowing power provides managers with greater discretion over resources that is often not used in the shareholders' interests.

The theory developed here explains (1) how debt-for-stock exchanges reduce the organizational inefficiencies fostered by substantial free cash flow, (2) how debt can substitute for dividends, (3) why "diversification" programs are more likely to be associated with losses than are expansion programs in the same line of business, (4) why mergers within an industry and liquidation-motivated takeovers will generally create larger gains than cross-industry mergers, (5) why the factors stimulating takeovers in such diverse businesses as broadcasting, tobacco, cable systems and oil are essentially identical, and (5) why bidders and some targets tend to show abnormally good performance prior to takeover.

---

21. Where growth is measured by increases in sales. See Kevin J. Murphy, "Corporate Performance and Managerial Remuneration: An Empirical Analysis," *Journal of Accounting and Economics* 7, Nos. 1-3 (April, 1985), pp. 11-42. This positive relationship between compensation and sales growth does not imply, although it is consistent with, causality.

22. See George Baker, "Compensation and Hierarchies" (unpublished, Harvard Business School, January, 1986).

23. Rents are returns in excess of the opportunity cost of the resources committed to the activity. Quasi-rents are returns in excess of the short-run opportunity cost of the resources to the activity.

24. See Stewart C. Myers and Nicholas S. Majluf, "Corporate Financing and Investment Decisions When Firms Have Information That Investors Do Not Have," *Journal of Financial Economics* 13 (1984), pp. 187-221.

The Role of Debt in Motivating Organizational Efficiency

The agency costs of debt have been widely discussed,[25] but the benefits of debt in motivating managers and their organizations to be efficient have largely been ignored. I call these effects the "control hypothesis" for debt creation.

Managers with substantial free cash flow can increase dividends or repurchase stock and thereby pay out current cash that would otherwise be invested in low-return projects or otherwise wasted. This payout leaves managers with control over the use of future free cash flows, but they can also promise to pay out future cash flows by announcing a "permanent" increase in the dividend.[26] Because there is no contractual obligation to make the promised dividend payments, such promises are weak. Dividends can be reduced by managers in the future with little effective recourse to shareholders. The fact that capital markets punish dividend cuts with large stock price reductions is an interesting equilibrium market response to the agency costs of free cash flow.[27]

Debt creation, without retention of the proceeds of the issue, enables managers effectively to bond their promise to pay out future cash flows. Thus, debt can be an effective substitute for dividends, something that is not generally recognized in the corporate finance literature.[28] By issuing debt in exchange for stock, managers bond their promise to pay out future cash flows in a way that simple dividend increases do not. In doing so, they give shareholder-recipients of the debt the right to take the firm into bankruptcy court if they do not keep their promise to make

---

25. See Michael C. Jensen and William H. Meckling, "Theory of the Firm: Managerial Behavior, Agency Costs and Ownership Structure," *Journal of Financial Economics*, V. 3 (1976), pp. 305–360; Stewart C. Myers, "Determinants of Corporate Borrowing," *Journal of Financial Economics*, V. 5, No. 2 (1977), pp. 147–175; and Clifford W. Smith, Jr. and Jerold B. Warner, "On Financial Contracting: An Analysis of Bond Covenants," *Journal of Financial Economics*, V. 7 (1979), pp. 117–161.

26. Interestingly, Graham and Dodd, in their treatise, *Security Analysis*, placed great importance on the dividend payout in their famous valuation formula: $V = M (D + .33E)$ (p. 454), V is value, M is the earnings multiplier when the dividend payout rate is a "normal two-thirds of earnings," D is the expected dividend, and E is expected earnings. In their formula, dividends are valued at three times the rate of retained earnings, a proposition that has puzzled many students of modern finance (at least of my vintage). The agency cost of free cash flow that leads to overretention and waste of shareholder resources is consistent with the deep suspicion with which Graham and Dodd viewed the lack of payout. Their discussion (Chapter 34) reflects a belief in the tenuous nature of the future benefits of such retention. Although they do not couch the issues in terms of the conflict between managers and shareholders, the free cash flow theory explicated here implies that their beliefs, sometimes characterized as "a bird in the hand is worth two in the bush," were perhaps well founded. See Chapters 32, 34, and 36 in Benjamin Graham and David I. Dodd, *Security Analysis: Principles and Technique* (New York, McGraw-Hill, 1951).

27. See Guy Charest, "Dividend Information, Stock Returns, and Market Efficiency-II, *Journal of Financial Economics* 6, (1978), pp. 297–330; and Joseph Aharony and Itzhak Swary, "Quarterly Dividend and Earnings Announcements and Stockholder's Returns: An Empirical Analysis," *Journal of Finance* 35 (1980), pp. 1–12.

28. Literally, principal and interest payments are substitutes for dividends. However, because interest is tax-deductible at the corporate level and dividends are not, dividends and debt are not perfect substitutes.

the interest and principal payments.[29] Thus, debt reduces the agency costs of free cash flow by reducing the cash flow available for spending at the discretion of managers.

Issuing large amounts of debt to buy back stock sets up organizational incentives to motivate managers to pay out free cash flow. In addition, the exchange of debt for stock also helps managers overcome the normal organizational resistance to retrenchment that the payout of free cash flow often requires. The threat of failure to make debt service payments serves as a strong motivating force to make such organizations more efficient. Stock repurchase for debt or cash also has tax advantages. Interest payments are tax-deductible to the corporation, the part of the repurchase proceeds equal to the seller's tax basis in the stock is not taxed at all, and that which is taxed is subject to capital-gains rates.

The control hypothesis does not imply that debt issues will always have positive control effects. For example, these effects will not be as important for rapidly growing organizations with large and highly profitable investment projects but no free cash flow. Such organizations will have to go regularly to the financial markets to obtain capital. At these times the markets will have an opportunity to evaluate the company, its management, and its proposed projects. Investment bankers and analysts play an important role in this monitoring, and the market's assessment is made evident by the price investors pay for the financial claims.

The control function of debt is more important in organizations that generate large cash flows but have low growth prospects, and it is even more important in organizations that must shrink. In these organizations the pressures to waste cash flows by investing them in uneconomic projects are most serious.

[The original paper contains a section here entitled "Evidence from Financial Transactions in Support of the Free Cash Flow Theory of Mergers," which appears in the "Appendix" to this article.]

The Evidence from Leveraged Buyout and Going-Private Transactions

Many of the benefits of going-private and leveraged buyout transactions seem to be due to the control function of debt. These transactions are creating a new organizational form that competes successfully with the open corporate form because of advantages in controlling the agency costs of free cash flow. In 1984, going-private transactions totaled $10.8 billion and represented 27 percent of all public acquisitions.[30] The evidence indicates premiums paid averaged over 50 percent.[31]

---

29. Two studies argue that regular dividend payments can be effective in reducing agency costs with managers by assuring that managers are forced more frequently to subject themselves and their policies to the discipline of the capital markets when they acquire capital. See Frank H. Easterbrook, "Managers' Discretion and Investors' Welfare: Theories and Evidence," *Delaware Journal of Corporate Law*, V. 9, No. 3 (1984b), pp. 540–571; and Michael Rozeff, "Growth, Beta and Agency Costs as Determinants of Dividend Payout Ratios" *Journal of Financial Research*, V. 5 (1982), pp. 249–59.

30. By number. See W.T. Grimm, *Mergerstat Review* (1985), Figs. 36 and 37.

31. See H. DeAngelo, L. DeAngelo and E. Rice, "Going Private: Minority Freezeouts and Stockholder Wealth," *Journal of Law and Economics*, V. 27, No. 2 (October, 1984), pp. 36–401, and Louis Lowenstein, "Management Buyouts," *Columbia Law Review*, V. 85 (May, 1985), pp. 730–784. Lowenstein also mentions incentive effects of debt but argues tax effects play a major role in explaining the value increase.

Desirable leveraged buyout candidates are frequently firms or divisions of larger firms that have stable business histories and substantial free cash flow (that is, low growth prospects and high potential for generating cash flows)—situations where agency costs of free cash flow are likely to be high. Leveraged buyout transactions are frequently financed with high debt; ten-to-one ratios of debt to equity are not uncommon. Moreover, the use of strip financing and the allocation of equity in the deals reveal a sensitivity to incentives, conflicts of interest, and bankruptcy costs.

Strip financing, the practice in which risky nonequity securities are held in approximately equal proportions, limits the conflict of interest among such security holders and therefore limits bankruptcy costs. A somewhat oversimplified example illustrates the point. Consider two firms identical in every respect except financing. Firm A in entirely financed with equity, and Firm B is highly leveraged with senior subordinated debt, convertible debt, and preferred as well as equity. Suppose Firm B securities are sold only in strips—that is, a buyer purchasing X percent of any security must purchase X percent of all securities, and the securities are "stapled" together so they cannot be separated later. Security holders of both firms have identical unlevered claims on the cash flow distribution, but organizationally the two firms are very different. If Firm B managers withhold dividends to invest in value-reducing projects or if they are simply incompetent, strip holders have recourse to remedial powers not available to the equity holders of Firm A. Each Firm B security specifies the rights its holder has in the event of default on its dividend or coupon payment—for example, the right to take the firm into bankruptcy or to have board representation. As each security above equity goes into default the strip holder receives new rights to intercede in the organization. As a result, it is quicker and less expensive to replace managers in Firm B.

Moreover, because every security holder in the highly levered Firm B has the same claim on the firm, there are no conflicts between senior and junior claimants over reorganization of the claims in the event of default; to the strip holder it is a matter of moving funds from one pocket to another. Thus, Firm B need never go into bankruptcy. The reorganization can be accomplished voluntarily, quickly, and with less expense and disruption than through bankruptcy proceedings.

Securities commonly subject to strip practices are often called "mezzanine" financing and include securities with priority superior to common stock yet subordinate to senior debt. This seems to be a sensible arrangement. Because of several other factors ignored in our simplified example, IRS restrictions deny tax deductibility of debt interest in such situations and bank holdings of equity are restricted by regulation. Riskless senior debt need not be in the strip because there are no conflicts with other claimants in the event of reorganization when there is no probability of default on its payment.

It is advantageous to have top-level managers and venture capitalists who promote the transactions hold a larger share of the equity. Top-level managers frequently receive 15 to 20 percent of the equity, and venture capitalists and the funds they represent generally retain the major share of the remainder. The venture capitalists control the board of directors and monitor managers. Managers and venture capitalists have a strong interest in making the venture successful because their equity interests are subordinate to other claims. Success requires, among other things, implementation of changes to avoid investment in low-return projects in order to generate the cash for debt service and to increase the value of equity. Finally, when the equity is held primarily by managers or generally by a small number of people, greater efficiencies in risk bearing are made possible by placing more of the risk in the hands of debt holders when the debt is held in well-diversified institutional portfolios.

Less than a handful of these leveraged buyout ventures have ended in bankruptcy, although more have gone through private reorganizations. A thorough test of this organizational form requires the passage of time and another recession.

Some have asserted that managers engaging in a buyout of their firm are insulating themselves from monitoring. The opposite is true in the typical leveraged buyout. Because the venture capitalists are generally the largest shareholder and control the board of directors, they have both greater ability and incentives to monitor managers effectively than directors representing diffuse public shareholders in the typical public corporation.

Evidence from the Oil Industry

The oil industry is large and visible. It is also an industry in which the importance of takeovers in motivating change and efficiency is particularly clear. Therefore, detailed analysis of it provides an understanding of how the market for corporate control helps motivate more efficient use of resources in the corporate sector.

Reorganization of the Industry Is Mandatory. Radical changes in the energy market from 1973 through the late 1970s imply that a major restructuring of the petroleum industry had to occur. These changes are as follows:

- a ten-fold increase in the price of crude oil from 1973 to 1979;
- reduced annual consumption of oil in the U.S.;
- reduced expectations of future increases in the price of oil;
- increased exploration and development costs;
- and increased real interest rates.

As a result of these changes the optimal level of refining and distribution capacity and crude reserves fell over this period, and since the late 1970s the industry has been plagued with excess capacity. Reserves are reduced by reducing the level of exploration and development, and it pays to concentrate these reductions in high-cost areas such as the United States.

Substantial reductions in exploration and development and in refining and distribution capacity meant that some firms had to leave the industry. This is especially true because holding reserves is subject to economies of scale, whereas exploration and development are subject to diseconomies of scale.

Price increases created large cash flows in the industry. For example, 1984 cash flows of the ten largest oil companies were $48.5 billion, 28 percent of the total cash flows of the top 200 firms in Dun's Business Month (1985) survey. Consistent with the agency costs of free cash flow, management did not pay out the excess resources to shareholders. Instead, the industry continued to spend heavily on exploration and development even though average returns on these expenditures were below the cost of capital.

Paradoxically, the profitability of oil exploration and drilling activity can decrease even though the price of oil increases if the value of the reserves in the ground falls. This can happen when the price increase is associated with reductions in consumption that make it difficult to market newly discovered oil. In the late 1970s the increased holding costs associated with higher real interest rates, reductions in expected future oil price increases, increased exploration and development costs, and reductions in the consumption of oil combined to make many exploration and development projects uneconomic. The industry, however, continued to spend heavily on such projects.

The hypothesis that oil-industry exploration and development expenditures were too high during this period is consistent with the findings of the earlier-mentioned study by McConnell and Muscarella.[32] Their evidence indicates that announcements of increases in exploration and development expenditures by oil companies in the period 1975–1981 were associated with systematic decreases in the announcing firms' stock prices. Moreover, announcements of decreases in exploration and development expenditures were associated with increases in stock prices. These results are striking in comparison with their evidence that exactly the opposite market reaction occurs with increases and decreases in investment expenditures by industrial firms, and with SEC evidence that increases in research and development expenditures are associated with increased stock prices.[33]

Additional evidence of the uneconomic nature of the oil industry's exploration and development expenditures is contained in a study by Bernard Picchi of Salomon Brothers. His study of rates of return on exploration and development expenditures for 30 large oil firms indicated that on average the industry did not earn "even a 10% return on its pretax outlays" in the period 1982–84. Estimates of the average ratio of the present value of future net cash flows of discoveries, extensions and enhanced recovery to expenditures for exploration and development for the industry ranged from less than .6 to slightly more than .9, depending on the method used and the year. In other words, even taking the cost of capital to be only 10 percent on a pretax basis, the industry was realizing on average only 60 to 90 cents on every dollar invested in these activities. Picchi concludes:

---

32. John J. McConnell and Chris J. Muscarella, "Corporate Capital Expenditure Decisions and the Market Value of the Firm," *Journal of Financial Economics*, V. 14, No. 3 (1985).

33. Office of the Chief Economist, Securities and Exchange Commission, "Institutional Ownership, Tender Offers, and Long-Term Investments," April 19, 1985.

> For 23 of the [30] companies in our survey, we would recommend *immediate* cuts of perhaps 25%–30% in exploration and production spending. It is clear that much of the money that these firms spent last year on petroleum exploration and development yielded subpar financial returns—even at $30 per barrel, let alone today's $26–$27 per barrel price structure.[34]

The waste associated with excessive exploration and development expenditures explains why buying oil on Wall Street was considerably cheaper than obtaining it by drilling holes in the ground, even after adjustment for differential taxes and regulations on prices of old oil. Wall Street was not undervaluing the oil; it was valuing it correctly, but it was also correctly valuing the wasted expenditures on exploration and development that oil companies were making. When these managerially imposed "taxes" on the reserves were taken into account, the net price of oil on Wall Street was very low. This provided incentives for firms to obtain reserves by purchasing other oil companies and reducing expenditures on non-cost-effective exploration.

High Profits Are Not Usually Associated With Retrenchment. Adjustment by the energy industry to the new environment has been slow for several reasons. First, it is difficult for organizations to change operating rules and practices like those in the oil industry that have worked well for long periods in the past, even though they do not fit the new situation. Nevertheless, survival requires that organizations adapt to major changes in their environment.

Second, the past decade has been a particularly puzzling period in the oil business because at the same time that changes in the environment have required a reduction of capacity, cash flows and profits have been high. This is a somewhat unusual condition in which the average productivity of resources in the industry increased while the marginal productivity decreased. The point is illustrated graphically in Figure 1.

As the figure illustrates, profits plus payments to factors of production other than capital were larger in 1985 than in 1973. Moreover, because of the upward shift and simultaneous twist of the marginal productivity of capital schedule from 1973 to 1985, the optimal level of capital devoted to the industry fell from Q_1 to Q_2. Thus, the adjustment signals were confused because the period of necessary retrenchment coincided with substantial increases in value brought about by the tenfold increase in the price of the industry's major asset, its inventory of crude oil reserves.

The large cash flows and profits generated by the increases in oil prices both masked the losses imposed on marginal facilities and enabled oil companies to finance major expenditures internally. Thus, the normal disciplinary forces of the product market have been weak, and those of the capital markets have been inoperative, during the past decade.

---

34. Bernard J. Picchi, "The Structure of the U.S. Oil Industry: Past and Future" (Salomon Brothers Inc.), July, 1985, emphasis in original.

Figure 1. Marginal Productivity of Capital in the Oil Industry: 1985 vs. 1973.

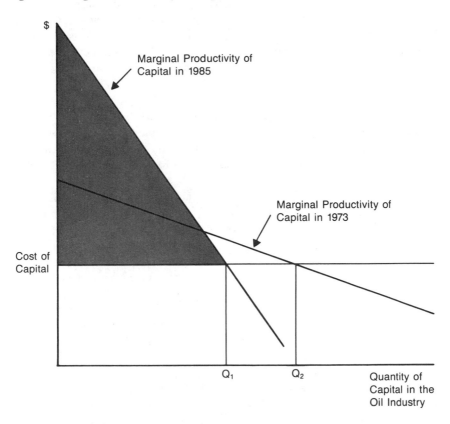

Third, the oil companies' large and highly visible profits subjected them to strong political pressures to reinvest the cash flows in exploration and development to respond to the incorrect, but popular, perception that reserves were too low. Furthermore, while reserves were on average too high, those firms which were substantially short of reserves were spending to replenish them to avoid the organizational consequences associated with reserve deficiencies. The resulting excessive exploration and development expenditures by the industry and the considerable delays in retrenchment of refining and distribution facilities wasted resources.

In sum, the stage was set for retrenchment in the oil industry in the early 1980s. Yet the product and capital markets could not force management to change its strategy because the industry's high internal cash flows insulated it from these pressures.

The fact that oil industry managers tried to invest funds outside the industry is also evidence that they could not find enough profitable projects within the industry to use the huge inflow of resources efficiently. Unfortunately these efforts failed.

The diversification programs involved purchases of companies in retailing (Marcor by Mobil), manufacturing (Reliance Electric by Exxon), office equipment (Vydec by Exxon), and mining (Kennecott by Sohio, Anaconda Minerals by ARCO, Cyprus Mines by Amoco). These acquisitions turned out to be among the least successful of the last decade, partly because of bad luck (e.g., the collapse of the minerals industry) and partly because of a lack of managerial expertise outside the oil industry.

The Effects of Takeovers.   Ultimately the capital markets, through the takeover market, have begun to force managers to respond to the new market conditions. Unfortunately, there is widespread confusion about the important role of takeovers in bringing about the difficult but necessary organizational changes required in the retrenchment.

Managers, quite naturally, want large amounts of resources under their control to insulate them from the uncertainties of markets.[35] Retrenchment requires cancellation or delay of many ongoing and planned projects. This affects the careers of the people involved, and the resulting resistance means that such changes frequently do not get made without the major pressures associated with a crisis. A takeover attempt can create the crisis that brings about action where none would otherwise occur.

T. Boone Pickens of Mesa Petroleum perceived early that the oil industry must be restructured. Partly as a result of Mesa's efforts, firms in the industry were led to merge, and in the merging process they paid out large amounts of capital to shareholders, reduced excess expenditures on exploration and development, and reduced excess capacity in refining and distribution.

The result has been large gains in efficiency. Total gains to the shareholders in the Gulf-Chevron, Getty-Texaco and Dupont-Conoco mergers, for example, were over $17 billion. Much more is possible. A study by Allen Jacobs estimates that, as of December 1984, the total potential gains from eliminating the inefficiencies in 98 petroleum companies amounted to roughly $200 billion.[36]

Recent events indicate that actual takeover is not necessary to bring about the required adjustments.

- The Phillips restructuring plan, in response to the threat of takeover, has involved substantial retrenchment and return of resources to shareholders; and the result was a $1.2 billion (20%) gain in Phillips' market value. It repurchased 53 percent of its stock for $4.5 billion in debt, raised its dividend 25 percent, cut capital spending and initiated a program to sell $2 billion of assets.
- Unocal's defense in the Mesa tender offer battle resulted in a $2.2 billion (35%) gain to shareholders from retrenchment and return of resources to shareholders. It paid out 52 percent of its equity by repurchasing stock with a $4.2 billion debt issue and will reduce costs and capital expenditures.

35. See Gordon Donaldson, *Managing Corporate Wealth* (Praeger, 1984).
36. Allen Jacobs, "The Agency Cost of Corporate Control: The Petroleum Industry," (MIT, unpublished paper, March, 1986).

- The voluntary restructuring announced by ARCO resulted in a $3.2 billion (30%) gain in market value. ARCO's restructuring involves a 35 to 40 percent cut in exploration and development expenditures, repurchase of 25 percent of its stock for $4 billion, a 33 percent increase in its dividend, withdrawal from gasoline marketing and refining east of the Mississippi, and a 13 percent reduction in its work force.
- The announcement of the Diamond-Shamrock reorganization in July 1985 provides an interesting contrast to the others and further support for the theory because the company's market value *fell* 2 percent on the announcement day. Because the plan results in an effective increase in exploration and capital expenditures and a reduction in cash payouts to investors, the restructuring does not increase the value of the firm. The plan involved reducing cash dividends by $.76/share (−43%), creating a master limited partnership to hold properties accounting for 35 percent of its North American oil and gas production, paying an annual $.90/share-dividend in partnership shares, repurchasing 6 percent of its shares for $200 million, selling 12 percent of its master limited partnership to the public, and *increasing* its expenditures on oil and gas exploration by $100 million per year.

Free Cash Flow Theory of Takeovers

Free cash flow is only one of approximately a dozen theories to explain takeovers, all of which are of some relevance in explaining the numerous forces motivating merger and acquisition activity.[37] The agency cost of free cash flow is consistent with a wide range of data for which there has been no consistent explanation. Here I sketch some empirical predictions of the free cash flow theory for takeovers and mergers, and what I believe are the facts that lend it credence.

The positive market response to debt creation in oil and other takeovers is consistent with the agency costs of free cash flow and the control hypothesis of debt.[38] The data is consistent with the notion that additional debt has increased efficiency by forcing organizations with large cash flows but few high-return investment projects to pay out cash to investors. The debt helps prevent such firms from wasting resources on low-return projects.

Acquisitions are one way managers spend cash instead of paying it out to shareholders. Therefore, free cash flow theory predicts which kinds of mergers and takeovers are more likely to destroy rather than to create value. It shows how takeovers are both evidence of the conflicts of interest between the shareholders and managers and a response to the problem. The theory implies that managers of firms with unused borrowing power and large free cash flows are more likely to undertake low-benefit or even value-destroying mergers. Diversification programs generally fit this category, and the theory predicts they will generate lower

---

37. See Roll, 1986, cited earlier.
38. See Robert Bruner, "The Use of Excess Cash and Debt Capacity as a Motive for Merger," (unpublished, Colgate Darden Graduate School of Business, December, 1985).

total gains. The major benefit of such diversifying transactions may be that they involve less waste of resources than if the funds had been invested internally in unprofitable projects.[39]

Low-return mergers are more likely to occur in industries with large cash flows where the economics dictate retrenchment. Horizontal mergers (where cash or debt is the form of payment) within declining industries will tend to create value because they facilitate exit; the cash or debt payments to shareholders of the target firm cause resources to leave the industry directly. Mergers outside the industry are more likely to have low or even negative returns because managers are likely to know less about managing such firms.

Oil fits this description and so does tobacco. Tobacco firms face declining demand as a result of changing smoking habits, but they generate large free cash flow and have been involved in major diversifying acquisitions recently—for example, the $5.6 billion purchase of General Foods by Philip Morris. The theory predicts that these acquisitions in non-related industries are more likely to create negative productivity effects—though these negative effects appear to be outweighed by the reductions in waste from internal expansion.

Forest products is another industry with excess capacity and acquisition activity, including the acquisition of St. Regis by Champion International and Crown Zellerbach by Sir James Goldsmith. Horizontal mergers for cash or debt in such an industry generate gains by encouraging exit of resources (through payout) and by substituting existing capacity for investment in new facilities by firms that are short of capacity.

Food-industry mergers also appear to reflect the expenditure of free cash flow. The industry apparently generates large cash flows with few growth opportunities. It is therefore a good candidate for leveraged buyouts, and these are now occurring; the $6.3 billion Beatrice LBO is the largest ever.

---

39. Acquisitions made with cash or securities other than stock involve payout of resources to (target) shareholders, and this can create net benefits even if the merger creates operating inefficiencies. To illustrate the point, consider an acquiring firm, A, with substantial free cash flow that the market expects will be invested in low-return projects with a negative net present value of $100 million. If Firm A makes an acquisition of Firm B that generates zero synergies but uses up all of Firm A's free cash flow (and thereby prevents its waste) the combined market value of the two firms will *rise* by $100 million. The market value increases because the acquisition eliminates the expenditures on internal investments with negative market value of $100 million. Extending the argument, we see that acquisitions that have *negative* synergies of up to $100 million in current value will still increase the combined market value of the two firms. Such negative-synergy mergers will also increase social welfare and aggregate productivity whenever the market value of the negative productivity effects on the two merging firms is less than the market value of the waste that would have occurred with the firms' investment programs in the absence of the merger. The division of the gains between the target and bidding firms depends, of course, on the bargaining power of the two parties. Because the bidding firms are using funds that would otherwise have been spent on low-or negative-return projects, however, the opportunity cost of the funds is lower than their cost of capital. As a result, they will tend to overpay for the acquisition and thereby transfer most, if not all, of the gains to the target firm's shareholders. In extreme cases they may pay so much that the bidding-firm share price falls, in effect giving the target-shareholders more than 100 percent of the gains. These predictions are consistent with the evidence.

The broadcasting industry generates rents in the form of large cash flows on its licenses and also fits the theory. Regulation limits the overall supply of licenses and the number owned by a single entity. Thus profitable internal investments are limited and the industry's free cash flow has been spent on organizational inefficiencies and diversification programs, making these firms takeover targets. The CBS debt-for-stock exchange and restructuring as a defense against the hostile bid by Turner fits the theory, as does the $3.5 billion purchase of American Broadcasting Company by Capital Cities Communications. Completed cable systems also create agency problems from free cash flows in the form of rents on their franchises and quasi-rents on their investment, and are thus likely targets for acquisition and leveraged buyouts.

Large cash flows earned by motion picture companies on their film libraries also represent quasi-rents and are likely to generate free cash flow problems. Similarly, the attempted takeover of Disney and its subsequent reorganization is consistent with the theory. Drug companies with large cash flows from previous successful discoveries and few potential future prospects are also likely candidates for large agency costs of free cash flow.

The theory predicts that value-increasing takeovers occur in response to breakdowns of internal control processes in firms with substantial free cash flow and organizational policies (including diversification programs) that are wasting resources. It predicts hostile takeovers, large increases in leverage, the dismantling of empires with few economies of scale or scope to give them economic purpose (e.g. conglomerates), and much controversy as current managers object to loss of their jobs or changes in organizational policies forced on them by threat of takeover.

The debt created in a hostile takeover (or takeover defense) of a firm suffering severe agency costs of free cash flow need not be permanent. Indeed, sometimes it is desirable to "over-leverage" such a firm. In these situations, levering the firm so highly it cannot continue to exist in its old form yields benefits. It creates the crisis to motivate cuts in expansion programs and the sale of those divisions that are more valuable outside the firm. The proceeds are used to reduce debt to a more normal or permanent level. This process results in a complete rethinking of the organization's strategy and structure. When it is successful, a much leaner, more efficient, and competitive organization results.

Some Evidence from Merger Studies

Consistent with the data, free cash flow theory predicts that many acquirers will tend to perform exceptionally well prior to acquisition and that exceptional stock price performance will often be associated with increased free cash flow which is then used for acquisition programs. The oil industry fits this description. Increased oil prices caused large gains in profits and stock prices in the mid-to-late

1970s. Empirical evidence from studies of both stock prices and accounting data also indicates exceptionally good performance for acquirers prior to acquisition.[40]

Targets will tend to be of two kinds: firms with poor management that have done poorly before the merger, and firms that have done exceptionally well and have large free cash flow that they refuse to pay out to shareholders. . . . In the best study to date of the determinants of takeover, Palepu (1986) finds strong evidence consistent with the free cash flow theory of mergers. He studied a sample of 163 firms that were acquired in the period 1971–1979 and a random sample of 256 firms that were not acquired. Both samples were in mining and manufacturing and were listed on either the New York or American Stock Exchange. He finds that target firms were characterized by significantly lower growth and lower leverage than the nontarget firms, although there was no significant difference in their holdings of liquid assets. He also finds that poor prior performance (measured by the net-of-market returns in the four years before the acquisition) is significantly related to the probability of takeover, and, interestingly, that accounting measures of past performance such as return on equity are unrelated to the probability of takeover. He also finds that firms with a mismatch between growth and resources are more likely to be taken over. These are firms with high growth (measured by average sales growth), low liquidity (measured by the ratio of liquid assets to total assets) and high leverage, and firms with low growth, high liquidity, and low leverage. Finally, Palepu's evidence rejects the hypothesis that takeovers are due to the undervaluation of a firm's assets as measured by the market-to-book ratio.[41]

V. High-Yield ("Junk") Bonds

The last several years have witnessed a major innovation in the financial markets with the establishment of active markets in high-yield bonds. These bonds are rated below investment grade by the bond rating agencies and are frequently referred to as junk bonds, a disparaging term that bears no relation to their pedigree. They carry interest rates that are 2 to 5 percentage points higher than the yields on government bonds of comparable maturity. High-yield bonds are best thought of as commercial loans that can be resold in secondary markets. By traditional standards

---

40. See the following two papers which were presented at the Conference on Takeovers and Contests for Corporate Control, Columbia University, November, 1985: Ellen B. Magenheim and Dennis Meuller, "On Measuring the Effect of Acquisitions on Acquiring Firm Shareholders, or Are Acquiring Firm Shareholders Better Off After an Acquisition Than They Were Before?"; and Michael Bradley and Gregg Jarrell, "Evidence on Gains from Mergers and Takeovers," See also Paul R. Asquith and E. Han Kim, "The Impact of Merger Bids on the Participating Firms' Security Holders," *Journal of Finance*, 37, pp. 1209–1228; Gershon Mandelker, "Risk and Return: The Case of Merging Firms," *Journal of Financial Economics*, V. 1, No. 4 (December, 1974), pp. 303–336; and T.C. Langetieg, "An Application of A Three-Factor Performance Index to Measure Stockholder Gains from Merger" *Journal of Financial Economics*, V. 6 (December, 1978), pp. 365–384.

41. Palepu (1986), presented at the Conference on Takeovers and Contests for Corporate Control, Columbia University, November, 1985.

they are more risky than investment-grade bonds and therefore carry higher interest rates. An early study finds the default rates on these bonds have been low and the realized returns have been disproportionately higher than their risk.[42]

High-yield bonds have been attacked by those who wish to inhibit their use, particularly in the financing of takeover bids. The invention of high-yield bonds has provided methods to finance takeover ventures like those companies use to finance more traditional ventures. Companies commonly raise funds to finance ventures by selling claims to be paid from the proceeds of the venture; this is the essence of debt or stock issues used to finance new ventures. High-yield bonds used in takeovers work similarly. The bonds provide a claim on the proceeds of the venture, using the assets and cash flows of the target plus the equity contributed by the acquirer as collateral. This basic structure is the common way that individuals purchase homes; they use the home plus their down payment as collateral for the mortgage. There is nothing inherently unusual in the structure of this contract, although those who would bar the use of high-yield bonds in takeover ventures would have us believe otherwise.

Some might argue that the risk of high-yield bonds used in takeover attempts is "too high." But high-yield bonds are by definition less risky than common stock claims on the same venture. Would these same critics argue that stock claims are too risky and thus should be barred? The risk argument makes logical sense only as an argument that the transactions costs associated with bankruptcy are too high in these ventures or that the promised yields on the bonds are too low and that investors who purchase them will not earn returns high enough to compensate for the risk they are incurring. This argument makes little sense because there is vast evidence that investors are capable of pricing risks in all sorts of other markets. It is inconceivable they are peculiarly unable to do so in the high-yield bond market.

In January 1986 the Federal Reserve Board issued a new interpretation of the margin rules that restricts the use of debt in takeovers to 50 percent or less of the purchase price. This rule reintroduces size as an effective deterrent to takeover. It was apparently motivated by the belief that the use of corporate debt had become abnormally and dangerously high and was threatening the economy.

This assessment is not consistent with the facts. Figure 2 plots three measures of debt use by nonfinancial corporations in the U.S. The debt/equity ratio is measured relative to three bases: market value of equity, estimated current asset value of equity, and accounting book value of equity measured at historical cost.

Although debt/equity ratios were higher in 1985 than in 1961, they were not at record levels. The book value debt/equity ratio reached a high of 81.4 percent in 1984, but declined to 78 percent in 1985. The fact that debt/equity ratios measured on a historical cost basis are relatively high is to be expected, given the previous decade of inflation. Maintenance of the same inflation-adjusted debt/equity ratio

---

42. Marshall E. Blume and Donald B. Keim, "Risk and Return Characteristics of Lower-Grade Bonds" (unpublished paper, The Wharton School, December, 1984).

Figure 2. Debt-to-Equity Ratios for Nonfinancial Corporations: 1961 to 1985.

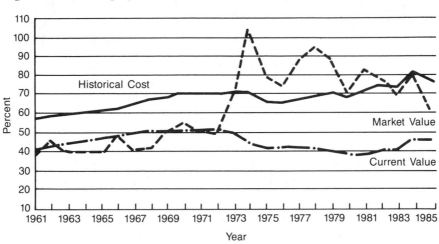

Source: Federal Reserve System [1986].

in times of inflation implies that the book value ratio must rise because the current value of assets in the denominator of the inflation-adjusted ratio is rising. The current value ratio, which takes account of inflation, fell from 50.7 percent in 1970 to 46.5 percent in 1985. The market-value ratio rose from 54.7 percent in 1970 to 80.5 percent in 1984 and plummeted to 60.8 percent in 1985. The 1985 market-value ratio was 45 percentage points below its 1974 peak of 105.2 percent. In short, the Federal Reserve System's own data are inconsistent with the reasons given for its restrictions on the use of debt.

High-yield bonds were first used in a takeover bid in early 1984 and have been involved in relatively few bids in total. In 1984, only about 12 percent of the $14.3 billion of new high-yield debt was associated with mergers and acquisitions. In 1985, 26 percent of the $14.7 billion of new high-yield debt was used in acquisitions.[43] Some of the acquisitions, however, such as the Unocal and CBS offers (both unsuccessful), have received intense attention from the media; and this publicity has fostered the belief that high-yield bonds are an important innovation in the takeover field because they help eliminate mere size as a deterrent to takeover. They have been particularly influential in helping to bring about reorganizations in the oil industry.

Historical default rates on high-yield bonds have been low, but many of these bonds are so new that the experience could prove to be different in the next downturn. Various opponents have proposed regulations or legislation to restrict the issuance of such securities, to penalize their tax status, and to restrict their holding by thrifts, which can now buy them as substitutes for the issuance of nonmarketable

43. Source: Drexel Burnham Lambert, private correspondence.

commercial loans. These proposals are premature. Policymakers should be wary of responding to the clamor for restrictions by executives who desire protection from the discipline of the takeover market and by members of the financial community who want to restrict competition from this new financing vehicle.

The holding of high-yield bonds by thrifts is an interesting issue that warrants further analysis. The recent deregulation of the banking and thrift industries presents many opportunities and challenges to the thrifts. Elimination of restrictions on interest paid to depositors has raised the cost of funds to these institutions. Thrifts have also received the right to engage in new activities such as commercial lending. Survival requires these institutions to take advantage of some of these new business opportunities.

The organizational costs of developing commercial lending departments in the 3,500 thrifts in the country is substantial. Thousands of new loan officers will have to be hired and trained. The additional wage and training costs and the bad-debt losses that will be incurred in the learning phase will be substantial. High-yield bonds provide a promising solution to this problem. If part of the commercial lending function can be centralized in the hands of investment bankers who provide commercial loans in the form of marketable high-yield debt, the thrifts can substitute the purchase of this high-yield debt for their commercial lending and thereby avoid the huge investment in such loan departments.

VI. The Legitimate Concerns of Managers

Conflicts of Interest and Increased Costs to Managers

The interests of corporate managers are not the same as the interests of corporations as organizations, and conflicts of interest can become intense when major changes in the organization's strategy are required. Competition causes change, and change creates winners and losers, especially in that branch of the managerial labor market called the takeover market.

Managers' Private Incentives Sometimes Run Counter to Overall Efficiency. The costs of takeovers have fallen as the legal and financial skills of participants in the takeover market have become more sophisticated, as the restrictions on takeovers imposed by antitrust laws have been relaxed, and as financing techniques have improved. Except for new regulatory constraints on the use of debt, this means that the largest of the Fortune 500 companies are now potentially subject to takeover. The abolition of mere size as a deterrent to takeover is desirable because it has made possible the realization of large gains from reallocating larger collections of assets to more productive uses.

This new susceptibility to takeover has created a new contracting environment for top-level managers. Many managers are legitimately anxious, and it will take time for the system to work out an appropriate set of practices and contracts reflecting the risks and rewards of the new environment. Some of the uncertainty of top-level managers formerly insulated from pressures from the financial markets will fade as they learn how their policies affect the market value of their companies.

The Desirability of Golden Parachutes

Unfortunately, a major component of the solution to the conflict of interest between shareholders and managers has been vastly misunderstood. I am referring to severance contracts that compensate managers for the loss of their jobs in the event of a change in control—what have been popularly labeled "golden parachutes."

These contracts are clearly desirable, even when judged solely from the viewpoint of the interests of shareholders; but they are also efficient from a social viewpoint. When correctly implemented they help reduce the conflicts of interest between shareholders and managers at times of takeover and therefore make it more likely that the productive gains stemming from changes in control will be realized. The evidence indicates that stock prices of firms that adopt severance-related compensation contracts for managers on average rise about 3 percent when adoption of the contracts is announced.[44] There is no easy way to tell how much of this could be due to the reduction in conflict between managers and shareholders over takeovers.

At times of takeover, shareholders are implicitly asking the top-level managers of their firm to negotiate a deal for them that frequently involves the imposition of large personal costs on the managers and their families. These involve substantial moving costs, the loss of position, power and prestige, and even the loss of their jobs. Shareholders are asking the very people who are most likely to have invested considerable time and energy (in some cases a life's work) in building a successful organization to negotiate its sale and the possible redirection of its resources.

It is important to face these conflicts and to structure contracts with managers to reduce them. It makes no sense to hire a realtor to sell your house and then penalize him for doing so. Yet that is the implication of many of the emotional reactions to control-related severance contracts. The restrictions and tax penalties imposed on these severance payments by the Deficit Reduction Act of 1984 are unwise interferences in the contracting freedoms of shareholders and managers; and they should be eliminated. Moreover, it is important to eliminate the misunderstanding about the purpose and effects of these contracts that has been fostered by past rhetoric on the topic so that boards of directors can get on with the job of structuring these contracts.

Golden parachutes can also be used to restrict takeovers and to entrench managers at the expense of shareholders. How does one tell whether a particular set of contracts crosses this line?

---

44. See R. Lambert and D. Larcker, "Golden Parachutes, Executive Decision-Making and Shareholder Wealth," *Journal of Accounting and Economics*, V. 7 (April, 1985), pp. 179–204.

The key is whether the contracts help solve the conflict-of-interest problem between shareholders and managers that arises over changes in control. Solving this problem requires extending control-related severance contracts beyond the chief executive to those members of the top-level management team who must play an important role in negotiating and implementing any transfer of control. Contracts that award severance contracts to substantial number of managers beyond this group are unlikely to be in the shareholders' interests. The contracts awarded by Beneficial Corp. to 234 of its managers are unlikely to be justified as in the shareholders' interests.[45]

It is particularly important to institute severance-related compensation contracts in situations where it is optimal for managers to invest in organization-specific human capital—that is, in skills and knowledge that have little or no value in other organizations. Managers will not so invest where the likelihood is high that their investment will be eliminated by an unexpected transfer of control and the loss of their jobs. In such situations the firm will have to pay for all costs associated with the creation of such organization-specific human capital, and it will be difficult to attract and retain highly talented managers when they have better opportunities elsewhere. In addition, contracts that award excessive severance compensation to the appropriate group of managers will tend to motivate managers to sell the firm at too low a price.

No simple rules can be specified that will easily prevent the misuse of golden parachutes because the appropriate solution will depend on many factors that are specific to each situation (for example, the amount of stock held by managers, and the optimal amount of investment in organization-specific human capital). In general, contracts that award inappropriately high payments to a group that is excessively large will reduce efficiency and harm shareholders by raising the cost of acquisition and by transferring wealth from shareholders to managers. The generally appropriate solution is to make the control-related severance contracts pay off in a way that is tied to the premium earned by the stockholders. Stock options or restricted stock appreciation rights that pay off only in the event of a change in control are two options that have some of the appropriate properties. In general, policies that encourage increased stock ownership by managers and the board of directors will provide incentives that will tend to reduce the conflicts of interests with managers.

VII. Targeted Repurchases

The evidence indicates takeovers generate large benefits for shareholders. Yet virtually all proposals to protect shareholders from asserted difficulties in the control market will harm them by either eliminating or reducing the probability of successful hostile tender offers. These proposals will also block the productivity increases that are the source of the gains.

---

45. Ann Morrison, "Those Executive Bailout Deals," *Fortune*, (December 13, 1982).

Most proposals to restrict or prohibit targeted repurchases (transactions pejoratively labeled "greenmail") are nothing more than antitakeover proposals in disguise. Greenmail is an appellation that suggests blackmail; yet the only effective weapon possessed by a greenmailer is the right to offer to purchase stock from other shareholders at a substantial premium. The "damage" to shareholders caused by this action is difficult to find. Those who propose to "protect" shareholders hide this fact behind emotional language designed to mislead. Greenmail is actually a targeted repurchase, an offer by *management* to repurchase the shares of a subset of shareholders at a premium, an offer not made to other shareholders.

Greenmail is the Trojan horse of the takeover battle in the legal and political arenas. Antitakeover proposals are commonly disguised as antigreenmail provisions. Management can easily prohibit greenmail without legislation; it need only announce a policy that, like Ulysses tying himself to the mast, prohibits management or the board from making such payments.[46]

VIII. Problems in the Delaware Court

Delaware courts have created over the years a highly productive fabric of corporate law that has benefited the nation. The court is having difficulty, however, in sorting out the complex issues it faces in the takeover area. The court's problems in settling conflicts between shareholders and management over control issues reflect a fundamental weakness in its model of the corporation, a model that has heretofore worked quite well. The result has been a confusing set of decisions that, in contrast to much of the court's previous history, appears to make little economic sense.[47]

---

46. Three excellent studies of these transactions indicate that when measured from the initial toehold purchase to the final repurchase of the shares, the stock price of target firms rises. Therefore, shareholders are benefited, not harmed, by the whole sequence of events. See Clifford Holderness and Dennis Sheehan, "Raiders or Saviors: The Evidence on Six Controversial Investors," *Journal of Financial Economics* (December, 1985), Wayne H. Mikkelson, and Richard S. Ruback, "An Empirical Analysis of the Interfirm Equity Investment Process." *Journal of Financial Economics*, V. 14 (December, 1985), and Wayne H. Mikkelson and Richard S. Ruback, "Targeted Repurchases and Common Stock Returns," (unpublished manuscript, June, 1986). There is some indication, however, that the stock price increases might represent the expectation of future takeover premiums in firms in which the targeted repurchase was not sufficient to prevent ultimate takeover of the firm. If so, it may well be that, much as in the final defeat of tender offers found by Bradley, Desai and Kim (Michael Bradley, Michael, Anand Desai and E. Han Kim, "The Rationale Behind Interfirm Tender Offers: Information or Synergy?" *Journal of Financial Economics*, V. 11 (April, 1983), pp. 183–206), all premiums are lost to those shareholders in firms for which the repurchase and associated standstill agreements successfully lock up the firm. The evidence on these issues is not yet sufficient to issue a final judgement either way.

47. See, for example, Moran v. Household Intl, Inc. 490 A.2d 1059 (Del. Ch. 1985) aff'd. 500 A.2d 1346 (Del. 1985) (upholding poison pill rights issue), Smith v. Van Gordom, 488 A.2d 858, (holding board liable for damages in sale of firm at substantial premium over market price), Unocal v. Mesa, 493 A.2d 946, 954 (Del. 1985) (allowing discriminatory targeted repurchase that confiscates wealth of largest shareholder), Revlon Inc. v. MacAndrews & Forbes Holdings Inc., 506 A.2nd 173, 180 (Del. 1986), (invalidation of Revlon's lockup sale of a prime division to Forstmann Little at a below-market price).

Altruism and the Business Judgment Rule

The Delaware court's model of the corporation is founded in the business judgment rule—the legal doctrine that holds that unless explicit evidence of fraud or self-dealing exists the board of directors is presumed to be acting solely in the interests of shareholders. . . . The courts must not apply the business judgment rule to conflicts over control rights between principals and agents. If the business judgment rule is applied to such conflicts, the courts are effectively giving the *agent* (management) the right unilaterally to change the control rights. In the long run, this interpretation of the contract will destroy the possibility of such cooperative arrangements because it will leave principals (stockholders) with few effective rights.

Recently the courts have applied the business judgment rule to the conflicts over the issuance of poison pill preferred stock, poison pill rights, and discriminatory targeted repurchases, and have given managers and boards the rights to use these devices.[48] In so doing the courts are essentially giving the agents (managers and the board) the right unilaterally to change critical control aspects of the contract—in particular the right to fire the agent. This has major implications for economic activity, productivity, and the health of the corporation. If the trend goes far enough, the corporation as an organizational form will be seriously handicapped.

Poison Pills

Poison pill securities change fundamental aspects of the corporate rules of the game that govern the relationship between shareholders, managers, and the board of directors. They do so when a control-related event occurs, such as a takeover offer or the acquisition of a substantial block of stock or voting rights by an individual or group. The Household International version of the poison pill rights issue is particularly interesting because it was a major test case in the area.

When the Household International board of directors issued its complicated right to shareholders, it unilaterally changed the nature of the contractual relationship with Household's shareholders in a fundamental way. The right effectively restricts the alienability of the common stock by prohibiting shareholders from selling their shares, without permission of the board, into a control transaction leading to merger at a price that involves a premium over market value of less than $6 billion. Since Household had a market value of less than $2 billion at the time, this was a premium over 300 percent—more than 6 times the average takeover premium of 50 percent common to recent times—a premium that is difficult to justify as in the shareholders' interests.

The November 1985 Delaware court decision upholding the Household International rights issue will significantly restrict hostile takeovers of firms that adopt similar provisions. Before that decision, 37 pills of various forms had been adopted.

---

48. Moran v. Household Intl., and Unocal v. Mesa.

Over 150 corporations adopted pills in the seven months following that decision.[49] Unlike most other antitakeover devices, this defense is very difficult for a prospective acquirer to overcome without meeting the board's terms (at least one who desires to complete the second-step closeout merger). An SEC study analyzed the 37 companies introducing pills between June 1983, when Lenox introduced the first one, and December 1985. Eleven of these 37 firms experienced control changes: five experienced a negotiated change in control while the pill was in effect (Revlon, Cluett Peabody, Great Lakes, Int., Lenox, and Enstar), two were taken over by creeping acquisitions (Crown Zellerbach and William Wright), two were taken over after their pills were declared illegal (AMF and Richardson Vicks), one (Superior Oil) was acquired after the pill was withdrawn in the face of a lawsuit and proxy fight by its largest holder, and one (Amsted) has proposed a leveraged buyout. The SEC study finds that "Announcements of (twenty) poison pill plans in the midst of takeover speculations have resulted in an average 2.4 percent net of market price declines for firms adopting the plans." The effects of another twelve plans adopted by firms that were not the subject of takeover speculation were essentially nil.[50]

Sir James Goldsmith recently gained control of Crown Zellerbach, which had implemented a rights issue similar to Household International's. Goldsmith purchased a controlling interest in the open market after Crown's board opposed his tender offer and refused to recall its rights issue. In this situation the acquirer must either tolerate the costs associated with leaving the minority interest outstanding and forsake the benefits of merging the assets of the two organizations, or incur the costs of the premium required by the rights on execution of the second-step closeout merger. The Crown case revealed a loophole in the Household/Crown version of the pill (which has been closed in newly implemented versions). Although Goldsmith could not complete a second-step merger without paying the high-premium required by the rights, he could avoid it by simply liquidating Crown.

Rights issues like Household's and Crown Zellerbach's harm shareholders. They will fundamentally impair the efficiency of corporations that adopt them, and for this reason they will reduce productivity in the economy if widely adopted.[51]

---

49. See Office of the Chief Economist of the SEC, "The Economics of Poison Pills," (March 5, 1986), and Corporate Control Alert, (February, March and April, May and June, 1986).
50. Ibid.
51. Another study of the effects of poison pills (Paul H. Malatesta and Ralph A. Walkling, "The Impact of Poison Pill Securities on Stockholder Wealth," (unpublished, University of Washington, 1985) also indicates they have a negative effect on stock prices. On average, stock prices fell by a statistically significant 2 percent in the 2 days around the announcement in the *Wall Street Journal* of adoption of a poison pill for a sample of 14 firms that adopted these securities between December 1982 and February 1985. This price decline, however, was smaller than the average 7.5 percent increase in price that occurred in the 10 days prior to the adoption of the pill. Firms adopting pills appear to be those in which managers and directors bear a substantially smaller fraction of the wealth consequences of their actions. In all but three of the firms the percentage of common shares owned by officers and directors was substantially below the industry average ownership of shares. The average ownership of firms in the same industry was 16.5 percent and for the firms adopting pills it was 7.5 percent.

A broad interpretation of the business judgment rule is important to the effectiveness of the corporation because a system that puts the courts into the business of making managerial decisions will generate great inefficiencies. The court has erred, however, in allowing the Household board, under the business judgment rule, to make the fundamental change in the structure of the organization implied by the rights issue without votes of its shareholders. It is unlikely the court would allow the board to decide unilaterally to make the organization a closed corporation by denying shareholders the right to sell their shares to anyone at a mutually agreeable price without the permission of the board. The Household International rights issue places just such a restriction on the alienability of shares, but only in the case of a subset of transactions—the control-related transactions so critical for protecting shareholders when the normal internal board-level control mechanisms break down. Several other poison pill cases have been heard by the courts with similar outcomes, but a New Jersey and two New York courts have recently ruled against poison pills that substantially interfere with the voting rights of large-block shareholders.[52] An Illinois District Court recently voided a poison pill (affirmed by the Seventh Circuit Court of Appeals) and two weeks later approved a new pill issued by the same company.[53]

The problem with these special securities and the provision they contain is not with their appropriateness (some might well be desirable), but with the manner in which they are being adopted—that is, without approval by shareholders. Boards of directors show little inclination to refer such issues to shareholders.

One solution to the problems caused by the Household decision is for shareholders to approve amendments to the certificate of incorporation to restrict the board's power to take such actions without shareholder approval. This is not an easy task, however, given the pressure corporate managers are bringing to bear on the managers of their pension funds to vote with management.[54] Even more problematic is the provision in Delaware law that requires certificate amendments to be recommended to shareholders by the board of directors.[55]

Exclusionary Self Tenders: The Unocal v. Mesa Decision[56]

The Delaware Supreme Court surprised the legal, financial, and corporate communities in the spring of 1985 by giving Unocal the right to make a tender offer for

---

52. Ministar Acquiring Corp. v. AMF Inc., 621 Fed Sup 1252, So Dis NY, 1985, Unilever Acquisition Corp. v. Richardson-Vicks, Inc., 618 Fed Sup 407, So Dist NY, 1985, Asarco Inc. v. M.R.H. Holmes a Court, 611 Fed Sup 468, Dist Ct of NJ, 1985, and Dynamics Corp. of America v. CTS Corporation.
53. Dynamics Corp. of America v. CTS Corp. *et al.* U.S. District Court, Northern District of Illinois, Eastern Division, No. 86, C 1624, (April 17, 1986), affirmed Seventh Circuit Court of Appeals Nos. 86–16–1, 86–1608, and Dynamics Corp. of America v. CTS Corp., *et al.* (May 3, 1986).
54. See Joe Koleman, "The Proxy Pressure on Pension Fund Managers," Institutional Investor, (July, 1985), pp. 145–147, and Investor Responsibility Research Center, Inc., Corporate Government Service: Voting by Institutional Investors on Corporate Governance Questions, 1985 Proxy Season, pp. 19–25.
55. 8 *Del C.* 242(c) (1).
56. This discussion is based on my article, "When Unocal Won over Pickens Shareholders and Society Lost," *Financier*, V, IX, No. 11 (Nov., 1985), pp. 50–53.

29 percent of its shares while excluding its largest shareholder, Mesa Partners II, from the offer. This decision enabled the Unocal management and board to avoid loss of control to Mesa. The decision imposed large costs on Unocal shareholders and, if not reversed, threatens major damage to shareholders of all Delaware corporations.

The Unocal victory over Mesa cost the Unocal shareholders $1.1 billion ($9.48 per post-offer share). This is the amount by which the $9.4 billion Mesa offer exceeded the $8.3 billion value of Unocal's "victory."[57] This loss represents 18 percent of Unocal's pre-takeover value of $6.2 billion. The $2.1 billion net increase in value to $8.3 billion resulted from Unocal's $4.2 billion debt issue which, contrary to assertions, benefits its shareholders. It does so by effectively bonding Unocal to pay out a substantial fraction of its huge cash flows to shareholders rather than to reinvest them in low-return projects, and by reducing taxes on Unocal and its shareholders.

For his services in generating this $2.1 billion gain for Unocal shareholders, T. Boone Pickens has been vilified in the press, and Mesa Partners II has incurred net losses before taxes—obviously a perversion of incentives.

In addition to Mesa's losses, shareholders of all Delaware corporations lose because the court's decision gives management a weapon so powerful it essentially guarantees that no Delaware corporation that uses it will be taken over by a tender offer. A determined board could, in the extreme, pay out all the corporation's assets and leave the acquirer holding a worthless shell. Because of this new power, shareholders are denied the benefits of future actions by Pickens and others to discipline managers whose strategies are wasting resources.

Society also loses. The decision will have a chilling effect on takeovers, blocking the productivity increases that are the source of the takeover gains and thereby handicapping Delaware corporations in the competition for survival.

Unocal's self-tender for 29 percent of its shares at $72 per share ($26 over the market price) was designed to defeat Mesa's $54 per share cash offer for 50.4 percent of Unocal's shares plus $54 per share in debt securities for the remaining 49.6 percent. The Unocal offer would have paid 59 percent of Unocal's pretakeover equity to other shareholders while denying participation to the 13.6 percent minority holding of Mesa Partners II. This would transfer about $248 million from Mesa's holdings to other Unocal stockholders—a classic case of corporate raiding that contrasts with the beneficial effects of the actions of takeover specialists like Pickens, Carl Icahn and Irwin Jacobs on other shareholders.

Faced with the threat of legalized expropriation of $248 million, Mesa accepted a settlement in which Unocal backed off from the Mesa exclusion. The settlement involved repurchase of part of Mesa's shares at the terms of the tender offer, a 25-year standstill agreement, a promise to vote its shares in the same proportion as other shares are voted, and constraints on Mesa's rights to sell its remaining shares.

---

57. The $8.3 billion value of Unocal securities held by its shareholders is calculated as $4.1 billion in stock (116 million shares at $34-7/8 on May 24, the first trading day after close of the offer), and $4.2 billion in Unocal debt trading at $73.50.

The essential characteristics of Unocal's exclusionary repurchase defense are now incorporated in newly popular poison pill plans called back-end plans.[58] These plans give shareholders a right to tender their shares for securities worth more than the market value of their stock when a shareholder exceeds a certain maximum limit of stock ownership that ranges from 30 to 50 percent. As with Unocal's exclusion of Mesa, the large shareholder is denied the same right to tender his shares. This threatens a shareholder who violates the holding limit with potentially large dilution of his holdings. It thereby limits the existence of large stock holdings.

"Protection" from Two-Tier Tender Offers.   The court ruled that the objective of Unocal's offer was to protect its shareholder against "a grossly inadequate and coercive two-tier, front-end-loaded tender offer" and against greenmail. This assessment of the situation was upside down. Paradoxically, the court's ruling imposed on Unocal shareholders exactly the evil it purported to prevent Unocal defeated Mesa's $1.1 billion higher offer precisely because Mesa's offer was a level $54 offer and Unocal's offer was an extreme front-end loaded two-tier offer—$72 for 29 percent of its shares in the front-end with a back-end price of $35 for the remaining 71 percent of the shares. (The back-end price was implicit, but easy to calculate and reported in the press at the time of the offer.) The effective price of the Unocal offer was therefore only $45.73 per pre-offer share (the weighted average of the front- and back-end prices).

Comparing the Unocal offer with SEC estimates of average minimums in two-tier tender offers indicates the extreme nature of the Unocal two-tier offer. Historically the average back-end premium on outside two-tier offers is 45 percent higher than the stock price measured 20 trading days prior to the offer.[59] This contrasts sharply with the *negative* back-end premium on Unocal's self tender of −25 percent. That is, the $35 back-end price was 25 percent below the Unocal market price of $46-3/8 twenty days before the offer.

The negative back-end premium on Unocal's offer means the holders of 20 million Unocal shares who failed to tender to the first tier of the Unocal offer were particularly hurt. As of the close of the offer they suffered total losses of $382 million, $215 million from the loss of $37.12/share on 29 percent of their shares,[60] plus a loss of $167 million from being denied the $54 in debt securities they would have received in the back of the Mesa offer.[61]

---

58. See Office of the Chief Economist of the SEC, "The Economics of Poison Pills" (March 5, 1986).

59. See Comment, Robert, and Gregg A. Jarrell, "Two-Tier Tender Offers: The Imprisonment of the Free-Riding Shareholder," (unpublished manuscript, March 1, 1986); an earlier version appeared as Office of the Chief Economist Securities and Exchange Commission, "The Economics of Any-or-All, Partial, and Two-Tier Tender Offers," *Federal Register*, June 29, 1984, pp. 26.751-26.761.

60. Calculated as the $72 value of the Unocal debt offered in exchange for 29% of their shares less the $34.875 post-offer closing price of the shares.

61. See Michael Bradley and Michael Rosensweig, "The Law and Economics of Defensive Stock Repurchases and Defensive Self-Tender Offers, (Unpublished manuscript, University of Michigan, 1985) for a thorough discussion of the issues involved in self-tender offers.

Protection from Targeted Repurchases. The court also erred in its concern over greenmail. In ruling to eliminate the threat of greenmail, the court in fact authorized Unocal to make a greenmail transaction that differs from the usual variety only in that it penalized, rather than benefited, the large-block holder (i.e., reverse greenmail). In authorizing this form of targeted repurchase, the court granted large benefits to managers who desire protection from competition but harmed shareholders.

One of the great strengths of the corporation is the long-held principle that holders of a given class of securities are treated identically in transactions with the corporation. The Unocal decision threatens to turn the corporation into a battleground where special-interest groups of shareholders fight over the division of the pie much as special interests in the public sector do. The result will be a much smaller pie.

Responsible boards of directors interested in the welfare of shareholders and the survival of the corporation as an organizational form will implement procedures to ban all targeted repurchases that carry premiums over market value.

IX. Conclusion

Although economic analysis and the evidence indicate the market for corporate control is benefiting shareholders, society, and the corporation as an organizational form, it is also making life more uncomfortable for top-level executives. This discomfort is creating strong pressures at both the state and federal levels for restrictions that will seriously cripple the workings of this market. In 1985 there were 21 bills on this topic in the Congressional hopper, all of which proposed various restrictions on the market for corporate control. Some proposed major new restrictions on share ownership and financial instruments. Within the past several years the legislatures of numerous states have passed antitakeover laws. This political activity is another example of special interests using the democratic political system to change the rules of the game to benefit themselves at the expense of society as a whole. In this case the special interests are top-level corporate managers and other groups who stand to lose from competition in the market for corporate control. The result will be a significant weakening of the corporation as an organizational form and a reduction in efficiency.

X. Appendix: Evidence from Financial Transactions in Support of the Free Cash Flow Theory of Mergers

Free cash flow theory helps explain previously puzzling results on the effects of various financial transactions. Smith [1986]* summarizes more than twenty studies of stock price changes at announcements of transactions that change capital structure as well as various other dividend transactions. These results are summarized in Table 2.

*See Cliff Smith, "Investment Banking and the Capital Acquisition Process," *Journal of Financial Economics* 15 (1986) for references to all studies cited in this Appendix.

For firms with positive free cash flow, the theory predicts that stock prices will increase with unexpected increases in payouts to shareholders and decrease with unexpected decreased in payouts. It also predicts that unexpected increases in demand for funds from shareholders via new issues will cause stock prices will increase with increasing tightness of the constraints binding the payout of future cash flow to shareholders and decrease with reductions in the tightness of these constraints. These predictions do not apply, however, to those firms with more profitable projects than free cash flow to fund them.

The predictions of the agency cost of free cash flow are consistent with all but three of the 32 estimated abnormal stock price changes summarized in Table 2. Moreover, one of the inconsistencies is explainable by another phenomenon.

Panel A of Table 2 shows that stock prices rise by a statistically significant amount with announcements of the initiation of cash dividend payments, increases in dividends, and payments of specially designated dividends; they fall by a statistically significant amount with decreases in dividend payments. (All coefficients in the table are significantly different from zero unless noted with an asterisk.)

Panel B of Table 2 shows that security sales and retirements that raise cash or pay out cash and simultaneously provide offsetting changes in the constraints bonding the payout of future cash flow are all associated with returns insignificantly different from zero. The insignificant return on retirement debt fits the theory because the payout of cash is offset by an equal reduction in the present value of promised future cash payouts. If the debt sales are associated with no changes in the expected investment program, the insignificant return on announcements of the sale of debt and preferred also fits the theory. The acquisition of new funds with debt or preferred is offset exactly by a commitment bonding the future payout of cash flows of equal present value.

Panel C shows that sales of convertible debt and convertible preferred are associated with significantly negative stock price changes. These security sales raise cash and provide little effective bonding of future cash flow payments for the following reason: when the stock into which the debt is convertible is worth more than the face value of the debt, management has incentives to call them and force conversion to common.

Panel D shows that, with one exception, security retirements that pay out cash to shareholders increase stock prices. The price decline associated with targeted large block repurchases (often called "greenmail") is highly likely to be due to the reduced probability that a takeover premium will be realized. These transactions are often associated with standstill agreements in which the seller of the stock agrees to refrain from acquiring more stock and from making a takeover offer for some period into the future.

Panel E summarizes the effects of security sales and retirements that raise cash and do not bond future cash flow payments. Consistent with the theory, negative abnormal returns are associated with all such changes. However, the negative returns associated with the sale of common through a conversion-forcing call are statistically insignificant.

Table 2. The Stock Market Response to Various Dividend and Capital Structure Transactions.[a]

Type of Transaction	Security Issued	Security Retired
Panel A: Dividend changes that change the cash paid to shareholders		
Dividend initiation[b]		
Dividend increase[c]		
Specially designated dividend[d]		
Dividend decrease[c]		
Panel B: Security sales (that raise cash) and retirements (that pay out cash) and simultaneously		
Security sale (industrial)[e]	debt	none
Security sale (utility)[f]	debt	none
Security sale (industrial)[g]	preferred	none
Security sale (utility)[h]	preferred	none
Call[i]	none	debt
Panel C: Security sales which raise cash and bond future cash flow payments only minimally		
Security sale (industrial)[e]	conv. debt	none
Security sale (industrial)[h]	conv. preferred	none
Security sale (utility)[h]	conv. preferred	none
Panel D: Security retirements that pay out cash to shareholders		
Self tender offer[j]	none	common
Open market purchase[k]	none	common
Targeted small holdings[l]	none	common
Targeted large block repurchase[m]	none	common
Panel E: Security sales or calls that raise cash and do not bond future cash flow payments		
Security sale (industrial)[n]	common	none
Security sale (utility)[o]	common	none
Conversion-forcing call[u]	common	cov. preferred
Conversion-forcing call[u]	common	conv. debt
Panel F: Exchange offers, or designated use security sales that increase the bonding of payout of		
Designated use security sale[p]	debt	common
Exchange offer[q]	debt	common
Exchange offer[q]	preferred	common
Exchange offer[q]	debt	preferred
Exchange offer[r]	income bonds	preferred
Panel G: Transaction with no change in bonding of payout of future cash flows		
Exchange offer[s]	debt	debt
Designated use security sale[t]	debt	debt
Panel H: Exchange offers, or designated use security sales that decrease the bonding of payout		
Security sale[t]	conv. debt	debt
Exchange offer[q]	common	preferred
Exchange offer[q]	preferred	debt
Security sale[t]	common	debt
Exchange offer[v]	common	debt

Note: Returns are weighted averages, by sample size, of the returns reported by the respective studies. All returns are significantly different from zero unless noted otherwise by *.
a. Summary of two-day average abnormal stock returns associated with the announcement of various dividend and capital structure transactions.
b. Asquith and Mullins (1983),
c. Calculated by Smith (1986, Table 1) from Charest (1978), and Aharony and Swary (1980).
d. From Brickley (1983).
e. Calculated by Smith (1986, Table 1) from Dann and Mikkelson (1984), Eckbo (1986), Mikkelson and Partch (1986).
f. Eckbo (1986).
g. Calculated by Smith (1986, Table 1) from Linn and Pinegar (1985), Mikkelson and Partch (1986).
h. Linn and Pinegar (1985).
i. Vu (1986).
j. Calculated by Smith (1986, Table 1) from Dann (1981), Masulis (1980), Vermaelen (1981), Rosenfield (1982).
k. Dann (1980), Vermaelen (1981).
l. Bradley and Wakeman (1983).

Average Sample Size	Average Abnormal Two-Day Announcement Period Return	Sign Predicted by Free Cash Flow Theory	Agreement with Free Cash Flow Theory?	Agreement with Tax Theory
160	3.7%	+	yes	no
281	0.9	+	yes	no
164	2.1	+	yes	no
48	−3.6	−	yes	no

provide off-setting changes in the constraints bonding future payments of cash flows.

248	−0.2*	0	yes	no
140	−0.1*	0	yes	no
28	−0.1*	0	yes	yes
249	−0.1*	0	yes	yes
133	−0.1*	0	yes	no
74	−2.1	−	yes	no
54	−1.4	−	yes	no
9	−1.6	−	yes	no
147	15.2	+	yes	yes
182	3.3	+	yes	yes
15	1.1	+	yes	yes
68	−4.8	+	no**	no**
215	−3.0	−	yes	yes
405	−0.6	−	yes	yes
57	−0.4*	−	no	yes
113	−2.1	−	yes	yes

future cash flows

45	21.9	+	yes	yes
52	14.0	+	yes	yes
9	8.3	+	yes	no
24	3.5	+	yes	yes
18	1.6	+	yes	yes
36	0.6	0	no	no
96	0.2*	0	yes	yes

of future cash flows

15	−2.4	−	yes	yes
23	−2.6	−	yes	no
9	−7.7	−	yes	yes
12	−4.2	−	yes	yes
81	−1.1	−	yes	yes

m. Calculated by Smith (1986, Table 4) from Dann and DeAngelo (1983), Bradley and Wakeman (1983).
n. Calculated by Smith (1986, Table 1) from Asquith and Mullins (1986), Kolodny and Suhler (1985), Masulis and Korwar (1986), Mikkelson and Partch (1986), Schipper and Smith (1986).
o. Calculated by Smith (1986, Table 1) from Asquith and Mullins (1986), Masulis and Korwar (1986), Pettway and Radcliffe (1985).
p. Masulis (1980).
q. Masulis (1983). These returns include announcement days of both the original offer and, for about 40 percent of the sample, a second announcement of specific terms of the exchange.
r. McConnell and Schlarbaum (1981).
s. Dietrich (1984).
t. As calculated by Smith (1986, Table 3) from Eckbo (1986), Mikkelson and Partch (1986).
u. Mikkelson (1981).
v. Rogers and Owers (1985), Peavy and Scott (1985), Finnerty (1985).
*Not statistically different from zero.
**Explained by the fact that these transactions are frequently associated with the termination of an actual or expected control bid. The price decline appears to reflect the loss of an expected control premium.

Panel F shows that all exchange offers or designated-use security sales that increase the bonding of payout of future cash flows result in significantly positive increases in common stock prices. These include stock repurchases and exchange of debt or preferred for common, debt for preferred, and income bonds for preferred. The two-day gains range from 21.9 percent (debt for common) to 2.2 percent (debt or income bonds for preferred).

Panel G of Table 2 shows that the evidence on transactions with no cash flow and no change in the bonding of payout of future cash flows is mixed. The returns associated with exchange offers of debt for debt are significantly positive, and those for designated-use security sales are insignificantly different from zero.

Panel H of Table 2 shows that all exchanges, or designated-use security sales that have no cash effects but reduce the bonding of payout of future cash flows result, on average, in significant decreases in stock prices. These transactions include the exchange of common debt or preferred or preferred for debt, or the replacement of debt with convertible debt. The two-day losses range from -9.9% (common for debt) to -2.4% (for designated-use security sale replacing debt with convertible debt).

In summary, the results in Table 2 are remarkably consistent with free cash flow theory, which predicts that, except for firms with profitable unfunded investment projects, prices will rise with unexpected increases in payouts to shareholders (or promises to do so) and will fall with reductions in payments or new requests for funds from shareholders (or reductions in promises to make future payments). Moreover, the size of the value changes is positively related to the change in the tightness of the commitment bonding the payment of future cash flows. For example, the effects of debt-for-preferred exchanges are smaller than the effects of debt-for-common exchanges.

Tax effects can explain some of these results, but not all—for example, the price changes associated with exchanges of preferred for common or replacements of debt with convertible debt, neither of which have any tax effects. The last column of Table 2 denotes whether the individual coefficients are explainable by these pure corporate tax effects. The tax theory hypothesizes that all unexpected changes in capital structure which decrease corporate taxes increase stock prices and vice versa. Therefore, increases in dividend and reductions of debt interest should cause stock price to fall and vice-versa. Thirteen of the 32 coefficients are inconsistent with the corporate tax hypothesis. Simple signaling effects, where the payout of cash signals the lack of present and future investments that promise returns in excess of the cost of capital, are also inconsistent with the results—for example, the positive stock price changes associated with dividend increases and stock repurchases.

If anything, the results in Table 2 seem too good. The returns summarized in the table do not distinguish firms that have free cash flow from those that do not have free cash flow. Yet the theory tells us the returns to firms with no free cash flow will behave differently from those which do. In addition, only unexpected changes in cash payout or the tightness of the commitments bonding the payout of future free cash flows should affect stock prices. The studies summarized in Table 2 do not, in general, control for the effects of expectations. If the free cash flow effects are large and if firms on average are in a positive cash flow position, the predictions of the theory will hold for the simple sample averages. If the effects are this pervasive, the waste due to agency problems in the corporate sector is greater than most scholars have thought. This helps explain the high level of activity in the corporate control market over the last decade. More detailed tests of the propositions that control for growth prospects and expectations will be interesting.

2

The Market for Corporate Control:
A Review of the Evidence

Peter Dodd
University of New South Wales

I. Introduction

From even the most casual reference to the popular financial press, it is clear there is an active market where the *control* of public corporations is traded. Headlines regularly announce proposals of corporate mergers and acquisitions. Tender offers have become a widespread, much publicized means of changing corporate control— and the size of the targets is becoming ever larger. Along with these fairly recent developments, the old-fashioned proxy fight now appears to be undergoing a dramatic revival. Once a phenomenon associated almost exclusively with small companies, proxy challenges have just succeeded in ousting directors of companies as large as Superior Oil and GAF. All these events, together with the less frequent, though increasingly common news of divestitures, spin-offs, and leveraged buyouts, are signs of the vigorous workings of a market for corporate control.

The existence of a well-functioning market for transferring corporate control has important economic implications. To many disinterested viewers, and no doubt to most incumbent managements whose jobs are threatened by such developments, the wave of mergers, acquisitions, and tender offers may seem to reflect the spectacle of managerial empire building, in which stockholders' interests are routinely sacrificed in a general management design to enlarge its own corporate domain. And boards of directors doubtless view proxy fights as an unwelcomed and unjustifiable nuisance, interfering with their efforts to run the company. But although this skepticism about acquiring managements and dissident stockholders may be justified in some—and perhaps many—cases, the market for corporate control provides the mechanism by which corporate assets can be channeled to those most efficient in using them. And this, as most economists would agree, is essential to the functioning of the economy as a whole.

The threat of takeover is also a crucial means of disciplining inept management, and of curbing the inevitable self-interest of those corporate managers who would prefer to pursue more private goals at their stockholders' expense. In this sense, the existence of an active market for corporate control is perhaps the best reply to the popular corporate criticism declaiming against the "separation of ownership and control." Such a market provides—ideally, at least, if not always in practice—a self-regulating, monitoring mechanism which ensures that management's interests cannot diverge too far from those of stockholders. In so doing, an efficient market for changing corporate control increases the wealth of all stockholders.

Such a market also contributes to the general economic welfare by providing the opportunity for firms to combine to form more efficient and profitable entities. Whether through economies of scale, improved access to capital markets, combination of complimentary resources, or any of the value-creating strategies that come under the term "synergies," mergers and acquisitions hold out the possibility of gains to stockholders of both acquired and acquiring firms. Critics of "big business" continue, of course, to view mergers and acquisitions as a net drain on the economy, wasting capital that could be channeled into more "productive" investment. But academic studies have demonstrated conclusively that such transactions— even after the expense of engaging the apparently "nonproductive" services of lawyers, accountants, and investment bankers—significantly increase the net wealth of stockholders.

A more controversial issue, both on Wall Street and in academic finance circles alike, concerns the pricing, and thus the profitability of corporate acquisitions to buying companies. The dramatic increase in acquisition purchase premiums over the past few years has raised questions about both (1) the efficiency of the market in pricing stocks and (2) the motives of managements of acquiring companies. If stock prices have not significantly understated the value of corporate assets, it is difficult to imagine how DuPont's recent acquisition of Conoco—at a price that represents a premium of over 100 percent above Conoco's pre-offer price— can turn out to be a profitable investment. More generally, in an efficient market in which current market prices reflect an unbiased estimate of companies' market values, is there an economic justification for the large acquisition premiums over market that are being paid?

This controversy has a direct bearing on larger questions about the effectiveness of the market for corporate control. How successful is the threat of events like tender offers and proxy fights in maintaining a reasonable unity of interest between management and stockholders? Some finance scholars have interpreted the large and growing purchase premiums as strong evidence that managements of acquiring companies systematically sacrifice the interests of their own stockholders. Acquisitions and tender offers are viewed as a management strategy to expand its own prestige, increasing their corporate fiefdoms at the expense of their own stock-holders. Others have argued that the premiums are justified by the increase in value that can be realized by consolidating control of the assets of the acquiring and acquired firms. According to this view, the premiums paid to the stockholders of acquired companies represent their "fair share" of the increase in value created by the combination.

In addition to the widespread skepticism about such large acquisition premiums, financial academics have expressed concern about the spread of the relatively new management strategies for warding off potential takeovers through "porcupine" amendments, "shark repellants," "standstill agreements," "golden parachutes," and targeted buybacks. Investment bankers are vigorously promoting such antitakeover "packages," and are finding that market receptive. Although purportedly designed to protect stockholders from "corporate raiders," it is hard to refrain from viewing such measures as a means of insulating management from the operation of this market for corporate control.

To be sure, corporate managements have never willingly acquiesced to hostile tender offers, even though they appear to hold out such benefits to their own stockholders. And in many cases, their resistance appears to have been justified by their willingness to accept higher offers down the road. But, the recent adoption of "antitakeover" measures, besides raising academic eyebrows, now appears to be provoking stockholder unrest. The successful proxy challenge at Superior Oil, which was aimed specifically at removing those barriers insulating management from the discipline of the market, may be only the most visible expression of stockholder disapproval, marking the beginning of a new era of stockholder activism.

Partly because of these relatively new developments, the market for corporate control has increasingly become the focus of research efforts in the U.S. The purpose of this article is to review the academic research bearing on questions like those introduced above: What are the real corporate motives for mergers and acquisitions, and who benefits from such transactions? What happens to the stock prices of companies resisting takeovers? What are the stock price consequences of proxy fights? Do they genuinely benefit current stockholders by threatening or displacing management, or are they merely obstructionist sound and fury, generated by opportunists and malcontents? What is the effect of the newly popular management "entrenchment" procedures on the stock prices?

This article will provide a brief overview of the large and growing body of research on such questions, as well as suggesting directions in which the market for corporate control is evolving.

II. The Economics of the Market for Corporate Control

Control of the corporation is a nebulous concept. There is a longstanding debate in law and economics about the relative roles of management and stockholders in controlling the public corporation. Critics of unfettered corporate enterprise like John Kenneth Galbraith have leveraged the premise of "separation of ownership and control" into the claim that the form of the public corporation effectively confers absolute decision-making power on corporate managers, insulating them from all responsibilities to stockholders. The very couching of the debate in terms of this "separation" is partly responsible for the proliferation of corporate and securities laws that now limit corporate actions.[1]

Such critics rightly point out that the form of the corporation has changed greatly from the days of the 18th-century "joint stock companies" described by Adam Smith. Although the 19th century saw a rapid growth in the numbers of corporations, they were mostly closely-held concerns, organized around and financed by a single entrepreneur or a small group of private investors. And, of course, when "insiders" hold a large fraction of the outstanding shares, ownership and control are effectively united, thus ensuring a strong commonality of interest.

To this day, there are still many corporations where the firm is owned and managed by a particular individual, or an influential group of investors, who clearly dictate the policies of the organization. For most large public corporations, however, the proportion of shares owned by insiders is small, and establishing who *ultimately* controls the firm is far from straightforward.

Beginning with the well-known arguments of Adolf Berle and Gardner Means,[2] many commentators have leaped from the observation that management holds only small proportions of shares to the conclusion that shareholders are therefore at the mercy of management. From there it is but a short step to the prescription that corporate activities be regulated by the federal government.

The most glaring inadequacy of this reasoning is its complete failure to consider why the public corporation has survived, indeed prevailed, as the form of organization of American business enterprise. In "Reflections on The Corporation as a Social Invention," William Meckling and Michael Jensen observe that

> Critics of the corporation are confronted by a striking historical phenomenon not readily reconciled with their views. The corporation has come to dominate production and commerce, not only in the United States, but in all of the world's highly developed nations. If the corporation is such a defective institution, how do we explain its chronicle of success? Freedom to choose among organizational forms provides an "organizational" test of survival just as markets provide a survival test for individual firms. . .The organizational forms that survive and prosper will be those that satisfy consumer demands at lowest cost.
>
> Wherever competition among organizational forms is open and unfettered, the large corporation has demonstrated its strength and durability.[3]

---

1. Richard Posner, the University of Chicago's erstwhile Professor of Law (now a Justice), makes this point in his *Economic Analysis of Law*, New York: Columbia University Press, 1972.
2. Adolf Berle and Gardner Means, *The Modern Corporation*. See also Berle, "Functions of the Corporate System," *Columbia Law Review*, Vol. 62, pp. 433–449.
3. In *Controlling the Giant Corporation: A Symposium*, published by the University of Rochester's Center for Research in Government Policy and Business, 1982, p. 84.

In proposing various forms of government control of the corporation, critics of "big business" almost invariably ignore the costs—in the form of reduced economic efficiency—of government-mandated changes of long-established institutional arrangements. Such institutions have evolved over time in response to a variety of market pressures, and they are in large part responsible for the corporation's success.

Corporate critics are right, of course, to insist that the traditional legal view of the corporation as a collection of assets "owned" by stockholders is grossly simplistic. In fact, the large modern corporation is an elaborate legal fiction, a complicated network of contracts binding a *number* of different parties to the production activities of the firm.[4] Stockholders are perhaps best represented as suppliers of capital, whose principal economic function is risk-bearing. They contract to be "residual" claimants, receiving the value of the remaining outputs only after the other inputs, or "factors of production," have been compensated. Their principal concerns are that the inputs of the firm are combined efficiently, and that the outputs are distributed scrupulously according to the specifics of the contracts. The individual stockholder, who typically holds an investment portfolio diversified across a number of firms, generally does not know much—nor perhaps even much care—about the day-to-day operations of the company.

Corporate decision-making, then, is primarily the province of professional managers hired to run the firm. But, as suggested above, and as most financial economists would agree, this specialization of functions has developed because of its efficiency. Although it has no doubt allowed some managers to exploit their stockholders, we can conclude that the benefits of such a development to the economy as a whole have far exceeded the costs.

Viewed in this light, then, "the separation of ownership and control," once the interventionist slogan of corporate critics, is transformed into a positive step in the evolution of the corporation toward greater economic efficiency.

But while it is undeniably more efficient to have professional managers controlling the day-to-day decisions of the corporation, stockholders and other contracting parties, such as employees, still require protection of their "investments." Part of this monitoring of management is accomplished through the board of directors, who are supposed to oversee corporate decision-making. But another part of this protection is provided through the contracts that bind stockholders, management, employees, and other parties. The level of protection provided by the contract determines the price at which different parties are prepared to invest. In the case of employees, this means the total level, form, and certainty of compensation that induces them to commit their "human capital" to the firm. In the case of stockholders, it refers to the price they will pay for the shares issued by the corporation.

---

4. See Michael C. Jensen and William J. Meckling, "Theory of the Firm: Managerial Behavior, Agency Costs, and Capital Structure, *Journal of Financial Economics* 3 (1976): pp. 305–60. See also Eugene Fama, "Agency Problems and the Theory of the Firm," *Journal of Political Economy*, 88, pp. 288–307.

One of the interesting implications of this analysis is that the *initiative* for providing monitoring devices, such as audited financial statements, comes not from investors, but rather from those entrepreneurs who wish to persuade potential investors to provide the funds for taking the firm public. The stronger the guarantees, the higher the price investors will pay for a given issue. And once the firm has become public, it remains in the interest of management to offer convincing promises of self-regulation, and to make good on them—at least up to the point that the benefits of added investor confidence outweigh the costs of providing such guarantees.[5]

Besides such specific contractual provisions, stockholders are also protected against mismanagement by a variety of institutional arrangements that have developed. Eugene Fama, the University of Chicago's well-known financial economist, argues forcibly that the primary mechanism that *constrains* corporate management to be efficient and scrupulous is the managerial labor market. Individuals both inside and outside the firm compete for management positions, and the existence of this market provides corporate managers with a powerful incentive to act in the interests of their stockholders. Although the precise mechanisms by which managers signal their value in this market is unclear, reference to the *Who's News* column in the *Wall Street Journal*, together with the proliferation of executive recruitment firms, suggests that this market is constantly at work.

The initiative for such management reshuffling, however, comes from the board of directors within the corporation. Typically composed of both top management and outside directors, the board is required to oversee the decision-making of management, and to replace managers or restructure the firm when it is being poorly run. Corporate boards also create compensation committees whose function is to design bonus schemes which furnish management with the proper incentives. Such programs offer stock options, or are tied to accounting measures of performance, and thus serve to unify the interests of management with those of stockholders.

But, if management does not respond to such incentives, and the board fails to respond to pressures for change, the market for corporate control then serves as a discipline of last resort. It is in this sense, as a protector of stockholder's wealth, that a freely functioning market for corporate control is an integral part of the corporate system. It is the operation of this market, together with well-designed compensation contracts and the labor market for management, that ensures that management's interests cannot diverge too far, and for too long, from the interests of their stockholders.

III. Transferring Corporate Control

I will assume throughout the rest of this discussion that ultimate responsibility for decision-making rests with the board of directors and, more precisely, with the coalitions of members which control that board. The mechanisms for transferring

---

5. Ross Watts and Jerold Zimmerman have developed this idea in their writings, which will be synthesized in their forthcoming book, *Positive Theories of Accounting*.

control of the corporation are those that effectively change the composition of the board. This allows us to concentrate on those transactions that tranfer control of the board: mergers, tender offers and proxy contests.

Before considering the similarities and differences between these transactions, it is important to note that many of the benefits of taking control of a corporation can be achieved without mounting a formal takeover campaign. For instance, it is possible to achieve synergistc benefits by designing joint ventures, which in effect are new business entities created by the corporate partners. It is also possible to negotiate long-term contracts to ensure the productive cooperation of two firms. The existence of these alternatives suggests that actual *voting control* of corporations must hold out benefits to acquiring firms that go beyond the operating synergies or cost savings provided by cooperative ventures and long-term contracts.

The most prominent mode of transferring control of corporate assets is, of course, the merger. Recall that a merger is a transaction in which one corporation (the acquirer) secures title to the stock or assets of another (the acquired). Consummation of a merger requires the approval of the acquired firm's board. If the board approves the transaction, it puts the merger proposal to a stockholder vote. Depending on the percentage of favorable votes required by the state corporate code, the merger is approved or rejected.

In effect, though, management has a veto power over all merger proposals and can refuse to put any proposal to a stockholder vote. Tender offers, by contrast, do not require the explicit approval of the incumbent management. A tender offer is a public offer made by the management of one firm (the bidder) to purchase a block of another (the target) firm's outstanding common stock. Tender offers are made directly to the target's stockholders. If enough stockholders tender, control of the corporation changes hands.

Proxy fights are a direct attempt by dissident stockholders to remove directors through a stockholder vote. It is a formalized voting procedure in which one or more parties oppose the re-election of the incumbent directors. Although the contestants often attempt to purchase blocks of the outstanding shares prior to the election, the outcome of the contest itself has no effect upon the distribution of ownership of the firm. Unlike mergers or tender offers, where control passes to those who can convince stockholders to trade their shares, in proxy contests most stockholders do not transfer ownership of their shares. Their incentive is simply to elect the management team that will enhance the value of their investment.

IV. Changes in the Market for Corporate Control: 1950s to the Present

The merger has long been and continues to be the most popular method of changing control. Beginning in the late 1960s, however, the number of tender offers per annum began to rival that of mergers (see Table 1). Prior to the 1960s, however, proxy fights were clearly the predominant means of *contesting* control of the corporation. In fact, the SEC files contain no record of tender offers prior to 1956.[6] Now, of course, the recent flurry of proxy fights aside, tender offers are much more commonly used for taking control of a corporation than proxy contests.

There is no completely convincing rationale for the eclipse of the proxy fight by tender offers, but changes in the regulatory climate provide a clue. My best guess is that, in the late 50s and 60s, the costs of waging a proxy war rose relative to those of making a tender offer (and the costs of tender offers then also included braving the social stigma attached to them), generating in effect a "demand" for tender offers as a substitute. In 1955, the SEC revised its proxy rules to require pre-examination of proxy materials, full disclosure of the identity of participants in the contest, and filing of proxy materials sent to stockholders. These rules became effective in January 1956, and were expanded in the Securities Act Amendment of 1964. Both of these regulations made proxy contests more costly, especially as the probability of litigation arising out of a contest increased with the broader disclosure requirements.

The emergence of tender offers is also associated with a significant change in the court's attitude to transactions transferring control. In a dramatic reversal of precedence, the court ruled in Perlman v. Feldman (1955) that proceeds from the sale of controlling interest in a corporation must be shared equally among all shareholders. This ruling effectively designated *control* an asset of the corporation. As early as 1952, one forward-looking commentator predicted the emergence of tender offers as a direct consequence of such a change in precedence:

> If a seller can be sued by other stockholders when he makes a sale in which
> they have not been included, he will probably insist that an offer be made to
> all stockholders of the corporation.[7]

In light of this evidence, then, it can be conjectured that the rise of tender offers in the late 1950s and early 1960s reflects the increase in the costs, both actual and potential, of proxy fights brought about by regulatory and legal changes. And, as I shall suggest later, the present resurgence of the proxy fight may well reflect a fairly large and recent increase in the costs of making tender offers.

V. The Evidence on Mergers and Acquisitions

Corporate critics have long contended that unregulated financial markets are incapable of ensuring that boards of directors effectively monitor corporate managements. A corollary of this view holds that mergers and acquisitions, far from being motivated by management's desire to increase stockholder wealth, are initiated by corporate managements acting in their own self interest to the detriment of stockholders.

---

6. The most extensive and complete data base on tender offers is that of the Managerial Economics Research Center at the University of Rochester. It was developed by Michael Bradley, Peter Dodd, and Richard Ruback.

7. Comment, *University of Chicago Law Review*, vol. 19 (1952), pp. 870.

Table 1. New York and American Stock Exchange Firms
Acquired in Mergers or Tender Offers or Involved in Proxy
Contests in the Period January 1963 through June 1982.

	Mergers	Tender Offers	Proxy Contests
1963	16	6	7
1964	27	4	6
1965	26	7	5
1966	35	10	3
1967	56	12	8
1968	14	23	4
1969	6	6	4
1970	19	4	3
1971	6	1	9
1972	14	3	5
1973	13	14	4
1974	9	21	2
1975	7	14	3
1976	9	11	4
1977	17	17	1
1978	26	21	1
1979	44	30	NA
1980	35	20	NA
1981	23	21	NA
June 1982	10	9	NA
Total	419	254	71
% of Population of firms	9.5	5.7	1.6

One of the most vocal of corporate critics, Adolf Berle, argued as early as 1932 that the market for corporate control exhibited the "megalomania" of corporate tycoons struggling to devour one another. The recent highly publicized billion dollar takeover battles for Conoco, Cities Service, Marathon Oil and Martin Marietta have rekindled these old arguments.

But while case studies are fascinating in their own right, they provide at best shaky foundations for generalizing—whether such generalizations apply to the natural sciences or the behavior of corporations. Responsible statements about the effectiveness of the market for corporate control should be based upon reasonably scientific evidence. And there is now a large and rapidly growing body of empirical evidence on the economic effects of mergers and acquisitions.

VI. The Methods

Before summarizing the conclusions of this research, however, it is important to start with a basic understanding of its methods, and the assumptions underlying their use.

The problem faced by researchers is finding a method for evaluating the effect of a corporate merger or acquisition on stockholder wealth. At first glance, it might appear that the success of an acquisition can be judged only by observing the performance of the combined firm over a long period of time; and that only by poring over masses of accounting data (including income statements and balance sheets for competitors as well as for the firms involved) compiled over, say, a five-year period can such a determination be reached.

The relationship between accounting and market values, however, is often a tenuous one. Modern finance theory says that the most reliable way of measuring the real economic performance of a company is to track its stock price against the performance of the market as a whole (and adjusted for risk). And, in measuring the economic value added (or subtracted) by an acquisition, we would ideally like to measure the market value of the corporation both with and without the acquired firm, and then compare.

Of course, once the acquistion is accomplished, it is impossible to know and thus to track what the value of the firm would have been *without* the acquisition. But modern theory enables us to get around this problem, maintaining that we need not wait for five years to pass in order to evaluate the market consequences of corporate deals. In an "efficient market," the expected value of an acquisition—to buying and selling stockholders alike—will be *estimated* by the market in changes in stock prices *immediately upon the announcement of the transaction* (and, because of leakage, some of that value will have been captured even before).

This is not to suggest that the market's immediate response never turns out, with hindsight, to be wrong. Both our theory and the evidence suggest, however, that there is a roughly 50–50 probability that the market's assessment will fall on the low or high side in estimating the eventual success of the transaction.[8] Such price reactions therefore should be interpreted as carrying investors' "unbiased" assessment of the future economic consequences of that acquisition. They express the collective judgment of the market.

Those already skeptical about the "efficiency" of the market might argue that because of the strong speculative influence of arbitrageurs following merger proposals and tender offers, there is even less reason to rely on market pricing to judge acquisitions. But the continuous presence of such "risk" arbitrageurs, driven by the lure of profits, provides a good illustration of how and why an efficient market works. When a proposed acquisition is first publicly announced, there is a good deal of uncertainty as to the eventual outcome of the transaction. In some cases the initial offer is completed as proposed, while in others competing higher bids materialize and the transaction is completed as a substantially higher price. In still other cases, the transaction is unsuccessfuly, the target firm is not acquired,

---

8. Richard Ruback and I showed that for a large sample of tender offers the market's initial assessment was unbiased: *over the five years following the transactions*, bidding firms earned on average *zero* abnormal returns. See "Tender Offers and Stockholder Returns: An Empirical Analysis, *Journal of Financial Economics*, vol. 5, pp. 351–74.

and the target stock price usually falls dramatically. Arbitrageurs betting on the outcome of the transaction provide an active market for such stocks. Those target stockholders wanting to avoid the risk of the transaction failing can sell their shares in the market after the offer has been made.

Modern finance, as well as common sense, predicts that the target's stock price will adjust at the time of the first public announcement of the offer to reflect the probability that higher competing bids will materialize—as well as the probability that the transaction will fall through completely. In some cases, the market guesses correctly and in others it does not. In each case, however, if the market's price reflects an "unbiased" guess about the outcome of the deal, there should be no evidence of mispricing when averaging across a large sample of transaction.

A study I performed in 1981 confirms that this, in fact, is what happens.[9] For a sample of 324 *proposed* mergers, the average market-adjusted return from buying a portfolio of all the target firms' stocks one day after the first public announcement, and holding for 60 trading days, was −0.2 percent. For 268 announced tender offers, the return was a little higher −0.31 percent. If an investor had purchased shares in each of the 592 target firms the day after the offer was announced, he would have earned a market-adjusted return of 0.03 percent. From these results, I conclude that "arbitraging" the outcome of acquisitions is a "fair game" (i.e., the chances of winning and losing are roughly equal). Without access to private information on the outcome of specific proposals, the expected return to this investment strategy is zero.

Extending this reasoning to the problem of evaluating the success of acquisitions, our tests assume that the market's immediate response—to buying companies and selling companies alike—contains an unbiased assessment of the net present value of that acquisition to stockholders. It impounds immediately those cash flow consequences that will only be realized in the future. For any given firm, of course, the market's response may be wrong. But all the players in the market have a powerful incentive to be right. If the market penalized Dupont too heavily for what it viewed as too good a deal for Conoco, then those stockholders who sold misread the long view. The short-run price response contains the market's best guess about the long-run view. If this were not so, then there would be opportunities for large profits to investors buying the DuPonts and U.S. Steels of this world.

It is also possible that there are other events affecting the company's stock price at the time of the acquisition. Across a large sample of firms, however, with acquisitions spread well over time, we can be fairly confident that such random effects will cancel out, and that no one set of events, whether good or bad, will confound the analysis.

---

9. In Peter Dodd, "The Effect on Market Value of Transactions in the Market for Corporate Control," *Proceedings of Seminar on the Analysis of Security Prices*, Center for Research on Security Prices, University of Chicago, May 1981.

VII. The Evidence on Target Firms

The evidence on the effects of acquisitions on target firm stocks is quite consistent across different studies. Both a study I conducted with Richard Ruback, as well as later tests by Michael Bradley, found that target shares rise dramatically on the announcement of a proposed tender offer. This is no surprise, of course, since the acquisition is always at an offer price above the current market price. For those transactions that are successfully completed, the stock price rises further over the interim as uncertainty about the outcome is resolved. Similarly large gains to target stocks in merger proposals have been documented in studies by Paul Asquith and myself.

Both Ruback's and my study of tender offers, and Asquith's study of mergers, report an interesting finding on target firms: over the periods 2 and 3 years *prior* to the acquisition, these target stocks experienced average abnormal *negative* returns of up to 15 percent. The marked failure of target firms to keep pace with the market suggests that, on average, such firms had not been performing up their potential. And this further suggests that acquisitions, provided the price is right, offer profitable investment opportunities for acquiring firms with more efficient managers or more profitable uses for the target's assets. (By contrast, the abnormal returns to shareholders of acquiring companies *prior* to the merger were consistently positive. Acquiring companies had apparently achieved good track records prior to their acquisitions, and their merger activity was the manifestation of a demonstrated ability to manage assets and growth.) Such evidence is consistent with our conception of the market for corporate control as imposing a discipline on management, and transferring corporate assets to more profitable uses.

Another striking result of our studies is that unsuccessful merger proposals and tender offers are associated with permanent positive revaluations of target shares. For 53 unsuccessful tender offers I examined, the average excess return over the 121 days around the transaction was 15.6 percent. It is clear that the attempted transfer of control has revealed information that results, on average, in a significant increase in the market value of a corporation's shares. Over two-thirds of these firms are subsequently acquired within five years and the revaluation could reflect the market's anticipation of these acquisitions. Alternatively the revaluation could reflect expectations of improved managerial performance following the attempted takeover.

The 108 cancelled merger proposals I studied were also associated with a positive overall revaluation. The gains to target stockholders were smaller than those in tender offers, but they were nevertheless significant.

Whether such a revaluation takes place, however, is very definitely a function of the type of cancellation. As noted earlier, merger proposals occur in a different institutional setting than tender offers. The management of the target firm can decide not to submit any proposal to a stockholder vote, and thus has effective veto power over any merger proposal. But not all cancellations are the result of target management's veto. It is possible for the bidding firm to reconsider its proposal (perhaps after getting access to "insider" information about the target during the negotiations) and to decide that the merger is no longer a good investment.

Of the 108 cancelled merger proposals, it is clear from the cancellation announcements that 34 were the result of vetoes by target management. For the remaining 74, the source of the cancellation cannot be determined. The overall impact of the transactions are vastly different for the two categories. In those proposals vetoed by target management, the excess returns to target stockholders over the 121 day period around the initial public announcement averaged 16.3 percent. In the 74 cases where either the bidder withdrew or the source of cancellation could not be determined, target stockholder returns were a −0.2 percent. From these results, we can conclude that there is a permanent revaluation associated with an average takeover bid rejected by the target management. This higher price reflects the fact that an unsuccessful acquisition attempt is often followed at a later date by a different, but successful bid. When the bidding firm withdraws, however, the target's stock price generally falls back to its level prior to the proposal.

VIII. The Evidence on Bidding Firms

The evidence on bidding firms is not nearly as conclusive, and studies using different samples have come up with conflicting results. Most studies have reported that the average abnormal return to bidding firms is close to zero, and that therefore the lion's share, if not all, of the gains from the transactions are earned by target stockholders. This would suggest that the market for corporate control is a competitive one, in which profits to buying firms are effectively bid to "zero"—that is, acquisitions earn on average "normal" rates of return for their stockholders, but no more.

In most cases the bidding firm is much larger than the target, and thus a comparison of *percentage changes* in value of the acquiring and the acquired firm's stock might not be appropriate. In order to measure the division of gains among buyers and sellers with greater sensitivity, researchers also estimated the *total dollar gains* (and losses) to both stockholder groups. Calculated in this fashion, the gains from acquisitions appear to be divided fairly evenly, on average, between buyers and sellers.

What these broad statistical averages conceal, however, is that announcements of acquisitions are associated with a surprising number of stock price declines. The results reported by both Bradley and Asquith show over 40 percent of bidding companies' stock prices falling on the announcement of the acquisition proposal. For some samples, such as the one I used in my 1980 study of mergers of NYSE firms over the 1972–1977 period, these negative returns to bidders are accentuated.

Recently, of course, some of the largest takeovers resulted in dramatic declines in stock price. DuPont's market value fell by almost 10 percent during its negotiations with Conoco. Similar declines were experienced by Gulf in their attempt to acquire Cities Service, and by U.S. Steel when acquiring Marathon Oil.

These well-publicized cases, together with the spectacle of Bendix's bid for Martin Marietta, have given new life to the old arguments for limiting management's autonomy. Some members of Congress and the SEC have also expressed concern that the market for corporate control is being abused by corporate managements. Such concern has magnified to the extent that a task force investigation has been initiated.

IX. Mergers and Acquisitions: 1979–1982

Implicit in this concern is the assumption that the market for corporate control has fundamentally changed in recent years. If this is the case, interpretation of the existing research must be cautious since most studies to date have looked at acquisitions that took place no later than 1977.

In order to determine whether the market for acquisitions has in fact changed, I attempted to update the existing evidence by examining returns to stockholders during the most recent wave of mergers and tender offers. Between January 1979 and June 1982, almost 200 New York and American Stock Exchange firms were acquired. For each of these transactions, I measured the returns (net of market movements) to buying and selling firm's stockholders over the period extending from 10 trading days before the first public announcement of the proposed acquisition through the day after the announcement.

The story for acquired firms is pretty much the same as reported for earlier periods: over this 11-day period target stockholders earned, on average, 27 percent in mergers and 39 percent in tender offers. The primary difference is that the premiums offered over market price, which have been increasing since the late 1960s, have become even larger. While some of the early increase in premiums was found to be associated with the passage of the Williams Act in 1968, and the various state tender offer laws that came after, the continued increase is difficult to explain.

This sharp and ever increasing growth of acquisition premiums seems to be reflected in the returns to bidding firms' stockholders. The average returns—which were slightly negative but still close to zero—are still fairly consistent with those of studies of earlier periods. But the percentage of bidding firms experiencing abnormal stock price declines rose sharply to 61 percent of firms bidding for mergers, and to 66 percent of companies making tender offers. On closer inspection, the results for bidding firms are quite revealing. Concentrating on just the week prior to (and including the day of) the public announcement of proposed acquisitions (i.e., −4 through 0), the negative abnormal returns to bidders in both tender offers and mergers are statistically significant (with t statistics of −2.3 and −2.2 respectively). Again, over 65 percent of both bidder samples recorded declines in stock price.

Thus, the stock market has clearly pronounced its judgment that a large proportion of tender offers have not served the best interest of the bidding companies' stockholders. And, the pervasiveness of negative stock price effects of acquisitions on bidding firms in the 1979–1982 period represents a marked change from the

Table 2. Percentage Abnormal Returns to Target and Bidder Stocks in Tender Offers and Mergers Between January 1979 and June 1982 (t Statistics in Parentheses).

Days	Tender Offers		Mergers	
	Targets	Bidders	Targets	Bidders
−10 through 0	38.99	−1.04	27.09	−0.73
	(7.0)	(−1.2)	(6.6)	(−1.1)
−4 through 0	33.76	−1.36	23.48	−1.31
	(9.0)	(−2.3)	(8.4)	(−2.2)
−1 through 0	22.01	−1.87	21.78	−0.16
	(9.2)	(−4.9)	(12.4)	(−0.4)

earlier evidence, providing ammunition for the critics of the market. The results are consistent with the notion that acquiring firms, on average, are paying too high a price.

Why more than half of bidding companies are willing to pay such high premiums over market—high, at least, in the market's collective judgment—to consummate these corporate unions is a mystery. Perhaps, of course, the stock market's response over the past three years has a significant downward bias to it. But if this is true, then there are profit opportunities which investors can systematically exploit by buying the shares of companies like DuPont and U.S. Steel. Both common sense, and a great deal of evidence accumulated about the way the market works, says that this is very unlikely.

On net, however, both mergers and tender offers have served to increase the wealth of stockholders as a whole. For even though bidding firms are larger than the targets on average, we also find that the dollar losses to bidding firms are far outweighed by the dollar gains to targets. This finding, substantiated by all past and present tests to date, implies that the assets of the combined firms are more valuable than when held by the individual firms prior to the acquisition. Contrary to the claims of those critics who argue that acquisitions and tender offers represent a net drain on the economy, total economic value is increased by mergers and acquisitions; and this suggests that the market for corporate control is fulfilling a valuable economic function by channeling corporate assets to more productive uses, or more efficient users.

X. Proxy Fights

A purer test of the effectiveness of the market for corporate control, as well as stronger testimony to its role in preserving stockholder value, is provided by a study of the stock price consequences of proxy contests.

Jerry Warner and I examined a sample of 96 proxy contests involving New York and American Stock Exchange firms between 1962 and 1977.[10] We found that these contests result, on average, in a positive stock price revaluation of over 8 percent. These returns are measured over the period extending from 60 days prior to the first public announcement of the contest until the results of the election are announced.

We began our study by classifying the 96 proxy contests into two groups, designated "control" and "participation," according to whether the dissidents proposed candidates for 50 percent or more of the available board seats. Of the 96 contests, 71 were for control of the board and 25 involved elections for less than 50 percent of the seats. In 56 of the 96 contests, dissidents won at least one seat. In 18 (or roughly 25 percent) of the "control" contests, dissidents won a majority. And in 45 (or 63 percent) of such contests, dissidents won at least one seat. In "participation" contests, dissidents won at least one seat in only 44 percent of the contests.

Proxy contests are often waged by former "insiders." In 37 of the 71 "control" contests, and in 4 of the 25 "participation" contests, the dissidents included either former board members or former high ranking officials of the firm. Such individuals typically leave the firm after a policy dispute with incumbent directors, and then later initiate the challenge.

Also, 16 of the proxy fights in the sample were led by outside firms (and 3 of these 16 contests were preceded by tender offers). The presence of either insiders or another firm seems to have a marked impact on the likelihood that the dissidents will be successful in winning seats. For example, in 29 of the 37 contests for control involving insiders, and in 10 of the 12 involving outside firms, dissident stockholders won seats. By contrast, dissident won seats in only 7 of the 23 contests not involving either insiders or other firms.

The results of our tests of the effects of proxy fights on stockholder wealth can be summarized as follows:

> Even though dissidents stockholders actually capture control in only 25 percent of the contests, over 75 percent of firms are more highly valued after the contest. On average, stockholders earn an 8.2 percent excess return over the duration of the contest.
>
> The significant positive abnormal returns are found in both control and participation contests. In control contests, stockholders earn 8.8 percent excess returns and in participation contests they earn 6.3 percent.
>
> The positive stock price performance over the duration of the contest does not appear to be affected by the outcome of the contest. In contests where dissidents win seats, the mean excess return is 8.1 percent, and in contests where dissidents win no seats, the average return is 8.2 percent.

---

10. Peter Dodd and Jerold B. Warner, "On Corporate Governance: A Study of Proxy Contests," *Journal of Financial Economics*, vol. 11, 1983.

Whether dissidents win majority or not, however, has a striking effect on the size of the positive revaluation. When dissidents win a majority of the board seats, the excess return is 12.8 percent on average, and for contests where they fail to win a majority, it is 7.7 percent.

The positive excess returns are earned prior to the public announcement of the contest, and most occur over the previous 40 days. The timing of the excess returns reflects the institutional mechanics of proxy contests, which require the dissidents to organize their team of experts (including lawyers, accountants, and public relations personnel) and to prepare the solicitations materials prior to public announcement. The results of our study suggest that news of the contest is known in the stock market well before the public announcement of the challenge.

The overall finding of positive abnormal performance is consistent with the proposition that proxy fights benefit stockholders by transferring corporate resources to more highly valued uses.

This positive share price performance is also found even in those contests where incumbents win all seats. Apparently, the fact of a challenge to management is associated with expectations of improved corporate performance. The outcome of the contest, however, does appear to influence stock prices somewhat. Upon the announcement of the election results, there is evidence of a small positive share price reaction when dissidents win seats, and a small negative reaction when they do not. Such evidence is consistent with the view that dissident representation was expected to improve profitability and increase stockholder wealth.

XI. Antitakeover Strategies: Protection of Stockholders or Management Entrenchment?

In response to the wave of takeovers in the late 70's, many corporations have adopted by-law and charter amendments which make it more difficult for potential acquirers to gain control. And even more recently, senior executives have also begun to grant themselves large bonus payments in the event their firm is acquired. These "porcupine amendments" (also known as "shark repellants") and "golden parachutes" have become standard components of comprehensive antitakeover strategies designed and marketed by investment bankers.

The widespread adoption of such measures has further fueled the debate about the genuineness of management's service to its stockholders. Such actions clearly increase the costs of changing corporate control, reducing the profitability and thus, presumably, the probability of takeovers.

Both the SEC and NYSE have severely criticized the introduction of the amendments, objecting that they effectively entrench existing management at the expense of their stockholders. Those corporations adopting the amendments have defended themselves by pointing to the apparent vulnerability of current stockholders who become minority holders when control is transferred by fractional tender offers.

Although the Williams Act and state statutes offer these stockholders some protection, charter amendments further restrict the actions that can be taken by a potential acquirer, thus increasing target management's power to control the outcome of any such proposal.

Also, because all proceeds from a successful tender offer are now required by law to be distributed equally among all tendering stockholders—regardless of which bid they initially accepted—all individual stockholders have an incentive to tender to the first bid, and not risk losing their gain. The antitakeover amendments allow target management to counteract this incentive to tender their shares (possibly) too soon by allowing them to negotiate on behalf of all stockholders for a higher price. And if the company is actually taken over, such amendments govern the dealings of the acquiring firm with remaining minority stockholders through "anti-squeeze out" provisions and "escape" clauses.

In defense of the practice of instituting "golden parachutes," it has been argued that guaranteed compensation agreements strengthen the incentive for target managers to act in their stockholders' best interests when faced with an acquisition proposal. There is some justification for this argument. But such provisions clearly increase the costs of acquiring the firm, thus reducing the expected profitability (and presumably the price paid for) the acquisition. And to the extent that potential bidding companies are deterred by such additional expenses, "golden parachutes" may be worth less to stockholders as a correction of management incentives than the loss resulting from the reduced probability of takeover.

XII. The Evidence

Researchers have collected data on the market's response to *announcements* of both charter amendments and guaranteed compensation contracts, and the evidence seems to refute the claim that either action harms stockholders. Scott Linn and John McConnell studies over 300 firms that introduced so-called antitakeover amendments and found slightly *positive*, though insignificant abnormal returns. Harry DeAngelo and Ed Rice found similar results for a sample of over 100 firms adopting supramajority voting rules, staggered boards, fair price and lock-up provisions.

In the case of "golden parachutes," Laureen Maines identified 93 firms that introduced severance compensation plans for executives within the past five years, and found no evidence of any negative stock price effects associated with the introduction of these plans. Similar results were obtained by Richard Lambert and David Larcker.

XIII. Partially Successful Transfers of Control: Standstill Agreements and Targeted Buybacks

Two other relatively new management practices have added to the managerial "entrenchment" controversy and, in these cases, the evidence appears to *support* the claims of critics.

Bidding firms often gain a large block of a target's outstanding shares but not enough to control the board. In an increasing number of these cases the bidder (now a substantial stockholder) and target managements enter into a voluntary contract, known as a "standstill agreement," which limits the former's ownership of target shares to some maximum (less than controlling) percentage for a stipulated number of years. Such contracts also often prevent the bidding firm from participating in a proxy contest against the incumbent board.

Standstill agreements are also often accompanied by repurchases of the bidder's block at a premium above the market price. And, in many cases, such "targeted buybacks" take place without standstill agreements.

Larry Dann and Harry DeAngelo (1981) recently studied 81 of these agreements and repurchases during 1971–1981. They find that both are associated with negative abnormal returns to the other target stockholders. Even those standstill agreements not accompanied by negotiated stock repurchases are associated with significant declines in target stock prices.

The evidence thus provides strong support that such actions serve only to insulate incumbent management from the threat of removal. By interfering with the workings of the market for corporate control, such entrenchment appears clearly to reduce the market value of remaining stockholders' shares. Although both standstill agreements and negotiated purchases are currently within the bounds of corporation law, the obviously detrimental effects of such practices on remaining stockholders can be expected to generate legal challenges, and possibly further battles for control.

XIV. New Directions for the Market for Corporate Control

The evidence reviewed in these pages provides overwhelming support for the argument that the existence of a market for corporate control benefits stockholders. Simply by holding out the possibility that control can change hands, and by providing the means for transferring assets to more profitable users or uses, this market increases the efficiency, and hence the wealth, of the economy as a whole.

Let me summarize this evidence briefly. First, the transfer of control achieved through mergers and tender has provided stockholders of acquired firms with large abnormal returns. Acquired companies tend to have underperformed the market, while acquiring companies tend to have outperformed the market, over the period 2 to 3 years prior to acquisitions. This is consistent with our conception of the market for control as disciplining inept management, and transferring assets to higher-valued uses. Furthermore, *unsuccessful* tender offers and mergers are often accompanied by permanent increases in target firms' stock prices (although not in those cases where bidding firms withdraw their bid), suggesting that the mere possibility of a company being sold increases stockholder value.

Proxy challenges, too, have resulted in significant increases for stockholders. This increase occurs whether the contests are successful or not—though increases are significantly larger in those contests where dissidents win majority control.

Thus, the mere threat of stockholder challenge appears to create market expectations of improved managerial performance.

These findings regarding mergers, tender offers, and proxy fights hold fairly consistently over the different time periods examined in our studies. But, more recent research suggests that the market for corporate control may be undergoing some important changes. As pointed out earlier, the operation of this market is profoundly affected by federal and state regulations, and many of the changes observed over the 50s and 60s can be explained by regulatory changes. For example, the substitution of the tender offer for the proxy fight as the predominant means for contesting corporate control in the 60s was in part attributable to restrictive legislation governing proxy fights. Such legislation greatly increased the costs, both out-of-pocket and expected, from waging proxy wars.

The recent flurry of proxy fights suggests, however, that the pendulum may have begun to swing the other way. Since the passage of the Williams Act in 1968, and the proliferation of state statutes governing tender offers, the size of acquisition premiums has become ever larger, thus increasing the costs of making tender offers. In fact, the size of the premiums have been increasing steadily throughout the 70s—a fact which cannot be explained by further regulatory and legal changes.

My own study of the most recent wave of acquisitions over the period 1979–1982 shows that the premiums paid over market to acquire companies have reached unprecedented levels. The stock market's response to buying companies was significantly negative in over 60 percent of the mergers and tender offers consummated during this period. Thus, the skepticism of finance theorists about the size of such premiums is being reinforced by the collective judgment of the market.

One plausible cause of this increase in acquisition premiums is an apparent stiffening of management resistance to takeovers. Increasingly popular "antitakeover" packages now feature "porcupine" amendments, "golden parachutes," defensive acquisitions, new stock issues to dilute control, privately negotiated repurchases, and standstill agreements. Although some of these provisions seem clearly intended to increase the costs—or, alternatively, to reduce the profitability—of takeovers, the market's response to announcements of charter amendments and guaranteed compensation contracts has been neutral. Furthermore, stockholders seem to endorse such measures directly by voting for them. In the case of "standstill agreements" and targeted repurchases, however, where the management motive of entrenchment seems to be pursued unambiguously at the expense of stockholders, the market's response has been decidedly negative. There seems to be little doubt that such provisions interfere with the operation of the market for control, and this clearly reduces the firm's value.

The spread of these relatively new antitakover procedures, then, may have a great deal to do with the current size of acquisition premiums. And this further significant increase may in large part explain the recent series of proxy contests. Two of these contests unseated directors of very large companies. And, perhaps just as significant, they succeeded by enlisting, for the first time, the support of large institutions, which have invariable backed management during proxy contests.

Although clearly arising out of stockholder dissatisfaction with current management, such proxy activity can be interpreted as an indirect response by stockholders to the rising costs, and thus the reduced probability, of changes in control achievable through tender offers. The challenge to Superior Oil was aimed specifically at removing antitakeover amendments, calling for the establishment of an independent committee of stockholders to evaluate all bids for over 45 percent of the company. To the extent that stockholders feel themselves increasingly shut off by management from recourse to the market for corporate control, this recent reawakening of the proxy war could well turn into a general resurgence.

3

Why Corporate Raiders Are Good News for Stockholders

Clifford G. Holderness
University of Rochester

Dennis P. Sheehan
Purdue University

The controversy over "corporate raiding" has become front-page news. It rages in corporate boardrooms, animates Wall Street investors, and has even been examined by Senate subcommittees. In the process, a handful of investors, branded "corporate raiders," have become perhaps the most visible of all participants in the market for corporate control. However, despite the scope and intensity of what now amounts to a national debate over the consequences of corporate raiding, little in the way of serious economic analysis or systematic evidence has been offered as a means of resolving the controversy.

Much of the media's attention to the takeover market tends toward the emotional. The opening statement of a recent article on corporate takeovers is representative: "As the American economic environment changed, predators emerged from under rocks and began to prey on healthy businesses. Is there no stopping them? Will they devour us all?"[1] Another article on the same subject is entitled "The Wasteful Games of America's Corporate Raiders."[2] The takeover process, as it has been portrayed by many financial journalists, Congressmen, and corporate executives, is simply a financial "shell game" in which unscrupulous raiders exploit helpless companies and their powerless stockholders. The perceived role of managers of target companies is ambiguous; they are viewed, alternatively (and sometimes simultaneously), as victims of the raiders and as co-conspirators in the process. About one thing, however, there seems to be little uncertainty: namely,

---

1. *Forbes*, March 11, 1985, p. 134.
2. *The Economist*, June 1, 1985, p. 73.

that the profits generated from the "raiding" process are all short-run gains, illusory "paper profits" which come at the expense of the long-run value of American corporations. The statement of a chairman of a major corporation aptly sums up the prevailing popular view of takeover challenges: "Disruption by raiders...is a horrible wrong. It's hurting the country. It's hurting the economic system."[3]

Although the popular press is seemingly unaware of its existence, there has been a substantial amount of academic research on corporate takeover and restructuring activity.[4] None of this research, however, has focused specifically on "corporate raiders." We decided therefore to study in a systematic way the investment activities of six well-known investors often cited as corporate raiders. They are Carl Icahn, Irwin Jacobs, Carl Lindner, David Murdock, Victor Posner, and the late Charles Bluhdorn. We arrived at this list of six after consulting with members of the financial community and reviewing news articles. Our goal was to identify those investors most widely perceived to be corporate raiders. One can reasonably argue that others should have been included in this list, but we are confident about the credentials of our chosen six.[5]

For example, an article in *Institutional Investor* stated that Carl Icahn has been called a " 'notorious corporate opportunist' and 'a racketeer, an unprincipled predator who will stop at nothing in his search for a quick buck.' "[6] Irwin Jacobs, to his critics, is "a corporate raider who has shown little talent for runnning the public companies he has acquired."[7] A former business partner was even less kind, calling Jacobs "a liar of the worst kind."[8] David Murdock comes off best in this cast of "villians," having been portrayed as a "usually friendly Los Angeles raider."[9] When Charles Bluhdorn was CEO of Gulf & Western, the company acquired the nickname Engulf & Devour.[10] Fellow stockholders brought suit against Carl Lindner alleging that he illegally borrowed corporate funds and then made unauthorized purchases of securities at "prices far above market value."[11]

The most notorious raiding reputation, however, belongs to Victor Posner. According to a *Barron's* article, he "is rarely identified without the tag 'corporate raider'."[12] Moreover, "few businessmen have suffered more abuse in recent years than Victor Posner."[13] To his numerous critics Posner has "all the talent of an

---

3. Andrew C. Sigler, Chairman of Champion International, as quoted in *Business Week*, March 14, 1985, p. 82.

4. For a summary of this research, see Michael C. Jensen and Richard S. Ruback, "The Market for Corporate Control: The Scientific Evidence," *Journal of Financial Economics*, Vol. 11, pp. 5–50 (1983).

5. The most glaring omission from this list is, of course, Boone Pickens. Our reason for excluding Pickens is that he was not very active in acquiring stock in other firms when we began our research.

6. *Institutional Investor*, October 1982, p. 147.

7. *Wall Street Journal*, October 27, 1982, p. 35.

8. *Fortune*, September 19, 1983, p. 160.

9. *Forbes*, March 4, 1985, p. 83.

10. *Forbes*, March 15, 1982, p. 31.

11. *Wall Street Journal*, January 9, 1980, p. 2.

12. *New York Times*, February 26, 1984, p. 6F.

13. *Barron's*, November 19, 1979, p. 55.

accomplished raider: boldness, ferocity, tenacity and greed. He may not be a promising candidate for charitable work, but for the provision of loot his credentials are excellent."[14]

As mentioned earlier, however, no systematic evidence has to our knowledge been offered to support such bald assertions. In fact, given the harshness of the accusation, one would at least have expected a clear, consistent definition of what it is that "corporate raiders" are supposed to do to those companies in which they buy an interest. But this is not the case. With a willing imagination, however, one can construct from news reports a sense of what is intended. Amongst the welter of negative connotations, the common implication appears to be that "corporate raiding" is an activity which reduces the long-run value of the "raided" companies and, thus presumably, of their stockholders' shares.

The most extreme form of raiding apparently centers around the "looting" of the corporate treasury. For example, following Victor Posner's acquisition of stock in Foremost-McKesson, a lawsuit was filed against him alleging that his goal was "to prey upon and defraud stockholders of a carefully chosen series of corporations by means of a corruptly conceived and maliciously executed strategy of corporate warfare."[15] It was further alleged that Posner had "taken over and looted at least eight corporations in approximately as many years."[16]

Another, perhaps less drastic, definition of raiding is that raiders use their corporate voting power to award themselves "excessive" compensation and perquisites. This possibility was raised by some when in 1978 Victor Posner earned at least $1.5 million in salary, bonus, and benefits from Sharon Steel Corporation,[17] and when Posner's daughter, who is a director of some of his companies, was provided an apartment at corporate expense.[18]

One could also define raiding to encompass instances where firms repurchase, typically at a premium over the market price, only the shares held by the so-called raider, the practice that has become known as "greenmail." Under this definition of raiding, it is not even necessary for an investor to gain a voting majority to effect transfers to himself from other stockholders.[19] A number of the six investors have had their shares repurchased in this manner. For example, Kaiser Steel Corporation repurchased shares held by Irwin Jacobs at $52 a share, while other Kaiser stockholders received only $40 a share.[20] And Carl Icahn is suspected of having

---

14. *Barron's*, November 19, 1979, p. 55.

15. Quoted in the *Wall Street Journal*, June 23, 1981, p. 1.

16. *Wall Street Journal*, June 23, 1981, p. 1.

17. *Forbes*, October 29, 1979, p. 34.

18. *Barron's*, November 19, 1979, p. 5.

19. To be sure, there is evidence, which we discuss later, that targeted repurchases in general tend to reduce the wealth of stockholders who are not offered the same opportunity. See Larry Dann & Harry DeAngelo. "Standstill Agreements, Privately Negotiated Stock Repurchases, and the Market for Corporate Control," *Journal of Financial Economics*, Vol. 11, pp. 275–300 (1983); Michael Bradley & Lee Wakeman, "The Wealth Effects of Targeted Share Repurchases," *Journal of Financial Economics*, Vol. 11, pp. 301–328 (1983).

20. *Wall Street Journal*, October 28, 1983, p. 6.

sold shares at large premiums back to Marshall Field & Co., Hammermill Paper Co., American Can Co., Owens-Illinois Inc., Phillips Petroleum Co., and Uniroyal Inc., among others.[21] Such "greenmail" repurchases, perhaps more than any other practice of corporate raiders, have prompted calls for legislative action.

Presented, then, with this uncertainty about just what "corporate raiding" is, we began our investigation of the six investors by posing two general questions: (1) Does the evidence support the hypothesis that the six are corporate raiders who systematically reduce the wealth of other shareholders? (2) If the evidence is not consistent with this claim, what market role do the six play?

As a first approach to resolving these questions, we measured the stock price changes associated with initial public announcements of stock holdings by any of the six investors from 1977 to 1982. Stock price changes were measured for both the firms the six were buying into ("target firms") as well as the firms used to make those purchases ("filing firms").

Why are the initial market reactions to these announcements useful indicators of anything? Regardless of how it is defined, "corporate raiding" seems to imply that stock acquisitions by the raider ultimately reduce the long-term wealth of other stockholders of target firms. In efficient capital markets like the New York and American Stock Exchanges, expected reductions in the value of corporate assets should be reflected in stock prices when it is first announced that a corporate raider has been accumulating stock in the firm. The evidence uncovered by our inquiry reveals, to the contrary, that stockholders of target firms earned statistically significant positive stock returns, on average, when it was first announced that one of our six controversial investors was accumulating stock.

To obtain additional insights into the long-run impact of the six investors on target firms, we also followed the market performance of, and the six investors' activities in, the target firms over a two-year period following their initial stock purchases. The evidence from this inquiry is likewise inconsistent with the hypothesis that the six have reduced the value of their target companies.

In short, our study finds no evidence that these six investors actually raid companies and thereby systematically reduce long-term stockholder wealth. If anything, based on our findings, they are far more deserving of the designation "corporate saviors." That much is clear. What is less clear is how these six controversial investors succeed in increasing long-run stockholder wealth. In the pages that follow, we explore this question and describe our study in more detail.

The Investigation

Initial Stock Price Changes.   Most of our analysis of the investments of the six controversial investors is based on information contained in filings required by the Securities and Exchange Commission (SEC). Under Regulation 13(d) any individual or company must file with the SEC within ten days of acquiring any security

---

21. *Wall Street Journal*, May 28, 1985, p. 6.

in a publicly traded firm if, after that acquisition, the individual or company owns more than 5 percent of the outstanding class of security.[22] These initial 13(d)s are available almost immediately in the SEC's public records room and are shortly thereafter published in the *SEC News Digest*.[23] It is through the filing of 13(d)s that the investing public presumably first learns of large new securities investments by any major investor. This seems a reasonable assumption because filings of 13(d)s are closely followed by several investor service firms and are often reported by the financial press.

To measure the stock market's response to the first announcement of large stock purchases by the six, we collected from the *SEC News Digest* all initial 13(d)s filed from 1977–1982 by any of the investors, or by any company with whom they were affiliated. We identified affiliated companies (listed in the Appendix) by searching two computer-based information services, the Dow Jones Free Text Search and the ABI/INFORM Data Base.[24] Together these services contain over 360,000 entries, including the text (from 1979 to present) of the *Wall Street Journal*, *Barron's*, and the *Dow Jones New Service*, plus abstracts of articles (from 1971 to present) from more than 500 journals, including *Business Owner, Business Week, Financial Analysts Journal, Forbes, Fortune, Institutional Investor*, and *Mergers and Acquisitions*. In this manner we identified 35 companies that were publicly known to be affiliated with, if not controlled by, one of the six investors for at least some period between 1977 and 1982. It is possible, of course, that any of the six investors might have had "hidden" interests in other companies that were used as vehicles to acquire stock. But because our study concerns the market's reaction to activities known to involve the six investors, no attempt was made to examine stock acquisitions by "hidden" affiliates.

From the initial sample of 155 13(d)s gathered from the *SEC News Digest*, we eliminated target companies not listed on either the New York or American Stock Exchanges; this allowed us to use computer listings of daily stock prices. The final sample of target firms contained 99 observations: 5 for Icahn, 5 for Jacobs, 21 for Lindner, 10 for Murdock, 31 for Posner, and 27 for Bluhdorn (see Table I for this data presented both by individual investor and for the six in aggregate).

We also measured the stock price changes of the firms filing these 13(d)s. Starting with the target firm sample of 99 observations, we again eliminated all observations when the filing firm was not listed on the New York or American Stock Exchanges. The final sample used to measure the stock price changes of

---

22. Securities are broadly defined in the regulations to include bonds and stocks (both voting and non-voting).

23. Subsequent 13(d)s must be filed with each 2% increase in the holdings of any security. Unless otherwise specified, references in this paper to 13(d)s are to initial filings.

24. The computer searches were also used to double-check the *SEC News Digest* for announcements of 13(d) filings and to search for expressions of intent by any of the six investors to acquire securities.

Table 1. Number of Initial 13(d)s Filed by the Six Investors or by Affiliated Companies.[a]

	Individual Investor						Aggregate— the Six Investors	Random Sample
	Icahn	Jacobs	Lindner	Murdock	Posner	Bluhdorn		
All initial 13(d)s from *SEC News Digest*	8	8	47	16	40	36	**155**	689
Target firm not on CRSP file or insufficient data (deletion)	3	3	26	6	9	9	**56**	534
Final sample of target firms	5	5	21	10	31	27	**99**	155
Filing firm not on CRSP file of insufficient data (deletion)	5	5	21	7	—	—	**38**	125
Final sample of filing firms	—	—	—	3	45[b]	24	**72**	30

a. During the period 1977–1982 and a random sample of initial 13(d)s from the period 1977–1981.
b. There are many observations for Posner because he often used multiple companies to buy stock in a single target firm. This was not true of the other investors.

the filing firms consisted of 72 observations: 3 for Murdock, 45 for Posner, and 24 for Bluhdorn.[25]

   To obtain a benchmark against which to evaluate our so-called raiders, we also examined the market's response to initial stockholdings by a group of "average," presumably less controversial, investors. To this end we collected a random sample of 689 13(d)s filed during 1977–1981, which resulted, after exclusions, in observations on 155 target firms. The final sample of random filing firms consists of 30 observations. The data for both the six investors and the random sample are summarized in Table 1.

The Event Study Methodology. We then used this data to determine what impact the six investors had on the stock prices both of their target and filing firms. The methodology we employed to make this determination is known as an "event study," and has been widely used by economists for many years. Because it is so well known and accepted, we provide only a brief overview here.[26]

25. There are many observations for Posner because he often used multiple companies to buy stock in a single target firm. This was not true of the other investors.
26. Readers interested in a more complete review of the event study methodology are urged to see G. William Schwert, "Using Financial Data to Measure the Effects of Regulation," *Journal of Law and Economics*, Vol. 24, pp. 121–58 (1981).

The goal in our investigation, as in any event study, is to isolate the impact of a specific event on a firm—in this case, the first public announcement of major stockholdings by any of the six investors. To this end, we measured the stock price changes, either positive or negative, associated with the initial public announcement that our six investors had been accumulating stock in the firm.

Because returns of individual firms tend to move with returns to the market as a whole, the first step in any event study is to adjust the individual stock return in question to remove this influence of covariance with the market return. The resulting stock price return is called the "market-adjusted" return and constitutes our best estimate of the impact of one of the six investors on a given firm.

We calculated market-adjusted returns for each of the 99 target firms in our sample and then summed the results to obtain a portfolio return. Lastly, we employed standard tests to see whether the market-adjusted returns of this portfolio were statistically significant or merely reflected the variation inherent in all stock prices.

We should also explain why, like so many other economists, we focused on stock price changes. A basic proposition of financial economics is that stock prices are the net present value of the market's current estimation of *all* future cash flows of the firm. Studies have shown that, contrary to some popular claims, stock prices do not focus exclusively on the short run but also reflect longer-term prospects.

For example, a recent study by John McConnell and Chris Muscarella showed that the market responds favorably to announcements of planned increases in capital expenditures and investments in R&D.[27] If the market were concerned only with the short run, stock prices would decline because such investment typically increases expenditures in the short run, thereby depressing short-term earnings. The benefits from capital spending programs generally do not show up in higher earnings until several years thereafter. The fact that stock prices increase on average with the announcement of such long-term investments is evidence that the market is quite capable of taking the long view of a company's prospects. In fact, it has every incentive to do so, for short-sighted investors selling out because of temporary earnings declines would be systematically providing their more far-sighted counterparts with profit opportunities.

It is on the basis of this logic, then, and the extensive body of empirical work on which the theory rests, that we began with the proposition that the stock price reaction to announcements of 13(d) filings by the six reflects the market's best estimate of the long-term impact these investors will have on the value of the target firm.

Follow-up Activities of the Six

Most event studies end at this point. In this case, however, we followed the activities of our six investors in their target firms for a period of two years following the initial 13(d). Of course, even two years may be considered less than the long

---

27. John McConnell and Chris Muscarella, "Corporate Capital Expenditure Decisions and the Market Value of the Firm," *Journal of Financial Economics* (Vol. 14, No. 3, 1985).

run. But, given that market prices are forward-looking, this extension of the time horizon of our tests provides much more perspective on how the six investors affected the value of the target firms.

Our follow-up investigation had a number of components. From the *SEC News Digest* we determined how many amended 13(d)s were filed by the six for each target firm. (Amended 13(d)s must be filed with each 2 percent increase in the holdings of any security.) In addition, the *Wall Street Journal Index* and the Dow Jones Free Text Search were reviewed for three categories of corporate activity: First, we investigated how often the investor's shares were repurchased by the target firm ("greenmail"). Second, it was determined how often the target firm was involved in a corporate "reorganization"—by which we mean mergers, takeovers, and going private transactions. Third, we attempted to determine whether the proposed reorganization was completed. We also searched for press reports that the six became active in the management of the target firm. (A summary of these follow-up activities can be found in Table 2).

Event Studies on Follow-up Activities In Target Firms.   To measure the market's reaction to the various follow-up activities by the six investors in the target firms, we divided the firms into four categories according to outcome: (1) target firms that were successfully reorganized (whether by the investor or by a third party) within two years of the initial 13(d); (2) those where a reorganization effort failed within the two years; (3) those where the target firm repurchased at least some of the investor's shares (greenmail), again within two years; and (4) all other target firms where we had two years of observations after the initial 13(d).

We then used the same event study methodology discussed earlier to evaluate each of these categories. For the first three categories, we measured market-adjusted returns to target firm stockholders associated with three types of events: 1) the announcement of the initial stock purchase, 2) "significant" intermediate events, and 3) the final event. Significant intermediate events are those instances (in the authors' opinion) when the investor revealed significant information about his future intention with respect to the target firm, or when the target firm's management revealed how they planned to respond to an investor's proposals for changes. (The announcement, on January 21, 1980, that Carl Icahn asked the President of Saxon Industries to either repurchase his shares or face a proxy fight is an example of an intermediate event.) The final event is defined as follows: for the successful reorganization category, it is the day on which the target firm's board announced its approval of reorganization; for unsuccessful reorganizations, the day on which the reorganization offer was publicly withdrawn; for repurchases, it is the day on which the target firm announced it would repurchase the investor's shares.

Finally, we calculated a measure of the net "event" returns to stockholders in target firms attributable to the controversial investors' stockholdings over the entire two-year period. This is the summation of stock price changes associated with the initial, intermediate, and final events for each category.

Table 2. Summary of Activities by the Six Investors in Target Firms for the Two Years After the Filing of 13(d), 1977–1982.

	Icahn	Jacobs	Lindner	Murdock	Posner	Bluhdorn	Aggregate—the Six Investors
Number of target firms followed for two years after initial 13(d)	3	4	16	9	26	15	73
Number of target firms repurchasing investor's shares	2	2	—	1	3	4	12
Reorganization of target firm[a]							
Number of attempted reorganizations by investor	—	2	1	2	—	1	6
Number completed	—	—	—	2	—	1	3
Number of attempted reorganizations by third party	1	—	4	—	5	2	13
Number completed	1	—	4	—	3	2	10
Number of news reports of investor involvement in management of target firm	2	0	3	3	2	0	10
Number of target firms where amended 13(d)s were filed	3	0	11	6	18	12	50
Average number of amended 13(d)s per target firm followed	3.6	0	2.1	1.8	3.3	5.2	2.7
Number of firms where no indication of any activity after initial 13(d)[b]	0	1	3	0	5	1	9

a. Reorganizations are defined in this paper to include mergers, tender offers, and going private transactions.
b. This means that for a target firm there were no repurchases of the investors' shares, no attempts to reorganize, no news reports of management by the investor, and no amended 13(d)s filed.

I. The Empirical Findings

The Myth of Corporate Raiding

The findings of our investigations, whether from the stock price changes associated with initial stock purchases by the six or from those over the two-year follow-up period, provide no support for the widely held view that the six are corporate raiders. As stated earlier, if the six investors in fact systematically reduced the wealth of other stockholders through corporate raiding, one would anticipate a negative market reaction, on average, to the first public announcements of stock-holding. These negative stock price changes would reflect the market's expectation that the six investors would expropriate corporate assets for their own purposes, or that these transfers had already been effectuated. But the initial stock price changes were, on average, significantly *positive* for target firms.

When the six investors are viewed as a group, perhaps the most striking finding is that over the day of and the day following the first public announcement of initial stockholding by any of the six investors, other stockholders in those target firms earned a positive return of 1.8 percent on average.[28] This, of course, does not mean that all firms experienced a stock price increase of 1.8 percent above the market return for that period: some had larger increases, some smaller, and for some firms the stock price changes were negative. (The range of market responses, in fact, was from a −10 percent change, in the worst case, to a positive 16 percent.) What our findings do indicate, however, is that the positive returns outweigh the negative, resulting in a portfolio return for the 99 target firms of 1.8 percent.

Table 3 and Figure 1 also indicate that stockholders in target firms realized large gains during the days immediately *preceding* the public announcements of initial stock purchases by the six investors. Stock price increases have been documented for the days preceding other corporate transactions, including mergers, tender offers, proxy contests, and going private reorganizations. As with these other corporate transactions, the stock price increases prior to the announcements suggest that the event-day returns underestimate the wealth increases of stockholders.

Accordingly, we measured the cumulative abnormal returns commencing forty days prior through forty days after the announcements of initial purchases. We also measured the abnormal returns over the period from ten days before through the announcement. Both findings are reported in Table 3 and confirm that announcements of initial stock purchases by the six investors are associated with gains for target firms' stockholders. Finally, it should be noted that the downward drift in stockholder returns from the event day through the end of the event period is statistically insignificant.

When the six are viewed individually, we again found no support for their raider image. On average there were no negative returns that are significant for any of the six investors when measured over any of the following periods: (1) the ten days preceding and the day following the 13(d) filing; (2) the day of the filing itself; and (3) over the eighty days surrounding the filing. (These findings are summarized in Table 3.)

The empirical evidence on the random sample of 13(d)s makes for an interesting comparison with the evidence on our six controversial investors. The six investors are associated with target firm announcement day returns that are statistically significantly larger than target firm returns associated with filings by random

---

28. The t-statistic for this finding is 3.7; the null hypothesis of a zero mean return can, therefore, be rejected at the .01 significance level.

Table 3. Market-Adjusted Returns in Target Firms for Various Parts of the Event Period Associated with the First Public Announcement of Stockholding.[a]

Event Period

	Ten Days Before Through the First Public Announcement of Stockholding	First Public Announcement of Stockholding	Forty Days Before Through Forty Days After the First Public Announcement of Stockholding
All Six Investors	5.9%	1.8%	6.7%
N = 99	(5.2)	(3.7)	(2.2)
Random Sample	3.4%	0.4%	5.8%
N = 155	(3.8)	(1.1)	(2.4)
Icahn	7.2%	2.4%	21.1%
N = 5	(1.5)	(1.2)	(1.6)
Jacobs	9.6%	3.8%	20.6%
N = 5	(1.9)	(1.8)	(1.5)
Lindner	1.8%	−1.7%	0.1%
N = 21	(0.7)	(−1.6)	(.02)
Murdock	9.9%	3.0%	12.2%
N = 10	(3.7)	(2.7)	(1.7)
Posner	7.0%	3.3%	3.3%
N = 31	(3.8)	(4.2)	(0.7)
Bluhdorn	4.9%	1.8%	7.9%
N = 27	(3.1)	(2.7)	(1.9)

a. By the six investors collectively, by a random sample of investors, and by individual investor (t-statistics are given in parentheses; sample sizes are denoted by "N =").

Figure 1. Cumulative Market-Adjusted Returns for Target Firms Six Investors and Random Sample*

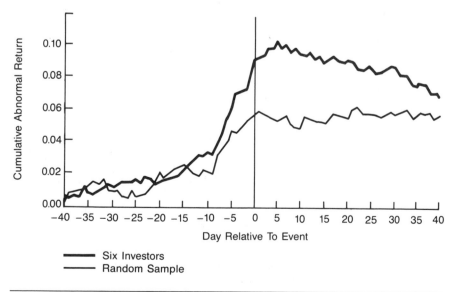

Six Investors
Random Sample

*From forty days before through forty days after the first public announcement of stockholding for the six investors (n = 99) (1977–1982) and for the random sample (n = 155 (1977–1981).

investors (1.8 percent for the six, 0.4 percent for the random sample). Over the eighty days surrounding the announcement of initial stockholding, the wealth increases associated with the six investors are larger than, although statistically indistinguishable from, those associated with random investors (6.7 percent for the six, 5.8 percent for the random sample). Hence, for stockholders in target firms, involvement by the six investors is, from some perspectives, more desirable—in the sense of being associated with larger wealth increases—than the presence of other, apparently less controversial, investors.

The Evidence on Filing Firms

As indicated earlier, we also measured stock price changes for firms controlled by or affiliated with one of the six investors purchasing stock in other companies and thus filing a 13(d) (hereafter "filing firms"). These returns are summarized in Table 4 and plotted in Figure 2. Although the event-day returns for the six are strongly positive, the cumulative returns are slightly negative (though the downward drift in cumulative returns after the event date lacks statistical significance). Table 4 and Figure 2 also contain findings for the random sample of filing firms, which serve as a benchmark to evaluate the findings on the six investors. All of these findings indicate that the six do not reduce the wealth of stockholders of firms that are used to acquire ownership positions in other companies. Perhaps the major conclusion to be drawn from these findings is that the six are not, as sometimes claimed, paying "too much" for the stock of other companies.

Figure 2. Cumulative Market-Adjusted Returns for Filing Firms Six Investors and Random Sample.*

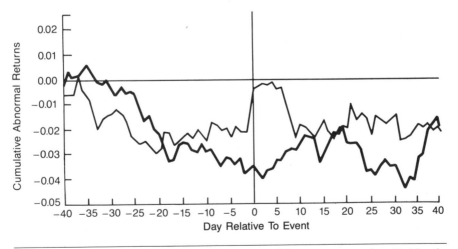

*From forty days before through forty days after the first public announcement of stockholding for the six investors (n = 72) (1977–1982) and for the random sample (n = 30) (1977–1981).

Table 4. Market-Adjusted Returns for Filing 13(d)s.[a]

Event Period

Sample	Ten Days Before Through the First Public Announcement of Stockholding	First Public Announcement of Stockholding	Forty Days Before Through Forty Days After the First Public Announcement of Stockholding
All Six Investors	1.9%	1.7%	−2.2%
N = 72	(1.4)	(3.0)	(−0.6)
Random Sample	−0.8%	0.4%	−2.0%
N = 30	(−0.6)	(0.8)	(−0.6)

a. For various parts of the event period for both the six investors (n = 72) (1972–1982) and for the random sample (n = 30) (1977–1981) (t-statistics are given in parentheses).

The Evidence on the Longer-Term

We found more empirical evidence inconsistent with the raiding hypothesis after reviewing the follow-up activities of the six investors in target firms. Regardless of what eventually happens to the target firm within the two years following an initial 13(d)—whether it is reorganized, a reorganization fails, the controversial investor's shares are repurchased, or even nothing at all happens—target firm stockholders, on average, earned positive returns (see Table 5).

Of particular relevance for the raiding hypothesis are the findings of our event study on targeted repurchases ("greenmail") involving the six investors. Like other studies, we found that the *announcements* of targeted repurchases are associated

Table 5. Average Event Day Market-Adjusted Returns for Initial, Intermediate, and Final Announcements for Target Firms of the Six Investors.

Type of Public Announcements	Successful Reorganization N = 13	Unsuccessful Reorganization N = 5	Repurchase N = 12	Other N = 39
Initial stock purchase	−0.3%	0.5%	4.1%	1.8%
	(−0.2)	(0.3)	(3.0)	(2.8)
Intermediate events	15.8%	12.8%	−0.4%	
	(3.5)	(3.7)	(−0.1)	
Final events	−1.2%	−3.4%	−1.3%	
	(−0.7)	(−1.9)	(−1.5)	
Total returns	13.0%	4.1%	3.2%	
	(3.1)	(1.0)	(1.8)	

with negative stock price changes for the firms making the repurchases.[29] These findings are certainly consistent with the widely-held view that targeted repurchases harm non-participating stockholders. However, the initial stock purchases that eventually led to those repurchases were on average associated with positive stock price changes of 4.1 percent over the two days surrounding the announcement of the initial purchase. And when the relevant initial stock purchases and significant intermediate events, as well as the "greenmail" repurchase itself, are all considered in aggregate, the total, net returns to target firm stockholders were a positive 3.2 percent.

Our findings on the total returns of those cases that terminate with repurchases are similar to those of Wayne Mikkelson of the University of Oregon and Richard Ruback of the Massachusetts Institute of Technology, who studied repurchases in general over the period of 1978–1980.[30] Using a different and larger sample, they found that the aggregate of the returns associated with the initial purchase, intermediate events, and the repurchase was a positive 2.0 percent. Our evidence, combined with that of Mikkelson and Ruback, casts a new light on "greenmail."[31]

II. If Not Raiders, Then What?

Given that we found no evidence that these six investors are corporate raiders in the sense of systematically reducing the wealth of other stockholders, we turn to the second of our two questions: If the evidence is inconsistent with raiding, what market role do the six play? Although our investigations failed to identify one precise role, there are two hypotheses that are consistent with some, if not all, of our findings.

Improved Management?

One hypothesis is that the six improve the management of target firms. This explanation, which stands directly opposed to the raiding hypothesis, holds that the six investors help bring about management changes that increase the target firm's expected net cash flows and hence increase its value. In fact, there are some that would argue that investors such as our six function, as a *Business Week* article put it, as "healthy whips over 'fat and complacent management.' "[32]

---

29. As reported in Table V, announcements of repurchases were associated with returns of -1.3%, $t = -1.5$. Equivalent results on the announcement of repurchases from other more general studies are as follows: Dann and DeAngelo (1983) (-1.8%, $t = -3.6$); Bradley and Wakeman (1983) (-1.2%, $t = -3.3$); Mikkelson and Ruback (1984) (-1.7%, $t = -4.2$).

30. Wayne Mikkelson and Richard Ruback, "Corporate Investments in Common Stock," *Journal of Financial Economics* (Vol. 14, No. 4, 1985).

31. Of course, the existence or non-existence of positive returns for shareholders is not the only point on which the "greenmail" debate will be decided. For example, one might argue that firms should not be empowered to create classes of shareholders who hold the same type of stock yet have different claims on the firm.

32. *Business Week*, March 4, 1985, p. 83.

These improvements in the management of target firms could result from either a change in corporate personnel (a new CEO, for example) or from a change in corporate policy (say, a decision to abandon a previously announced acquisition or to stop investing corporate capital to maintain unprofitable operations). In a number of cases, we found that the six investors became directly involved in the management of a target firm. A few examples of direct involvement by the six follow.

After David Murdock purchased stock in Cannon Mills Company, he "moved quickly to cut costs at Cannon, which he says had archaic management. He fired dozens of front-office employees one Friday on a half-hour's notice, laid off an estimated 2,000 millworkers, and warned the rest in a video-taped speech to work harder or lose their jobs."[33]

After Irwin Jacobs bought Watkins Company, he "brought in new managers who doubled sales to around $50 million and made Watkins profitable."[34]

Carl Lindner bought stock in Penn Central, was then elected to its board, and one year later became its chairman (before eventually selling his stock). This appears to be in keeping with the Lindner management approach, which purportedly is "to keep his finger on as many details as possible and be contemptuous of management depth."[35]

Carl Icahn is open about his potential involvement in management changes: "Critics can call me what they want—corporate raider or predator. But I believe that I have functioned as catalyst for change. . ."[36] This might provide an insight into Icahn's attempt to gain control of TWA. In the face of TWA's management claims that he would dismantle the company, Icahn responded that "while he had considered selling TWA's planes, cutting routes and adding to TWA's debt, he now says he wants control to operate the airlines for the long term and even expand it." "TWA has a great future," he said in an interview.[37] He did announce, however, that if his attempted takeover was successful, he would fire TWA's president.[38]

In some cases, one of the six did not institute the management change himself, but instead backed proposals for changes by other stockholders. When Irwin Jacobs bought stock in Walt Disney Productions, for example, he did not become directly involved in management, but he did announce his opposition to a planned acquisition which had already been opposed by several other major Disney stockholders and by some directors.[39]

Although no love is lost between "raiders" and incumbent management in contests for control, some target firm managers have grudgingly admitted that attempted takeovers changed their outlook on what management course was best

---

33. *Wall Street Journal*, March 2, 1983, p. 1.
34. *Fortune*, September 19, 1983, p. 160.
35. *Fortune*, January 1977, p. 130.
36. *Business Week*, December 12, 1983, p. 116.
37. *Wall Street Journal*, May 28, 1985, p. 6.
38. *Wall Street Journal*, June 10, 1985, p. 4.
39. *Wall Street Journal*, July 30, 1984, p. 4.

for the firm. Raymond Watson, Disney's chairman during its recent takeover attempt by Irwin Jacobs, said that the challenge to management by stockholder dissidents "woke us up, though I hate to give credit to something like that. I think the company is stronger."[40] Thomas Pownall, chairman of Martin Marietta during the celebrated Bendix-Martin Marietta battle, later characterized that battle as "useful." "It became apparent to us that we really did need to shed some less productive operations."[41] Thus, the prospect of a takeover may be sufficient to induce management changes that benefit stockholders.

Perhaps the strongest evidence that these six investors improve the management of target firms comes from the positive market response to the first public announcement of stockholding by one of the six investors. This favorable response is consistent with the argument that the market expects the six to improve the management of target firms and thereby increase net cash flows. Additional empirical evidence consistent with the improved management hypothesis comes from the activities of the six investors following their initial stock purchases. If they were expected by the market to bring about management changes, then we would look for them to play some management role, or somehow "be heard from," after their initial stock purchases. In other words, they should not be "passive" investors.

That our six investors generally take some kind of active role is consistent both with the general impression we received from examining financial press reports and with the empirical evidence reported in Table 2. In only ten target firms out of the 73 in our sample was there no public indication of any activity during the two years following an initial stock purchase. Moreover, in at least ten (again, out of 73) target firms, one of the investors assumed a direct and publicly-visible management role. In six other cases, one of the investors attempted to reorganize a target firm, while in 13 other instances a third party attempted the reorganization after one of the six became a stockholder. Overall, 13 target firms were successfully reorganized within the two years following an initial stock purchase by one of the investors.

Management *changes*, to be sure, do not necessarily guarantee improvements in the sense of increasing a target firm's expected net cash flows and thus its market value. The findings from our event studies on the follow-up activities, however, are consistent with the hypothesis that the majority of the management changes in our sample were in fact improvements. Successful reorganizations, which could be a prelude to the introduction of a new management team, are associated with the largest wealth gains (measured as total announcement-day returns) for target firms' stockholders (13.0 percent).[42] On the other hand, when it was announced that a reorganization effort was withdrawn, target firm stockholders suffered wealth losses of 3.4 percent—perhaps because management changed proposed by the

40. *Business Week*, March 4, 1985, p. 82.
41. *Forbes*, March 11, 1985, p. 44.
42. Jensen and Ruback, cited in note 4, suggest this possibility.

controversial investor, and anticipated by the market, had been rejected. (Nevertheless, the total, net return to stockholders from the three events was still a positive 4.1 percent on average.) Lastly, even the 12 cases of "greenmail" repurchases could be consistent with the improved management hypothesis if the initial purchase and the subsequent repurchase increased the scrutiny of the target firm's management. This scrutiny, in turn, could have resulted in more effective monitoring of management, and perhaps even in a subsequent reorganization attempt (as happened with Disney).

Thus, our empirical evidence is consistent with the hypothesis that the six are associated with improved management of target firms. But what are the implications of the empirical evidence for filing firms? In particular, do stockholders of firms filing 13(d)s suffer wealth losses perhaps because of diseconomies of scale in management caused by these stock investments? The empirical evidence is inconsistent with this view. For those filing firms affiliated with one of the six investors, statistically significant negative returns were not observed over the eighty-day event period. Indeed, the event day abnormal returns are both positive (1.7 percent) and larger than the returns for a random filing firm (0.4 percent).

Superior Security Analyst?

An alternative, though not mutually exclusive, hypothesis holds that the six investors systematically identify and purchase undervalued stocks. This superior security analyst hypothesis is occasionally reflected in statements by and about the six. Carl Lindner, for example, has been described as "an 'asset player' who has a nose for undervalued situations and guts to buy when other people are scared,"[43] Victor Posner "says he prefers to buy stocks that are 'low multiples of earnings, never above 10 times (earnings).' "[44] Irwin Jacobs' investor groups "look for undervalued situations. [Says Jacobs] 'I like to buy dollars for 50 cents. . .I'm an asset-oriented individual. Intangibles carry zero on the balance sheet for me.' "[45]

Stock purchases by the six could be based either on non-public information about target firms or on skills they have in interpreting publicly-available information about target firms. The positive abnormal returns to stockholders in target firms associated with the first public announcements of stockholding by the six are consistent with either version of this hypothesis. Moreover, it is possible that some investors systematically possess more valuable private information than others or have greater skills at interpreting publicly-available information on target firms. If the market is aware of this, then the hypothesis could explain the observed differences in initial stock price changes for different investors filing the 13(d).

Other findings, however—most notably the direct involvement of the six investors in management and the targeted repurchases of their shares—cannot be explained by the superior security analyst hypothesis. This explanation has relevance

---

43. *Fortune*, January 1977, p. 138.
44. *Wall Street Journal*, June 23, 1981, p. 1.
45. *Wall Street Journal*, January 28, 1985, p. 6.

only for stock purchases and does not address follow-up activity in target firms. It should be noted, however, that the evidence on the follow-up activities is not inconsistent with the superior security analyst hypothesis. Indeed, it is possible, given all of the empirical evidence uncovered by our investigations, that the "improved management" and the "superior security analyst" hypotheses work best together in explaining the success of these six investors in raising stockholder values.

The improved management and superior security analyst hypotheses describe mechanisms by which the six investors were able to generate positive returns. Clearly, both hypotheses require the existence of undervalued firms, but, equally clearly, neither explains why firms are undervalued. Perhaps the most plausible explanation for the undervaluation of assets is a failure by management to put the assets at its disposal to their highest-valued use. As long as the market expects management to employ assets in a suboptimal manner, then investors lower their assessment of the market value of a company. This potentially explains why some firms sell below their book value or even below the liquidation value of their net assets.

Thus, in one sense, our two mechanisms are connected. The six investors studied here, as well as other "corporate raiders," may be the catalyst necessary to allow potential asset values to be realized. They can do this by being active investors and taking a direct role in the management of the firm, or they may be able to do this simply by spotting stocks that are undervalued and investing, thereby giving a signal to the market that increased scrutiny of the target firm may yield benefits.

III. Conclusion

No sensible person would argue that these six investors are not pursuing their own self-interest by accumulating stock in a given firm. They are by their own admission. The key question is: Does that pursuit of self-interest increase the wealth of other individuals? Is Adam Smith's invisible hand at work here? Our investigations into the activities of six controversial investors show the answer to be an unequivocal yes.

Specifically, our investigations show that announcements of initial stock purchases were associated with statistically significant increases in the wealth of target firms' stockholders. Moreover, these increases, at least for the announcement day, exceeded the increases associated with initial stock purchases by random (typically less controversial) investors.

The activities of the six in target firms over a two-year period after they file an initial 13(d) are likewise consistent with wealth increases for other stockholders. Even in those cases when the investors' shares were repurchased by the target firm (so-called "greenmail"), target firms' stockholders experienced statistically significant wealth increases when events from the initial purchase through the repurchase are examined. In short, if "corporate raiding" implies the reduction in wealth of other stockholders, the empirical evidence reported in this paper lends no support to the corporate raider image attached to these six investors.

While the empirical evidence is inconsistent with the raiding hypothesis, the precise market role of the six is less clear. One reasonable interpretation of the evidence is that the six investors help bring about management changes that increase the value of corporate assets. Although our investigation of the follow-up activities of the six sheds some light on these management changes, more research is needed to identify their precise nature, and to ascertain whether the investors helped cause these changes or whether they merely anticipated them. Additional research is also needed to see to what extent, if any, the positive returns resulted because these investors are able to identify undervalued stocks. Finally, additional research is needed to answer what is arguably the biggest mystery uncovered by our investigations: Given that the six investors are on average associated with increases in the wealth of other stockholders, how did they ever obtain the label of "corporate raider," and why has that label persisted?

PART II

Corporate Restructuring

4

The Restructuring of Corporate America:
An Overview

Gailen L. Hite
Columbia University

James E. Owers
University of Massachusetts

Until fairly recently, modern corporate finance theory has rested securely on the premise that managers of public corporations act, on the whole, so as to maximize the wealth of their stockholders. In 1976, however, two finance professors at the University of Rochester, Michael Jensen and William Meckling, raised important questions about this foundation of financial economists' thinking. In a paper entitled "Theory of the Firm: Managerial Behavior, Agency Costs, and Ownership Structure," Jensen and Meckling pointed a new direction for research in finance by exploring the potential conflict of interest between management and stockholders—and the resulting loss of value—in the large, widely-held public corporation.

The intent of the Jensen-Meckling paper, to be sure, was not to challenge, much less to overturn, this fundamental assumption about corporate management's behavior. In fact, the standard conception of management as stewards of stockholder savings has served, and continues to serve, the academic finance profession remarkably well. It has been upheld by the findings of all but a handful of the studies that now swell the body of finance literature.

The real contribution to finance scholarship of the Jensen-Meckling argument was to draw attention to matters of corporate organization—matters which, up to that point, had been largely neglected by financial economists. In the course of

The authors would like to thank Don Chew, the editor of this journal, for his editorial assistance and safeguarding of the English language.

re-examining this old problem of the "separation of ownership from control," Jensen and Meckling redirected our focus by viewing the corporation as a "nexus of contracts" among stockholders, managers, employees, regulators, and others. The resulting change in finance scholars' way of looking at the corporation has given rise to a new line of research attempting to explain how and why certain features (read "contracts") of the modern corporation have evolved into their present form.

In the real world, meanwhile, a host of changes—ever larger divestiture waves, the revival of the proxy war, the growing popularity of leveraged buyouts, wholesale corporate liquidations, and the proliferation of new varieties of spin-offs and split-ups—all this seems to be confirming the appropriateness of this new direction in financial research. For much of this "restructuring" activity can be explained only by looking more carefully at the contractual relationships, both explicit and implicit, among management, stockholders, regulators, and other corporate constituencies. Such restructurings seem to be making profound changes in existing corporate "contracts"—contracts which themselves have evolved and are continuously evolving through time. And, on the basis of the market's enthusiastic endorsement of these restructuring transactions, such changes promise to make the corporation a more efficient vehicle for creating and storing stockholder value.

The recent divestiture activity, for example, suggests in part an unraveling of much of the conglomerate activity of the 60s. The emphasis of strategic planning has fallen increasingly on sharpening the "corporate focus" by identifying a company's strengths or comparative advantages, and by eliminating those businesses that do not offer a good "strategic fit." (There has also, of course, been a large merger wave in recent years. But, with the glaring exception of a few very large, highly-publicized, diversifying takeovers, we suspect that most strategic acquisitions have been combinations of firms with complementary resources, prompted by prospects of real business "synergies.")

The growing number of divestitures also provides evidence of what seems to be a general corporate trend toward more streamlined, decentralized, "entrepreneurial" organizations. This trend is probably even more clearly illustrated, however, by the recent flurry of spin-offs and split-ups. Such transactions, which simply divided a corporation into a number of separate firms with no change in proportional ownership, suggest that a new kind of arithmetic has come into play. Whereas corporate management once seemed to behave as if $2 + 2$ were equal to 5, especially during the conglomerate heyday of the 60s, the wave of reverse mergers seems based on the counter proposition that $5 - 1$ is 5. And, as suggested, the market's consistently positive response to such deals seems to be providing broad confirmation of the "new math."

Even more radical restructurings have enriched their stockholders not by concentrating the focus of corporate operations, but rather by completely dissolving the current organizational structure. In choosing total liquidation, such companies have decided they are worth more "dead than alive" and have accordingly self-destructed, selling off their assets piecemeal.

Last, and perhaps most surprising, the growing number and size of companies going private suggest that even the very form of the public corporation is being tested. The proliferation of leveraged buyouts may be telling us that management compensation committees of public corporations could be doing far more to strengthen management incentives to perform. Also, the large amounts of leverage supported in these deals contain the suggestion that either (1) some public companies may be significantly underleveraged or (2) the private corporation per se has considerably more debt capacity than its public counterpart.

To return to our earlier statement, we feel that much of the underlying corporate motivation for such widespread restructuring can only be understood by looking more closely at how management and stockholders (and regulators) are linked in the structure of the public corporation. To understand *how* and *why* the organizational structure changes through time, it is important to address five key questions: (1) How do the composition and responsibilities of the management team change as a result of the restructuring? (2) How do the managerial compensation and incentive structure change? (3) How does the ownership of the residual equity claims change? (4) If assets are exchanged, as in the case of a sell-off, how are the new assets employed? (5) What factors lead to the obsolescence of the old and the adoption of the new, presumably more efficient, contractual structures?

We will explore some of these issues in this discussion of sell-offs, liquidations, spin-offs, and leveraged buyouts. But first we present a case study of Dillingham Corporation, a company which executed each of these four transactions in a massive reorganization. The following account is based on reports published in *The Wall Street Journal*.

I. The Dillingham Case

From late 1978, when Dillingham began to sell off some of its properties, through 1983, when management took the company private in a leveraged buyout, the company went through a remarkable series of structural changes. In orchestrating these changes, management brought about a dramatic increase in the value of its stockholders' claims.

Before undertaking this general restructuring, Dillingham was a diversified firm involved in real estate, energy, maritime, and construction activities. In December 1978, the press carried a report that Dillingham was selling its Fabri-Value unit to the Grinnell division of IT&T and its Reef Cattle Management unit to an Australian investor. The latter operation had been losing money, but losses on such foreign operations were not deductible against U.S. taxable income. The capital loss on the sale, however, was deductible.

To assess the effect of these announcements on Dillingham's stockholders, we computed the rate of return on the shares on the day of the announcement and on the following day when the press carried the report. Adjusted for general stock market movements over that two-day period, Dillingham's stock price increased 7.8 percent.

In July 1979, management announced the suspension of its coal mining activities at its Canmore mines in Canada due to operating losses. The market's response was to raise Dillingham's stock price by 5.1 percent (again, adjusted for market movements).

Ten days later, management initiated a continuing tender offer at the prevailing market price for all blocks of its Dillingham stock owned by holder of 50 shares or less. Management cited the disproportionate costs of servicing small accounts as the justification for the repurchase offer. While less than 1 percent of the outstanding shares were eligible, the announcement of the potential elimination of 2000–3000 small accounts generated an abnormal return of 3.5 percent for shareholders.

In April 1980, Harry Weinberg, a private Honolulu investor owning 10 percent of Dillingham's outstanding shares, sought representation on Dillingham's board. It was rumored that Mr. Weinberg would try to bring about a merger of Dillingham with Alexander and Baldwin, a company in which he held a 13 percent stake. Dillingham's board postponed the annual meeting to prepare a proposal to reduce the board from 15 to 3 seats, according to which the unseated directors would assume new roles on an advisory council. The share price rose 9.3 percent at the time of the announcement of this anti-takeover move, and 3.2 percent more when the shareholders approved the plan denying Mr. Weinberg representation on the board (unless he upped his stake to 25 percent of the outstanding shares.)[1]

Although unsuccessful in his bid to gain minority representation on the board, Mr. Weinberg did raise questions about whether Dillingham's stockholders were benefiting to the fullest extent possible from the company's extensive real estate holdings in Hawaii. After a careful study of the real estate operations, management proposed a partial liquidation of the Hawaiian properties on March 17, 1981. In the week of this announcement, Dillingham stock rose a market-adjusted 39.4 percent!

Two weeks later, when the board expanded the plan to sell nearly all the Hawaiian land holdings, the price jumped another 9.6 percent. The plan called for the following series of moves: the transfer of the properties to a newly formed limited partnership, Ala Moana Hawaii Properties; the spin-off of the limited partnership interest to existing stockholders; the liquidation of the properties; and the distribution of the cash proceeds to the limited partners (that is, the original Dillingham stockholders).

Even after Dillingham disposed of the Ala Moana shopping center, its "crown jewel," the stage had been set for a battle for control of the firm. On April 29, 1981, a group of Singapore investors bought a 5.7 percent stake, triggering a stock price rise of 4.7 percent. On September 25 the stake was increased to 9.6 percent and prices jumped another 7.5 percent.

---

1. That Mr. Weinburg was unable to obtain a board seat and yet stock prices rose is not atypical. In a study of proxy contests, Dodd and Warner found that stock prices tend to rise upon the announcement of these contests, regardless of whether the dissidents are successful in acquiring board representation.

The following day management announced a cash repurchase tender offer for 3 million shares, about 20 percent of the total then outstanding, at the then current market price of $12⅜. Although a spokesman for the board denied that the offer was related to the purchases of the Singapore investors, the board announced that only 1.6 million had been tendered. During the offer period, share prices fell 11 percent as the probability of a premium takeover bid declined.

On December 29, 1981, the board approved a change in the by-laws that provided for limitations on the rights of foreign owners. The board noted that U.S. maritime law required a minimum of 75 percent U.S. ownership to secure Maritime Administration-guaranteed financing and to retain the right to trade between U.S. ports. The change gave the directors the right to suspend voting rights and dividend payments on foreign holdings in excess of 20 percent on the outstanding shares. The by-law change left share prices unchanged.

In May of 1982 the firm repurchased all 1.5 million shares owned by the Singapore investors in a privately negotiated transaction at $14 per share when the current market price was $11.50 per share. The agreement included a "standstill" provision under which the selling group agreed not to acquire additional shares in Dillingham. The block repurchase and standstill agreement were greeted with a market-adjusted price decline of 3.3 percent.

Then, in September 1982, management announced a continuing plan to buy back additional shares in open market and private transactions in the following year. The market price of Dillingham shares jumped 3 percent upon this announcement and continued to climb another 17 percent through the middle of November.

On November 17, 1982 management announced a plan to take the company private in a deal arranged by Kohlberg, Kravis, Roberts & Co. The offer to public shareholders was made at $25 per share when the market price was $17⅝. The return to stockholders was more than 25 percent at the time of the announcement (and roughly 40 percent by the time the deal was actually consumated). The leveraged buyout provided equity positions for senior management and no plans to dispose of any lines of business. Lowell Dillingham, chairman and a member of the founding family (which held 20 percent of the outstanding shares), described the proposal as a "unique opportunity to serve the best interests of all the company's constituencies, particularly shareowners and employees."

Summing Up Dillingham

Over this four-year period in Dillingham's history, we found that the company's public stockholders earned an *abnormal* return of 185 percent (which excludes the effect of the general market appreciation over this period). Of this total gain, more than 160 percent preceded the announcement of the leveraged buyout proposal. There can be little doubt that this restructuring of Dillingham greatly increased stockholder wealth. What seems even more remarkable, though, is that even *after* the 160 percent abnormal price run-up, management expected enough additional gains from going private to be willing to pay 40 percent premium over the already dramatically increased market value of the company.

While the restructuring of Dillingham is an interesting case, we do not wish to imply that such gains accompanied most—or even the majority—of such restructuring transactions in recent years. To make general statements, we must examine data from larger samples of transactions. But before turning to this larger body of evidence, it is worthwhile noting two important features of the Dillingham case study. First, the stock price reactions to restructuring announcements have often been quite large, suggesting large expected gains from changes in corporate organizational structure and productive activities. Second, restructuring transactions—sell-offs, liquidations, spin-offs, and management buyouts—do not always occur as separate, isolated events but sometimes as a sequence of actions in a major restructuring plan.

II. Sell-offs

Over the last decade mergers and acquisitions have captured the imagination and focused the energy of many academic researchers in finance. The financial press has been equally preoccupied with business combinations and their potential effect on the economy and financial markets. With all this attention on multi-billion dollar acquisitions, it has been easy to overlook the extent of divestiture activity—the massive paring and shedding by American conglomerates of their divisions, subsidiaries, and smaller business units. In 1983, for example, W.T. Grimm reported 2533 mergers and acquisitions. What is less well known is that 932, or more than one-third of this total, were sales of operating assets from one corporation to another. As can be seen from Table 1, while total acquisition activity has increased since 1980, divestitures have increased slightly faster than the total.

A "sell-off" of assets in exchange for cash or securities is simply a "reverse" merger from the point of view of the divesting firm. From previous academic research we know that mergers, on average, create value for stockholders, though the lion's share of the gains generally go to the stockholders of the acquired firms. Divestitures also typically result in significant, positive abnormal returns for sellers and positive, but insignificant, gains for buyers. (For a more detailed discussion of studies of divestitures, see Scott Linn and Mike Rozeff's article, Chapter 8.)

Table 1. Acquisition and Divestiture Trends: 1980–83

	Total Number of Transactions	Divestitures Included in Totals	Divestitutes as a Percent of Totals
1980	1,886	665	35%
1981	2,395	830	35%
1982	2,346	875	37%
1983	2,533	932	37%

Source: W.T. Grimm & Co. Chicago

But this finding begs the question: if the merger of corporate assets increases the combined value of the two operations, how can the divestiture of previously acquired assets also create new value?

For the sale of a business unit to benefit existing shareholders, the selling price must exceed the present value of the cash flows the unit will generate if retained within the organization. That is, the assets must be more valuable to the buyer than to the seller. This difference in value can result from synergies, the creation of scale economies for the buyer, or superior management. Alternatively, to the extent that the operations no longer "fit" with the seller's other activities, a sale may also create value by eliminating negative synergies (or what Linn and Rozeff call "anergies").

Our rationale for sell-offs might appear to be at odds with press reports of divestitures motives. For example, in 1974 Motorola announced the sale of its TV business to Matsushita Electric, a Japanese consumer electronics firm. The stockholders of Motorola enjoyed a market-adjusted gain of 21.9 percent. Management explained that the TV unit "hadn't achieved appropriate profit objectives in recent years." But how does simply selling a "loser" benefit shareholders? Shareholders don't escape losses by selling—they simply receive lower prices for the assets of losing operations.

A more plausible explanation is that Matsushita expected to turn the division into a "winner." But competition in the acquisition market forced Matsushita to share the expected gains with Motorola's stockholders. In fact, Matsushita's stock price actually declined when the deal was announced—though by a barely detectible 0.2 percent.

Another possible explanation is that divestitures represent corrections of prior acquisition mistakes. Linn and Rozeff find that divestiture "waves" follow one to two years after merger waves. This finding, however, should not necessarily be interpreted as challenging the value of merger activity. A firm may acquire another company with the intention of reorganizing the acquired firm, and getting rid of those businesses that don't complement the primary business lines. Also, changes in technology and product markets may cause combinations which were once valuable to become inefficient. A sell-off may simply indicate that the divested resources now have higher values in other uses.

Our point here is that the divestiture of previously acquired businesses may be consistent with many explanations besides the "admission of prior mistakes" hypothesis. At the current time we have no systematic evidence on why firms acquire and then divest business units. Nor do we have reason to believe that a single, simple explanation will cover all such cases.

In summary, our general finding is that the change of ownership and control in corporate sell-offs increases the wealth of the shareholders of divesting companies. We view the sell-off of a subsidiary, division, line of business, or other operating assets as a mechanism for transferring assets to higher-valued uses in other corporations. The gains may result from synergies or economies of scale offered by the buyer. Or the management of the buying firm may have a comparative advantage in monitoring and controlling the management of the subsidiary.

III. Liquidations

An extreme form of sell-off is the liquidation of assets. A liquidation represents a sale of assets and should not be confused with a decision to "shut down" or abandon an operation. The assets are sold to another firm, and the proceeds are distributed to stockholders instead of being re-invested in new operating assets. Liquidations may be either partial or total. In the latter case the original firm ceases operations. We confine our attention here to total liquidations.

The interesting feature of total liquidations is the recognition by management that the existing organizational structure is no longer viable. In short, the firm is "worth more dead than alive." Not only do the assets have a higher-valued use elsewhere, but they are more valuable after being divided and sold off in a piecemeal fashion.

We examined a sample of 25 total liquidations occurring between 1963 and 1982. All 25 cases were voluntary dissolutions—that is, none of the firms were in bankruptcy. Although one might expect that these firms were performing poorly just before liquidation, this was not the case. During the period from 50 trading days through 5 trading days prior to the liquidation proposal, these firms experienced no abnormal price movements on average. That is, they did as well as expected given the general stock market performance.

In the trading week ending with the liquidation proposal, the average market-adjusted return was 9.0 percent, a statistically significant result. While the average gain was substantial there was wide variation among the sample. For example, the list of 16 gaining firms was topped by a 58.6 percent gain for National Silver in 1980 and a 56.7 percent gain for Reeves Telecom in 1979. At the other extreme were losses of 12.5 percent for Telecor in 1978 and 11.5 percent for Reliance Manufacturing in 1964. Both Telecor and Reliance are special cases, however, since both had previously announced plans to find a merger partner. Their stock prices had initially risen in anticipation of a takeover. When the takeover plans fell through, the companies announced their intentions to liquidate. Presumably, their liquidation values were below the market's expectation of their value as a takeover candidate.

The market's strongly positive response to these corporate self-liquidations suggests that, in most of these cases, the curent organizational structure was not leading to the most efficient use of the firm's assets and that dissolution was a higher-valued strategy. Management presumably recognized that continued operations would produce a substandard return on assets—one lower than the opportunity cost of capital. Concluding, furthermore, that the business was no longer viable as a going concern and could not profitably be sold as such to another corporate bidder, it elected to sell off its assets in parts and distributed the proceeds to stockholders.

IV. Spin-offs

In its purest form, a spin-off involves a separation of the operations of a subsidiary from its parent into separate corporations, with no change in ownership of the equity claims. For example, a firm may form a subsidiary corporation and transfer assets to the new entity in return for all the stock certificates. The new shares are then distributed to the original stockholders of the parent on a pro-rata basis.[2] The two firms separate, and the subsidiary's management is vested with autonomous decision-making authority.

The distinctive feature of pure spin-offs is that parent company management gives up control of the subsidiary operations while shareholders maintain their proportional ownership of both operations. The interesting questions raised by such transactions are these: What can be accomplished with two separate, free-standing units that cannot be achieved under a unified organizational structure? Why can subsidiary management be more effective as heads of an independent unit than as subordinates reporting to parent company management?

In an article which appears later in this issue, Katherine Schipper and Abbie Smith document a significantly positive market reaction to such spin-offs. In speculating about the reasons for this positive investor response, they state that expected tax savings and the ability to avoid regulatory interference seem clearly to have motivated a number of these transactions. But for the majority of spin-offs, the answer seems to lie in the diversity of operations within the firm. Schipper and Smith suggest that there may be large expected gains from simplifying a complicated conglomerate structure, decentralizing decision-making, and replacing an original set of compensation contracts which governed the conglomerate with two different sets of contracts, each tailored to the specific circumstances of the separate unit.

In our own work we found three reasons for spin-offs frequently given by management. The most common was a desire to "get back to basics, to the lines of business we know best." An organizational structure that is well-suited to certain operations may not profitably accommodate other, different business units. For one thing, compensation arrangements tied to the stock price of the parent may have little effect on the incentives of managers of a small division. If the division is spun off, new contracts tied directly to the stock price of the unit may be used to provide a much more effective means of motivating managers.

A second common motive was to circumvent implicit contracts with outside regulatory agencies by separating regulated and unregulated lines of business. For example, having a bank subsidiary may bring non-bank operations under the eye of banking authorities. Or in the case of rate-of-return regulated industries, such

---

2. Occasionally the term "spin-off" is used to refer to the initial public offering of the stock of a subsidiary. If less than 100% of the subsidiary shares are sold, the remainder is typically distributed to parent company stockholders at a later date.

as public utilities, regulators may effectively "tax" income of profitable unregulated operations by figuring subsidiary returns into the allowable rate-of-return calculations for regulated operations.

The desire to reduce tax liabilities seems to have provided the impetus for the formation and spin-off of royalty trusts, particularly in the oil and gas industry. The strategy is most often associated with Boone Pickens and Mesa Petroleum, and figured prominently in the recent proxy fight to restructure Gulf Oil. The ostensible motivation was to remove the double layer of taxation (first at the corporate level and then at the stockholder level on dividends) on distributed oil and gas income.

As a matter of curiosity we looked at the market reaction to the two Mesa spin-off announcements. For the two days surrounding the first spin-off proposal in 1979, the price of Mesa rose 9.7 percent after adjustment for general market movements. Surprisingly, however, when Mesa announced the offshore trust in 1982, the market-adjusted price declined by 14.4 percent upon the announcement. If both of these spin-offs were truly motivated by the desire to reduce taxes paid on oil and gas revenues, then we are at a loss to explain the recent bid by Mesa to reacquire the properties spun off in the 1979 transaction. It would seem that bringing the revenues back under the corporate umbrella would result in higher tax liabilities.[3]

A third reason for spin-offs was to facilitate mergers. In such cases, either the parent or a subsidiary was the target of a friendly takeover bid. The bidding company seeking only part of the target's assets arranged for the spin-off to precede the merger consummation. As an example, the spin-off of Houston Oil Trust by Houston Oil & Mineral was part of its plan to be acquired by Tenneco. The idea came out of a disagreement between the two companies' managements about the amount of "proven" gas reserves in Houston's U.S. producing wells.[4] The royalty trust was spun off to Houston's stockholders. Tenneco lowered its bid from $1.6 billion to $422 million in Tenneco stock because it was acquiring a much smaller fraction of the original asset base.

Another, and perhaps the most common, motive for spin-offs relies on the inability of investors to recognize the value of "hidden" corporate assets—those assets whose market values, though substantially above book values, are not reflected in corporate financial statements. Companies with valuable real estate holdings are often held to be undervalued for this reason, and are thus cited as prime candidates for spin-off. This line of reasoning is presented by Dan Palmon and Lee Seidler of New York University:

---

3. Perhaps Mesa is anticipating tax write-offs from exploration and drilling in excess of other production income. If so, Mesa could be "purchasing" taxable income to fully use the excess write-offs. This would be comparable to U.S. Steel's acquisition of Marathon prior to taking substantial write-offs for discontinued operations.
4. See the recent article, "How a Royalty Trust Proved a Leaky Shelter and Angered Investors," *The Wall Street Journal*, April 6, 1984, p. 1.

> Properties are shown at constantly declining historical cost net book values
> on the balance sheet, when they are often worth considerably more than cost.
> Reported income is understated because of the same requirement. These two
> [effects] combine to mislead investors in the opinion of managements, and tend
> to cause share prices to be unduly depressed.

In a crude test of this hypothesis, we looked at a sample of spin-offs of real estate subsidiaries.[5] In six cases in which *real estate firms* announced spin-offs of real assets, we found two-day abnormal returns of 0.3 percent—that is, virtually no response. But when we examined a sample of 20 *industrials* spinning off real estate subsidiaries, we found two-day average, market-adjusted returns of 9.1 percent.

When viewed together, these two sets of results do not seem to support the notion of a "real estate discount," of a systematic failure by investors to recognize the underlying cash profitability of real estate operations. The fact that the market does not appear to reward real estate companies spinning off real estate properties suggests that investors *are* capable of establishing the value of real assets within a larger corporate structure. It is only when the real assets are part of a diverse or conglomerate structure that the market responds positively. (Also, remember that the upward revaluation of the common stocks occurs when the spin-off plan is first *announced*. The subsidiary is not yet reporting separate financial information allowing investors to revise their valuations. Under the real estate discount story, it seems the revaluation would occur later, after investors see the separated operating results.)

Our findings do provide support, however, for our contracting-based argument presented earlier: namely, that the potential gains from spin-offs are larger when the divested unit consists of operations not closely related to the parent company's primary lines of business. Different operating units may not operate as efficiently as possible under a single, all-encompassing set of contracts. Such diversity of businesses may create the economic rationale for separating the operations into more homogeneous units with specialized contracts.

Stated more plainly, spin-offs seem part of a growing corporate design to promote decentralized, "entrepreneurial" management decision-making—while at the same time preserving a large, overarching diversified corporate structure.

V. Going Private[6]

In recent years, many large U.S. public corporations have transformed themselves into private companies. W.T. Grimm reports that in 1979 there were 16 buyouts of major firms totalling $600 million. By 1983, the number of transactions reached

---

5. See Hite, Owers, and Rogers (1983).

6. This discussion is based in large part on DeAngelo, DeAngelo, and Rice (1983) and private discussions with the authors and Terry Smith.

36, and the dollar magnitude exceeded $7 billion. Many Wall Street analysts are predicting an even larger dollar volume in 1984 as the size of the deals becomes ever larger.

The term "going private" covers a wide range of transactions, all of which result in a new organizational structure with closely-held or private ownership. The ownership claims of a diverse group of outside stockholders are replaced by equity claims concentrated in the hands of a small group of investors, including the managers of the restructured firm.

In a "pure" going private transaction, management or a dominant owner-manager purchases the ownership rights of outside stockholders and reorganizes the firm as a closely-held operation. In such cases, the purchase of outside equity is accomplished by the management team without participation of a third-party equity investor.

In their published study of such management buyouts, Harry DeAngelo, Linda DeAngelo, and Ed Rice (henceforth DDR) report that for their sample of 45 buy-outs, insiders typically owned just over half the total number of shares prior to the going private bid. Although management may borrow on personal account to effect the purchase, corporate leverage generally increases very little in these deals. DDR examined the financing mix of 13 transactions and found that the median debt-to-assets ratio increased modestly from .26 before to .30 after the buyout.

Several explanations of the potential gains from going private have been offered. Most obvious is the savings from eliminating the registration, listing, and other stockholder-servicing costs associated with outside ownership. Especially for companies with relatively small capitalization, the direct costs of public ownership can be significant.

Perhaps most important, though, are the incentive effects of combining owner-ship and control in the management team purchasing the firm. As owners, the managers have a much greater stake in corporate profitability. Furthermore, besides increased equity ownership, compensation contracts can be restructured with greater flexibility in the absence of outside shareholders.

Consider a simple case in which a key operating executive owns 10 percent of the firm's shares and receives a fixed salary. Suppose an opportunity arises that would increase current cash flow by $1.00 but would require longer hours for the manager in question. With a fixed salary, the manager must trade off his 10¢ share in the gain against the personal value of the extra leisure forgone. If he values his leisure at more than 10¢ he will not have the incentive to undertake the action. Increasing that manager's percentage ownership is likely to induce extra effort, and thus to align management's interests more closely with those of stockholders.

Another possible means of resolving this potential conflict between management and stockholders is to provide the manager with an incentive compensation contract that allows him to capture the gains from his extra effort. Of course, in the real world, conditions will be far more complicated than those in our simple example; and it will be a difficult task to determine the extent of any single executive's con-tribution to actual results. But there is probably an even greater impediment to adopting such a compensation scheme in the public corporation: namely, that a disproportionate share of cash flows going to a single executive will probably appear "excessive" to some stockholders, leading to costly legal actions in which the judicial system is asked to determine the "fairness" of such compensation. (The costs of such litigation aside, the courts are not likely to view an executive's marginal contribution to the value of his or her firm as their principal criterion of "fairness.")

The advantages of going private in such situations include, then, additional flexibility in compensation contracting and a reduction in monitoring costs. In a private corporation, a manager can contract for a "disproportionate" share of the cash flows—one more closely matched to his marginal contribution to firm value—without fear of costly legal interference from outside shareholders. Also, the fact that other equity participants are typically insiders, too, should reduce the costs of determining the direct linkage between performance and results.

In short, we would expect to see very detailed contracts among the new owner-managers in companies going private, with the distribution of operating profits linked more closely to managerial performance than to ownership proportions.

VI. The Leveraged Buyout

Unlike the "pure" going private deals we have been discussing, leveraged buyouts involve participation by third-party equity investors and substantial amounts of borrowings. In a sample of 23 leveraged buy-out proposals, DDR report far smaller management ownership fractions than in pure going private transactions. In their profile of the average firm acquired through a leveraged buyout, management owns just over $13 million of a total market value of $83 million (these market values are calculated 40 trading days prior to the proposals). From DDR's data one gets the impression, not surprisingly, that insider ownership proportion declines as the size of the deal increases. Furthermore, for five transactions for which they had detailed financial information, they report an increase in the median debt-to-assets ratio from .11 to .86.

Leveraged buyouts are thus different from "pure" going private transactions by virtue of their third-party equity participation, lower management ownership fractions before the buyout, and significantly larger increases in debt after the reorganization.

Henry Kravis of Kohlberg, Kravis, Roberts & Co., a pioneer in arranging leveraged buyouts, provides some insight into the typical contractual structure. Kravis and his partners put up equity, sell an interest to the target firm's management, and arrange loans for the balance of the purchase price. The existing management remains in place, while Kravis and his partners provide financing and control the board of directors. As he puts it,

> Our approach is that we do not know how to run a company. We know that
> we are very good at financing, we are financially oriented. We know how to
> control a company and we know when it is getting off course. We know how

> to set long-range goals for companies and we know how to maximize value
> in a company. But the day-to-day running of a company is not in our interest.[7]

The buyout specialist plays a key role as an intermediary among management, equity investors, and lenders. Management no longer needs to deal with a diverse group of small stockholders, but instead with the specialist as a representative of outside equity. The advantage of this arrangement is that specialized management incentive contracts, which would be very expensive for a diverse stockholder group to enforce, can now be efficiently monitored by the specialist.

One of the most visible aspects of leveraged buyouts is the dramatic increase in debt ratios. In some cases, once conservatively leveraged public companies (or their divisions) lever their private equity as high as 10 to 1. What can explain this turning "upside down" of corporate capital structures?

One argument holds that buyout candidates typically have low amounts of debt. Perhaps they are underleveraged, and the restructuring takes advantage of unused "debt capacity." While we do not have a precise theory of optimal capital structure, we seriously doubt that such a dramatic increase in debt usage could arise *solely* from a previous failure to make the maximum use of debt financing. In fact, some financing theorists would argue that going private reduces corporate debt capacity because managements holding a large equity stake have even stronger incentives than otherwise to take actions which benefit themselves, as stockholders, at the expense of lenders.

A second possible explanation for the extensive use of debt financing is that interest payments offer a tax advantage. One wonders, however, why management did not exploit this advantage as a public company. Also, the additional depreciation write-offs provided by the step-up of assets after the buyout should make the tax deductions from interest payments less valuable as a tax shield.

There is one other very important reason why we find both the unused "debt capacity" and "tax advantage" explanations to be implausible—or certainly not exhaustive: the first order of business after the company goes private is to start paying down the debt.[8] The arguments citing the tax advantage of debt and the unused debt capacity of public companies both imply that not only will debt be advantageous at the time of the takeover, but it will continue to be valuable after the firm is private. If large amounts of debt are taken on during the buyout and reduced shortly thereafter, then it seems that leverage has no longer-range purpose, but functions principally as part of the *mechansim* to take the company private. Remember that part of the expected gains from the buyout comes from the elimination of shareholders. The use of large amounts of debt may simply be the means of achieving the desired concentration of ownership among a small group of equity participants, who in turn exercise control through the buyout specialist.

---

7. See "The Entrepreneur Series: Henry R. Kravis," *Hermes*, Fall, 1983.
8. Ibid.

anagements—there
se in the process.

ratios also provide the potential
o lenders. The extensive restric-
s are themselves strong evidence

Here again, the buyout specialist
e debt market for future buyouts,
e contracts. He must be sensitive
ation." Also, should the leveraged
venants, the costs of renegotiating
ialist who serves as intermediary

, outside equity participants, lend-
an we have indicated. But because
are not readily available to finan-
come to light, they should provide
ling of incentive contracting.

ion Effects of Volun-

eeze-outs and Stock-

y Contests," *Journal*

Management (1984).
Spin-off Announce-

Sellers," unpublished

y Spin-off," unpub-
TX.
ior, Agency Costs,
976), pp. 305–360.
cientific Evidence,"

nces," unpublished

Prices: The Anergy
84 forthcoming).
rices," unpublished

Companies and a
(1978), pp. 776–790.
cements on Share-

Wealth: The Case
), pp. 437–467.
Bond Covenants,"

nlining their operations by selling
ee-standing companies out of sub-
mply calling it quits and liquidating
ng from public to private ownership

simply be a fad, the brainchild of
pon impressionable corporate man-
mmarized here, and more fully in
tructuring transactions create signifi-
changes may in fact reflect a major
form—an evolution toward greater
effective in generating and storing

estructuring, it is useful to focus on
g the different constituencies of the
ers in large conglomerates may be
means of improving the new owner's
performance. Spin-offs may also help
ting management with greater auton-
wards than was possible as a united

ement and third-party leveraged buy-
from the separation of ownership and
ignificant. Given the large premiums

paid in such restructurings—premiums voluntarily offered by n
seems little doubt that corporate values are expected to incre

VIII. References

Alexander, G., P. Benson, and J. Kampmeyer, "Investigating the Valua
tary Corporate Sell-offs," *Journal of Finance* (1984).

DeAngelo, H., L. DeAngelo, and E. Rice, "Going Private: Minority F
holder Wealth," *Journal of Law Economics* (1984).

Dodd, P., and J. Warner, "On Corporate Governance: A Study of Pro:
of Financial Economics*, 11, pp. 401–438.

Hearth, D., and J. Zaima, "Voluntary Divestitures and Value," *Financia*

Hite, G., and J. Owers, "Security Price Reactions around Corporate
ments," *Journal of Financial Economics*, 12 (1983), pp. 409–43(

Hite, G., and J. Owers, "Sale Divestitures: Implications for Buyers and
manuscript (1984), Southern Methodist University, Dallas, TX.

Hite, G., J. Owers, and R. Rogers, "Separation of Real Estate Assets I
lished manuscript (1984), Southern Methodist University, Dallas

Jensen, M. and W. Meckling, "Theory of the Firm: Managerial Beh;
and Ownership Structure," *Journal of Financial Economics*, 3 ({

Jensen, M. and R. Ruback, "The Market for Corporate Control: The {
Journal of Financial Economics, 11 (1984), pp. 5–50.

Klein, A., "Voluntary Corporate Divestitures: Motives and Consequ
Ph.D. dissertation (1983), University of Chicago, Chicago, IL.

Linn, S., and M. Rozeff, "The Effects of Voluntary Spin-offs on Stock
Hypothesis," *Advances in Financial Planning and Forecasting* (1'

Linn, S., and M. Rozeff, "The Effects of Voluntary Sell-offs on Stock I
manuscript (1984), University of Iowa, Iowa City, IA.

Palmon, D., and L. Seidler, "Current Value Reporting of Real Estat
Possible Example of Market Inefficiency," *The Accounting Review*, 53

Miles, J., and J. Rosenfeld, "The Effect of Voluntary Spin-off Annou;
holder Wealth," *Journal of Finance*, 38 (1983), pp. 1597–1606.

Schipper, K., and A. Smith, "Effects of Recontracting on Shareholde
of Voluntary Spin-offs," *Journal of Financial Economics*, 12 (198

Smith, C., and J. Warner, "On Financial Contracting: An Analysis o:
Journal of Financial Economics, 7 (1979), 117–161.

5

Royalty Trusts, Master Partnerships, and Other Organizational Means of "Unfirming" the Firm

John W. Kensinger
University of Texas at Austin

John D. Martin
University of Texas at Austin

> The separation of ownership from control produced a condition where the interests of owner and ultimate manager may, and often do, diverge, and where many of the checks which formerly operated to limit the use of power disappear. . . . (Adolph Berle and Gardiner Means, *The Modern Corporation and Private Property*, 1932)

> Once an industry has ceased to advance—[it] soon embarks on a career of decadence. . . . (Arthur F. Burns, *Production Trends in the U.S. Since 1870*, 1934)

The separation of ownership from control is a sometimes distressing characteristic of the modern corporation, and the social and economic consequences of such a division have been debated since the days of Adam Smith. The dialogue continues today in the current controversy over the level of executive pay and the quality of management's service to its stockholders. The capital market now appears to be playing a prominent role in devising solutions to problems caused by the separation of ownership from control. Although there is a tendency to think of corporations as living forever, the capital market in fact sees to it that they are mortal. Once a corporation's economic usefulness is over, it changes significantly or passes out of existence—sometimes by bankruptcy, but more often by a restructuring intended to achieve a higher market value.

Not long ago it was widely accepted by corporate strategists that the ideal corporation consisted of a portfolio of projects at various stages of development which was balanced such that the cash flows from the mature projects were just used up to nourish fledgling projects.[1] In popular slang, the "cash cows" were milked to feed the "rising stars." As they grew old, "cash cows" became "dogs," joining the stars that never took off. Over this menagerie stood the corporate managers who involved themselves in strategic planning, deciding which new projects to finance. If their own organization was not generating enough cash to support its rising stars, they might go out into the market to buy someone else's cash cow. If, on the other hand, they had lots of cash cows but too few deserving new projects, they might buy another company's rising star.

This approach did not stand the test of time—mainly because investors have a much broader spectrum of opportunities than do corporate managers who have set a goal of investing internally. Stockholder discontent with the old model has helped fuel the recent wave of corporate takeovers, particularly in the oil industry. Simply put, investors have declared their preference to milk the cash cows themselves.

I. The "Unfirming" of the Firm

There is a body of academic literature, whose province is often referred to as the "theory of the firm," which has developed the idea that the formation of a corporation removes resources from the control of markets and places them under the discretionary control of the firm's management.[2] A reversal of this process, one which returns resources to the control of the marketplace, might be called "unfirming" the firm.

Why could this be a valuable process? A number of finance scholars have suggested that a company's financing policy, its dividend policy, and even the structure of its executive compensation plan are largely determined by the extent and promise of its investment opportunities.[3] Firms with considerable growth opportunities are often able to attract lots of capital from investors while offering such investors little in the way of dividends or cash return. On the other hand, firms with limited investment opportunities find themselves pressured by investors to pay dividends, or return their capital through some other channel. Furthermore, it is a natural extension of this argument to say that the "unfirming" of the organization itself will follow upon the exhaustion of a viable set of internal investment opportunities. Such a circumstance need not necessarily be taken as a bad reflection upon management. The economic or institutional environment can change and, in the process, can remove natural growth opportunities from an organization which was formed for a once-needed purpose. When this happens it is time for that organization to undergo the process of releasing its resources back into the marketplace.

---

1. See, for example, Michael Porter, *Competititve Strategy* (Free Press, 1980).
2. See, for example, A.M. Spence, "The Economics of Internal Organization: An Introduction," *Bell Journal of Economics* (Spring 1975), pp. 163–72.
3. See, for example, Clifford Smith and Ross Watts, "The Investment Opportunity Set and Corporate Policy Choices," Unpublished manuscript, University of Rochester, 1986.

Corporate takeovers and proxy fights are well-publicized means of forcing restructuring upon unwilling managers, which often accomplish the task of returning resources to the control of markets. But while these quite visible restructuring activities have been receiving a high level of public attention, another kind of restructuring has been quietly taking place out of the public spotlight, with the cooperation of management. Often using non-corporate organizational forms, this quiet restructuring provides explicit contractual terms for the disposition of cash flows generated by a firm's operations, thus assuring investors that management is cut out of decisions about how to reinvest the cash flows. This represents "unfirming" with respect to control of capital, one of the major factors of production. If the cash flows are reinvested outside of it, the firm will gradually diminish—or, if you will, become "unfirmed" with respect to the other factors of production.

Whoever has discretionary power over the reinvestment of its operating cash flows has fundamental power over the future of a firm, and any reorganization which improves the process of allocating corporate cash flow is potentially quite valuable. Because the cash flows are the property of investors, reinvestment should be guided by their interests rather than the preferences of management. Ideally, management compensation would be designed such that management's interests mesh completely with those of investors. Unfortunately, this is not easy to accomplish. When managers' interests cannot be united with those of investors, there may be large benefits to moving to organizational forms which place reinvestment decisions squarely in the hands of equity investors.

Limited partnerships, for example, are a set of organizational forms which by their very nature accomplish the task of putting investors back into the driver's seat, while still providing limited liability. The extreme use of financial leverage in leveraged buyouts (LBOs) and debt-equity swaps, which substantially transforms the organization, is yet another means to the same end.

We begin with a look at the oil industry, where this quiet restructuring has been under way for several years. We then look at signs of it in other fields, in the form of R&D limited partnerships and marketing partnerships. Finally, we look at potential implications of all this "unfirming" for investment professionals.

II. "Unfirming" in the Oil Industry

Because it is so big and so tumultuous, the oil industry has been in the public eye frequently in the recent past. T. Boone Pickens in particular has been a hero to some and a villain to others for his efforts to restructure the oil industry by means of takeover threats and proxy fights. Yet, at the same time, he and other oil industry innovators have experimented successfully with a quieter means of restructuring oil firms: by spinning off cash-producing assets into royalty trusts and then, after a change in the tax laws, into limited partnerships. Tax benefits have been strong motivators, attracting managers by the promise of increased profits from their operations; but there is another fundamentally important reason for the success of such moves. Choosing to place productive assets within such organizational forms produces profound changes in the contractual relationship between owners and managers. Besides restructuring by means of non-corporate organizational forms, oil industry innovators have also made use of leveraged stock repurchases to accomplish the same ends within the corporate organizational form.

Royalty Trusts and Limited Partnerships

In the traditional model of the corporation, managers are expected not only to run existing operations efficiently, but also to take primary responsibility for deciding how to reinvest the cash flows. They may decide to pay cash dividends, which the stockholders are then free to reinvest as they see fit, but managers nevertheless have first crack at the money.

Limited partnerships and royalty trusts work on a completely different basis.[4] When a corporation becomes a managing partner, management is charged with the efficient operation of existing enterprises (indeed, it holds complete sway in such matters), but it may be cut out of the reinvestment decision. Unlike corporate management, the managing partner in a limited partnership has limited discretion in dividend/reinvestment matters. Revenues and expenses are credited directly to the partners' individual accounts according to a fixed contractual formula. Once the accounting decisions are made, the individual partners receive their pro rata share of the cash produced by the partnership assets, and the reinvestment decisions are their own.

Limited partnerships are very flexible organizational forms which convey to investors the corporate advantage of limited liability, but without double taxation. There is a wide latitude possible in the terms that can be stated in the partnership agreement. After the agreement is entered into, however, the general partners' discretion over the use of partnership assets is bound by its terms. These partnerships have a finite life, with a well-defined set of conditions for their demise. All legal expenses and revenue accrue directly to the partners' accounts and for tax purposes are consolidated with other income; but the limited partners cannot be held liable for any more than the original amount invested. Although limited partners give up day-to-day control of the enterprise in exchange for limited liability, they still have access to the partnership ledgers to monitor compliance with the agreement and can vote in extraordinary circumstances (such as the removal of the general partner). Furthermore, the partnership agreement spells out explicitly how the partnership profits are to be paid out to the partners.

In some cases, however, the general partner may enjoy considerable discretion in the early years of the partnership. Boone Pickens has even parlayed this kind of discretion into takeover attempts.[5] Typically such partnerships are structured

---

4. Since the Tax Reform Act of 1984, new royalty trusts do not enjoy the same desirable tax advantages as their predecessors and have fallen out of favor, but limited partnerships were not affected.

5. For example, Mesa Partners II was the major stockholder in Unocal during the recent takeover attempt. Then in January 1986, Mesa Limited Partnership made a run at KN Energy, the Colorado-based natural gas concern.

to take maximum advantage of the tax situation. By recomputing the tax basis of depletable properties, for example, the partnership may generate large losses in the early years. These losses are credited to the individual partners' accounts according to the partnership agreement. Subsequent profits must be credited up to a predefined point before cash payments begin to flow to limited partners. During the early years there may be substantial cash flows within the partnership over which the general partner exercises reinvestment discretion. As time passes, however, that discretion irresistibly erodes. Moreover, even the temporary existence of management discretion over reinvestment of partnership cash flows is dictated by purely tax considerations rather than economic ones.

In some cases the limited partners' shares, called "units," can be bought and sold.[6] Such limited partnerships are often referred to as Master Limited Partnerships, and some are even listed on the New York Stock Exchange. Unlike common stock, however, the market value of partnership units is expected to decline as the lifespan of the partnership draws to a close. Investors buy them for their cash flows rather than for anticipated price increases.

But because the IRS often will not make guarantees about tax treatment before an investment is made in a limited partnership, there is some risk that favorable tax treatment might be denied after the fact. Nevertheless, it is possible to put together a variety of reasonable, arms-length arrangements that are within the spirit of the partnership laws and which have a high probability of being treated as such by the tax authorities. It is certainly possible for such arrangements to include liquidity for the limited partners through securitization of their partnership units.

---

6. Active trading of limited partnership units need not necessarily jeopardize the tax status of the partnership because this alone will not cause it to be treated as a corporation for tax purposes. Tax law allows a duly constituted limited partnership to be treated as such so long as it does not have more of the characteristics of a corporation than of a partnership. The determination is made by the answers to four questions. If the answer is yes to more than two of them, then partnership is taxed as a corporation. The questions are as follows:

- Does the partnership have continuity of life?
- Is there centralization of management in the partnership?
- Is there limited liability for all members of the partnership?
- Do all partners have free transferability of partnership interests? (26CFR 301.7701-2)

When partnership units are traded publicly, the answer to the last question is not necessarily yes. If only the limited partners have the power of substituting someone else for themselves in the partnership, but one of the general partners does not, then the attribute of free transferability may not be judged to be present. Furthermore, even if the answer to the last question were "yes," an answer of "no" on at least two others would preserve partnership tax treatment. The third question will rate a "no" so long as the general partner bears full liability for the obligations of the partnership, and treasury regulations contain detailed guidelines for making this determination. The partnership will usually be judged not to have continuity of life as long as it is set up so that at least one member (a general partner) is crucial to its survival. Only if the partnership were set up so that it could survive the death or bankruptcy of the general partner would continuity of life normally be judged to be present. Finally, limited partners are not expected to have any involvement with management. Therefore, as long as the general partner is diligently involved as manager, centralization of management would not normally be judged to be present.

Leveraged Stock Repurchases

In terms of scope, it is hard for partnerships to match the dramatic effect on stockholder value of leveraged stock repurchases such as those that Boone Pickens forced on Phillips Petroleum and Unocal. Similar consequences also resulted in the case of Gulf and Chevron, in which Chevron ended up borrowing heavily in order to buy out its Gulf stockholders. These events all had something very basic in common: stockholders came out of them with a substantial wealth increase, in cash. (Also, it came in the form of capital gains for most of them, so the maximum tax rate anyone had to pay was 20 percent.) Those investors were then free to choose how to reinvest this capital, selecting from the full array of opportunities in the marketplace.

Where did this wealth increase come from? Much of it came from the tax benefits of leverage, but that is not the whole story. Besides its favorable tax effect, the leverage fundamentally narrowed the range of management discretion. Michael Jensen coined the term "control hypothesis" to explain this effect of leverage, and it goes as follows:[7] In the case of oil firms with large creditors to satisfy, corporate cash flows become committed to interest and debt retirement payments for a significant period into the future. New projects thus have to compete for external funding rather than be sustained by the cash flows from the oil fields. Besides the tax effect, then, leverage brings with it a change in the process by which management's actions are monitored, and thus changes the way managers are motivated. The mountain of debt forces the cash to flow out of the firm instead of circulating within it.

If there is any danger that management might not be as demanding in scrutinizing internal investments as is the marketplace, then this change increases the probability that the cash flows will find their way to the highest-valued uses. After the leveraged stock repurchases, there was much less of a chance that Phillips or Unocal might buy a Reliance Electric or a Montgomery Ward or a Kennecott Copper.[8] (Nor would their managements be able to indulge in the temptation to get into the office products business, as did Exxon, with so little success.) With cash flows committed to debt service, management had its wings clipped and stockholders had their money. As one would expect, managers were less happy about it than stockholders.

Some people raise the concern that diverting cash flows from oil and gas production into the marketplace might be detrimental in the long run. That is, our oil supply may eventually be depleted without a replacement of reserves. Phillips management, for example, lamented the effect of the "crushing mountain of debt" upon their exploration efforts, claiming that pleasing the financial marketplace requires short-run maximization of cash flows at the expense of long-run economic viability.

---

7. Michael C. Jensen, "Agency Costs of Free Cash Flow, Corporate Finance and Takeovers," *American Economic Review* (May 1986).
8. As did Exxon, Mobil, and Sohio, much to their chagrin.

The marketplace, however, is the ultimate source of resources for commitment to any venture. When the market puts a high enough value on oil and gas exploration, new drilling partnerships can be formed quickly. Meanwhile, there are opportunities in electronics, robotics, artificial intelligence, and bioengineering (to name just a few) which are more appealing to investors. In fact, a recent study of the impact of new internal investments upon corporate stock values found strong evidence contradicting the claims of Phillips's management. The study found that announcements of capital expenditures by corporations resulted, on average, in increases in stock values. By contrast, announcements of expenditures for new exploration by integrated oil companies over the period 1981–83 resulted in declines in share values.[9]

Ultimately we come to the question of whether to let resources be allocated by market processes or by corporate managers. So long as corporate management is able to provide returns commensurate with investors' expectations, the equity of the firm will rise, or at least keep pace with the market. In this sense, the answer *is* effectively decided by the market.

Why the Oil Industry?

Until recently, this activity has been concentrated in the oil industry, where there have been many instances of producing oil properties being spun off or sold off to partnerships.[10] Such actions represent the simplest model for "unfirming" because the assets involved are depleting mineral resources which cannot be replaced once they are used up.

There is no possibility of considering an oilfield as having an indefinite lifespan. In the oil industry, depletion allowances provide funds for new exploration in different places, whereas in the industrial sector depreciation allowances can be interpreted as providing for replacement of worn-out machines with similar new ones, such that the factory is continually renewed. Another way of expressing this point is to say that ownership of an oil well translates into the right to a decreasing series of payments with a finite life, whereas ownership of a factory might be thought of as entitlement to a series of steady or increasing payments with an indefinite life.

In the oil industry, investors who own partnership units can reinvest cash flows in exploration partnerships, if they so desire, or in any other available investment opportunity that appeals to them. Whether or not they decide to invest in replacement of oil-producing assets has no effect on the efficiency of ongoing operations. In the factory, however, decisions about replacement of worn capital equipment

---

9. John J. McConnell and Chris J. Muscarella, "Corporate Capital Expenditure Decisions and the Market Value of the Firm," *Journal of Financial Economics* (1986).

10. For example, Apache Petroleum and May Energy are limited partnership spin-offs whose partnership units are traded on the New York Stock Exchange. Mesa Petroleum has spun off several such partnerships, and in December 1985 shareholders voted to spin off most of Mesa's remaining assets into a new Mesa Limited Partnership.

can have profound impact on the efficiency of ongoing operations. The oil patch is simpler than the world of factories, and so is a natural place to see the first move toward new organizational forms.

III. "Unfirming" in Other Industries

Now, however, "unfirming" has begun to spread into more complex endeavors. This is happening in a variety of ways. R&D limited partnerships are being established as an alternative for financing the most fundamental type of investment. Marketing partnerships are beginning to appear as a follow-up to RDLPs for the purpose of producing and distributing specific new products. Finally, LBOs and employee stock ownership plans (ESOPs) are being used to take many corporations private.

R&D Limited Partnerships

After a modest beginning the late 70s, research and development limited partnerships (RDLPs) have matured rapidly, accounting for a significant proportion of the financing for private-sector R&D in recent years.[11] RDLPs are particularly significant because they enable investors to focus their funds on the development of tomorrow's business activities. They also give the marketplace much greater control over the process of innovation.

Even more recently, with strong encouragement and support from the U.S. Department of Commerce, a few firms have experimented with limited partnerships formed for the purpose of promoting and marketing a specific product.[12] Bruce Merrifield, Assistant Secretary of Commerce for Productivity, Technology, and Innovation, has thrown the resources of the Commerce Department behind an effort to help overcome the initial barriers to forming partnerships for the purpose of manufacturing and marketing specific products.

These marketing partnerships are in essence very simple. They are business organizations formed for the purpose of bringing a specific product or group of products to market. The general partner may manufacture the product itself, or contract its manufacture to a third party. The general partner also contracts with third parties for advertising and promotion.[13] The partnership owns the trademark

---

11. For a review of RDLPs and a discussion of their contribution to the set of organizational possibilities, see John Martin and John Kensinger, "An Economic Analysis of R&D Limited Partnerships," Chapter 16.

12. Energy Sciences Corporation offers an example. It recently developed a data networking system which sends data via low-frequency radio signals over existing phone or power lines, while leaving normal utility services undisturbed. The development was financed largely with RDLPs. Now the company is preparing a marketing campaign financed by what it calls "technology marketing partnerships." For more details, see *Financial Planning* (October 1985), pp. 181–8.

13. Each partnership is a network organization. The sports shoe marketer Nike is an example of such a network hub. Nike contracts its manufacturing to offshore factories, itself serving as developer and marketer of products. An issue of *Business Week* (March 3, 1986) predicted that network organizations are the wave of the future. Partnerships can function in this role just as well as corporations can, but with a product-specific lifespan and less management discretion over reinvestment of cash flows.

and brandname supported by its advertising, and has an exclusive distributorship for the product. It earns revenues from royalties or commissions paid out of sales by the manufacturer. In some cases they are set up with an option for the manufacturer to buy out the distributorship for a lump sum.

Though there can be great tax advantages generated by these arrangements, the real economic importance of their existence is that they provide a project-specific organizational alternative to the corporation. It is possible for a product to be developed by one partnership and brought to market by another, with heavy reliance upon capital raised in the public market. Four major investment banking firms are now actively engaged in managing R&D efforts through limited partnerships, and some of them are studying the possibilities of marketing partnerships as a means of following up on R&D efforts.[14]

Leveraged Buyouts

What Boone Pickens accomplished through leveraged stock repurchases at Phillips Petroleum and Unocal, the firm of Kohlberg Kravis Roberts has achieved in other industries through LBOs. There have been many explanations offered for the LBO phenomenon, each of which may have some element of truth. Without claiming to offer the definitive explanation, we can note the following common results.

First of all, stockholders are able to sell their holdings at a significant premium over current market value. The payment comes to most of them in the form of a capital gain, thereby minimizing taxes. After paying taxes, these stockholders are immediately free to reinvest the cash in the most attractive opportunities available in the marketplace.

Managers gain a shot at ownership and, without changing jobs, go to work for a new boss—themselves. They are free of the burden of reporting to a large group of public shareholders. In place of the shareholders, however, management must answer to the LBO specialist, whose group generally takes a strong position on the board of directors. Finally, in place of a host of public shareholders demanding ever-increasing earnings and dividends, the managers have to placate a small group of creditors who demand that every stray penny be applied to repayment of the debt used to finance the buyout.

In short, managers do not escape monitoring. They merely exchange one form of monitoring for another. Nor do they escape pressure. In fact, it might seem that the pressure on managers increases as a result of the leverage. They do have the advantage that the bite taken from cash flows by income tax is reduced, giving them more to work with. But they are most definitely not "their own men"—not at least until the burden of debt is reduced to comfortable levels. Without a base of public equity to build upon, and with cash flows committed to debt support, their access to expansion capital is severely limited. New projects will not have access to the milk from the old cash cow, and long-term growth is put on hold.

---

14. They are Merrill Lynch, Morgan Stanley, E.F. Hutton, and Prudential-Bache.

Some have objected that the LBO process will stifle the growth of the general economy. But it must not be forgotten that the stockholders got an infusion of cash at the very beginning. They will be reinvesting in growth opportunities elsewhere. In addition, the creditors of the newly-private company will be receiving cash, which they will be able to reinvest in the best available opportunities. Only when the debt is repaid will the managers—at that point certainly older and perhaps wiser—once again have access to the cash spigot to finance internal expansion projects. Then it will be their own money they are spending, and they may be more demanding about the prospects for potential projects than when they were employees of a public corporation.

Whatever hypothesis one offers to explain why LBOs are happening, they have a common result: Decisions to reinvest corporate operating cash flow are effectively transferred from corporate managers to the marketplace.

Employee Stock Ownership Plans

Besides the garden-variety LBO, there is another new player on the scene. Leveraged Employee Stock Ownership Plans (ESOPs) have served as the vehicle for several recent buyouts. In these arrangements a special trust is formed to purchase stock and credit it to the accounts of individual employees.

The Tax Reform Act of 1984 added two very attractive new sweeteners for leveraged ESOPs.[15] Since January 1985, dividends paid to stock owned by an ESOP have been tax deductible. In addition, lenders need pay income tax on only half of the interest paid to them by an ESOP. Thus ESOPs are able to borrow at low interest rates in order to buy stock in the employer corporation. Finally, employer corporations are allowed to make tax-deductible contributions of cash to ESOPs, and through 1987 may even earn tax credits in addition. With these incentives, an ESOP can borrow the money to finance a buyout of an employer's stock with the employer's guarantee on the loan. Debt support payments come from dividends and employer cash contributions, so the entire amount—principal as well as interest—can be tax-deductible. Through such an arrangement it is possible for the corporation to eliminate income tax entirely, and thus make the entire pre-tax cash flow of the corporation available for debt retirement. Only if the corporation retained earnings for new investment would there be any need to pay income tax.

This represents a significant turning of the tax tables. Because paying dividends resulted in double taxation, income tax laws formerly acted to keep cash inside a company. In the case of a buyout by a leveraged ESOP, however, the tax penalty is instead levied against retention of earnings for reinvestment.

Besides giving employees a chance to own their companies, the new ESOPs do two other important things. First, they put cash into the hands of stockholders, who then make the reinvestment decisions themselves. Second, leveraged ESOPs

---

15. For a complete analysis of the benefits, see Andrew Chen and John Kensinger, "Financing Innovations: Tax-deductible Equity," *Financial Management* (Winter 1985), pp. 44–51.

commit the firm's cash flows to debt retirement, and divert the milk from the cash cow into the marketplace where it can nourish the highest-valued new ventures.

A Potential New Alternative to the Corporation

This quiet restructuring is laying the foundations of a new alternative for organizing economic activity.[16] In this alternative investors still enjoy limited liability, but relinquish much less power to managers. Investors are the direct recipients of cash flows from mature operations. They are then free to choose whether or not they wish to provide funding for the development of new products by participating in RDLPs. If development efforts are successful, investors may choose to participate in manufacturing and marketing by means of other partnerships. Alternatively, the partnership's rights may be sold or licensed to a manufacturer/marketer.

For those situations in which the corporate form of organization is most efficient, the possibility of bringing up new companies through venture capitalists or business incubators is attractive. It gives investors more choice and more control than the alternative of building new divisions within old corporations.

In such a complex of small, specialized organizations the primary role of managers is to run existing operations efficiently. In order to increase the assets under their management they must compete by creating alluring new oppportunities to be offered in the marketplace, where capital investment decisions ultimately should be made.

IV. The Unfirming Movement: Summing Up

As Michael Jensen has pointed out forcefully, corporations have been a powerful productive tool for organizing society's resources.[17] Nevertheless, there is a major source of mischief built into all corporations. They have no built-in provision to dissolve themselves when their economic purpose has been served. In the extreme, it is possible to visualize a very productive corporation which has built up great wealth and has paid off all its debts, but which, because of a change in the environment, has no natural growth opportunities. With the threat of bankruptcy eliminated by the retirement of all debt, it is possible for the management to dissipate stockholder value in a series of ill-fated attempts to take the organization into new products and new markets where it has no competitive advantage.

A takeover or proxy fight could avert such a catastrophe. A leveraged buyout could transfer the wealth to stockholders and divert the cash flows generated by the firm during its declining years away from internal investments. Reorganizing the firm as a set of limited partnerships could also accomplish this redirection of cash flows. These last two alternatives are voluntary, and derive value from the assurance they provide the capital market that management is committed to

---

16. The authors develop this concept in another paper, "Merchant Adventurers in the Information Age," unpublished manuscript, University of Texas at Austin, 1986.
17. See Michael C. Jensen, "The Takeover Controversy: Analysis and Evidence," Chapter 1.

returning the resources of the firm to market control. Without some sort of contractual commitment, investors would have to discount for the possibility that management might try to perpetuate the firm beyond its useful life.

Why would managers perpetuate the firm beyond its useful life—past the point where it has an economic advantage that justifies its control over resources? Managers feel commitments to many other corporate stakeholders than the investors who contributed capital.[18] They are typically far closer to the corporation's employees, for example, than they are to its investors. Likewise, they are likely to feel closer ties to the community which houses the corporation than they do to a faceless and widely dispersed group of public investors. It can be very difficult, therefore, for them to visualize a future in which their corporation does not exist in a familiar form.

When the purpose for which a corporation was conceived has been served, there are strong pressures, both emotional and political, to redirect the corporation's resources into some new set of activities, even though they may not be the most efficient employment of the resources. This sort of conflict can present some very thorny issues; but it ultimately leads to the question of whether to let the marketplace achieve the highest-valued use of the world's resources, or try to slow down progress and avoid making difficult decisions.

We use the word "unfirming" to refer to the process of returning resources to the control of the marketplace. "Unfirming" is a very healthy process when it removes resources from lower-valued uses and moves them to higher-valued ones. "Unfirming" is under way in the oil industry not only through the highly-visible means of corporate takeovers and proxy fights, but also through less visible means. These include the transfer of producing assets into limited partnerships, as well as the use of heavy debt financing in leveraged share repurchases. The effect is to reduce management discretion over the reinvestment of cash flows from oil properties and return control to investors.

"Unfirming" is under way in other industries, too. Leveraged buyouts (LBOs) return capital to stockholders immediately, reduce the tax bite from corporate cash flows, and divert future cash flows away from internal reinvestment, sending them back into the marketplace. The net result is to reduce management's discretionary power over the capital resources of the firm and return that power to the marketplace. At the same time, the marketplace is receiving some very interesting new investment opportunities.

In addition to the venture capital partnerships and initial public offerings which have for several years provided a means for financing new and innovative activities, new organizational forms are evolving. With the help of the U.S. Department of Commerce and several major investment banking firms, R & D Limited Partnerships are coming of age. They are now capable of infusing several hundred million dollars per year into efforts to develop new products and technologies, and soon

18. Bradford Cornell and Alan Shapiro, "Corporate Stakeholders and Corporate Finance," unpublished manuscript, University of California at Los Angeles, September 1985.

will be capable of marshalling billions. RDLPs are also spawning a follow-on, in the form of marketing partnerships formed for the purpose of contracting for the production of new products and distributing them. Investors flush with cash from the "unfirming" of mature operations now have a variety of opportunities to underwrite new growth; and as we have pointed out repeatedly, they have a far more sumptuous array of such choices in the marketplace than do corporate managers seeking to reinvest internally.

V. Implications of "Unfirming" for Institutional Investors

Although in an ideal world investors might all make their own decisions, there are many things in the real world that make them decide to turn their decision-making over to professionals. The costs in time, money, and energy involved in choosing and rebalancing a portfolio are often prohibitive. One alternative is to grant significant discretionary control to the managers of firms. Since firms typically have a very limited universe of internal investment opportunities compared with the vast array now available in the marketplace, it makes more sense for investors to transfer some of this control to professional portfolio managers. The rise of new organizational forms which "unfirm" the corporation therefore has profound implications not only for investors and corporate managements, but also for investment professionals.

As the present "unfirming" movement progresses, institutional investors will gain increasing influence over the deployment of resources in the economy. Roles which once were associated with managers of diversified corporations—strategic planning and choosing promising new projects, for example—will shift to portfolio managers as the universe of investment opportunities expands. Stated in technical terms, as the financial markets become more complete, investment professionals will gain greater influence over basic resource allocation decisions.[19] Rather than betting on a team of general managers, the bets will be increasingly on specific products, technologies, and the skills of specialized professionals in engineering, science, and marketing.

---

19. We use the term "complete" in the sense of the breadth of the set of investment opportunities made available in the capital market. As R&D and other traditional activities of firms are spun off into limited partnerships, the set of investment vehicles is expanded, and the market becomes more complete.

6

Competitive Decline and Corporate Restructuring:
Is a Myopic Stock Market to Blame?

J. Randall Woolridge
Pennsylvania State University

I. Myopic Markets or Myopic Managers?

In recent years many observers have attributed the competitive decline of U.S. industry in world markets to corporate management's preoccupation with short-term performance. In a classic *Harvard Business Review* article, for example, Robert Hayes and William Abernathy accused managment of being short-sighted and not keeping their companies technologically competitive over the long run.[1] The emphasis on short-term profitability is predicted by some to have disastrous long-term implications, leading ultimately to the "de-industrialization of America."[2]

Corporate managers, however, respond to this charge by putting the blame on capital markets. Investors, they argue, are short-sighted, compelling management to sacrifice long-term investment and maximize current earnings—or else face the threat of takeover. Andrew Sigler, CEO of Champion International, has become one of the most prominent spokesmen for this view. "There is intense pressure for current earnings," Sigler says, "So the message is: Don't get caught with long-term investments. And leverage the hell out of yourself. Do all the things we used to consider bad management."[3] And Sigler's statement appears to have struck a

---

1. Robert H. Hayes and William J. Abernathy, "Managing Our Way to Economic Decline," *Harvard Business Review*, (July–August 1980), pp. 67–77.
2. "Will Money Managers Wreck the Economy," *Business Week*, (August 13, 1984), pp. 86–93.
3. See Judith H. Dobrznyski, "More Than Ever, It's Management for the Short Term," *Business Week*, (November 24, 1986), pp. 92–3.

sympathetic chord in many of America's top executives. In a survey of 100 CEOs of major corporations, 89 agreed that America's competitive edge has been "dulled" by its failure to emphasize long-term investment, and 92 percent of this group felt that Wall Street's preoccupation with quarterly earnings was the cause.[4]

In the meantime, academic theory suggests that investors have strong incentives to take the long view of corporate performance; and what evidence we have supports this theory. Michael Jensen, in fact, has turned the popular "short-term" argument on its head by asserting that "managers may behave myopically but markets do not." As Jensen argues,

> There is little formal evidence on the myopic managers issue, but I think this phenomenon occurs. Sometimes it occurs when managers hold little stock in their companies and are compensated in ways that motivate them to take actions to increase accounting earnings rather than the value of the firm. It also occurs when managers make mistakes because they do not understand the forces that determine stock values...There is much evidence inconsistent with the myopic markets view, and none that supports it.[5]

The purpose of this article, then, is to evaluate current claims about the allegedly destructive role of the capital markets in corporate restructuring and the competitive decline of U.S. industry. My approach is to review the existing theory and evidence, and then introduce two further pieces of evidence. The first examines the market response to announcements of corporate long-term investments of several kinds (joint ventures, major capital expenditures, product strategies, and largescale R & D projects) to see if the markets actually penalize companies for committing capital to undertakings with distant, uncertain payoffs. The second is a less formal attempt to estimate the fraction of current stock prices that reflect corporate cash flows expected beyond a five-year horizon. Taken together, these two experiments provide suggestive evidence about the time horizon used by investors in valuing securities.

II. Some Background

The capital markets in this country have become dominated by large financial institutions. Recent statistics indicate that pension and mutual fund managers now control some 60 percent of all common shares and, on average, account for 80 to 90 percent of all daily trades.[6] According to the popular "short-term argument," the quarter-to-quarter performance figures of institutional investment managers, which are often reported in the financial press, are very important in retaining old accounts and in attracting new investors. Presumably, in pursuit of competitive

---

4. Business Bulletin, *Wall Street Journal*, (June 12, 1986), p. 1.
5. Michael Jensen, Chapter 1.
6. For statistics and a discussion of the dominance of institutional investors in the markets, see Michael Blumstein, "How the Institutions Rule the Market," *The New York Times*, (November 25, 1984), Section 3, p. 1.

quarterly performance figures, money managers follow investment strategies that place a premium on short-term corporate performance, which forces corporate managers to focus constantly on quarter-to-quarter earnings per share at the expense of long-term competitive growth. As Peter Drucker writes (in a *Wall Street Journal* editorial entitled "A Crisis of Capitalism"):

> Everyone who has worked with American managements can testify that the need to satisfy the pension fund manager's quest for higher earnings next quarter, together with the panicky fear of the raider, constantly pushes top managements toward decisions they know to be costly, if not suicidal, mistakes. The damage is greatest where we can least afford it: in the fast-growing middle-sized high-tech or high-engineering firm that needs to put every available penny into tomorrow—research, product development, market development, people development, service—lest it lose leadership for itself and for the U.S. economy.[7]

The short-term orientation of managers is said to manifest itself in several ways. Managers are accused of being risk averse, forsaking investments with longer-run payoffs such as research and development expenditures. They are blamed for boosting short-term earnings, potentially at the expense of long-term growth, through financial innovations such as sale/lease backs and common stock repurchases. In addition, managers are said to concentrate their efforts in merger and acquisition activity and other "financial games," instead of devoting their attention to strategic product market issues. Other common charges against management are these: strategic decisions in product development are purely market-driven, showing little imagination; managers are biased towards buying productive resources and processes from others and against developing new productive resources and processes to gain competitive advantage; and, finally, innovation is discouraged by the short-term orientation of managers, which instead fosters imitation and backward integration because of their more predictable results.

The debate over the investment time horizon of the market, and its alleged role in the competitive decline of U.S. industry, is only one strand of a much larger contemporary issue in corporate America: namely, corporate governance. Managerial performance in creating value for shareholders has come under close scrutiny in the markets, and those firms which fall short risk being taken over. Indeed, the market for corporate control has heated up with growing numbers of hostile tender offers and proxy fights.

Managers have responded in essentially two different ways. One response has been to restructure their companies themselves through various actions aimed at increasing shareholder value. These restructurings have included redeploying or selling assets (and thereby allowing these resources to be employed in higher-valued uses), divesting or selling off poorly performing divisions (again, to some other corporate user who anticipates improving performance), decreasing uneconomic

---

7. Peter Drucker, "A Crisis of Capitalism," *The Wall Street Journal*, (September 30, 1986), p. 31.

overhead, strategically repositioning primary business units, and making efficient use of cash and leverage (which often includes some form of settlement with shareholders).

The second class of managerial reactions to the increase in takeover activity has been to seek protection from the corporate control market through contracting agreements with corporate boards, and through regulatory proposals that alter the regulation of tender offers and change shareholder voting procedures and other corporate governance rules. Overall, as managers have come under greater pressure to perform on behalf of shareholders, the relationship between management and shareholders has become increasingly strained.[8]

Many observers have debated the merits of the current restructuring of corporate America. Managers argue that they must balance the interests of stockholders with those of other corporate stakeholders, such as employees, suppliers, customers, and communities. Hicks B. Waldron, chairman of Avon Products, makes the point this way:

> We have 40,000 employees and 1.3 million representatives around the world. We have a number of suppliers, institutions, customers, communities. None of them have the democratic freedom as shareholders do to buy or sell their shares. They have much deeper and more important stakes in our company than our shareholders.[9]

As such, management claims it must be protected from "overzealous" institutional stockholders who demand immediate results—and from corporate raiders and their allies, Wall Street arbitrageurs, who stand willing to pounce on firms whose short-term performance and stock price falters.

Managers contend that they need patient investors who are willing to accept the risks of long-term equity investment.[10] To illustrate this point, they cite such statistics as the relatively high turnover rates on institutional stock portfolios (over 60 percent, on average, in recent years) and stock returns in Japan, where stocks have grown over sixfold since 1970 (and turnover rates are one-third those of U.S. institutions.)[11] Andrew Sigler, cited earlier, is somewhat more succinct in his

---

8. For example, see C. Power and V. Cahan, "Shareholders Aren't Just Rolling Over Anymore," *Business Week*, (April 27, 1987), pp. 32–33.

9. See Bruce Nussbaum and Judith Dobrzynski, "The Battle for Corporate Control," *Business Week*, (May 18, 1987), pp. 102–109.

10. John G. Smale, chairman and CEO of Procter & Gamble Co., recently wrote on the responsibilities of shareholders. Whereas he does not specify what shareholders' responsibilities actually are, he makes the distinction between 'traditional shareholders' and 'temporary owners,' who ". . . play a role that can lead to the acquisition of corporate assets through creative financing for the purpose of reaping a quick profit." See John G. Smale, "What About Shareholders' Responsibility?," *The Wall Street Journal*, (October 16, 1987), p. 20.

11. For an extended version of the "patient investor" argument, see Donald Frey, "The U.S. Needs Patient Investors," *Fortune*, (July 7, 1986), pp. 125–126; and Karen Pennar, "Is the Financial System Shortsighted?," *Business Week*, (March 3, 1986), pp. 82–3.

evaluation of the short-term perspective of institutional investors: "What right does someone who owns the stock for an hour have to decide a company's fate. That's the law, and it's wrong."[12]

According to T. Boone Pickens, however, management's short-term theory is "pure hokum." "Increasing acceptance of the short-term theory," Pickens argues,

> has freed executives to scorn any shareholders they choose to identify as short-termers. Executives aim their contempt not only at the initiators of takeover attempts but at the arbitrageurs and the institutional investors who frequently trade in and out of stocks.[13]

Institutional investors themselves vigorously object to the notion that they are "only short-term" investors and insist that they are only interested in portfolio value gains which, given the forward-looking nature of the market, result from enhanced future prospects.[14] At the same time, however, they profess to be "fed up" with corporate managers who mismanage assets and then hide behind the "cloak" of social responsibility. It goes without saying that institutional investors oppose management entrenchment procedures—the proxy process, poison pills, greenmail, golden parachutes, staggered boards, and dual classes of common stock—all of which serve to reduce the discipline imposed on management through the market for corporate control. In articulating what is probably the position of most institutional investors, Richard M. Schlefer of the Collge Retirement Equities Fund says, "We view tender offers as a kind of free, competitive market for management. The best managers will end up running a company."[15]

III. The Market Response to Strategic Investment Decisions

With few exceptions, the short-term theory of managerial and capital market behavior is inconsistent with the contemporary literature in finance and economics. Economic theory suggests that an active market for managerial labor and corporate control compels managers to maximize shareholder wealth over the long run which, among other things, entails making strategic investment decisions today which ensure growth tomorrow. In addition, many empirical studies have demonstrated

---

12. B. Nussbaum and J. Dobrznyski, "The Battle for Corporate Control," *Business Week*, (May 18, 1987), pp. 102–109.

13. T. Boone Pickens, "Professions of A Short-Termer," *Harvard Business Review*, (May–June 1986), pp. 75–79. A rebuttal to Pickens arguments is provided in W. Law, "A Corporation Is More Than Its Common Stock," *Harvard Business Review*, (May–June 1986), pp. 80–83.

14. Seely argues that corporations should actually court institutional investors. He claims that higher levels of institutional common stock ownership leads to higher stock liquidity and lower market-related volatility. Furthermore, he maintains that "overowned" stocks have outperformed "underowned" stocks, and that "underowned" stocks are more vulnerable to takeovers since these companies tend to have a low profile on Wall Street and therefore have been neglected by institutions. See Michael Seely, "In Praise of Institutional Investors," *Fortune*, (April 15, 1985), p. 167.

15. See Bruce Nussbaum and Judith H. Dobrzynski, "The Battle for Corporate Control," *Business Week*, (May 18, 1986), pp. 102–109.

that the capital markets, full of institutional as well as individual investors looking to take advantage of arbitrage opportunities, do not systematically misprice securities.

Therefore, security prices are presumed to provide an unbiased estimate (that is, neither too high nor too low, on average) of long-term investment value. Consequently, whereas managers continue to make their case in the financial press that long-term investments are "hazardous" in today's capital markets, most economists would be reluctant to blame the capital markets for inducing myopic behavior by managers.

Economic Theory and Real Corporate Investment

According to traditional valuational theory, the market value of a firm is equal to the sum of (a) the net present value of cash flows generated from assets in place and (b) the net present value of expected cash flows from investment opportunities that are expected to be available to and undertaken by the firm in the future. The market value of a firm changes as the market receives either general market or firm-specific information which changes the market's expectations about either (a) or (b) above.

As such, upon announcement of corporate strategic investment decisions, the market provides its immediate, "best guess" about the effect of these strategic investment decisions on the present value of all future cash flows. In a competitive and efficient market, arbitrageurs should prevent any systematic mispricing of securities.

In economists' model of a perfectly competitive industry, entry and exit are assumed to be costless, products are undifferentiated, and there are increasing marginal costs of production. In such an environment, products are sold strictly on the basis of price, each firm produces up to the point where price equals marginal cost, and the long-run industry equilibrium is reached in which price equals average cost (including a charge for capital, or "normal" level of profit). In equilibrium, total revenues equal total costs for the industry and individual firms alike; and because costs include the required return on the capital employed by each firm, in the long-term actual and required returns on capital are equal.

In perfectly competitive factor and product markets, then, strategic investment decisions with positive net present values do not exist; that is, the factors associated with strategic investment decisions are priced in factor and product markets void of imperfections such that the net present value of these decisions is zero. If a strategic investment decision is perceived to have a positive net present value, it instantaneously attracts new entrants to the industry, which in turn increases factor prices and capacity and drives product prices down. Higher factor prices and lower product prices reduce returns to all the firms, which forces weaker firms to leave the industry. With fewer competitors, factor prices decline and product prices rebound, increasing returns for the surviving firms until once again actual and required returns are equal. As such, in this perfectly competitive environment, the search by corporative planners for strategic investments with positive net present values is doomed to failure.

The ability of strategic investment decisions to generate positive net present values rests, then, on "imperfections" in product and factor markets. It is these "imperfections" that permit one firm to gain competitive advantage over others in its industry. Firms can gain competitive advantage through strategic decisions which allow the firm to become the low-cost producer or to differentiate its product on the basis of service or quality such that customers are willing to pay a premium for the product. These competitive advantages form "barriers to entry" to potential entrants and result in an imperfectly competitive market in which strategic investment decisions with positive net present values are possible.[16]

The Hypotheses

In this study, I am defining strategic investment decisions as those corporate resource allocations that involve a substantial commitment of capital with the expectation of an uncertain payoff in the future.[17] By definition, therefore, these decisions are made in anticipation of increasing long-term growth at the expense of lower short-term earnings.

The stock market reaction to announcements of strategic investment decisions can be thought of as having two components: (1) a price reaction which reflects general, overall factors influencing managerial strategic decisions and firm valuation;

---

16. Alan Shapiro, for example, has identified five major areas where strategic investment decisions can create, preserve, or enhance barriers to entry and generate positive net present values. These areas are (1) economies of scale; (2) product differentiation; (3) cost advantages; (4) access to distribution channels; and (5) government policy. (See Alan Shapiro, "Corporate Strategy and the Capital Budgeting Decision," *Midland Corporate Finance Journal*, (Spring 1985), pp. 22–36).

17. Research into the valuation impact of strategic investment decisions is concentrated in the area of intercorporate acquisitions. For a review of the evidence on intercorporate mergers and tender offers and shareholder returns, see Michael Jensen and Richard Ruback, "The Market for Corporate Control: The Scientific Evidence," *Journal of Financial Economics*, (April 1983), pp. 323–329.

Several recent studies, however, have evaluated the market's response to the kinds of strategic investment decisions that I am considering in this paper. For example, John McConnell and Chris Muscarella examined the reaction of stock prices to 658 announcements of increases and decreases in the dollar amount of planned capital expenditures and discovered that announcements of increases (decreases) in capital budgets are associated with significantly positive (negative) abnormal stock returns for industrial firms. (See John McConnell and Chris Muscarella, "Corporate Capital Expenditures Decisions the Market Value of the Firm," *Journal of Financial Economics*, (July 1985), pp. 399–422.) John McConnell and Tim Nantell investigated the relationship between joint venture formation and announcement day stock returns. Their sample included 210 firms involved in 136 joint ventures over the 1972–79 time period. They discovered joint venture formations to be associated with significantly positive announcement day returns. (See John McConnell and Timothy Nantell, "Corporate Combinations and Common Stock Returns: The Case of Joint Ventures," *Journal of Finance*, (June 1985), pp. 519–536.) Gregg Jarrell, Ken Lehn, and Wayne Marr analyzed the relationship between research and development (R&D) expenditures and stock prices as part of a larger study of institutional stock ownership, long-term investments, and tender offers. Using a sample of 62 R&D announcements taken from the *Wall Street Journal*, over the 1973–83 period, they found these announcements to be associated with significantly postitive stock returns. (See Greg Jarrell, Ken Luhn, and Wayne Marr, "Institutional Ownership, Tender Offers, and Long-Term Investments," The Office of the Chief Economist, Securities and Exchange Commission (April 19, 1985).)

and (2) price reactions to individual situations in which the market reacts positively or negatively to a strategic announcement based on (a) the information available to investors at the time of the announcement (for example, to what extent was the strategy announcement expected?) and (b) the perception of the market regarding the soundness of the strategic investment decision.

How, then, should the market be expected to respond to such announcements? I have laid out the alternative hypotheses as follows:[18]

Positive Stock Price Reactions

Shareholder Value Maximization (SVM)   Traditional finance theory posits that managers seek to maximize the market value of the firm. According to this hypothesis, managers are compelled by market forces to make strategic investment decisions aimed at maximizing shareholder value. Therefore, strategic investment announcements are interpreted by investors as managerial decisions with expected positive net present values and therefore are accompanied by significantly positive abnormal stock returns;

Neutral Stock Price Reaction

Highly Competitive Markets (HCM)   The ability of strategic decisions to generate positive net present values and to increase stock prices rests on imperfections in factor and product markets which permit a firm to gain competitive advantage over others in the industry. However, equilibrium in a perfectly competitive market requires that the level of factor and product prices be set such that strategic decisions cannot generate positive net present values. Whereas the assumptions of a perfectly competitive world are unduly restrictive, it is possible that, in a highly competitive market, products and factors are priced so as to virtually eliminate excess returns. In such a market, strategic investment decisions with positive net present values would be rare, and thus strategic announcements would be accompanied by no change in stock prices; and

---

18. Several comments on these hypotheses and tests are in order: (1) in the tests which follow, the stock price reaction to strategic investment announcements may reflect some or all of the specific and general considerations discussed here. However, only the dominant general factor influencing stock prices can be determined. Specific factors are presumed to average out over the sample; (2) while the lack of any statistically significant stock price movement is consistent with both the HCM and the REM hypotheses, it is also consistent with other joint and confounding hypotheses. As such, strict inferences in this case are not possible; and (3) it is arguable that a negative strategic announcement/stock return relationship is also consistent with some theories of managerial behavior which conflict with the SVM hypothesis. An alternative interpretation of negative stock returns is that managers may be engaging in activities with negative net present values. These may result from traditional agency problems in which managers' intersts conflict with those of stockholders. For capital expenditures, this argument is similar to Malatesta's size-maximization hypothesis for stock returns of acquiring firms in mergers. As such, this hypothesis would be supported in this study if stock prices are discovered to react negatively to capital expenditures announcements. See Paul Malatesta, "The Wealth Effect on Merger Activity and the Objective Functions of Merging Firms," *Journal of Financial Economics*, (April 1983), pp. 155–181.

Rational Expectations Market (REM)   In a rational expectations market environment, security prices reflect investors' expectations that managers will undertake strategic investments to provide for future growth and increase in shareholder value. As such, according to this hypothesis, security prices do not react to announcements of strategic investment decisions, even though investors may believe that these investments have positive net present values; and

Negative Stock Price Reaction

Myopic Stock Market (MSM)   Many observers have argued that investors in the U.S., especially the large and powerful financial institutions, are too short-sighted, focusing on quarter-to-quarter earnings and thereby preventing managers from pursuing strategies aimed at long-term competitive advantage and growth. According to MSM hypothesis, strategic investment announcements which involve decisions with long-term payoffs (such as research and development and capital expenditures) at the risk of reducing short-term earnings result in a significant decrease in stock prices.

The Data

To examine the relationship between strategic investment decision announcements and stock prices, I gathered a large sample of strategic investment announcements from articles appearing in the *Wall Street Journal*. With the aid of a computer, I searched the "What's News" column (over the period June 1972 to December of 1984) for announcements that appeared to indicate a major corporate strategic investment. When a likely candidate was located, I then read the article to determine the strategic nature of the announcement and whether or not other significant information was also published. In cases where the announcements included other information concerning a firm's sales or earnings, or if other announcements concerning sales or earnings appeared in the *Wall Street Journal* within one day of the strategic investment decision announcement, they were excluded from the sample.

After this winnowing process, I was left with 634 strategic announcements made by 347 different companies operating in 81 different industries.[19] These announcements were then classified into one of four general areas based on their strategic orientation: (1) joint ventures, (2) research and development expenditures, (3) product strategies, and (4) capital expenditures for expansion or modernization. These four general categories were refined further into more specific subcategories (all of which are listed in Table 1).

---

19. By year, the sample breaks down as follows:

Year	No.	Year	No.	Year	No.	Year	No.	Year	No.
1972	40	1975	35	1978	56	1981	32	1984	44
1973	93	1976	28	1979	25	1982	49		
1974	33	1977	84	1980	40	1983	75		

As may be expected, the annual number of the strategic investment decision announcements is closely related to the level of overall economic activity.

Table 1. Strategic Investment Announcements.

Category	Number of Announcements
Joint venture formation	161
Research and development	39
Shared assets/resources	35
Asset construction	87
Research and development	45
Advances	27
Initial expenditures	18
Product strategies	168
New product/old business line	105
New product/new business line	39
Old product/new geographic market	24
Capital expenditures	260
General capacity expansion construction	194
Plant modernization construction	31
Capital budgets increases	35

The four general categories may be summarized as follows:

Joint ventures. Joint ventures are typically employed when two or more firms lack a necessary component to compete in a particular market. The purposes behind joint venture formation take many forms, which range from joint research projects aimed at developing new technology, to joint production projects to take advantage of the engineering strengths of more than one firm, to joint marketing efforts to gain access to new markets. Management and development costs are usually shared by the firms, as are the profits from the venture. Joint ventures reduce the risk and potential financial losses inherent in new projects, but at the expense of reduced rewards if the project proves to be successful.[20]

The sample of joint venture formations was further broken down according to the purpose behind formation, e.g., research and development, shared resources, and asset construction.

---

20. Strategists like the joint venture concept. According to one theorist, joint ventures are one of twelve "grand strategies" which "serve to provide the basis for achieving long-term objectives" (see J. Pearce, "Selecting Among Alternative Grand Strategies," *California Management Review*, (Spring 1982), pp. 23–31). Michael Porter describes joint venture as a type of "long-term alliance which broadens the effective scope of the firm's value chain" (Michael Porter, *Competitive Advantage* (NY: the Free Press, 1985).

Research and development expenditures. A number of studies report that R&D expenditures exert a strong positive impact on profitability.[21] But, a significant time gap exists between when the expenditures are made and when they affect profitability. One study found that peak profits accrued four to six years after R&D spending occurred.[22] However, the returns from R&D expenditures are uncertain and can fluctuate considerably from year to year.

The sample of R&D announcements were further classified according to information contained in the announcement: some announcements involved expenditures to new R&D projects, while others provided details on commitments to ongoing R&D projects and programs.

Product strategies. The Development and launching of new products, as well as entrance into new markets with existing products, are strategic decisions which are essential for long-run growth. However, they both involve a commitment of resources and, as such, are risky and costly in the short run.

The product strategy announcements fall into three categories: new product introductions into old business lines, the introduction of new products into new business lines, and the introduction of old products into new geographic markets.

Capital expenditures. Like other strategic investment decisions, the commitment of funds for capital projects is necessary to ensure the long-term vitality of a business firm. Capital expenditures are provided for projects such as capacity expansions, plant modernization, as well as general expenditures to update equipment. Like R&D expenditures, the returns on capital expenditures are uncertain and may not come until some time in the future. In addition, after a capital project is undertaken, short-term earnings will be depressed until the project is completed and begins to generate revenues or reduce operating costs.

Capital expenditures are further categorized as follows: general capacity expansion construction (including mining and exploration), plant modernization projects, and general increases in capital budgets.

The Results

With the aid of a computer, I calculated stock price changes in response to the entire sample of strategic announcements both in the two-day period surrounding the public announcement and over a period of 30 trading days following the announcement. These returns were adjusted for the overall market return (as measured by the return for the S&P 500), and then averaged across the entire sample. Average,

21. See H. Grabowski and D. Mueller, "Industrial Research and Development, Intangible Capital Stocks, and Firm Profit Rates," *Bell Journal of Economics*, (Fall 1978), pp. 328–342; Z. Griliches, "Productivity, R&D, and Basic Research at the Productivity Rates," *American Economic Review*, (May 1983), pp. 215–218; and Edwin Mansfield, "How Economists See R&D," *Harvard Business Review*, (November–December 1981), pp. 98–106.
22. Sherer, cited in note 21.

Table 2. Common Stock Returns Around Strategic Investment Announcements

	Day	Mean Raw Return	Percent Greater Than 0	Market-Adjusted Return	T-Stat	Cumulative Market-Adjusted Return
N = 634	− 1	+0.360	46.53	+0.295	+2.95	+0.360
	0	+0.350	51.42	+0.355	+4.27	+0.710
	+30	—	—	—	—	+0.984
Panel A: Joint	− 1	+0.526	48.45	+0.384	+1.92	+0.384
venture formations	0	+0.447	51.55	+0.399	+2.02	+0.783
N = 161	+30	—	—	—	—	+1.412
Panel B: Research	− 1	+1.042	57.78	+0.944	+2.47	+0.944
and development	0	+0.400	48.89	+0.251	+0.93	+1.195
expenditures	+30	—	—	—	—	+1.456
N = 45						
Panel C: Product	− 1	+0.421	50.60	+0.402	+2.29	+0.402
strategies	0	+0.487	54.76	+0.440	+2.84	+0.842
N = 168	+30	—	—	—	—	+0.350
Panel D: Capital	− 1	+0.099	40.77	+0.058	+0.36	+0.058
expenditures	0	+0.194	49.62	+0.290	+2.45	+0.348
N = 260	+30	—	—	—	—	+1.499

market-adjusted returns were also calculated for each of the four categories of investment described above.[23] The results are summarized in Table 2.

All Strategic Investment Announcements. For the entire sample of 634 strategic investment announcements, the market-adjusted returns (MMARs) over the two-day period surrounding the announcement average a positive 0.7 percent. (The MMARs for days −1 and 0 were .295% (t=2.95) and .355% (t=4.27), respectively, which are the two largest MMARs over the 32-day period (day −1 to day +30). Over this 32-day period these stocks outperformed the S&P 500 by about 1 percent.

Joint Venture Formations. As shown in Table 2, the average, two-day, market-adjusted return to 161 announcements of joint ventures was a positive 0.8 percent, roughly the same as the market response to the broad sample. Over the thirty-two day period following (and including) the announcement days, the cumulative excess market return to joint venture formations was 1.4 percent. (The largest positive response to subcategories of joint ventures (not shown in the Table) were those in which assets or resources were to be shared.)

---

23. In all cases, the announcements appeared in the *Wall Street Journal* on day 0. However, in some instances, the announcements were actually made on day −1. Therefore, returns on these two days should provide an indication of the market's evaluation of the announced strategic investment decision.

Research and Development Expenditures. The two-day market returns to 45 announcements of R&D expenditures averaged a positive 1.2 percent (reflecting MMARs for day −1 and day 0 of .944% and .251%). As in the case of joint ventures and the overall sample, there is no evidence of stock price declines in the subsequent 30 days.

The subsample statistics indicate that the announcements of expenditures on ongoing R&D programs, as opposed to new projects, were received more positively by the market.

Product Strategies. For 168 announcements of product strategy announcements, the market's two-day response averaged 0.8 percent, again mirroring the market reaction to the broad sample. (In addition, the returns for the two-day event period represent the largest average price movements over the entire 32-day period.) Most of these gains, however, are lost over the following 30-day period, and the cumulative average return becomes slightly negative.

The subsample results indicate that the market responds positively to the announcements of new product introductions, be they in old or new business lines. The most positive market response is associated with the introduction of new products in old business lines.

Capital Expenditure Announcements. For 260 announcements of large capital spending programs, the average two-day, market-adjusted return was 0.35 percent. (The return of .29 percent on day 0 is the largest over the 32-day period.) In addition, these stocks outperformed the S&P 500 by almost 1.5 percent over the 32-day period. As such, there is no evidence of a subsequent price decline following capital expenditure announcements.

Within the subcategories, expenditures for general capacity expansion and for capital budget increases were received most positively by investors.[24]

Summary of Findings

The consistently positive stock market reaction to announcements of various types of corporate strategic investment decisions provides significant support for the proposition that these announcements are interpreted by investors as managerial decisions with expected positive net present values. Thus, the results support the hypothesis that management is encouraged by market forces to make strategic investment decisions aimed at maximizing shareholder value.

The results offer no support for the propositions that (1) product and factor markets are so highly competitive that investment returns approximate the cost of capital and that (2) security prices reflect investors' expectations that managers will undertake profitable strategic investments aimed at providing for future growth

---

24. The positive returns associated with capital expenditure announcements, and especially the results for the capacity expansion subsample, provide evidence against the size-maximization hypothesis, as discussed in Malatesta (1983) and footnote number 18.

Table 3. Some Examples of the Market's Response to Strategic Announcements.

Company	Date	Nature of Announcement	2-Day Return
Imperial Chemical	3/9/77	Plan to build two plants in Britain at total cost of $181 million	5.51%
Union Camp	8/31/77	Plan to spend $250 million to double output of linerboard mill	4.13%
Reynolds Metals	9/15/78	Plan to spend $70 million to expand sheet-and-plate plant	2.01%
Washington Post	5/22/78	Joint venture to build and operate newsprint mill costing $100 million	2.50%
Motorola	8/12/81	Plan to spend $120 million to expand semiconductor plant in Scotland	2.42%
Westinghouse	4/2/82	Increased capital spending by 33%, to $800 million, to enter cable TV market	1.56%
J.C. Penney	2/1/83	Plan to spend $1 billion over next 5 years to modernize 450 stores	7.15%
DuPont	8/12/83	Plan to spend $100 million on R&D to improve automotive/industrial coatings	2.54%
PSA	11/17/83	Purchase of 20 British Aerospace 100-seat jets for $300 million	2.23%
Wang Labs	4/18/84	Plan to acquire 15% interest in InteCom to pursue joint marketing & product development	6.41%
Federal Express	7/30/84	Plan to spend $1.2 billion next 10 years to expand new ZapMail service	2.27%

and increases in shareholder value. In addition, and more important, these results contradict the popular notion that the markets are myopic, focusing on quarter-to-quarter earnings to the exclusion of considerations of long-term competitive growth.

IV. The Fundamental Valuation of Common Stocks

The positive reaction of stock prices to corporate strategic investment decisions suggests that the market looks well beyond the next quarter in setting security prices. Nonetheless, critics of the market claim that day-to-day security price fluctuations, generated to a large extent by the buying and selling of institutional investment managers pursuing short-term trading profits, do not reflect long-term corporate prospects. As noted by Alfred Rappaport, however, "it's important to distinguish between the daily scurrying of investors and the forces that determine market prices."[25]

---

25. See Alfred Rappaport, "Don't Sell Stock Market Horizons Short," *The Wall Street Journal*, (June 27, 1983), p. 22. In this article Rappaport discusses the results of a study which is similar in form to the analysis that follows.

According to the fundamental valuation theory presented earlier, the current price of a security is equal to the present value of all future cash flows to investors. The discount rate, which reflects the risk of the security and the time value of money, represents investors' required rate of return. Using this model, and using both current dividends and accounting earnings as proxies for expected net cash flows (which should be reasonable, at least over a broad sample of firms), we can perform a little experiment to assess the investment time horizon of the stock market.

Table 4 provides recent and projected data for the Dow Jones Industrials. For each security, the data given include the stock price, the P/E ratio, current dividends and earnings, and Value Line Investment Survey's estimated beta and 5-year projected dividends' and earnings' growth rates. Using the Capital Asset Pricing Model (CAPM) to estimate investors' required rate of return, the present value of the next five years of dividends and earnings is computed.[26] Comparing each of these figures to the current stock price provides an estimate of the proportion of the current price which may be attributed to short-term (next five years) versus long-term (beyond five years) dividends and earnings. Those proportions of the current stock price attributable to dividends and earnings beyond 5 years I am calling the "Long-term Value Indices" ("LVI"'s—"LVID" for dividends and "LVIE" for earnings).

With the Dow Jones Industrials valued at a P/E of 14, which approximates the historic range, the average LVID is about 80 percent and the average LVIE is 55 percent. As might be expected, companies with poorer growth prospects tend to have lower LVIs, and vice-versa.[27] Rappaport reported similar LVI results, which he summed up in the following manner:

> In short, prices behave as if the market cares most about companies' long-term prospects, even though the financial community appears to emphasize short-term financial results. The most plausible explanation of this seeming paradox is that investors often see long-term implications in current information, including reported earnings, and use the latest results to reassess a company's prospects.

Overall, these results suggest that the market places considerable emphasis on a company's long-term prospects in valuing securities. As noted by Rappaport, high LVIs are an indication of the market's confidence in the ability of well-managed companies to gain and sustain a competitive advantage in the future.

---

26. In applying the CAPM, the interest rate on five-year Treasury securities was employed as the risk-free rate of interest and a market risk premium of 2.5% was assumed. The latter estimate was provided by a major investment banking firm.

27. In his broader-based study, Rappaport reports the lowest LVIs for public utilities and the highest LVIs for companies in the electronic components, medical instruments, retail drugs, radio-TV transmitting equipment, and electronic computers industries.

Table 4. Long-Term Value Indexes Dow Jones Industrials March 1988.

Company	Stock Price	Beta	P/E	Current Earnings	Earnings Yield	Projected Earnings Growth	Pres Val Next 5 Yr Earnings
Allied Signal	$32.75	0.95	13	$2.60	7.9%	5.5%	$11.38
Alcoa	$45.38	1.25	11	$4.14	9.1%	17.5%	$24.55
American Express	$26.00	1.45	21	$1.25	4.8%	16.5%	$7.12
AT&T	$29.38	0.80	16	$1.85	6.3%	16.5%	$11.02
Bethlehem Steel	$19.88	1.45	80	$0.25	1.3%	NMF	
Boeing Company	$47.88	0.95	16	$3.00	6.3%	10.5%	$15.05
Chevron Corp.	$43.75	0.95	18	$2.50	5.7%	6.5%	$11.24
Coca-Cola	$38.00	0.95	16	$2.45	6.4%	11.0%	$12.46
Dupont	$86.75	1.15	12	$7.39	8.5%	12.0%	$38.09
Eastman Kodak	$41.38	0.85	12	$3.55	8.6%	23.5%	$25.36
Exxon Corp.	$42.25	0.75	13	$3.20	7.6%	4.5%	$13.80
General Electric	$43.88	1.05	18	$2.43	5.5%	11.0%	$12.27
General Motors	$70.00	1.00	—	$10.00	14.3%	3.0%	$40.69
Goodyear Tire	$58.13	1.20	8	$7.70	13.2%	23.0%	$52.94
IBM	$116.13	0.95	13	$8.72	7.5%	12.5%	$46.18
International Paper	$43.25	1.25	12	$3.60	8.3%	22.5%	$24.34
McDonald's Corp.	$47.38	1.00	17	$2.85	6.0%	15.5%	$16.31
Merck & Co.	$163.25	0.90	24	$6.68	4.1%	22.0%	$45.72
Minnesota Mng.	$59.00	1.05	15	$3.95	6.7%	13.5%	$21.34
Navistar Int'l.	$5.50	1.25	25	$0.22	4.0%	NMF	
Phillip Morris	$93.00	1.05	12	$7.80	8.4%	21.0%	$51.45
Primerica	$29.13	1.00	9	$3.30	11.3%	17.5%	$19.91
Procter & Gamble	$82.63	0.85	18	$4.59	5.6%	11.0%	$23.50
Sears & Roebuck	$36.25	1.30	8	$4.50	12.4%	12.0%	$22.96
Texaco	$42.25	0.75	26	$1.65	NMF	2.0%	
USX Corp.	$32.88	0.95	26	$1.25	3.8%	NMF	
Union Carbide	$23.88	NMF	11	$2.17	9.1%	NMF	
United Technologies	$40.63	1.10	9	$4.35	10.7%	9.5%	$21.02
Westinghouse	$53.25	1.30	10	$5.12	9.6%	12.5%	$26.48
Woolworth (F.W.)	$45.13	1.10	12	$3.80	8.4%	14.0%	$20.74
Mean[a]	$55.67	1.04	14	$4.45	8.1%	13.8%	$24.64

a. All mean figures exclude companies with incomplete data.
b. Key assumptions—Risk-free interest rate equals 8.00%
　　　　　　　　—Market risk premium equals 2.50%

V. Concluding Comment

This study provides evidence that (1) common stock prices react positively to announcements of corporate strategic investment decisions and (2) the market appears to place considerable emphasis on prospective long-term developments in valuing securities. These results contradict the popular press accounts which blame the competitive decline and corporate restructuring of U.S. industry on a myopic stock

			Dividends Per Share		
Long-Term Value Index[b] (LVI)	**Current Dividend**	**Dividend Yield**	**Projected Dividend Growth**	**Pres Val Next 5 Yr Dividends**	**Long-Term Value Index[b] (LVI)**
65.3%	$1.80	5.5%	6.0%	$7.98	75.6%
45.9%	$1.20	2.6%	7.0%	$5.36	88.2%
72.6%	$0.76	2.9%	11.0%	$3.74	85.6%
62.5%	$1.20	4.1%	5.0%	$5.23	82.2%
	NIL	NIL	NIL		
68.6%	$1.40	2.9%	9.5%	$6.84	85.7%
74.3%	$2.40	5.5%	2.5%	$9.66	77.9%
67.2%	$1.20	3.2%	5.5%	$5.25	86.2%
56.1%	$3.40	3.9%	7.0%	$15.30	82.4%
38.7%	$1.80	4.4%	7.0%	$8.26	80.0%
67.3%	$2.00	4.7%	6.5%	$9.12	78.4%
72.0%	$1.40	3.2%	11.0%	$7.07	83.9%
41.9%	$5.00	7.1%	9.0%	$24.00	65.7%
8.9%	$1.60	2.8%	4.0%	$6.61	88.6%
60.2%	$4.40	3.8%	11.0%	$22.38	80.7%
43.7%	$1.20	2.8%	9.0%	$5.66	86.9%
65.6%	$0.50	1.1%	13.0%	$2.67	94.4%
72.0%	$3.84	2.4%	20.0%	$24.94	84.7%
63.8%	$2.12	3.6%	11.0%	$10.71	81.9%
	NIL	NIL	NIL		
44.7%	$3.60	3.9%	18.5%	$22.23	76.1%
31.6%	$1.60	5.5%	5.5%	$6.98	76.0%
71.6%	$2.80	3.4%	6.0%	$12.50	84.9%
36.7%	$2.00	5.5%	5.5%	$8.55	76.4%
	NIL	NIL	NIL		
	$1.20	3.7%	10.0%	$5.94	81.9%
	$1.50	6.3%	3.0%		
48.2%	$1.40	3.4%	8.5%	$6.58	83.8%
50.3%	$1.72	3.2%	13.0%	$9.01	83.1%
54.0%	$1.32	2.9%	14.0%	$7.20	84.0%
55.3%	$2.30	3.8%	9.1%	$9.99	82.1%

market. They are in fact strong evidence for the opposing claim (widely held by financial economists) that the popular "short-term theory" is, as Boone Pickens says, "pure hokum."

7

The Growing Role of Junk Bonds in Corporate Finance

Kevin J. Perry
Baring America Asset
Management Company

Robert A. Taggart, Jr.
Boston University

The growing volume of newly-issued "junk" bonds has been among the most controversial of recent developments in corporate finance. Preferring to call them "high yield" bonds, their promoters extol them as an essential cog in the revitalization of American industry.[1] Their critics, by contrast, denounce them as "securities swill" and have called for restrictions on investment in junk bonds by financial institutions and on the issuance of junk bonds in hostile takeover attempts.[2]

What are junk bonds, and why have they aroused such heated and conflicting emotions? What are the capital market conditions that have fueled the growth in junk bonds? What factors should a corporate treasurer consider in deciding whether to issue junk bonds? The present article seeks to shed light on these questions.

I. Recent Growth of the Junk Bond Market

Junk bonds are those rated below Ba by Moody's or below BBB− by Standard and Poor's. That is, they are bonds with below investment grade ratings. Unrated corporate bonds are usually included in the junk bond category as well.

Under their broadest definition, junk bonds include private placements and public issues, convertible and straight debt, low-rated municipal bonds and even

---

1. Because of its more widespread popular usage, the term "junk bonds" is used throughout this article.
2. See Felix G. Rohatyn, "Junk Bonds and Other Securities Swill," *The Wall Street Journal*, April 18, 1985.

Table 1. New Issues of Junk Bonds ($Billions).

Year	(1) Newly-Issued Public Straight Junk Bonds[a]	(2) Exchange Offers and Private Issues Going Public[b]	(3) Total Junk Bond Issuance n(1)+(2)m	(4) Total Public Bond Issues by U.S. Corporations[b]	(5) (1) as % of (4)	(6) (3) as % of (4)
1987	28.9	n.a.	n.a.	219.1	13.2	n.a.
1986	34.3	11.3	45.6	232.5	14.8	19.6
1985	15.4	4.4	19.8	119.6	12.9	16.6
1984	14.8	0.9	15.8	73.6	20.1	21.5
1983	8.0	0.5	8.5	47.6	16.8	17.9
1982	2.7	0.5	3.2	44.3	6.1	7.2
1981	1.4	0.3	1.7	38.1	3.7	4.5
1980	1.4	0.7	2.1	41.6	3.4	5.0
1979	1.4	0.3	1.7	25.8	5.4	6.6
1978	1.5	0.7	2.1	19.8	7.6	10.6
1977	0.6	0.5	1.1	24.1	2.5	4.6

a. From Drexel Burnham Lambert (1987). 1987 figure from *Investment Dealer's Digest*.
b. From *Federal Reserve Bulletin*, 1987 figure from *Investment Dealer's Digest*.

low-rated preferred stock. For the most part, however, this article focuses on the largest segment of the market: public, straight debt issued by U.S. corporations.

Junk bonds have existed ever since the first bond ratings were published by John Moody in 1909. In fact, junk bonds were a significant source of corporate funds throughout the pre-war period, accounting for 17 percent of total rated, publicly issued straight corporate debt during the years 1909–43. Downgradings during the Depression swelled the supply of junk bonds so that they grew from 13 percent of total corporate debt outstanding in 1928 to 42 percent in 1940.[3]

Junk bonds were less widely used as a source of corporate funds in the early postwar years. Between 1944 and 1965, for example, they accounted for only 6.5 percent of total corporate bond issues,[4] and from the mid-sixties to the mid-seventies they were used even less frequently. By 1977, junk bonds accounted for only 3.7 percent of total corporate bonds outstanding and most of these were "fallen angels" or bonds initially issued with investment grade ratings and subsequently downgraded.[5]

In 1977, however, the market began to change, as newly-issued junk bonds started to appear in larger volume. Although this has been widely heralded as the birth of the new-issue junk bond market, it is perhaps more accurately viewed

3. As reported by Thomas R. Atkinson, *Trends in Corporate Bond Quality* (New York: National Bureau of Economic Research, 1967).
4. Ibid.
5. As reported by Edward I. Altman and Scott A. Nammacher, *Investing in Junk Bonds* (New York: John Wiley & Sons, 1987).

Table 2. Estimated Ownership of Junk Bonds December, 1986.

Type of Investor	Estimated Holdings ($ Billions)	% of Total
Mutual funds	40	32
Insurance companies	40	32
Pension funds	15	12
Individuals	15	12
Thrift institutions	10	8
Other (foreign investors, securities dealers, etc.)	5	4
Total	125	100

Source: Rasky (1986)

as a resurgence of the flourishing market of the prewar years. In either case, the growth of new issues, as documented in Table 1, has been impressive, particularly since 1983.[6]

Between cumulative new issues and additional fallen angels, the total amount of junk bonds outstanding has been estimated at about $125 billion by the end of 1986, and at about $137 billion by the middle of 1987.[7] This represents more than 20 percent of the entire corporate bond market. Approximately one-third of all junk bonds outstanding consisted of fallen angels as of year-end 1986.[8]

On the investor side, the junk bond market is primarily institutional. More than 50 mutual funds now specialize in holding junk bonds and these, together with other nonspecialized mutual funds, hold nearly one-third of junk bonds outstanding. The estimated ownership distribution of junk bonds as of December, 1986, is shown in Table 2.

II. Investment Characteristics of Junk Bonds

Presumably, the attraction that junk bonds hold for investors is a high expected return. Expected returns are impossible to measure, and realized returns are an imperfect proxy because of their substantial variation from year to year. Over longer

---

6. It is true that new issues of junk bonds were much reduced in the wake of the stock market crash of October 1987. After running slightly ahead of the 1986 pace for the first three quarters of 1987, new issues of junk bonds totaled only $4.4 billion in the fourth quarter, compared with $8.7 billion for the comparable period in 1986. Often overlooked, however, is the fact that corporate debt issues in general were much reduced in the fourth quarter of 1987. Thus junk bond issues still represented 11.7 percent of total corporate debt issues for the fourth quarter of 1987, not much different from their share for 1985 and 1986.

7. The 1986 estimate was provided by Drexel Burnham Lambert ("The Case for High Yield Securities." April 1987) and the 1987 estimate by Edward I. Altman, in "Analyzing Risks and Returns in the High Yield Bond Market," *Financial Markets and Portfolio Management*, Zurich, Switzerland.

8. See Susan F. Rasky, "Tracking Junk Bond Owners," *The New York Times*, December 7, 1986.

periods, however, junk bonds do seem to offer higher average realized rates of return. For the period 1977 to 1986, for example, a study of Marshall Blume and Donald Keim calculated an annualized compound monthly rate of return of 11.04 percent for an index of junk bonds, compared with 9.6 percent for an index of AAA- and AA-rated corporate bonds and 9.36 percent for an index of long-term Treasury bonds.[9]

In exchange for these higher returns, investors in junk bonds can expect to bear higher levels of risk. Their lower ratings, of course, suggest a higher risk of default.[10] In addition, junk bonds tend to have fewer restrictive covenants than other bonds, and they are frequently subordinated. Thus junk bondholders have less flexibility to accelerate the bankruptcy process in the event that the borrower's condition deteriorates, and they stand lower in the line of creditors if bankruptcy does occur.

Measured default rates are, in fact, higher for junk bonds than for corporate bonds generally. For the period 1970 through 1986, a recent study by Ed Altman calculates the junk bond default rate (that is, par value of defaulting junk bonds divided by total junk bonds outstanding) as 2.22 percent, compared with 0.20 percent for all straight, public corporate debt. Influenced by the LTV and Texaco bankruptcies, the junk bond default rate was 3.39 percent for 1986 and 4.69 percent for 1987 (through August 31).[11]

The default rate, however, is probably not the best measure of the risk of holding junk bonds. Losses on defaulting bonds are rarely equal to their entire par value. For the period 1974 to 1986, for example, the weighted average default loss was 1.10 percent, compared with a default rate of 1.67 percent for the same period. In addition, junk bonds and investment grade bonds have different sensitivities to interest rate changes and to fluctuations in the value of the issuing firm's assets.

The importance of these additional factors is illustrated by Blume and Keim's finding that, for the period 1977 to 1986, their junk bond index had a lower standard deviation of monthly returns than did their indices of either high-grade corporates or long-term Treasuries (2.86 percent versus 3.73 percent and 4.02 percent respectively).[12] Thus, after the fact, junk bonds actually had lower total risk than did their investment-grade counterparts. This seemingly paradoxical result may be attributed to two factors.

---

9. Marshal E. Blume and Donald B. Keim, "Lower Grade Bonds: Their Risks and Returns," *Financial Analysis Journal* 43 (July/August, 1987), pp. 26–33. A similar return relationship prevailed during 1987, even though junk bonds were hurt by the October stock market crash. The return on the Drexel Burnham Lambert Composite Index of high yield was 5.41 percent for all of 1987, as opposed to −0.35 percent for comparable-duration treasury bonds (for the fourth quarter alone, analogous return figures were 2.73 percent for junk bonds versus 6.73 percent for treasuries).

10. In the Blume and Keim return calculations, default losses are already recognized to the extent that bonds in default are retained in the index as long as they have quoted market prices.

11. See Altman (1988), as cited in note 7.

12. Blume and Keim (1987), cited in note 9.

First, since junk bonds have higher coupon rates, they have shorter "durations" than investment grade bonds. That is, the weighted average of the times at which cash is received over the life of the bond is shorter for a junk bond.[13] This in turn implies that junk bond values are less sensitive to interst rate fluctuations than the values of investment grade bonds. Since the 1977–86 period was one of substantial interest rate fluctuations, this factor may have dominated the relative variability of realized bond returns.

Second, junk bonds are typically protected by smaller equity cushions than investment grade bonds, and thus are more sensitive to fluctuations in the value of the issuing firm's assets. The value of the assets in turn reflects the present value of the operating cash flows they generate. As a result, the variability of junk bond returns is more heavily influenced by sector, industry, and firm-specific factors than is that of investment grade bonds. However, much of the risk stemming from these fluctuations may be diversifiable. Thus the risk of a large portfolio or index may be substantially less than the average risk of the individual bonds.

Taken as whole, the investment characteristics of junk bonds are unlike those of either high grade bonds or common stocks. Their lower sensitivity to interest rate changes and the diversifiability of a substantial portion of their risk make them unlike high-grade bonds. Like common stocks, junk bond values move up and down with the value of the issuing firms' assets. Unlike common stocks, however, this upward movement is truncated for junk bonds beyond a certain point. This is because most junk bonds are callable; and if the issuing firm's creditworthiness improves dramatically, it will find it advantageous to call the bonds and refinance at a lower rate.

In the final analysis, investing in junk bonds may be most akin to a covered call option strategy, whereby a portfolio manager buys common stocks but also writes call options on those stocks. If the stocks fail to appreciate, the portfolio manager still receives the premium income from having written the call options. If the stocks do appreciate, however, the portfolio's upside potential is limited, because the stocks will be called away.

In a similar fashion, junk bond's high current yield affords the investor some protection against the possibility that the firm's assets will decline in value. If, on the other hand, the firm's fortunes improve substantially, the junk bondholders participate to some degree, but that participation is limited by the fact the firm will ultimately call the bonds away.

---

13. Over the period 1978–83, for example, Altman and Nammacher (1987), cited in note 5, calculated an average duration of 8.53 years for bonds in the Shearson-Lehman Long-Term Government Bond Index versus 6.64 years for their junk bond index. For further discussion and applications of the duration concept, see Stephen Schaefer, "Immunization and Duration, A Review of Theory, Performance and Applications," *Midland Corporate Finance Journal* 2 (Fall, 1984), pp. 41–58.

III. Capital Market Conditions and the Rise of the Junk Bond Market

Capital Markets in the 1970s and 80s

It is natural to wonder why junk bonds suddenly regained a significant share of the total corporate debt market after having been relatively dormant for a number of years. Several key factors emerged in the 1970s and 80s that brought about fundamental changes in the overall capital market environment. These same factors were conducive to the growth in junk bonds.

The first factor has been increasing competition on an international scale. Industry boundaries and firms' market shares have become more fluid; and the financial services, transportation, communications and energy industries, as well as major segments of U.S. manufacturing, have all undergone extensive restructuring. Deregulation has been a factor in several of these industries. In banking, for example, the erosion of interest rate ceilings has forced banks to compete on a broader scale in financial markets. It could be argued that these and other moves toward deregulation have often been a response to, rather than a cause of, increased competitive pressure. Whatever their source, these pressures have generated substantial capital market activity in the form of mergers and divestitures, issues and repurchases of securities, and the start-ups of new firms and liquidation of old ones. Regulatory changes that have given financial institutions greater flexibility should also be mentioned. For example, the ERISA standards of 1973 for pension fund investments essentially replaced the "Prudent Man" rule with a rule of reasonable compensation for risks incurred. This allowed pension fund to compete more broadly for investment opportunities.

A second important factor has been uncertain inflation and interest rate volatility. As exemplified by the response to the Federal Reserve's switch from interest rate to money supply targets in October 1979, the prices of fixed income securities have become more variable. This has spurred investors to seek protection against sudden changes in rates and has induced them to increase their portfolio turnover. For corporations, changing inflation rates have contributed to sharp fluctuations in the availability of internal funds relative to total financing needs. Thus many firms have found themselves moving in and out of the capital markets more frequently, and facing high variable conditions when doing so.

The third important factor in changing capital market conditions is at least partially motivated by the first two. Securities issuers have greatly expanded the range of their potential sources of funds. In part, the increasingly global nature of competition in many industries has led to raising funds on an international scale as well. This is exemplified by the growth of the Eurobond markets, in which U.S. corporations raised an average of $28.4 billion in both 1986 and 1987, up from just $300 million in 1975. In addition, the need to move in and out of markets more frequently has led to an emphasis on reducing the costs of external financing. Since 1982, corporations have taken advantage of the shelf registration rule

Table 3. Composition of Credit Market Debt Raised by U.S. Nonfinancial Corporations.

Period	1977–83	1984–86
Total credit market debt raised ($ Billion)	$565.4	$535.1
Proportion of credit market debt accounted for by (%):		
Bank loans	40.6%	32.7%
Commercial paper	4.4	4.0
Finance co. loans	11.0	11.6
Tax-exempt bonds	12.9	6.5
Corporate bonds	25.9	43.7
Mortgages	2.1	0.5
Other	3.0	0.0
Total	100.0	100.0
Note: Credit market debt as % of total sources of funds	23.3	36.3

Source: Federal Reserve Flow of Fund Accounts

(Rule 415) to cut their underwriting costs. They have also sought to raise funds in public markets, where possible, circumventing more costly borrowing through financial intermediaries.

This disintermediation has been especially apparent in recent years, as indicated in Table 3. As the corporate bond market has expanded, the share of corporate debt financing accounted for by bank loans has declined. Although it is less apparent in the table, use of the commercial paper market by the most creditworthy corporations has also eroded banks' traditional lending relationships with their prime customers. These developments, combined with competition from foreign banks and other financial institutions, have turned prime lending into more of a low-margin commodity business. The banks have thus been forced to turn to lower grade credits in an attempt to maintain their profitability.

The Influence of Capital Market Conditions on the Junk Bond Market

The same factors that have molded capital market developments more generally have been important contributors to the recent growth of the junk bond market. Let us consider in turn the impact of these factors on investors, underwriters, and issuers of junk bonds.

Hurt by unexpected inflation during the 1970s, investors have sought higher returns and greater flexibility. Thus junk bonds, with their premium yields and shorter durations, grew more attractive by the late 1970s. This attractiveness was enhanced by the widely-noticed performance of Keystone's B4 Fund, a pioneer junk bond fund that inspired the start-up of other such funds.

Investors also found that traditional loss-protection measures were inadequate in a rapidly changing environment. High credit quality, for example, offered little protection against volatile interest rates. Similarly, restrictive covenants in bond indentures proved insufficient to guard against the losses imposed by massive corporate restructurings.[14] As a result, investors have increasingly emphasized liquidity relative to credit quality or contractual provisions. Despite their higher default risk and fewer restrictive covenants than other corporate bonds, junk bonds' attractiveness to investors has thus been greatly enhanced by the development of a liquid secondary market.

In this sense, the rise of the junk bond market has paralleled the "securitization" phenomenon more generally. Because little or no secondary market existed, mortgages, auto loans, and other receivables were formerly held to maturity by their originators or by specialized intermediaries. Increasingly, however, they have been packaged as asset-backed securities, and a more active secondary market has developed. In a similar vein, junk bonds are akin to medium- or long-term loans that might formerly have been originated and held by commercial banks and insurance companies. With the development of a secondary market, however, they are now more widely traded.

Changing capital market conditions have also rapidly eroded the stigma that was formerly attached to junk bond underwriting and trading. As in commercial banking, prime-quality underwriting has become more of a low margin business as worldwide competition, shelf registration and issuer pressure have all combined to squeeze profits. This has in turn sparked a search for new opportunities. Merger and acquisition advising is one such opportunity that has been pursued by many securities firms. Providing investment banking services to below-investment grade companies, which comprise about 95 percent of all U.S. corporations, is another natural target.

The latter opportunity was especially attractive to Drexel Burnham Lambert in the late 1970s, since it did not have a strong investment grade client base. It did, however, have a well-established junk bond trading operation under the direction of Michael Milken. Thus it had already developed a network of investors and and expertise in secondary market-making.

When Drexel Burnham began underwriting junk bonds in 1977, it was therefore able to provide investors with the liquidity they needed to make these securities attractive. Drexel quickly became, and remains today, the leading underwriter of junk bonds; but other firms have recognized the potential profitability of the business and have entered the market as well.

Junk bonds also afforded Drexel Burnham a way to enter the lucrative merger and acquisition business and thus to participate in the restructuring boom. The firm began financing leveraged buyouts with junk bonds in 1981 and hostile takeover bids in late 1983. Drexel was able to capitalize on its established investor network to mobilize large amounts of funds within very short periods. Again, competitors have followed suit or have come up with alternative means of raising cash quickly, such as committing their own capital in the form of "bridge loans."

---

14. See S. Prokesch, "Merger Wave: How Stock and Bonds Fare." *The New York Times*, January 7, 1986.

Finally, capital market conditions of recent years have also enhanced the appeal of junk bonds for issuers. Junk bond underwriting spreads are high, typically falling in the three to four percent range, compared with less than one percent for investment grade issues.[15] Still, there are reasons to believe that junk bond financing can offer cost advantages to issuers.

Investors, for example, appear to be willing to accept lower expected returns in exchange for greater liquidity.[16] Hence, investors' ability to trade their bonds in a secondary market can lower the cost of junk bond financing relative to negotiated debt, for which secondary trading is thin or nonexistent. This should be particularly the case in recent years, as volatile market conditions have dictated increased investor emphasis on liquidity.

In addition, rapidly changing financing needs and competitive situations have necessitated flexibility for issuing corporations. In this respect, the implicit cost of junk bond financing may have been less than that of other sources in recent years. For example, junk bonds have allowed lower-grade firms to raise larger amounts of money in a shorter period than would be possible from negotiated sources. Junk bonds also tend to have fewer restrictive covenants and more liberal call provisions than many types of negotiated debt. Recent market conditions have apparently created a willingness on the part of some investors to make these concessions in exchange for greater liquidity. In fact, it could be argued that investors' demand for liquidity has greatly facilitated the placement of junk bonds from the largest leveraged buyouts.

IV. The Role of Junk Bonds in Corporate Financial Policy

Given that junk bonds have established a solid position in the corporate debt market, we now examine their role in corporate financial policy. When should a corporation consider issuing junk bonds?

Stewart Myers' "pecking order" theory provides a useful starting point.[17] Myers notes that a firm's managers typically know more about its true value than other capital market participants. If the managers act in the interests of their existing shareholders, they will thus try to issue securities at times when they know them to be overvalued. Recognizing this incentive, however, market participants will then interpret securities issues as a sign that they are overvalued. That in turn reduces the amounts they are willing to pay for the securities.

This problem of unequal information gives rise to a pecking order of sources of funds. Internally generated funds are unaffected by the problem, since their use entails no new securities issues. The closer a company's debt securities are

---

15. As reported by Henny Sender, "Don't Junk the High-Yield Market Yet," Institutional Investor 21 (March, 1987), pp. 163–66.

16. See Yakov Amihud and Haim Mendelson, "Asset Pricing and the Bid-Ask Spread," *Journal of Financial Economics* 17 (December, 1986), pp. 223–49.

17. See "The Capital Structure Puzzle," *Journal of Finance* 39 (June, 1984), pp. 575–92. Reprinted in *Midland Corporate Finance Journal* 3, Fall 1985, pp. 6–18.

to being riskless, the less severe is this problem as well. This is because the value of riskless securities will be unaffected by revisions in the estimated value of the company's assets. Riskier securities such as equity, however, will clearly be affected by investors' perceptions of firm value. Since the mere fact of their issuance is likely to lead to downward revisions in their value, managers will be reluctant to issue these securities.

The pecking order, then, implies the following rules for financial policy: (1) Use internal funds first, until these have been exhausted; (2) to the extent that external funds must be relied upon, issue debt first, the less risky the better; (3) issue common stock only as a last resort, after all debt capacity has been exhausted.

Junk bonds occupy an intermediate position in this pecking order. They are more susceptible to the investor information problem than investment grade debt, but less so than common stock. For a firm that needs large amounts of external financing for its current investment plan, junk bonds can allow the firm to fully use its available debt capacity and thus avoid an equity issue.

At what point is debt capacity used up? While it is difficult to identify a given firm's optimal debt ratio with any precision, finance theory does suggest certain characteristics that will lead some firms to have higher debt capacities then others.[18]

The first of these is the firm's tax-paying status. The tax-deductibility of interest is one of the potential advantages of debt. Firms pay for this advantage, however, because the more debt they issue in the aggregate, the more they bid up the returns on debt securities relative to equity. Thus firms that already have large tax shields (for example, from depreciation and loss carry forwards) relative to their cash flow would find little tax benefit from additional debt, even though they would be implicitly paying for this benefit. For such firms, debt capacity is likely to be relatively low.[19]

A second important determinant of debt capacity is the riskiness of the firm's assets. The costs of bankruptcy and of resolving conflicts of interest among security holders are closely related to the perceived probability of default. The fact that a company's bonds are rated below investment grade is, of course, itself an indication that perceived default risk is relatively high. Hence, issuers of junk bonds should carefully weight the potential costs of bankruptcy and claimholder conflicts against the dilution that might be entailed by an equity issue. In particular, a firm that plans to return to the debt markets on a regular basis in the future should be wary of increasing its debt ratio suddenly and sharply through the issuance of junk bonds today. To the extent that this undermines the value of its already outstanding bonds, the firm can expect investors to extract a penalty yield or more stringent convenants the next time it return to the market.

---

18. For a discussion of these characteristics, see Stewart C. Myers, "The Search for an Optimal Capital Structure," *Midland Corporate Financial Journal* 1 (Spring, 1983), pp. 6–16.

19. Since the new tax law reduces nondebt tax shields by eliminating the Investment Tax Credit and lengthening allowable depreciation schedules, it may tend to increase debt capacity for many firms.

A third factor affecting a firm's debt capacity is the composition of its assets. A firm whose value stems largely from assets already in place is likely to have a greater debt capacity than one for which future investment opportunities comprise a substantial portion of current market value. This is because debt that is issued now can weaken the firm's incentive to undertake those future investments. The riskier is the firm's currently outstanding debt, the more the future projects will tend to bolster the bondholders' position. Because they must share the value of these projects, however, equityholders' willingness to undertake them will be less than if they captured the entire value themselves. In the face of this potential problem, firms with significant future growth opportunities will tend to rely less heavily on debt financing today.

The foregoing analysis suggests that the ideal junk bond issuer is a firm that can take full advantage of the interest tax shields, that does not have a potential for severe bankruptcy costs or conflicts among security holders, and that has a total market value that is largely attributable to assets in place. One such firm would be the prototypical leveraged buyout candidate: a firm with a mature business that generates a high but relatively steady level of cash flows. Another might be a younger firm that has already cleared the hurdles of developing its product and establishing a market position but that now needs capital to finance its major expansion phase.

One other factor should also be considered by the potential junk bond issuer. The arguments advanced above concerning debt capacity and the pecking order of funds sources do not distinguish between public and private debt. Hence the issuer must decide whether it is better to rely on the public market or to negotiate a private agreement with a financial institution. The more highly the issuer values the flexibility entailed by call provisions and less restrictive covenants, the more the choice will tend toward public debt. The public market will also be favored the more investors are willing to make yield concessions in exchange for the possibility of secondary trading.

V. Public Policy Issues

If junk bonds are simply one possible choice in an entire spectrum of funds sources, why have they aroused such controversy in publicy policy circles? The general economic conditions described earlier—especially worldwide competitive upheaval and uncertain inflation combined with interest rate volatility—have been accompanied by many painful dislocations. Although total employment has expanded, the wave of restructurings has brought plant closings and loss of jobs in a number of industries and localities. Changes in control have extended the threat to job security to the most senior executive ranks. Competition and volatile market conditions have also aroused fears over the safety of the financial system. These developments have in turn generated heated debate over such issues as industrial policy and the regulation of financial institutions. And because they are a highly visible product of the same economic forces that have caused these dislocations, junk bonds have become enmeshed in the same policy debates.

However, the true contribution of junk bonds to these perceived policy problems may be more symbolic than real. Their very label tends to surround junk bonds with the unsavory aura that makes them a convenient target. Their real influence is less easy to detect.

Consider, for example, the role of junk bonds in financing mergers and acquisitions. This has been the subject of several congressional hearings and various restrictions on junk bond financing of hostile takeover bids have been proposed.[20] Sometimes lost amidst the furor, though, is the fact that junk bonds account for only a small fraction of all merger and acquisition financing. The peak occurred in 1986, when junk bond issues were related to 7.8 percent of the $190 billion in total merger financing (*Mergers and Acquisitions,* 1987). This was up from 4.3 percent in 1985 and 2.6 percent in 1984. Merger and tender offer transactions have accounted for at most 41 percent of public junk bond issue proceeds in any given year, this occurring in 1986.

It cannot be denied that the availability of the junk bond market has strengthened the credibility of takeover threats, allowing larger amounts of funds to be raised in a shorter time period than was previously thought possible. Nevertheless, merger-related activity does not absorb a majority of the proceeds from junk bond issues, and bank loans are a far bigger source of merger financing than junk bonds.

The junk bond market has also been discussed frequently in conjunction with the recent insider trading charges, and revelations connected with the Boesky scandal have apparently triggered some decreases in junk bond prices, at least temporarily.[21] While the SEC has recommended that charges be brought against Drexel Burnham and several of its employees, however, no systematic involvement of junk bond market participants in insider trading has been established as yet. Furthermore, as with mergers and acquisitions generally, the issue is broader than junk bonds. Tender offers can create opportunities for insider trading, but it is not clear why offers that will be financed with junk bonds are more susceptible to such opportunities than others.

Consider finally the connection between junk bonds and the safety of the financial system. Some have argued that junk bonds represent part of a general weakening of corporate financial strength in recent years. However, it is at least debatable whether such weakening has in fact occurred.[22] When measured in market value

---

20. To date, the only restriction actually imposed has been the Federal Reserve Board's 1986 determination that a shell corporation, set up for the purpose of making a takeover bid, is subject to margin requirements under Regulation G. The impact of this ruling is limited, however, by numerous stated exceptions. See M. Langley and J.D. Williams, "Fed Board Votes 3-2 to Restrict the Use of 'Junk' Bonds in Takeovers," *Wall Street Journal* (January 9, 1986).

21. Estimates of these price decrease range from one to four percentage points (see Randall Smith, "Junk Bonds Lag Market Since Boesky Case, But Exact Gap Proves Difficult to Measure," *The Wall Street Journal*, December 4, 1986). Much of these losses, however, appear to have been recouped within about two months (see Randall Smith, "Junk Bonds Retain Strength and Discount Latest Fallout From Insider Trading Scandal," *The Wall Street Journal*, February 18, 1987).

22. See, for example, Robert A. Taggart, Jr., "Corporate Financing: Too Much Debt?," *Financial Analysis Journal* 42 (May/June, 1986), pp. 35-42.

terms, the ratio of debt to total capital for U.S. nonfinancial corporations has actually declined by more than 20 percent since 1974. Even if it were conceded that U.S. corporations have relied too heavily on debt financing, it should be noted that junk bond issues account for only six percent of the total credit market debt that companies have raised during the period 1977–1986.

It has also been argued that junk bond investments can weaken the safety of financial institutions. Acting on these arguments the state of New York has recently moved to limit unapproved junk bond investments by insurance companies.[23] Given their default risk, it is of course true that an ill-conceived junk bond investment program can lead to trouble. But the number of ways to make risky investments is almost unlimited. They include, for example, issuing short-term debt and investing in long-term Treasury securities that are free of default risk. Limiting junk bond investments, but not other investments, is unlikely to significantly enhance the safety of financial institutions.

VI. Conclusion

The rapid growth of the junk bond market has been impressive, but controversial. Most of the controversy stems from the fact that the market development has coincided with the rise of such emotional policy issues as industrial restructuring and corporate control. It has been argued here, however, that the junk bond market is a product of the same forces—international competition, volatile capital market conditions, and the search for new funds sources—that have given rise to these policy issues. It is a symptom rather than a cause of those forces.

For the corporate treasurer, the development of this market represents a significant financial innovation. It allows companies that do not qualify for investment grade bond ratings to tape the public market and thus to take advantage of investors' willingness to pay for liquidity. For such firms, access to the junk bond market can be an important alternative to privately negotiated debt.

---

23. See Johnnie L. Roberts, "New York Limits Assets Insurers Put in Junk Bonds," *The Wall Street Journal*, June 1.

8

The Corporate Sell-Off

Scott C. Linn
University of Iowa

Michael S. Rozeff
University of Iowa

I. Introduction

For decades the glamor, wealth and suggestion of economic power that attend corporate mergers and acquisitions have captured the attention of the media, academics and, inevitably of course, regulators. But while the spotlight has been focused principally on mergers and acquisitions, the divestiture has quietly become an important phenomenon in the management of corporate resources. In fact, the recent prominence of the divestiture is probably the most visible sign of that massive reallocation of corporate assets that has come to be known as "the restructuring" of corporate America.

The rising importance of the divestiture or "sell-off"—by which we mean the sale of a subsidiary, division or product line by one company to another—is seen most readily in the growing volume of such deals. In 1983 alone there were some 932 divestitures of more than $500,000 in assets. And in every year since 1971 sell-offs have amounted to at least 35 percent of the number of mergers.[1] Besides the increasing volume and dollar value of these transactions, the roster of well-known companies selling off large businesses also attests to the divestiture's rising favor among corporate strategies. In 1983, for example, General Electric sold its metallurgical coal business, RCA Corporation its finance company, and Dun & Bradstreet its television stations.

While academic studies have provided extensive documentation of the valuation consequences of mergers and acquisitions, it is only recently that studies of corporate divestitures have begun to appear in the corporate finance literature.

---

1. See the *Mergerstat Review* published by W.T. Grimm & Co.

Partly because financial economists have scanted divestitures, but also no doubt because of the strong hold of the "conventional wisdom" on Wall Street thinking, myth and unexamined assertion are rife in published commentaries on sell-offs. The popular accounts of Esmark's sale of Vickers Energy Company are a case in point. Esmark's common stock gained significantly in price when this sale was announced. Why? Echoing a Wall Street commonplace, Eugene Brigham (in the most recent edition of what is perhaps the most widely distributed finance text every published)[2] argued that the market was thinking of Esmark as primarily a meat packing and consumer products company. Investors thus collectively overlooked Esmark's large holdings of oil reserves, resulting in a significant undervaluation of Esmark stock. Once the sale was announced, however, the market came to its senses.

This explanation is inconsistent, of course, with the central premise of modern finance theory: the efficiency of capital markets. In an efficient stock market, a company's current stock price reflects the market's unbiased estimate, using all publicly available information, of future expected cash flows from the company's operations. In the case of Esmark, there seems no reason to doubt that many people knew about the company's ownership of Vickers, and were aware of the value of Vickers if it were sold to another company. What the market did not know was *if* and *when* the sale would take place. The revaluation of Esmark occurred only when it became clear that Vickers would be sold.

But if market ignorance and a resulting undervaluation of Esmark's stock was not the reason why the stock price rose on the announcement of the sale, then what was? Our answer is simply that Vickers was worth more to several potential buyers than to Esmark, and that Esmark took advantage of this discrepancy in value by selling Vickers in a competitive market. Through the sale Esmark captured at least a portion of Vickers' increased value.

II. Two Cases of Successful Sell-Offs

A small amount of economic analysis should help place in perspective the two examples which follow, as well as serving as prologue to further discussion of the basic questions: Why do companies divest? and what are the market consequences of so doing?

If the selling company is rational, then it should certainly not expect to lose anything by the sale. A subsidiary will therefore not be sold for any price less than its current worth to the seller. Of course, some companies do make mistakes, so that the best we can hope to observe is that *on average* selling companies do not lose as a result of the sales.

Stated more positively, we assume that corporate managements sell off subsidiaries in order to strengthen their companies and add value for their stockholders. If management's plans are fulfilled (on average), and if the market is reasonably

---

2. *Financial Management*, (Chicago Press, 1982).

efficient, then this should show up in an upward revaluation of the selling company's shares *at the time the market learns of the sale*. In sum, economic logic tells us that we should observe sell-offs accompanied by gains (or at worst no losses) in the prices of selling company shares. Were we consistently to see price decreases in response to divestiture announcements, we would seriously have to wonder why managements en masse were taking actions that seemed to harm their shareholders.

A similar logic obtains for the buying company. If the buying company pays a price for the subsidiary that is reasonable in view of the returns that can be earned on its investment, then at the very least the buying company should not lose from the purchase. But if the buyer's operations form an especially good "fit" with the operation, such that the divested subsidiary is worth far more to the buyer than to the seller (and provided competing bids don't drive the subsidiary's price too high), then the market may expect significant gains to the buyer to result from the combination. Under this set of circumstances, the stock of the buyer will also rise.

A prime example of a well-structured sell-off—one in which the buyer as well as the seller appeared to benefit—was the sale by Warner-Lambert of Entenmann's, the bakery business, to General Foods. The price was $315 million. The sale was announced on October 6, 1982, and the stock price of Warner-Lambert closed up $2 to 24⅜ on that day. General Foods' stock increased $2⅛ to $41⅜. After accounting for market price movements, the wealth increase to General Foods' stockholders was about $44 million. The gain to Warner-Lambert shareholders was approximately $101 million.

We can draw several inferences from these market responses. Since Warner-Lambert was paid a total of $315 million for Entenmann's and since the stock increased by roughly $100 million in value, the implied value of the subsidiary to Warner-Lambert prior to the sale was about $215 million. This means that the percentage "premium" paid by General Foods Corp. was about $100/$215, or 47 percent above its value to Warner-Lambert.

Even with such a large premium, the stock market apparently approved of the acquisition. In fact the $44 million gain in the value of General Foods' stock suggests that the market believed the present value of Entenmann's (future expected cash flows) as part of General Foods was some $359 million, or $44 million greater than the cost of $315 million. Stated another way the implicit value of the benefit/cost ratio to General Foods was $359/$315 or 1.14.

What accounts for these wealth increases? Why was the market valuing Entenmann's more highly as part of General Foods than Warner-Lambert? Security analysts noted that General Foods would be able to reduce the materials and manufacturing costs of Entenmann's. The President of General Foods, Philip Smith, stated that General Foods would increase the distribution of Entenmann's products, providing coverage of up to about 60 percent of the country (a marked increase from the 36 percent coverage prior to the sell-off). He was also quoted as saying that the bakery would very clearly earn a rate of return above its cost of capital. Hence it is understandable that General Foods' stock went up.

What about Warner-Lambert, why did its stock price rise? Entenmann's was a profitable company for Warner-Lambert, one which it had nurtured from its start as a regional baker. Despite its current level of profitability, it had the potential to become even more profitable in someone else's hands, someone that could take advantage of buying, manufacturing and distribution economies. Because of competition among potential buyers, Warner-Lambert was able to capture some of the potential gains that would come from the buyers' more efficient handling of the company.

Another plausible reason for the gain in Warner-Lambert's stock was that the market viewed its exit from the baking business as a signal that it possessed profitable investment opportunities that it wished to pursue in the health-care area. It is possible that the presence of Entenmann's was somehow interfering with these plans.

A second example of a sell-off benefiting both buyer and seller was the sale of INA Corp. of Hospital Affiliates International to Hospital Corp. of America. When this sale was announced on April 20, 1981, INA common rose $1 7/8 to $45 3/4, while Hospital Corp. increased $2 3/4 to $42 1/2. In dollar terms the wealth increase of the INA common was about $75 million while the market value of Hospital Corp. rose by $126 million. The subsidiary was sold for $65 million. In this case the implicit premium paid by the buyer was only 13 percent ($75/$575).

Both companies gave clues as to why their stocks rose. Hospital Corp. pointed out that economies of scale resulting from the acquisition would provide substantial savings in overhead and operating expenses. It noted that the companny would now be able to enter four new states and extend operations in several others.[3] INA Corp.'s chairman and chief executive officer made it clear that the sale now made it possible for INA Corp. to allocate more resources, both management and capital, to its strategic plan to expand various insurance lines. This suggests not only that the subsidiary was worth more to someone else, but that its presence in the selling company was interfering with the pursuit of more profitable opportunities.

III. Why Divest?

One popular corporate motive for divestitures is that they are a means of raising capital. But such an explanation does not tell us very much. Obviously sell-offs do not increase a company's *sources* of capital since they simply exchange one set of assets for another. A sell-off does, however, increase the company's working capital in that long-term assets are usually exchanged (at least in part) for cash. For example, the sale by International Harvester Co. of its Solar Turbines International division to Caterpillar Tractor Co. may have been motivated by such a reason. The proceeds of the sale ($505 million) were used to cut Harvester's short-term

---

3. Another possibility is that the market expects Hospital Corp.'s acquisition to confer some monopolistic advantage. We do not believe, however, that an increase in monopoly power explains the gains to Hospital Corp. For one thing, its share of the market was small even after the purchase. Secondly, it did not buy hospitals in the same locations as its own hospitals. Third, the stock price of its largest rival (Humana) did not change when the acquisition was announced.

debt by half. Because the division sold had been consistently profitable, the problem apparently was an asset/liability structure in which fixed assets were financed by too much short-term debt.

But however logical this explanation might seem, it really relies on the existence of some unexplained capital market "imperfection" that prevented Harvester from otherwise (and more cheaply) reorganizing its financing. The sale of fixed assets to increase working capital seems an expensive way of obtaining cash as compared with borrowing or an equity issue. Thus we strongly doubt that this motive for divestiture is a pervasive one.

Our review of sell-offs indicates, moreover, that the great majority involve healthy companies that have adequate access to the capital markets. Even in the Harvester case there are signs that the sale of the unit was not simply out of distress. Harvester had found that the use of turbines for its vehicles was impractical. Meanwhile there were active bidders for the division and Harvester was able to realize a sale price of almost 2.5 times its book value.

One sometimes reads that a sell-off is undertaken in order to repay debt and strengthen the balance sheet. But, as with divestitures undertaken to raise working capital, we find it implausible that this is a widespread motive for sell-offs. For one thing, this seems an expensive way to change one's debt/equity ratio. The sale of assets obviously involves a disinvestment decision. Like the case for sell-offs as a means of increasing working capital, this explanation seems to confuse the results of sale with its cause. The real cause may simply be that the seller feels it can obtain a good price for the subsidiary. The fact that the newly liquid assets are used to pay down debt is merely a secondary, an incidental effect—one, at any rate, that should not be expected to increase stock value.

Divesting companies also sometimes offer as their motive the desire to get out of capital-intensive businesses. Gulf & Western, for example, cited the capital intensity of its cement subsidiary when it was sold. It is clear, however, that excessive capital requirements per se do not explain sell-offs. Obviously the buying company is willing to undertake the capital requirements of the subsidiary. And if the subsidiary were actually or potentially profitable, the seller could obtain financing for it. We are thus inclined to regard this explanation as a way of saying that the subsidiary does not fit with the remaining operations of the company and its causing a real diseconomy of some sort.

A fourth prominent reason for sell-offs is that the unit is "losing money." We interpret this more broadly to mean that the rate of return from the unit's activities is less than the required rate of return. A lack of profitability in this sense may be signaled by more readily available indicators, such as disappointing sales volume, a slowdown in the sales growth rate, a decline in market share, or a technological change which lowers profit margins and makes a unit unprofitable.

In all of these instances, however, a sell-off is not necessarily the optimal response to the problem. There are any number of alternatives to divestiture of a sub-performing business. Profitability might be restored through changes in product pricing, alterations in product line, further investment in the operation, or cost reduction. And, in cases where a business is worth no more to any prospective buyer than the liquidation value to the seller, then closing down the unit and selling off the assets may be the best solution.

The important point here is that getting rid of an unprofitable business should not necessarily increase the market value of the company. In an efficient market, the presence of a unit that is detracting from stockholder value (that is, not earning its required rate of return) should already be reflected in the value of the parent company's shares. The stock price should already be marked down such that, at that reduced value, new or prospective shareholders expect to earn a normal rate of return on their investment in the company's shares. If at this point the company is able to sell the unit for exactly its value (to the seller), there should be no gain or loss in the value of the selling company's shares. It is only when the selling company is able to locate a buyer who expects to restore the unit's profitability, or to take advantage of some other unexploited feature of the subsidiary, that real gains should be expected from selling out.

In other words, selling a subsidiary *merely* because it is "unprofitable" or "losing money" should benefit the selling company only if it receives more than the unit's present worth as part of that company. When companies use this language to justify sell-offs, it probably means that they are unable to restore profitability, and that the assets are worth more when put to different uses or in the hands of more efficient users. The other possibility is that the presence of the money-losing subsidiary is somehow interfering with the remaining operations of the company. Casting off this corporate albatross, so to speak, may allow the remaining units to operate more profitably, and this too should cause the seller's shares to increase in price.

A fifth rationale for sell-offs is that the seller wishes to sell unrelated units or units that do not fit with its strategic plan. Or, put slightly differently, the seller wants to concentrate its resources in areas of operations that it knows best. This kind of explanation can also be interpreted as saying that the unit is producing diseconomies that would be removed if the unit were sold. Since these diseconomies are present only when the unit is run in conjunction with the other units of the company, they constitute "negative synergies," or what we have elsehwere termed "anergies."[4] Ridding the company of such "negative synergies" should cause the share price to rise.

Sixth, and finally, we come to the motive which we think prompts the majority of corporate divestitures (as well as explaining the market's positive response to them): namely, that the divested unit is worth more as part of another company (or even as a stand-alone unit) than as part of its present organization. We presented two cases earlier. But as additional examples, consider the sales by U.S. Steel and Holiday Inns of their shipping subsidiaries. Both operations were sold to maritime companies, and both transactions were probably motivated by the ability of the buyers to operate the subsidiaries more economically.

---

4. See our paper "The Effects of Voluntary Spinoffs on Stock Prices: The Anergy Hypothesis."

Of this list of common motives for sell-offs, then, only two make economic sense: removal of diseconomies and the presence of buyers willing to purchase the unit for more than its value to the seller, the sale of an unprofitable unit per se should not be expected to add to stockholder value. Only if the sale is to a bidder who expects to restore profitability, or if the sale removes diseconomies, would we anticipate a stock price increase (although the market may interpret even uneconomical sales as part of a general restructuring plan, reflecting management's long-run commitment to improving profitability). Finally, those motives that view a sell-off solely as a means of raising capital (or increasing working capital) or strengthening the balance sheet should not, in and of themselves, have a significant effect on stockholder value.

IV. The Evidence on Sell-Offs

Methods of Study

We earlier described two instances of divestiture in which the capital market clearly perceived that both the buyer and the seller added value for their stockholders. Although case studies help us to understand the market consequences of some individual events, broad generalizations about the market's response to sell-offs must rely upon studies that have examined large samples. It is to the findings of those studies that we now turn.

Studies of divestiture, like most research in modern finance, attempt to measure the effects on stock prices of *announcements* of the event in question—in this case, sell-offs. Assuming that the current price of a company's stock reflects the market's assessment of its prospective cash flows and that the market reacts quickly and unbiasedly to news, the immediate stock price reaction to a sell-off announcement can be seen as conveying the market's perception of the *long-run* cash flow consequences of the sell-off. That perception may not prove to be accurate, but it will be "unbiased"—that is, neither too high nor too low on average. A rise in the selling company's stock price carries, of course, the market's seal of approval and a decline signals its skepticism. The same logic holds for the buying company as well.

There are two factors, however, which tend to obscure the market's true reaction to a sell-off: (1) our inability to determine precisely when the market first learns that a sell-off has been decided upon, and (2) the daily movements of the market itself that tend to sweep along individual stocks. In practice, these problems are overcome by (1) relying upon the earliest dates on which the sell-offs are publicly announced and by (2) removing statistically that part of a stock's price movement that can be accounted for by market movements. The studies discussed below use various benchmark models to calculate the expected percentage change in a divesting or buying firm's stock price, conditional on the general market return, both on and around the day on which the divestiture is announced in the financial press.

The difference between a company's actual and its expected return on the announcement date is called the "abnormal return" to stockholders, and it is interpreted as the market's assessment of the expected cash flow consequences of the forthcoming sell-off.

Involuntary Sell-Offs

Divestitures are generally voluntary, but sometimes they are forced upon the firm as the result of some regulatory action. James Ellert, Donald Kummer, and Peggy Wier have each studied the impact on firms of divestitures forced by Federal antitrust actions. They all conclude that involuntary divestitures tend to reduce the value of the stocks of the affected firms. Ellert, for example, finds that the average abnormal percentage change in the market value of the equity of 205 defendants in antitrust merger was −1.86 percent during the month that the merger complaint was filed. Furthermore this result was significantly different from zero.[5]

Why do these declines in market value occur? Three main possibilities come to mind. The first is that the market expects that in a forced sale the seller will not obtain a fair price. Although this might be reasonable if the sale is hurried or if the assets find no ready market, we do not expect such conditions to be pervasive. As a general rule there should be enough competition among buyers to ensure a fair price for the subsidiary.

A second possibility is that the regulators are right, and that the forced sale actually takes away some monopolistic advantage possessed by the selling company. If this were the case, though, we would expect the stock prices of *rival* companies to fall as well, since the break-up of monopolies is supposed to result in generally lower industry prices. Studies by Robert Stillman and Bjorn Eckbo have addressed this issue by examining the effects of antitrust complaints on the shares of rival firms, and both find no evidence to support this claim.

A third, and to us the most likely, possibility is that forced divestitures destroy generally efficient asset structures—ones built up over the years to take advantage of synergies and economies of combination. In this case, forced divestitures would be expected to increase costs and decrease cash flows, thereby causing stock prices to decline.

Voluntary Sell-Offs

The results of the most recent available academic studies of *voluntary* sell-offs are summarized in Table 1. Each of the five studies finds that during the two-day period ending with the day on which the announcement of the sell-off is printed in the *Wall Street Journal*, the stocks of the sellers gain on average relative to the market. The average price increase is about one to two percent, a result which

---

5. Kummer finds that for the period covering one month before through one month after the complaint filing, firms involved in horizontal, and horizontal–vertical mergers lose −6.3% and −55%, both statistically significant.

Table 1. The Effect on the Seller's Stock Values of Voluntary Sell-Offs[a] (t-Statistics in Parentheses).

Author(s)	Days	Average Abnormal Returns	Period Sampled	Sample Size
Alexander, Benson, and Kampmeyer (1984)	−1 through 0	.17% (.67)	1964–1973	53
Hite and Owers (1984)	−1 through 0	1.5% (4.33)	1963–1979	56
Klein (1983)	−2 through 0	1.12% (2.83)	1970–1979	202
Linn and Rozeff (1984)	−1 through 0	1.45% (5.36)	1977–1982	77
Rosenfeld (1984)	−1 through 0	2.33% (4.60)	1963–1981	62

a. Each study utilizes daily return data.

is statistically significant.[6] These findings probably understate the positive effect of sell-offs because most of the studies also indicate that the selling firm's shares rise by an additional one to three percent in the month prior to the sell-off announcement.

On balance, then, the market appears to feel that divestiture decisions by management serve stockholder interests.

In an attempt to learn more about why the market responds positively to divestitures. April Klein divided her sample according to whether the sell-off announcement contained information about the price of the sale. She found that only the group of firms that announced sale prices of the divested assets experienced average gains (of 2.41 percent). Those companies that announced sell-offs but did not provide a transaction price showed virtually no stock price movement (−.06 percent). We checked this finding on our own sample and found similar results. Those companies announcing prices rose about 2.95 percent while prices of those that did not rose only 0.49 percent.

What is the meaning of these findings? Klein contended that the revelation of the sales price to the market was

> a way to convey favorable information about the market value of the divested assets, and hence the firm. The information can be either that the value of the assets increases on transfer of ownership or that the firm sells assets undervalued by the market.[7]

---

6. The study of Gordon Alexander, et al. is an exception in this regard.
7. "Voluntary Corporate Divestitures: Motives and Consequences," University of Chicago, 1983, p. 31.

Table 2. The Effects of Announcing the Sale Price and the Motive for the Sale on the Seller's Stock Value (Average Abnormal Daily Returns Over Days -1 through 0).

Price Announced	Motive Announced	
	yes	no
yes	3.92% (N=14)	2.3% (N=21)
no	.70% (N=15)	.37% (N=27)

As suggested earlier, the latter explanation is inconsistent with the premise of efficient markets. And, again, with so much evidence testifying to the sophistication of markets, we should certainly be reluctant to rely upon pervasive undervaluation of assets as an explanation of the market's systematically positive responses to sell-offs.

We fully agree that providing a transaction price to the market fixes the increase in value that arises from a transfer of ownership. But why is publication of a price *necessary* for the market to raise the value of the selling company's shares? Once the stock market learns that a sale is contemplated, its knowledge of the market for those real assets should enable it to make an educated guess about the value of the assets in an open-market sale. Recently, for example, Esmark's announcement of a potential leveraged buyout was accompanied in the *Wall Street Journal* by analysts' estimates of the market values of Esmark's subsidiaries. If analysts are generally capable of making such estimates (and there seems little reason to doubt this capability), then there should be some form of stock market reaction regardless of whether the sale price is announced.

One possible explanation of this result is that companies choose not to announce selling prices when they are unable to obtain a selling price that exceeds the divested unit's worth to the seller. Since we see no reason why companies should behave in this way, however, this explanation does not seem persuasive.

A second possibility is that the presence of a sales transaction price is a "proxy" for one or more other variables. For example, many of the divestiture announcements contain statements of motive as well as the price of the sale. To test whether the disclosure of motive also influences the market's response, we read all the announcement articles in our sample and classified them into four categories according to the presence or absence of a transaction price and the presence or absence of a motive for the sale. Table 2 contains the results.

It is clear that although the publication of the sales price is still highly correlated with abnormal returns to shareholders, a published statement of the motive for divestiture also plays an important role. The abnormal returns roughly double when the announcement discloses a motive for the sell-off—regardless of whether a sales price is given. For those cases when the sales price is given, the abnormal return increases from 2.3 percent to 3.92 percent when a motive for the sale is also announced.

Pursuing a somewhat different approach to this question, Gailen Hite and James Owers found that when previously announced proposals for sell-offs are cancelled, the divesting firms' stocks give up all of their earlier gains. Hite and Owers interpret this evidence as inconsistent with the hypothesis that the announced sell-off and sales price convey new information to the market about the subsidiary's true worth. If such information truly caused the market to revalue the shares, the selling company's stock would retain its price gain.

On the other hand, however, we find it somewhat hard to understand why *all* the gains are lost. For this seems to suggest that the market has ruled out almost all possibility of a sale in the future. At a minimum the market has learned from the proposal that the selling company is willing to sell the subsidiary. Perhaps the company's unsuccessful testing of the market demand for its assets means that a sale is simply a dead issue for the foreseeable future.

The explanation of this puzzle, as well as that posed by Klein's findings, will have to await further research.

V. Some Aggregate Data on Sell-Offs

Before concluding, let's look briefly at some general patterns of divestiture activity to see what such patterns suggest, if anything, about the corporate motives for selling off businesses.

Sell-offs, it turns out, can be divided into two categories: those associated with a previous merger and those that are not. We believe this breakdown is a useful one because of the evidence that so many divestitures are associated with previous mergers. As stated earlier, the ratio of divestitures to mergers has been about one to three. Figure 1 shows a plot of major combinations—mergers and acquisitions—and divestitures since 1963. These data show clearly the famous merger wave of the late 1960s, with a peak of over 6,000 mergers in 1969. There also is a divestiture wave that peaks in 1971 at almost 2,000 divestitures.

The fact that the divestiture curve has roughly the same shape as the merger curve, but displaced by several years, is no statistical accident. We converted the data to annual percentage changes (or rates of change) for each series and found a strong statistical relationship between the annual rate of change in merger activity in any given year, and the annual rate of change in divestitures *two years after*. In other words, if the rate of mergers jumps we expect that the rate of divestitures will rise sharply within one to two years thereafter. Conversely, if the merger rate declines we can predict that the divestiture rate will fall several years later.

One can also point to specific cases in which companies active in the merger area have also been active in the divestiture area. In the five years ending with 1982, such prominently acquisitive companies as ITT, Genesco, Beatrice Foods, and W.R. Grace had each no less than 12 divestitures.

Figure 1. Numbers of Mergers and Divestitures, 1963–1983.

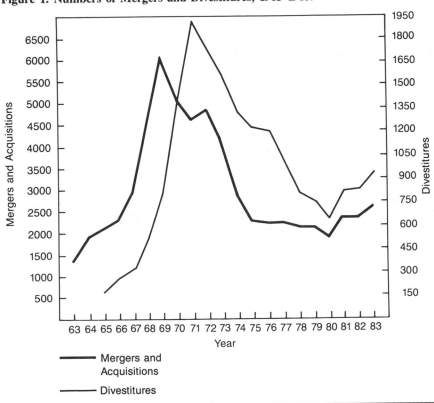

Source: W.T. Grumm & Co.

The performance of the stock market also appears to have a marginal relationship to the divestiture rate. Buyers and sellers of subsidiaries seem to transact more frequently when the market is high relative to historical levels. Using regression analysis, we found that in years when the stock market fell—such as 1966, 1969 and 1973–1974—the rate of divestiture fell below what one would have predicted given the previous merger rates; and when stocks performed well there was a tendency for more divestitures to occur. This relation was very strong during the period 1966–1977, but did not appear to hold during 1978–1982.[8] On balance, though, the data seem to show that the stock market environment, or perhaps the overall business environment as represented by the stock market, influences the rate of divestiture.

What does the relationship between divestitures and mergers tell us? On an aggregate basis, the fact that sell-offs increase within such a short time period after mergers suggests that acquiring companies quickly decide to "prune down"

8. Despite the fact that the stock market has risen in four of the last five years, the rates of divestiture have been less than what one would expect given the changes in the numbers of mergers. Perhaps this is just an artifact of the current depressed levels of both mergers and divestitures.

the companies they have bought or merged with. Indeed it is quite possible that they have the intention to do this even at the time of the merger. In other words, they may really wish to acquire only a part of the company they buy. And, for one reason or another, purchase of the entire company may have been the least costly way of obtaining the portion they wanted. Alternatively, merging companies may buy another firm with the idea that restructuring it will increase its productivity. The buyer's management may intend to carry out a reorganization that the previous management was unwilling to undertake. Still another possibility is that the bidder discovers after the acquisition that some pieces do not "fit" and would be worth more as part of some other company.

VI. Conclusion

The evidence suggests that voluntary sell-offs, on average, create value for divesting companies' stockholders. Some analysts explain the stockholder gains to selling firms by arguing that divestitures force the market to recognize the value of previously undervalued assets. But, while the jury may still be out on this question, the abundant testimony of modern finance to the efficiency of the market in pricing assets should cause us to view this argument with some skepticism.

A more plausible explanation of the stock price increases is that the divested assets are worth more to someone else than to the current owner, and that competition among firms for those assets allows the selling firm to obtain "economic rents" from the sale. Stockholder value may also be created, in some cases, by selling a unit whose continued presence is causing diseconomies or "negative synergy" in the selling firm.

A value-enhancing corporate policy, therefore, calls for continual review of the assets of the firm, assesssing both the internal effects of a unit's continued presence and the external market for these assets. The rules to guide such strategic thinking are fairly simple:

1. If an operation is worth more as part of some other company or companeis, then management should consider selling it.
2. Selling an unprofitable operation does not necessarily add value for stockholders. Buyers can be expected to come forth only if they see the opportunity to restore profitability, and earn a rate of return on their investment—the acquisition price—equal to or greater than their cost of capital. Although the sale itself may provide a positive signal to the market that management is paying greater attention to profitability, the economic value of the firm increases only if the sale price is greater than the value of the expected cash flows to the seller.
3. If no buyers are found, and the prospects for future profitability are dim, then the piecemeal liquidation of the operation's assets may be the best solution. In fact, as some of the research cited earlier by Gailen Hite suggests, some entire companies have proved to be worth more "dead than alive." There may be many others which would best serve their stockholders' interests by either partially or, in extreme cases, totally liquidating their assets.

VII. References

Alexander, Gordon J., George Benson and Joan M. Kampmeyer, "Investigating the Valuation Effects of Announcements of Voluntary Corporate Selloffs," *Journal of Finance*, 39 (1984), pp. 503–517.

Eckbo, Bjorn E., "Horizontal Mergers, Collusion and Stockholder Wealth," *Journal of Financial Economics*, 11 (1983), pp. 241–274.

Ellert, James C., "Mergers, Antitrust Law Enforcement and the Behavior of Stock Prices," *Journal of Finance*, 31 (1976), pp. 715–732.

Hite, Gailen L. and James E. Owers, "Corporate Asset Divestitures: Implications for Buyers and Sellers," Southern Methodist University (1984).

Klein, April, "Voluntary Corporate Divestitures: Motives and Consequences," University of Chicago (1983).

Kummer, Donald R., "Valuation Consequences of Forced Divestiture Announcements," *Journal of Economics and Business* (1978), pp. 130–136.

Linn, Scott C., and Michael S. Rozeff, "The Effects of Voluntary Spinoffs on Stock Prices: The Anergy Hypothesis," *Advances in Financial Planning and Forecasting*, 1 (1984).

Linn, Scott C., and Michael S. Rozeff, "The Effect of Voluntary Divestiture on Stock Prices: Sales of Subsidiaries," University of Iowa (1984).

Rosenfeld, James D., "Additional Evidence on the Relationship Between Divestiture Announcements and Shareholder Wealth," Emory University (1984).

Stillman, Robert, "Examining Antitrust Policy Towards Horizontal Mergers," *Journal of Financial Economics*, 11 (1983), pp. 225–240.

Wier, Peggy, "The Costs of Antimerger Lawsuits: Evidence from the Stock Market," *Journal of Financial Economics*, 11 (1983), pp. 207–224.

9

The Corporate Spin-Off Phenomenon

Katherine Schipper
University of Chicago

Abbie Smith
University of Chicago

Introduction

With a frequency that seems ever increasing, the financial press reports shareholder or management proposals based on the premise that some companies are worth more divided than whole. Trans World Corporation and Gulf Oil Corporation offer two recent examples. In February 1984, after shareholders rejected a proposal to split Trans World Corporation into as many as five companies, the airline business (TWA) was separated from the rest of the firm through a public offering of a minority interest in TWA, followed by a spin-off of the remaining shares. One motive offered for the spin-off was that the airline's losses might otherwise "swamp" Trans World's profitable units—which include Hilton International, Canteen Corporation and Century 21.[1] Several analysts also predicted that both Trans World Corporation and TWA would be more valuable apart than combined. Two reasons were given. First, because the airline's unions would henceforth not be able to point to the profits of other divisions as a source of subsidies to airline operations, the airline would be better able to extract concessions from its unions. Second, it was argued that some of the other divisions were in industries that command relatively high price-earnings multiples, and that association with the airline was causing the earnings from these industries to be capitalized at a lower multiple.[2]

---

1. See "Trans World Corporation's Plan to Spin-off TWA was Prompted by Fears on Losses," *Wall Street Journal*, October 28, 1983.
2. See "Trans World, Soon to be Shorn of its Airline, Appears to Offer More Attractive Prospects," *Wall Street Journal*, December 30, 1983.

In the case of Gulf Oil, the proposal was to create a royalty trust and spin off the shares to the current owners of Gulf. The proposal was based on a study that claimed the royalty trust might result in a package of securities with market value nearly 60 percent larger than Gulf's then current equity value.[3]

It is probably too soon to evaluate the effects on shareholders of the spin-off of TWA by Trans World. And, given the defeat of Boone Pickens's proposal for a royalty trust (not to mention the recent takeover of Gulf by SOCAL), we will never know how the Gulf proposal would have worked out. Nevertheless, there have been enough corporate spin-offs in the last twenty years to allow us an at least preliminary answer to the question: Is the whole ever worth *less* than the sum of its parts? And if the answer is yes, then the obvious question arises. Why? What are the benefits to shareholders from such "negative mergers?"

On the basis of three empirical studies of the shareholder wealth effects of voluntary spin-off announcements, the answer to the first question appears to be yes.[4] The real cause of this consistently positive market reaction, however, is not always clear. Some spin-offs hold out the promise of significant tax or regulatory advantages. But, for the majority of these transactions, the benefits are much more elusive. A spin-off, after all, merely creates two (or more) companies where before there was one, generally without any obvious major operating or managerial changes (the kind of changes that financial economists like to designate as "real" as opposed, say, to changes produced by financial or accounting sleights of hand). Some analysts have argued that spin-offs enable the market to assess the real worth of assets whose value have become obscured by the complexities of conglomerate corporate structures. But, to believers in efficient markets, the systematic gains to shareholders at the time of spin-off announcements continue to be something of a mystery.

In this article, we review the available evidence documenting the market's response to spin-offs. But before turning to the results of the studies, and the light they cast on this market enigma, we start by explaining what a spin-off is, and how it differs from the other forms of corporate restructuring that have recently begun to proliferate. Then we discuss some of the professed corporate motives for spin-offs, offering what we believe are the most plausible explanations for the market's positive reaction. Finally, we present and interpret the results of our own study of the stock market's response to 93 voluntary spin-off announcements between 1963 and 1981.

---

3. See "Pickens' Mesa Group, Gulf Wage Stiff Campaigns for Proxy Victory," *Wall Street Journal*, November 23, 1983.

4. See G. Hite and J. Owers, "Security Price Reactions around Corporate Spin-off Announcements," *Journal of Financial Economics*, December 1983; J. Miles and J. Rosenfeld, "The Effects of Voluntary Spin-off Announcements on Shareholder Wealth," *Journal of Finance*, December 1983; K. Schipper and A. Smith, "Effects of Recontracting on Shareholder Wealth: The Case of Voluntary Spin-offs," *Journal of Financial Economics*, December 1983.

II. What is a Spin-off?

There are several ways in which a firm can be partly or completely separated into two or more parts. We will restrict our focus here to "pure" voluntary corporate spin-offs. In such spin-offs, management distributes shares of a subsidiary, usually pro rata, to the shareholders of the parent company as a dividend in kind. Hence the spin-off does not alter shareholders' proportional ownership of the subsidiary and the parent. The spin-off does, however, separate the common stock of the parent and subsidiary companies for subsequent trading.

The term "spin-off" is also sometimes used by the business press to describe a variety of corporate structural changes which differ from the spin-off as defined above. Spin-offs are often confused, for example, with divestitures. In a divestiture (as described in the article immediately preceding), the divesting firm sells a set of net assets to another firm, and is generally paid in cash or marketable securities (sometimes including stock of the buying firm).

Spin-offs should also be contrasted with "split-ups," in which a firm separates into several parts, distributes the stock of these parts to its shareholders and ceases to exist. And both spin-offs and split-ups can be further distinguished from "split-offs," in which stock of a subsidiary is distributed to one or more of the parent firm's shareholders in exchange for their parent company stock. A "split-up" can be structured to have the same consequences as a spin-off, that is, the emergence of two separate firms with the same owners. A "split-off," however, alters ownership because some shareholders exchange ownership of the parent for ownership of the subsidiary.

Finally, the term "spin-off" is also sometimes applied to financing arrangements in which a parent firm offers a percentage of the shares of a subsidiary for public sale. These public offerings generally differ from spin-offs in that effective control of the subsidiary is maintained by the parent. Also unlike spin-offs, such partial public offerings generate a cash inflow from the sale of the minority interest.

Spin-offs can be either taxable as dividends or tax-free. By "tax free" we mean that shareholders receive shares of the subsidiary but pay no tax until the shares are sold. For a spin-off to be tax free, Section 355 of the tax code requires that there be a business purpose, as opposed to tax avoidance, for the spin-off. It also requires that both the subsidiary and parent be actively engaged in some business for at least five years preceding the spin-off, that the subsidiary be at least 80-percent owned by the parent, and that the parent distribute all its subsidiary securities without a pre-arranged plan for these securities to be resold.

Because a spin-off can be regarded as simply another form of stock dividend, the SEC has not always required registration of the stock distributed in a spin-off. But during the late 1960s, there were allegations that private companies were using "shell corporations" and spin-offs to go public without SEC registration. Specifically, a private company could merge with a public "shell" and then arrange to have its stock distributed to the shareholders of the "shell." Through this process, the once private firm could have its shares traded in the over-the-counter market without registration. The popularity of this mechanism was evidenced by the appearance in the *Wall Street Journal*, between July 15 and October 10 of 1969, of 25 advertisements to buy, and 19 advertisements to sell, such corporate shells.[5]

The SEC responded by effectively requiring registration of stock issued in spin-offs. Furthermore, the Commission suspended trading and even sued certain firms for violations of the Securities Acts. Thus, there was a shift in the regulatory environment during 1969–70 which resulted in more disclosure about firms engaged in spin-offs. This shift was probably most noticeable in the over-the-counter market.

Our attention, however, will be directed mainly to spin-offs by American and New York Stock Exchange companies. The motive for spin-off described above, and the resulting regulatory reaction, do not seem to be central to the resurgence of spin-offs we have witnessed in the past few years. Nor do they appear to have influenced the market response to spin-offs by NYSE and ASE firms reported in academic studies.

III. Possible Sources of Shareholder Gains from Spin-offs

Several explanations have been offered for the stock price increases associated, on average, with voluntary spin-off announcements. One of the most straightforward is that shareholder gains arise from creditor losses. As developed by Dan Galai and Ron Masulis,[6] this hypothesis contends that parent firm bondholders lose in a spin-off because they have no claim on the assets which are spun off solely to stockholders. This reduction in bondholders' collateral implies a transfer of wealth from bondholders to stockholders.

Galai and Masulis point out, however, that any redistribution of wealth from bondholders to stockholders would be reduced to the extent that spin-offs are anticipated by bondholders. In fact, contractual arrangements existing prior to the spin-off may make the Galai-Masulis argument irrelevant. If the spun-off entity is legally separate from the parent (that is, a subsidiary as opposed to, say, a division), the debts of the parent and the entity to be spun-off are also legally separate *before* the spin-off. Creditors of one legal entity thus have no claim on the assets of the other, unless such a claim is provided for in the indenture agreement.

Also casting doubt on Galai and Masulis's hypothesis is their implicit assumption that debt is *not* assigned to the spun-off entity. In practice, debt is often transferred to the subsidiary in a spin-off. Depending on what debt is spun off, the original creditors of the parent may actually benefit from—or at worst will be unaffected by—such a spin-off. For example, what was junior debt of the total company before the spin-off sometimes becomes senior debt of either the spun-off company or the parent. In such a case, bondholders would have a claim with higher priority, but on a smaller asset base, than before. The expected net effect of such a spin-off

5. See A. Hershman, "The Spin-off: One Minus One Equals Three?" *Dun's Review*, March 1969, and L. Orlanski, "Going Public Through the Back Door and the Shell Game," *Virginia Law Review*, 1972.
6. D. Galai and R. Masulis, "The Option Pricing Model and the Risk Factor of Stock," *Journal of Financial Economics*, 1976.

on the value of that debt would be uncertain—possibly negative, possibly positive. Most important, however, many bond covenants contain provisions which limit dividends and forbid asset dispositions of any kind. Because spin-offs are dividends in kind and are also considered asset dispositions, they are subject to the usual constraints that creditors write into debt covenants.

Tax and Regulatory Advantages

A second possible source of shareholder gains from spin-offs lies in their expected effects on taxes, and on regulatory or legal constraints that bind the firm. Three examples follow.

1. After a spin-off, one or both of the "new" companies' tax or regulatory status may differ from that of the original firm. Companies with certain types of assets can take advantage of the tax code by spinning off those assets. Prime examples include the formation and spin-off of REIT's and natural resource royalty trusts. These trusts pay no income taxes and pay 90 percent of their income as dividends to shareholders. The 1980 Annual Report of Southland Royalty, for instance, makes the statement that its royalty trusts "were created in order to afford shareholders a more advantageous method of participating in ownership of Southland's long-lived producing oil and gas properties," and goes on to describe the tax-saving mechanism in some detail. Royalty trusts thus allow oil and gas producers to shelter much of their income from taxation while, at the same time, allowing them to retain direct ownership of the oil and gas reserves (which, of course, allows shareholders to benefit from unexpected increases in oil and gas prices).[7]

2. If a parent spins off a regulated utility subsidiary, ratemaking commissions may grant rate increases sooner, or grant larger rate increases, than otherwise because the spun-off utility can no longer be subsidized by cash flow from unregulated operations. This motive was explicitly stated in the 1980 Annual Report of the Philadelphia Suburban Corporation:

   > First of all, we think there has been some confusion on the part of the public and the regulatory authorities over the needs of the water company when viewed against the success of the unregulated portions of the company. There have been repeated suggestions that the water company derives significant benefits from its association with [the unregulated portion of the business]—benefits which should be reflected in lower rates.

   Southern Union offers another example of a firm spinning off a poorly performing regulated business to prevent cross-subsidization by profitable business lines. In 1982, the company's New Mexico gas utility was earning as low as 2.5 percent on its equity base, and there was speculation that the utility would be spun off to strengthen the utility's appeal for rate relief.[8]

---

7. See D. Levin, "Royalty Trusts, an Issue in the Gulf Oil Dispute, Seen Drawing Those Who Expect Oil Price Rise," *Wall Street Journal*, October 21, 1983.

8. See G. Anders, "Southern Union Draws Investor Interest on Belief Utility Spinoff Will Boost Parent's Earnings," *Wall Street Journal*, April 14, 1982.

3. A parent that spins off a foreign subsidiary enables that subsidiary to circumvent restrictions placed by Congress on U.S. fims operating abroad. For example, Sea Containers' 1974 Annual Report described its reason for the spin-off of a foreign subsidiary as follows:

> We do not pay bribes nor do we conceal the true nature of our expenses. We do pay our agents commissions and fees in 41 countries in connection with the business they generate for us. We are genuinely concerned that the outcome of the current revelations of questionable payments abroad by U.S. companies will be regulation by Congress of companies which operate the way we do, and this could again make us uncompetitive with foreigners.... We feel the best defense is to segregate out a portion of our foreign activities and separate [that portion] from Sea Containers Inc. to allow the former to grow in overseas markets without interference by the whims of the U.S. government.

Changes in Managerial Focus, Accountability and Incentives

The tax and regulatory advantages described above are probably significant for only a small portion of the companies spinning off business units. What accounts, then, for other spin-offs—those which seem to have been prompted neither by taxes nor regulatory concerns?

Among the most popular explanations for the positive stock market reaction to spin-offs is the notion that investors have a predilection for the "pure play." That is, investors are better able to understand and evaluate single-industry stocks; accordingly, they pay higher prices for companies as separate entities than as parts of diversified firms. Or, put, somewhat differently, investors have apositive distaste for the complexity of conglomerates, and thus systematically discount their values.[9]

Such an argument, however, seems to run against the grain of efficient markets theory. In a sophisticated market, with its incentives to identify undervalued companies, there are enough analysts adept at untangling consolidated financial statements to ensure that conglomerates will trade at fair value. We shouldn't expect diversified companies to sell consistently below a value which reflects the sum of the values of their component businesses simply because the market is incapable of understanding them.

There may indeed by a systematic investor preference for "pure plays." But such a preference, we suspect, reflects less the inability of analysts to comprehend conglomerates than the markets' skepticism about the quality of management decision-making, controls and incentives in large, sprawling organizations. In short, investors may be unsure about how well diversified firms are being managed. If there are management inefficiences that result from the conglomerate form *per se*, then the market may systematically assign higher prices to the parts

---

9. See M. Greenebaum, "Making the Most of Unnoticed Assets," *Fortune*, June 15, 1981.

when separated than combined. This explanation, moreover, is completely consistent with the information efficiency of the stock market.[10]

Some recent work in accounting and finance has focused attention on the potential improvements in managerial incentives from "disentangling" the performance of the segments of a company. This line of research highlights management incentive and performance problems that can arise when managers are spread too thin, are trying to operate several highly disparate segments, or when the exceptional performance of a given segment is lost in the consolidated financial statements. And, as this research would suggest, spin-offs may offer the most direct solution to these problems. By reducing the number and complexity of operations under a single management group, spin-offs may promise major improvements in management's efficiency in employing assets. The simplification of information flows may allow managers to exert tighter control over existing operations, and to allocate the resources of the firm more effectively.

Some Casual Evidence

In the course of our own research, we found that 19 of the 93 companies in our sample offered explanations for their spin-offs which support the idea that removing a poor business "fit" and sharpening the corporate focus is expected to improve management's productivity. For example, in 1981 Itek Corporation spun off its eyeglass-manufacturing business, Camelot Industries Corporation, from its defense electronics and graphics business. The attention Itek's management devoted to the struggling eyeglass division prior to the spin-off apparently detracted from Itek's other operations. Mistakes such as gross overstocking of inventory in its graphics division and cost overruns in its government-contract business might have been avoided in the absence of the demands placed on management by the vision products division.[11] In the 1981 Annual Report, Itek's management reported:

> With the separation of vision products, Itek is once again entirely a high technology company. While the separation of vision products was costly, we are now in a position to totally dedicate our efforts and resources where Itek has expertise and leadership.

Besides eliminating some of the distractions inherent in a diversified enterprise, a spin-off may also improve efficiency by strengthening managers' incentives to act in the shareholders' interests. Because a spin-off separates the parent and the spun-off subsidiary, it allows for a more effective evaluation and control of managerial performance in each business. For example, a spun-off subsidiary, as an independent public firm, will issue complete, audited financial statements. Before the spin-off the subsidiary's operating results are buried in consolidated statements or, at most, given only partial disclosure as a business segment.

---

10. "Information efficiency" means that the stock price of a firm fully reflects all public information.
11. See "Itek: Shedding Its Eyeglass Division and Focusing on High-Tech Lines," *Business Week*, November 8, 1982.

The other gauge of performance that a spin-off makes possible is the stock price of the spun-off subsidiary. Stock prices reflect the collective judgment of investors about management's effectiveness in employing corporate assets. To the extent that executives' rewards can be linked to their companies' stock prices, the capital market can be used to monitor executives' actions.[12]

Some kind of incentive scheme, whether tied to stock prices or, more likely, to accounting results, was found to exist in most of the firms spinning off subsidiaires *before* the spin-off was announced. But the incentive effects of such compensation arrangements are typically diluted in diversified firms. The influence of a particular segment's operations on corporate income and share price is presented together with the results of other units, often operating in different industries. By "unbundling" these effects, a spin-off can improve managerial accountability, and stock options and stock purchase plans can provide a very effective means of motivating subsidiary management by providing a much more direct link between managerial performance, share prices, and management rewards.

The improvement of managerial incentives as a motive for spin-off was stated explicitly by six of the firms in our sample. For example, the president's letter to shareholders in the 1980 Annual Report of Peabody International describes the incentive effects of Peabody's spin-off of GEO International:

> Speaking from personal experience, one of the most exciting benefits has been a rekindling of the entrepreneurial spirit and initiative within both Peabody and GEO. Managers in both companies now feel that their individual efforts can make a significant difference in bottom line results.

Similarly, the management of Valmac Industries cited the improvement of incentives in both firms as a motive for spinning off Distribuco, its food distribution subsidiary:

> The poultry processing business has been subject to seasonal and cyclical fluctuations and the cotton merchandising business is subject to cyclical fluctuations also, some of which are beyond the control of management, while the food division business is somewhat more constant and is not subject to such external factors.

> The corporate separation will enable the management of both companies to more clearly measure results of efforts of employees of each company, and to provide an incentive, through stock options, stock purchase plans, and through direct payments to reward the efforts.

> —1974 Annual Report

---

12. The importance of stock price as a measure of performance in contracting with managers is discussed in E. Fama and M. Jensen, "Separation of Ownership and Control," *Journal of Law and Economics*, June 1983 and in D. Diamond and R. Verrecchia, "Optimal Managerial Contracts and Equilibrium Security Prices," *Journal of Finance*, May 1982.

IV. The Evidence on the Shareholder Effects of Spin-Offs

To measure the effects of spin-offs on shareholders, we estimated the "abnormal return" (the return over and above that expected from market movements) to common stock of 93 firms that announced voluntary spin-offs between 1963 and 1981. Over the two-day period including the day before and the day of the spin-off announcement, shareholders earned abnormal positive returns of 2.84 percent. (Standard statistical tests indicate a confidence level of 99 percent associated with this result.) Sixty-one announcements were associated with positive abnormal returns, 51 with returns of at least 1.0 percent. Moreover, the size of the abnormal return was associated with the relative size of the subsidiary being spun off; that is, larger spin-offs (relative to the size of the company) resulted in larger abnormal returns. Similar results were also obtained by Gailen Hite and Jim Owers (1983) for a sample of 123 spin-offs, and by Jim Miles and Jim Rosenfeld (1983) for a sample of 55 spin-offs. Both of these studies also report that larger shareholder gains are associated with the spin-off of larger subsidiaries (where size is measured in terms of equity values relative to the parent firm).

The Bondholder Rip-off Revisited

As suggested, one potential source of these gains are the bondholder losses resulting from the wealth transfer mechanism described earlier. A transfer of wealth from bondholders to shareholders would be caused by an unanticipated reduction in bondholders' collateral. A wealth transfer upon a spin-off announcement is much less likely, however, if (1) the spun-off firm already exists as a legal subsidiary: (2) bondholders' collateral is protected by a debt covenant constraint on dividends; or (3) debt is allocated to both parent and subsidiary.

We attempted to determine the extent to which these conditions were present in our sample of companies, and our findings were as follows:

- Of 82 spun-off subsidiaries for which there was information available, 27 were created at the time of the spin-off from divisions that had not been legally separate. The rest were subsidiaries established or acquired more than a year in advance, or formed from existing subsidiaries.
- General dividend constraints or specific requirements that lenders approve spin-offs were known to exist for 34 sample firms. However, the nature of debt covenants could not be identified for about half the sample.
- Finally, debt was assigned to subsidiaries in at least 64 of the 93 sample spin-offs. The mean ratio of the book value of debt to total assets for 45 of these 64 spun-off subsidiaries (again, those for which information was available) was .51. The range of debt to assets for this subsample was .03 to .89.

To gain more direct evidence on the effect of spin-offs on bondholders, we also examined bond price and bond rating changes around spin-off announcements. If the market's positive reaction to spin-offs was the result of wealth transfers from creditors to shareholders, then we would expect spin-off announcements to lead to declines in both bond prices and ratings. Of the 62 spin-off announcements associated with gains to shareholders, we were able to obtain price data for 26 bonds of 13 firms. For only 11 of these 26 bonds was there evidence of a decline in value upon the announcement.

We found ratings for 19 bonds of 16 firms. Only two bonds (both of the same firm) experienced a decline in bond rating during the year after the spin-off announcement.

Needless to say, our results are not suggestive of a widespread reduction in bondholder collateral caused by spin-offs. Furthermore, this finding is supported by results of Gailen Hite and Jim Owers, who actually find *positive* risk-adjusted returns (though not statistically significant) to bondholders at the time of spin-off announcements.

The Evidence on Tax- and Regulatory-Motivated Spin-Offs

Eighteen, or nearly 20 percent of our 93 sample firms stated motives for spin-offs consistent with the realization of tax or regulatory advantages. The average abnormal return to shareholders of these 18 firms was a positive 5.07 percent, nearly twice that of the entire sample. These spin-offs, however, do not account for the total gains to the sample; that is, they are not "driving" the average results. (This statement is based on a standard test for differences in shareholder gains between the "tax-regulatory" subsample of 18 announcements, and the rest of the sample.) While regulation and taxation provide powerful motives for certain companies to spin off a subset of their net assets, relatively few firms have the special characteristics necessary to realize tax and regulatory benefits from a spin-off. To repeat, such tax and regulatory benefits arise primarily from the special tax treatment accorded real estate investment trusts and royalty trusts; from removing the possibility that a rate-regulated utility may be subsidized by the operations of a nonregulated business; and from removing legal and tax restrictions on the actions of U.S. firms operating abroad.

Some Indirect Evidence on the Management Efficiency Hypothesis

We have also speculated that separating a firm into two or more segments may increase management efficiency by allowing managers to concentrate on a single line of business. The opportunity for such efficiency gains would be most likely to exist in companies with complex operations. In order to provide a crude test of this hypothesis, we reasoned that, among our sample of spin-off companies, we should expect to find a disproportionate number where there has been a past increase in the complexity of the firm's operations, as measured by the number and diversity of businesses to be managed. In fact, we found that our sample of spin-off firms is characterized both by diversity of operations and by recent expansion. For the average firm, over the five years before the spin-off announcement, sales (adjusted for inflation) grew at an annual rate of 20 percent, and the number of employees grew at a rate of 19 percent.[13] Also, more significantly, in 72 of the 93 spin-offs we examined, the parent and its spun-off subsidiary were in different industries. This is perhaps the strongest evidence we have that the desire to segregate distinct business lines, presumably for reasons of improved management efficiency (although the possibility of market undervaluation of conglomerate assets cannot be ruled out), is behind the recent spin-off movement.[14]

V. Closing Remarks

We have documented a statistically significant positive average share price reaction for a sample of 93 voluntary spin-off announcements on the American and New York Stock Exchanges between 1963 and 1981. There are, we think, three plausible explanations of this favorable market response: (1) tax savings; (2) loosening of regulatory constraints; and (3) improvements in managerial efficiency, accountability and incentives brought about by reducing the number of diversity of operations under one management. We also consider, though mainly to dismiss, the explanation that such gains to shareholders represent wealth transfers from bondholders. There is little evidence to suggest that spin-offs consistently cause unanticipated reductions in bondholder collateral.

A good number of the spin-offs in our sample (at least 18 of the 93) seem clearly to have been motivated by expected tax or regulatory advantages. The most common tax advantages arise from the formation and spin-off of REITs and natural resource royalty trusts, both of which continue to be exempt from corporate income tax (though legislation rumblings about such "loopholes" are now faintly audible).

Finally, spin-offs may improve management efficiency by sharpening focus and strengthening incentives. Breaking off a single segment from a diversified enterprise frees the segment managers and the parent firm managers to concentrate on fewer lines of business. The segment can operate and be evaluated independently of the parent's operations. Spin-offs also allow for a much more direct link between segment managers' efforts and corporate results, whether measured in terms of reported net income or, perhaps more important, the share price of the spun-off business. Investors' apparent willingness to pay more for the firm divided than whole may, in many cases, reflect their judgment that each of the parts, because simpler, will be better managed.

---

13. As a benchmark, we computed growth rates in inflation-adjusted sales and number of employees for a random sample of non-spin-off firms (over the same time periods as for the spin-off sample). The growth rates are 13 percent (sales) and 7 percent (employees).

14. Nine of the twenty-one "similar" parent-subsidiary spin-offs were probably intended to relax regulatory or tax constraints. Of these, three spun off a foreign subsidiary. An additional six separated a natural resource royalty trust from an operating company or separated a regulated natural resource firm from an unregulated one.

VI. References

Baiman, S. and J. Demski, "Economically Optimal Performance Evaluation and Control Systems," *Journal of Accounting Research*, 18 (1980), Supplement, pp. 184–220.

Coase, R.H., "The Nature of the Firm," *Economica* IV (1937), pp. 386–405, Reprinted in: *Readings in Price Theory*, 1952 (Irwin, Homewood, IL).

Diamond, D. and R. Verrecchia, "Optimal Managerial Contracts and Equilibrium Security Prices," *Journal of Finance*, 37, May 1982, pp. 275–287.

Eger, C. "An Empirical Test of the Redistribution Effect in Pure Exchange Mergers," Unpublished working paper (1982), (Stanford University, Stanford, CA).

Fama, E. and M. Jensen, "Separation of Ownership and Control," *Journal of Law and Economics*, June 1983, 301–325.

Galai, D. and R. Masulis, "The Option Pricing Model and the Risk Factor of Stock," *Journal of Financial Economics* 3, nos. 1–2, Jan/March 1976, pp. 53–82.

Hershman, A., "The Spin-off: One Minus One Equals Three?," *Duns Review* 93, no. 3, March 1969, pp. 31–33.

Hite, G. and J. Owers, "Security Price Reactions Around Corporate Spin-off Announcements," *Journal of Financial Economics*, Vol. 12 (1983).

Jensen, M. and W. Meckling, "Theory of the Firm: Managerial Behavior, Agency Costs and Ownership Structure," *Journal of Financial Economics* 3, no. 4, Oct. 1976, pp. 305–360.

Klein, A., "Voluntary Corporate Divestitures: Motives and Consequences," Unpublished Ph.D. dissertation, June 1983, (University of Chicago, Chicago, IL).

Miles, J. and J. Rosenfeld, "An Empirical Analysis of the Effects of Spin-off Announcements on Shareholder Wealth," *Journal of Finance*, (1983).

Mishkin, W., ed., *Techniques in Corporate Reorganization* (Presidents Publishing House, New York) (1972).

Orlanski, L., "Going Public Through the Back Door and the Shell Game," *Virginia Law Review* 58, no. 8 (1972), pp. 1451–1487.

Schipper, K. and R. Thompson, "Evidence on the Capitalized Value of Merger Activity for Acquiring Firms," *Journal of Financial Economics* 11, nos. 1–4, April 1983, pp. 85–120.

10

Equity Carve-Outs

Katherine Schipper
University of Chicago

Abbie Smith
University of Chicago

Late in 1981 Condec Corporation filed a prospectus describing a plan to sell to the public slightly over 20 percent of the equity in its wholly-owned subsidiary, Unimation, Inc. In this "equity carve-out" (also known as a "partial public offering"), Condec sold 1.05 million common shares of Unimation at $23 each, thereby raising $22.5 million in new equity capital (after fees and expenses). The purpose of the offering, as stated in the prospectus, was to use "$19.4 million to repay all [of Unimation's] outstanding long-term indebtedness to Condec, and the remainder to provide working capital." The market's response to Condec's announcement resulted in a 19 percent stock price increase (after taking account of market movements).

Why did Condec choose this relatively unusual method of raising capital instead of, say, selling more of its own common equity? Why, furthermore, did the market respond so favorably to the announcement of the offering—especially since announcements of common stock offerings generally signal bad news to investors?

In this article, we attempt to provide answers to these questions based on our own recently published study of 76 equity carve-out announcements by New York and American Stock Exchange companies over the period 1965–1983.[1] Our study finds, in brief, that the stockholders of parent companies earn on average almost 2 percent positive market-adjusted returns during the five-day period surrounding announcements of the carve-outs—and almost 5 percent if an additional two weeks

---

1. See Katherine Schipper and Abbie Smith, "A Comparison of Equity Carve-outs and Seasoned Equity Offerings: Share Price Effects and Corporate Restructuring," *Journal of Financial Economics* 15 (1986), pp. 153–186.

preceding the announcement are included. In contrast, the stock prices of companies announcing seasoned equity offerings fall some 3 percent or more, on average, around the time of announcement, and announcements of convertible debt offerings provoke an average negative reaction of 1 or 2 percent. Thus, according to the findings of recent research, equity carve-outs represent the only form of new equity financing by public companies which results, on average, in an increase in shareholder wealth.

I. The Popular Argument

One popular explanation for the positive market reaction to equity carve-out announcements is that carve-outs allow investors to evaluate exceptional corporate growth opportunities on a stand-alone basis. This explanation would imply that Condec, a large, defense-oriented conglomerate, decided to carve out 20 percent of Unimation, a robot manufacturer, to reinforce the market's perception of the value of that subsidiary and thus, presumably, to increase the market's valuation of Condec, as a whole. As another example, MGM/UA's 1982 carve-out of its Home Entertainment Group has been described as a means of "cash[ing] in on the craving of investors for a share in what may become an enormous market for pay television and home videos."[2] Commenting on this same transaction, an analyst at Bear Stearns stated that such a partial public offering provided "a way for studios to enhance their own valuations and for investors to get a piece of the fast-growing market [for home video]."[3]

The assumption underlying this explanation seems to be that investors are attracted to subsidiary growth opportunities when these are isolated from the consolidated entity (that is, available for separate purchase). By creating a separate public market for Unimation's common stock, the popular argument seems to run, the carve-out allowed Condec to benefit by allowing direct investment in the growth opportunities of the robot subsidiary.

A variant of this popular argument holds that investors might value a specific investment opportunity more highly when set apart from a conglomerate if and when it offers them a scarce commodity; that is, a so-called "pure play." It might be difficult for investors to invest in, say, stand-alone public robotics manufacturers. (Such an advantage is likely to last only as long as there are few "pure plays" around.) This variant is illustrated, in the case of Unimation, by the following analysis:

> The Unimation offering is among the first opportunities for substantial investment in the growing robot industry and it attracted considerable interest when it was announced last month. Most robotics companies that are publicly traded over the counter are too small to attract major investors. (*Wall Street Journal*, November 27, 1981)

---

2. From "The Old Razzle-Dazzle," *Forbes*, February 14, 1985, pp. 43–44.
3. From "MGM/UA Movie-distributing Unit's Rise Has Other Studios Studying Its Strategy," *Wall Street Journal*, October 21, 1983.

In this article, we argue that although equity carve-outs may indeed create securities which have scarcity value, there are also other explanations for the market's positive response to partial public offerings. First of all, equity carve-outs may overcome the problem of the information gap between insiders and investors that attends all seasoned equity offerings. They may also provide more information to the market about the subsidiary, thereby stimulating new investor demand (not to mention the interest of potential corporate acquirers). Perhaps more important, however, is that although the parent company generally retains a majority interest in the "carved-out" subsidiary, equity carve-outs are often accompanied by important changes in management responsibilities and incentive contracts. Expected improvements in performance from changes in managerial accountability and incentives may partially explain the market's positive reaction.

In the pages that follow we shall explain more precisely what an equity carve-out is, and how it differs from and resembles both spin-offs and seasoned equity offerings. We then review our own recent research on carve-outs, and discuss differences between equity carve-outs and conventional parent equity offerings that might account for the systematically negative response to the latter and the generally positive response to the former. Last, we take a look at what happens to subsidiaries after they have had partial public offerings. Seldom do carved-out subsidiaries remain unchanged for very long, with the public simply maintaining its minority interest in the firm. Instead they are generally either reacquired by the parent, completely spunoff, acquired by management through an LBO, or acquired by some other firm. We attempt to make sense of these developments.

II. The Market Reaction to Related Events: Seasoned Equity Offerings and Spin-Offs

An equity carve-out resembles a primary offering of seasoned stock in that cash is received from the investing public. Several recent studies of the market's response to seasoned equity offerings have confirmed average negative returns to stockholders of 2 to 3 percent over the two-day period surround the announcement of the issue.[4]

---

4. The share price reaction of NYSE and ASE listed firms to an announcement of a public offering of seasoned common stock is the subject of the following published studies, all of which appeared in Volume 15 (1986) of the *Journal of Financial Economics*; Ronald Masulis and Ashok Korwar, "Seasoned Equity Offerings: An Empirical Investigation"; Paul Asquith and David Mullins, "Equity Issues and Offering Dilution"; and Wayne Mikkelson and Megan Partch, "Valuation Effects of Security Offerings and the Issuance Process." The share price reactions to public offerings of convertible debt claims on NYSE and ASE listed firms were examined by Larry Dann and Wayne Mikkelson in "Convertible Debt Issuance, Capital Structure Change and Financing-Related Information: Some New Evidence," *Journal of Financial Economics* 13 (1984). The results of these studies are as follows: For offerings by industrial firms, a statistically significant negative average abnormal stock return of 2 or 3 percent is documented in the two-day period ending with the *Wall Street Journal* announcement date. In the case of equity offerings by public utilities, the return is smaller (less than one percent), but still negative and statistically significant. Furthermore, a negative average share price effect of an increase in outstanding common equity through exchange offers and conversion of debt to common stock is documented

In addition, our own study of carve-outs found that for those companies which had a seasoned common stock offering within five years of a carve-out, the average price reaction to the parent stock offering was −3.5 percent over the five-day period ending with the announcement.

Many of the features which distinguish a subsidiary equity offering from a seasoned equity offering represent similarities with a voluntary spin-off.[5] In a spin-off, distinct equity claims of a wholly-owned subsidiary are distributed as a dividend to the consolidated entity's shareholders and begin to trade in public equity markets. Thus, in both spin-offs and equity carve-outs, a subsidiary's equity claims begin to trade separately from equity claims on the consolidated entity. Studies of the market reaction to announcements of corporate spin-offs all document positive abnormal returns of about 3 percent in the two-day period ending with the *Wall Street Journal* announcement date.[6]

A subsidiary equity offering differs in two respects from a corporate spin-off. First, as mentioned, whereas in a spin-off the subsidiary stock is distributed to the existing shareholders of the consolidated entity, the equity carve-out is a sale of subsidiary stock which raises new capital. Second, in a spin-off the parent company typically relinquishes control over the subsidiary by distributing all of the subsidiary stock. In an equity carve-out, the parent company typically does not relinquish control over the subsidiary; instead a public minority interest is created. Because a subsidiary equity offering partly resembles both a seasoned equity

---

by the following studies: Ron Masulis, "The Effects of Capital Structure Changes on Security Prices," Unpublished doctoral dissertation, University of Chicago, 1978; and Wayne Mikkelson, "Convertible Calls and Security Returns," *Journal of Financial Economics* 9 (1981).

Conversely, evidence exists that an increase in share price is associated with a *reduction* in outstanding common equity through repurchases of shares and exchange offers; Larry Dann, "Common Stock Repurchases: An Analysis of Returns to Bondholders and Stockholders," *Journal of Financial Economics* 9 (1981); Ron Masulis, "Stock Repurchase by Tender Offer: An Analysis of the Causes of Common Stock Price Changes, *Journal of Finance* 35 (1980), pp. 305–319, (as well as the Ph.D. dissertation cited above); and Theo Vermaelen, "Common Stock Repurchases and Market Signalling: An Empirical Study," *Journal of Financial Economics* 9 (1981). Thus, the evidence suggests that an increase in outstanding equity is associated on average with a decrease in stock price, and a decrease in equity is associated with an increase in stock price.

5. A subsidiary equity offering also resembles a divestiture in that cash is received. However, a divestiture does not in general initiate the trading of subsidiary stock. Two studies (G. Alexander, P. Benson and J. Kampmeyer, "Investigating the Valuation Effects of Announcements of Voluntary Corporate Selloffs," *Journal of Finance* 29 (1984); and April Klein, "Voluntary Corporate Divestitures: Motives and Consequences," Unpublished doctoral dissertation, University of Chicago, 1983) both report positive abnormal returns of about 1 percent or less in a three-day period (Klein) and a two-day period (Alexander et al.) ending with the announcement of the divestiture in the *Wall Street Journal*.

6. See Katherine Schipper and Abbie Smith, "Effects of Recontracting on Shareholder Wealth: The Case of Voluntary Spin-offs," *Journal of Financial Economics* 12 (1983); Gailen Hite and James Owers, "Security Price Reactions around Corporate Spin-off Announcements," *Journal of Financial Economics* 12 (1983); and J. Miles and J. Rosenfeld, "An Empirical Analysis of the Effects of Spin-off Announcements on Shareholder Wealth," *Journal of Finance* 38 (1983).

offering (associated with a negative share price reaction) and a corporate spin-off (asociated with a positive reaction), it was not obvious ex ante what the market's reaction to carve-outs would be.

III. The Market Reaction to Equity Carve-Outs

Our study examined the stockmarket's response to 76 announcements of equity carve-outs by 63 NYSE and ASE firms over the period 1965 to 1983.[7] These announcements were clustered in the late 1960s through 1972 and in the early 1980s; there were no announcements in the five years 1973–1977.[8] This pattern differs from the pattern of seasoned common stock offerings reported in three recent studies; in these samples about one-fourth to one-third of common stock offerings over the same 19-year period occurred in the five-year period 1973–1977.[9] The pattern of equity carve-outs does, however, conform roughly to that of initial public offerings.[10]

In our sample of 76 carve-out announcements, 37 of the announcements state that the firm "has proposed" or "is considering" offering a portion of a subsidiary to the public. The remaining 39 report that an offering has been filed with the SEC. Some of these provide no details, while others describe what is being offered, when and why. Regardless of the nature of the announcement, our share price reaction tests are based on the date the earliest announcement about the subsidiary equity offering appears in the *Wall Street Journal*. To increase the likelihood that the test period captures the first public disclosure of information about the subsidiary equity offering, the test period is defined as the five trading days ending with the day of the *Wall Street Journal* announcement.

Seventy-three percent of the carve-out offerings were underwritten. The percentage of the subsidiary's equity offered ranged from 4 percent to 75 percent, with 81 percent of the sample with available data falling between 10 percent and 50 percent. The proceeds of the offerings ranged from $300,000 to $112,200,000.

---

7. Although there are 76 carve-out announcements, there are actually 81 subsidiaries in the sample because four announcement dates account for nine subsidiaries. That is, three announcement dates involve two subsidiaries each and one date involves three subsidiaries. The number of parents (63) is also less than the number of announcements because of multiple carve-outs by the same firm. The largest number of carve-out announcements by a single firm is three (by W.R. Grace); ten firms announced at least two carve-outs. Of the 81 subsidiaries in the announcement sample, eight were not carved-out during the sample period, which ends in December 1983. Thus, carve-outs of eight subsidiaries were announced and later cancelled. Details of the sample selection procedures can be found in Schipper and Smith [1986], cited in footnote 1.

8. While it is possible that a number of carve-outs occurred during 1973–1977 that we were not able to find, we do not think this is likely. Every initial public offering on the SEC's *Registrations and Offerings Statistics* tape for the years 1973–77 was checked and none was a carve-out by an NYSE or ASE listed firm.

9. See footnote 4 for full citations of the three studies of the market's response to announcements of seasoned equity offerings.

10. See Jay Ritter, "The 'Hot Issue' Market of 1980," *Journal of Business* 57 (1984).

Carve-out proceeds as a percentage of the parent's common equity value ranged from 3 percent to 69 percent, with a median of about 8 percent.[11]

A subset of 26 sample firms also made a total of 39 public offerings of their own common stock or convertible debt (hereafter called "parent equity") within five years of their subsidiary equity offerings. Parent equity issues of sample firms were identified by searching the *Wall Street Journal Index* for each of the five years prior to, the year of, and, where possible, the five years following that firm's announcement of a subsidiary equity offering. The share price reactions to these 39 announcements are measured by the abnormal stock returns (percentage price changes adjusted to general market movements) over the five-day period ending with the date of the *Wall Street Journal* announcement.

The market reactions to the 76 equity carve-out announcements in our sample were estimated by calculating abnormal stock returns over the five-day period leading up to the *Wall Street Journal* announcement.[12] In addition to measuring five-day returns, we also measured cumulative average abnormal stock returns for the 76 carve-out announcements over an 85-day period beginning 44 days before the *Wall Street Journal* announcement and ending 40 days after. (These returns are shown in Figure 1.) During the period starting 13 days before the announcement, the cumulative abnormal return drifts upward at an increasing rate from +0.8 percent to +4.95 percent at the announcement day. The cumulative abnormal return is nearly level in the subsequent eight weeks, ending with a value of +4.45 percent 40 trading days after the announcement.

In the case of the 39 sample firms which issued either seasoned equity or convertible debt within five years of the carve-outs, the cumulative return drops from +0.2 percent four days before the announcement of the offering of parent equity to −3.3 percent on the announcement day (see Figure 1). In the eight weeks following the announcement of the parent equity offering, the return drifts downward to −4.7 percent by 40 trading days after the announcement.[13]

---

11. The market value of parent common equity is measured by share price multiplied by the number of outstanding common shares at the end of the month preceding the carve-out announcement.

12. For details of the procedures used to compute abnormal returns and to perform statistical tests, see the appendix to Schipper and Smith [1986], cited in footnote 1.

13. t-tests for the significance of abnormal returns do not imply rejection at the .05 level (two-tailed) of the null hypothesis that the abnormal return is zero within the periods before or after the carve-out announcement. However, the t-statistic of +2.55 in the five-day announcement period leads to rejection of the null hypothesis of zero abnormal returns at better than the .02 level (two-tailed). Similarly, the abnormal returns before and after the announcement of the parent equity offerings are not significantly different from zero at the .05 level (two-tailed). However, the abnormal return of −3.5 percent in the five-day event period is significantly different from zero at better than the .01 level (two-tailed).

The difference in the cumulative abnormal returns over the event period for the announcement of 76 subsidiary equity offerings versus 39 parent equity offerings is +5.3 percent, significant at better than the .005 level (one-tailed). The average difference in the cumulative abnormal returns in the five-day event period for 26 matched pairs of subsidiary and parent equity offerings by the same firm is +5.5 percent, also significant at better than the .005 level (one-tailed). For these pairwise comparisons, each subsidiary equity offering announcement is matched, if possible, with a parent equity offering

Figure 1. The Stock Market Response to Announcements of Equity Carve-Outs and Parent Equity Offerings.

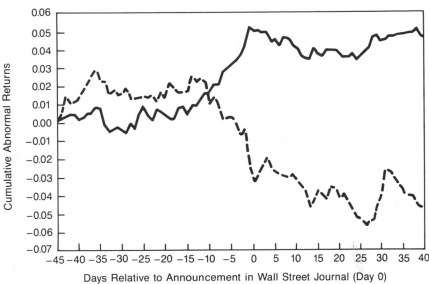

Cumulative abnormal returns for 76 equity carve-out announcements made during the period 1967–1983 are shown by the solid line. Cumulative abnormal returns for 39 seasoned equity offering announcements made by the same firms are shown by the broken line. Market model parameters are estimated for each sample firm over trading days −280 to −161 relative to the announcement in the *Wall Street Journal*.

The variation in the market reaction to both the sample of carve-out announcements and the sample of parent equity offering announcements is considerable. Abnormal returns at carve-out announcements range from −12.1 percent to +19.5 percent, with a median of +1.6 percent. About two-thirds of these returns (50 to 76) are positive. In contrast, about 69 percent of abnormal returns (27 of 39) at the announcement of parent equity offerings are negative. The median abnormal return for this sample is −2 percent, and the range is from −16 percent to +17.5 percent.[14]

---

announcement by the same company. If more than one parent equity offering was available for matching, priority was given to common stock over convertible debt offerings, and to proximity to the subsidiary equity offering announcement date.

14. Previous tests of share price reactions to announcements of offerings of seasoned equity have used a two-day event period (e.g. Asquith and Mullins [1986], Dann and Mikkelson [1984], Masulis and Korwar [1986], and Mikkelson and Partch [1986]), all cited earlier in footnote 4. Because many of our announcements refer to SEC filings, we use a five-day event period. A two-day period, however, is reasonable for the 37 *Wall Street Journal* announcements of intentions to undertake an equity carve-out. For this subsample, the average two-day abnormal return is +1.2 percent (t = 1.91) and the median

IV. Why, Then, The Different Market Response to Equity Carve-outs?

There are three differences between equity carve-outs and parent equity offerings which might account for the market's positive response to the former: (1) the separation of subsidiary investment projects from those of the parent firm for external financing; (2) the creation of a public market for subsidiary common stock; and (3) the restructuring of asset management and incentive contracts.

Separate Financing for Subsidiary Investments

An offering of seasoned parent equity simply increases the number of outstanding equity claims on the consolidated assets. In contrast, an initial subsidiary equity offering "carves out" the assets of the subsidiary from the assets of the original entity. Thus, an equity carve-out allows a subsidiary to obtain separate funding for subsidiary growth opportunities.[15] The equity securities publicly offered represent claims on the cash flows of the subsidiary projects only.

If parent equity had instead been offered to finance the subsidiary's investment projects, the offered securities would represent a joint claim on both the parent and subsidiary projects. By separating the subsidiary projects from those of the parent, a carve-out may reduce the asymmmetry of information between managers and investors about the asset base underlying the securities offered.[16]

The separate financing of subsidiary projects by an equity carve-out is expected to have a positive share price effect under either of two circumstances: (1) information is publicly revealed about the subsidiary's planned investment in a positive net present value project without negative implications about the value of the other assets of the consolidated firm; (2) separate financing implies that management will not forgo *future* positive net present value projects.

Support for viewing some carve-outs as a means of financing growth opportunities of the subsidiary apart from the parent company is found in the stated motives for our sample carve-outs. In the case of 59 of the 81 subsidiaries whose carve-outs were announced, we were able to find stated motives by reading annual reports,

---

two-day abnormal return is +1.7 percent. A binomial test of the null hypotheses of an equal portion of positive versus negative two-day event period abnormal returns results in a z-statistic of + 2.48, which is significant at the .007 level. In the entire sample, however, the two-day event period does not appear to capture the initial information release. For the entire sample of 37 intention announcements and 39 announcements that a registration statement has been filed, the two-day abnormal return is +.7 percent (t = 1.59). These significant tests should be interpreted with caution, as they are not independent.

15. Other mechanisms for separate financing of investment projects include spin-offs and sales of limited partnership interests to finance research and development. In some cases, the tax code provides special incentives for the latter financing mechanism.

16. For a discussion of the information asymmetry financing problem, and why it may pay to fund growth opportunities separately from assets-in-place, see Stewart Myers and Nicholas Majluf, "Corporate Financing and Investment Decisions When Firms Have Information That Investors Do Not Have," *Journal of financial Economics* 9 (1984).

10-Ks, registration statements, prospectuses and articles in the financial press. For 19 of these 59, at least part of the declared motivation was to enable the subsidiary to obtain its own financing for expected growth.

Additional support for viewing some carve-outs as a means of financing growth opportunities of the subsidiary is found in the nature of some of the carve-outs. In six cases, registration statements or prospectuses described a specific growth opportunity to be funded with the proceeds of the subsidiary equity offering. For example, Interferon Sciences was formed by National Patent Development in 1981 to develop its interferon program. The parent contributed basic technology and patents, which were reported as having a book value of about $600,000 or $.20 per share. Shortly thereafter, 25 percent of Interferon Sciences was offered to the public at $10 a share; the proceeds were $10 million. The stated purpose of the offering was to finance the development of the interferon technology transferred by the parent to its subsidiary. Thus, Interferon Sciences represented primarily a growth opportunity, with virtually no assets-in-place. Other projects included investments in Atlantic City casinos, Hawaiian condominiums, oil drilling, and bioengineering products. In each case, the parent firm apparently rejected the option of funding the project by issuing parent equity and chose to offer separate equity claims on the growth opportunity by means of a carve-out.

Assuming that one purpose of a carve-out is to finance investment projects, a measure of the relative size of those projects is the proceeds of the carve-out offering as a percentage of the market value of parent equity. This size measure, it turns out, is positively correlated with the share price reactions of parent firms; that is, the larger the carve-out as a percentage of the total equity of the consolidated company, the larger in general was the positive market reaction.[17]

To provide evidence of the anticipated growth of carved-out subsidiaries, we computed the P/E ratios of 70 subsidiaries with available data at the time of or immediately after the carve-out. Relative to their parent firms, the carved-out subsidiaries had high P/E ratios. The median subsidiary P/E ratio was 21.7 (after excluding negative values caused by losses). In contrast, the median contemporaneous P/E ratio of the parent firms was 15. For the 58 parent-subsidiary pairs with available P/E ratios, the subsidiary had the higher P/E ratio in 43 cases (74 percent).[18]

---

17. The Spearman rank correlation between our size measure and the five-day abnormal returns associated with carve-out announcements is .27, which is significant at better than the .05 level (two-tailed).

18. A Wilcoxon test of the null hypothesis that the two samples are drawn from populations with the same median generates a t-statistic of 3.83, leading the rejection of the null hypothesis at better than .01 probability level. Hence, subsidiary P/E ratios tend to exceed the P/E ratios of the corresponding parent firms. Furthermore, these high subsidiary P/E ratios cannot be explained by low levels of risk. Of the 23 sample subsidiaries with returns on the CRSP Daily Excess Returns Tape within two years after the equity carve-out, 14 (61 percent) belong to the three highest of ten beta portfolios (6, 5, 3 respectively). It also is unlikely that the high P/E ratios can be attributed to the use of highly conservative accounting methods to measure subsidiary earnings. Through 1982, earnings figure reported in subsidiary registration statements were not required to include such corporate costs as interest, taxes, amortization of purchased goodwill, and certain administrative costs. It was not until 1983 that the SEC issued "carve-out accounting" rules that require proportionate allocation of these corporate costs

Creation of a Public Market for Subsidiary Stock

An equity carve-out initiates public trading of the common stock of the previously wholly-owned subsidiary. The subsidiary is thus subject to all financial and other reporting requirements of public companies (for example, 10-Q and 10-K reports and proxy statements filed with the SEC, and annual reports issued to stockholders). These requirements can impose considerable costs on the parent company's stockholders. These costs consist of direct costs of preparing audited financial statements and other required reports for the subsidiary, as well as any indirect costs of disclosing proprietary information to subsidiary competitors.

Such costs, however, may be more than offset by the benefits to parent stockholders of the increased supply of and demand for information about the subsidiary's growth opportunities. The carve-out of subsidiary stock *commits* the subsidiary to supply audited periodic financial reports prepared in accordance with prescribed measurements and disclosure rules, as well as other nonfinancial information about firm activities (such as the information in proxy statements). By making possible an equity investment in the subsidiary alone, the carve-out also increases the incentives of both individual investors and potential acquiring firms to gather and analyze information about subsidiary activities. The increase in both the supply of and demand for information about the subsidiary may increase the perceived value of subsidiary stock to individual and corporate investors.

Such an improvement in investor understanding is cited as a motive for 14 equity carve-outs in our sample. It is also cited in a recent announcement by Perkin-Elmer Corporation of its plan to carve-out and sell to the public up to 19 percent of its minicomputer business, which was named Concurrent Computer Corporation. According to a *Wall Street Journal* report, the chairman of Perkin-Elmer said the carve-out plan "is intended to improve the visibility of Perkin-Elmer computers and thus improve sales and help attract investors."[19]

Perkin-Elmer completed the equity carve-out in January 1986 and described its advantages to parent company shareholders in a full-page *Wall Street Journal* advertisement with the following copy:

> Higher visibility and a sharp, singular focus will help concurrent Computer Corporation attract and retain a strong, motivated management team. And lead to increased recognition in the financial community where shareholders will be able to benefit from its full potential.
>
> As the Perkin-Elmer Data Systems Group, our computer business was not accorded its true value. Yet, in just one week after its initial offering, the market

---

to the subsidiary's earnings statement. Hence it is likely that the high subsidiary P/E ratios in our sample are indicative of high anticipated growth in subsidiary earnings. However, the high P/E ratios may also reflect the low earnings figures of young firms due to high research and development expenses and depreciation charges.

19. From "Perkin-Elmer Organizes New Computer Firm," *Wall Street Journal*, November 14, 1985.

has placed Concurrent Computer Corporation's worth at nearly a quarter of a billion dollars—enriching Perkin-Elmer's ownership as the major shareholder.[20]

The Restructuring of Asset Management and Incentive Contracts

Many carve-outs are associated with a major restructuring of managerial responsibilities and incentives. Divisions are often regrouped into a new subsidiary for the public offering with a consequent realignment in the responsibilities of various managers. Furthermore, the incentive contracts of subsidiary managers are usually revised to incorporate subsidiary share prices and profits as measures of performance. Such internal structural shifts are seldom associated with seasoned equity offerings.

Stated motives for 11 of 59 sample subsidiaries mentioned a change in corporate focus through a restructuring program or a reduction by the parent of investment in the line of business of the carved-out subsidiary. Also worth noting is that 38 of the 73 carved-out subsidiaries (52 percent) had been formed as little as one year before the carve-out.[21] The formation of the new subsidiaries typically involved combining the operations of existing units, divisions or subsidiaries under a single management. Finally, management responsibilities in 12 cases were changed to the extent that one or more persons resigned a top management position with the parent to become president or CEO of the subsidiary.

Two pieces of qualitative evidence suggest that changes in the incentives of subsidiary managers are important considerations in carve-outs. The first is 10 statements of motive which focus on the improvements in managerial incentives associated with a public market for subsidiary shares. For example, in W.R. Grace's explanation of its decision to carve out a 27 percent interest in its El Torito restaurant chain, Charles Erhart, vice-chairman of Grace, said the environment at Grace inhibited the entrepreneurial style of El Torito's management. "These are people-sensitive businesses. They [El Torito management] are independent cats who need a piece of the action to motivate them."[22]

The second piece of evidence concerns the use of subsidiary share prices and profit figures in contracts with subsidiary managers. Of the 63 sample carve-out subsidiaries for which data are available, 59 (that is, 94 percent) adopted incentive compensation plans based on the subsidiary's stock—generally stock option plans. Most of these adoptions occurred within one year of the carve-out. In addition, at least 23 subsidiaries adopted incentive plans based on subsidiary net income.

This evidence suggests that restructuring of managerial responsibilities and incentives is frequently associated with equity carve-outs. To the extent the market

---

20. *Wall Street Journal*, February 19, 1986.
21. Of the 32 subsidiaries in existence at least 1 year before the equity carve-out announcement, 17 had been previously acquired, 4 had been formed as part of a joint venture, and 11 were formed from existing divisions.
22. *Business Week*, December 19, 1983, contains additional information.

expects such restructuring to lead to improvements in management's efficiency in using corporate assets, we would expect a favorable share price reaction.[23]

V. After the Carve-Out

Carved-out subsidiaries often experience some form of change in ownership following the carve-out. For our entire sample of 73 carve-outs, all but 14 of the subsidiaries as of February 1986 had undergone further changes since the initial public offering.[24]

One common fate of carved-out subsidiaries is complete separation from the parent by one of the following means: spin-off, purchase by the subsidiary of its stock held by the parent, leveraged buyout, sale to another firm, and bankruptcy/liquidation. Of the 73 carve-outs in our sample, 30 had separated from their parents by one of the above means as of February 1986 (see Table 1). Fifteen of these 30 separations involved the outright sale of the subsidiary to another firm. Four were acquired by management in leveraged buyouts (though all of these occurred after November 1984, reflecting the newness of the LBO phenomenon).

---

23. The principle of "informativeness," as developed by Shavell and by Holmstrom (See S. Shavell, "Risk Sharing and Incentives in the Principal and Agent Relationship" and B. Holmstrom, "Moral Hazard and Observability," both in the *Bell Journal of Economics* 10 (1979), maintains that any (costless) variable which is marginally informative about an agent's actions can be used to increase the efficiency of the contract with the principal. Hence, if the subsidiary share price contains additional information about subsidiary managers' actions, agency theory suggests that the efficiency of managers' contracts can be improved by linking compensation to the subsidiary stock price performance.

This requirement does not appear to be overly restrictive. The aggregation of the parent company with the subsidiary company for purposes of equity market valuation and financial reporting (i.e., presentation of consolidated financial statements) is likely to result in loss of information about the subsidiary's management's production, investment, and financing decisions. The contracting gains which may result from disaggregating agent performance measures for unrelated operations is discussed in the context of responsibility accounting in the following study: S. Baiman and J. Demski, "Economically Optimal Performance Evaluation and Control Systems," *Journal of Accounting Research* 18 (1980), Supplement, pp. 184–220. Although the performance of the subsidiary and the parent company may be measured separately with internal (managerial) accounting procedures even before the equity carve-outs, in general such "divisional" accounting measures are unlikely to contain all the information contained in the subsidiary share price with respect to subsidiary mangement's actions. On this last point, see D. Diamond and R. Verrecchia, "Optimal Managerial Contracts and Equilibrium Security Prices," *Journal of Finance* 37 (1982), pp. 275–287.

24. At the time of the original carve-out announcement, the market does not appear to respond differently to those carve-outs which later undergo some kind of restructuring. For carve-outs announced before 1983, a Mann-Whitney test for differences in abnormal returns at announcements of carve-outs that were later restructured versus those that remain unchanged results in a z-statistic of .82, which is not significant at conventional levels. Thus, there is not an ex ante perceived difference, in terms of impact on shareholder wealth, between carve-outs that were later reacquired, divested, spun-off or liquidated and those that have not undergone some further ownership or structural change.

Parent firm share price reactions to announcements that subsidiaries are being divested or reacquired are small and positive. For a sample of eight divestiture announcements, the two-day average abnormal return is 2.8 percent (t = 1.88). For a sample of 13 reacquisition announcements, the two-day average abnormal return is 0.6 percent (t = .55). These results are consistent with little or no revision in market expectations associated with restructuring announcements.

Table 1. Ownership Changes for 73 Subsidiaries Carved-Out During 1965–1983[a].

	Number	Number of Years Between Carve-out and Event	
		Average	Range
Reacquisition by parent			
Transaction complete	26	5.1	2–12
Proposal pending	2	5.5	5–6
Transaction proposed but failed	1	3	NA
Separation from parent			
Spin-off or purchase by subsidiary of its shares held by parent	7	5	1–12
Leveraged buyout complete or pending	4	3.5	1–5
Sale to another firm	15	6.7	1–19
Bankruptcy or liquidation	4	3.75	1–7
Total	59[b]		

a. These data cover the period from the carve-out announcement through February 1986.
b. We found no information for five subsidiaries. Nine subsidiaries (of which eight were carved-out in 1983) have had no ownership changes.

The length of the period between the carve-out and the separation varies considerably within our sample. Some separations occurred almost immediately (that is, within one or two years), while one divestiture occurred 19 years after the carve-out. The average period, however, is approximately four or five years for most of these changes.

The fact that so many carve-outs are followed by complete separation suggests that management may have originally intended the carve-out as a way of advertising the subsidiary—that is, as an intermediary stage in a process whose final goal was divestiture. The parent may have expected that the disclosure associated with a public market for subsidiary shares would eventually lead to a greater understanding (and thus willingness to pay a higher price) on the part of the potential acquirers.[25] For example, some insurance executives speculated that the 1985 carve-out of 49 percent of Fireman's Fund by American Express was "a way to attract higher bids for a sale of its entire interest in Fireman's Fund."[26]

25. As stated in footnote 24 earlier, parent firm share price reactions to announcements that subsidiaries are being divested are small and positive. For a sample of eight divestiture announcements, the two-day average abnormal return is 2.8 percent (t = 1.88).
26. See "Fireman's Fund Stock Offer Set by Parent Firm," *Wall Street Journal*, June 26, 1985. The carve-out offering was completed in October 1985 at $27.75 a share. By February 25, 1986, Fireman's Fund stock was selling at about $37.75 a share, to capitalize on this gain, American Express announced a plan to offer as many as 10 million shares plus warrants for another 10 million shares. (See "American Express Plans to Reduce Stake in Fireman's Fund by Second Offering," *Wall Street Journal*, February 26, 1986).

Only slightly less common than complete separation, however, is the reacquisition of carved-out subsidiaries by the parent. In our sample, 26 subsidiaries were reacquired and another reacquisition is pending. Why do companies reacquire carved-out subsidiaries? One possible explanation is that the original carve-out decision was a mistake. An alternative explanation, however, is that reacquisition is attractive if the objectives of the carve-out can be accomplished with only a temporary public market for subsidiary shares. For example, the need for external equity financing of subsidiary growth will decline if the subsidiary's investment projects mature to the point where they generate sufficient profits for internal equity financing. The objective of informing individual investors and potential acquirers about a subsidiary's growth potential through audited subsidiary financial statements and other reports, as well as the increased incentives for private information collection, may be achieved by a temporary public market for subsidiary stock. Even the contracting gains associated with incorporating subsidiary stock price in the incentive contracts of subsidiary managers may be temporary.

One example of a carve-out followed quickly by a reacquisition proposal is the case of First Data Resources. American Express sold 25 percent of First Data for $14 a share in September 1983, and announced a plan to reacquire the shares for $36 a share (27 times earnings) in August 1985. The reacquisition was announced as part of a plan to narrow the corporate focus on consumer financial services. While some analysts speculated that the reacquisition might imply that the original carve-out was a mistake, the president of American Express, Louis Gerstner, Jr. disputed this point by saying that the equity ownership taken by First Data management as part of the 1983 carve-out offering helped stimulate the subsidiary's rapid growth. (In the first six months of 1985, First Data's income was nearly 50 percent higher than in 1984.)[27]

The MGM/UA carve-out of its Home Entertainment Group mentioned earlier in this article was also followed by a reacquisition. Late in 1984 MGM/UA proposed a reacquisition at $28 in notes or MGM/UA stock; the carve-out offering price was $12. It might be concluded from this proposal that the original purpose of the carve-out had been served and there was no longer a need for a public market for HEG stock.[28]

Subsequent ownership changes are easier to accomplish if the parent retains control of its carved-out subsidiary. In our sample, parent firms typically offered only a minority interest to the public, while retaining a majority or supermajority interest. Some of the parent companies in our sample also maintain control over

---

27. See "American Express Seeks Rest of Concern," *Wall Street Journal*, August 22, 1985.

28. These reacquisitions often involve premia over the current market price of subsidiary shares or lawsuits by minority stockholders to increase the reacquisition price, or both. In the case of the Home Entertainment Group, settlement of a shareholder suit resulted in a reacquisition for $28 in cash (*Wall Street Journal*, April 24, 1985).

As mentioned in footnote 24, parent firm share price reactions to announcements that subsidiaries are being reacquired are small and positive. For a sample of 13 reacquisition announcements, the two-day average abnormal return is 0.6 percent (t = .55).

the carved-out subsidiary by creating a special class of stock which increases the parent's voting power. For example, the parent might create and hold 100 percent of class B common stock carrying four votes while issuing common stock with one vote in a carve-out. These kinds of special stock arrangements were found in 15 of the 73 subsidiaries in our sample.

Besides facilitating ownership changes, there are two other advantages to the parent of maintaining a majority or supermajority voting interest in a carved-out subsidiary. First, effective control allows any existing operating and/or financial synergies to be maintained (although it is possible that the absence of operating synergies, in many cases, is an important motive for the carve-out in the first place). Second, 80 percent voting control of the subsidiary is required if the subsidiary is to be consolidated for tax purposes. Tax consolidation is beneficial if operating losses or tax credits which would otherwise go unused by either the parent or subsidiary can be used to offset taxable income of the more profitable firm, thereby reducing taxes to the consolidated entity.

The benefits of tax consolidation were cited in the case of Trans World Corporation's 1983 carve-out of its airline subsidiary. After the carve-out, public ownership was 19 percent of the common stock and 5 per cent of the voting control (the parent retained preference shares with 10 votes apiece). Because the airline subsidiary generated both tax losses and investment tax credits that could be used to shield earnings of other units from taxation (as long as a consolidated tax return was filed), this arrangement was described as "having cake and eating it too."[29] Presumably, the "cake" came from the $78 million cash generated by the offering, which permitted the subsidiary to purchase new equipment, especially Boeing 767's.

VI. Summary and Conclusions

We recently completed a study of 76 equity carve-out announcements by public companies traded on the New York and American Stock Exchanges. Our results indicated that in the five-day period culminating with the announcement of such carve-outs, the stock prices of parent companies announcing the carve-outs outperformed the market by almost 2 percent on average; the size of the average reaction is a positive 4 to 5 percent if an additional two weeks preceding the announcement are included.

In contrast, announcements of public offerings of parent common stock and convertible debt by a subset of the same companies have been associated with average shareholder losses of over 3 percent. Such a negative reaction to announcements of *parent* equity offerings is consistent, furthermore, with prior research on the stock price effects of changes in outstanding equity through public sale or repurchase of common stock and convertible debt, debt conversion, and exchange offers to current security holders.[30] Initial public offerings of subsidiary

29. See "Let Them Eat Stock," *Forbes*, April 25, 1983.
30. See footnote 4 earlier for a review of this research.

stock are thus the only means of raising outside equity capital (of which we are aware) which appear to communicate a positive signal to the stock market.

How do we account for this difference in the market's response to announcements of carve-out and seasoned equity offerings?

An equity carve-out, first of all, allows public investment in subsidiary growth opportunities apart from an investment in the parent's assets. Such a security, by offering investors a "pure play," may have scarcity value if such opportunities are typically buried within a conglomerate structure.

A partial public offering also appears to offer an effective means of overcoming the financing problem caused by the potential information gap between insiders and public investors which appears to make conventional equity offerings quite expensive. Still another possibility is that the equity carve-out may improve public understanding of the subsidiary's growth opportunities. By making the subsidiary a public company, the carve-out may increase the supply of and demand for information about the subsidiary. Periodic, audited financial statements prepared by the subsidiary in accordance with regulations are issued to the public. Investors accordingly may have added incentives to analyze publicly available data and to search for private information about the subsidiary because of the new opportunity to trade subsidiary stock. Also, the readily observable market price of subsidiary stock may attract an acquiring firm and facilitate negotiations concerning the purchase price. If such an increased flow of information increases the perceived value of subsidiary stock to individual or corporate investors, it may partially explain the more favorable share price response to equity carve-outs than to parent equity offerings.

Alternatively, the market may be saying that the conglomerate is an inefficient organizational structure for capitalizing on such growth opportunities, and for providing the entrepreneurial climate necessary to do so. Equity carve-outs often are associated with a major restructuring of managers' responsibilities and incentive contracts, and the market may associate such restructuring with improvements in management's efficiency in putting corporate assets to their most valuable uses.

11

Going Private:
The Effects of a Change in Corporate Ownership Structure

Harry DeAngelo
Linda DeAngelo
University of Michigan

Edward M. Rice
University of Washington

I. Introduction

In a "going private" transaction, the entire equity interest in a public corporation is purchased by a small group of investors that includes members of the incumbent management team. In some of these management buyouts, current managers obtain 100 percent equity ownership of the newly private company. In others, management shares equity ownership with a small group of outside investors, which typically places representatives on the private company's board of directors. Besides contributing equity capital, these outside investors generally arrange other financing for the acquisition of the publicly held stock. Deals with third-party investors almost always involve substantial borrowing by the private company and thus are commonly known as "leveraged buyouts."

Whether structured as a leveraged buyout or otherwise, going private transactions simply rearrange the ownership structure of a single operating entity. They involve no obvious "synergies"—no economies of scale or vertical integration—of the kind that potentially characterize, and are often used to justify, a business combination of two operating companies. Because there is no possibility for the usual "synergistic" gains, critics of management buyouts argue that going private cannot possibly create sufficient value *both* to provide public stockholders adequate compensation for their ownership interest in the firm and to make the transaction profitable from management's perspective. Furthermore, because management is itself the purchaser of its company's publicly-held shares, it has an obvious incentive to place its own interest ahead of the welfare of its public stockholders. And, therefore, if management buyouts leave the size of the corporate "pie" unchanged, and if we assume that management benefits from the deal (which seems reasonable since they propose it), then public stockholders are bound to lose.

Our own study of going private transactions, however, does not support this argument. Rather, it indicates that public stockholders benefit substantially from the typical buyout. In the average buyout proposal, the management group bids a price for the outstanding shares that significantly exceeds the market price prior to (and immediately after) the announcement of the offer. Therefore, at least according to the market's assessment, public stockholders appear to be getting a good deal. Furthermore, the willingness of corporate management to buy out the public stockholders at a premium over market suggests that going private may actually increase the size of the corporate "pie" for some companies. This possibility raises a related question: what expected benefits underlie these value increases?

There appear to be several potential advantages from a management buyout which, taken together, may create sufficient new value to enrich *both* managers and public stockholders in the process. For one thing, going private can result in significant savings by eliminating the costs of registration, listing, and stockholder servicing incurred by publicly traded companies. Second, and perhaps more important, management's increased ownership interest after the buyout provides it with stronger incentives to perform, which can lead to significantly greater firm profitability. Furthermore, private companies seem to have more flexibility in adopting compensation packages which recognize and thus stimulate individual effort.

In the past few years, the number and size of public companies (or their divisions) receiving leveraged buyout proposals seem to have increased dramatically. This leveraged buyout phenomenon suggests that going private *per se* may increase debt capacity. The typically heavy reliance on debt financing in these deals, together with the "step-up" of largely depreciated assets, may provide significant tax benefits. Also potentially valuable in leveraged buyouts is the fact that largely passive public stockholders are replaced by knowledgeable investors who, with their substantial interest in the resulting private firm, often participate in the financial management of that firm. Moreover, the monitoring service provided by these buyout specialists may also add significant value by increasing managerial productivity.[1]

II. Public Stockholder Returns from Going Private: The Evidence

We recently completed a study of 72 companies that proposed to go private during the period 1973–1980. We identified these firms by inspecting each issue of *The Wall Street Journal* over that period. Forty-nine of these proposals were by companies listed on the AMEX at the time of the proposal, and the other 23 were

---

1. A more thorough discussion of these issues (as well as a detailed statistical analysis) can be found in our earlier paper (DeAngelo, DeAngelo, and Rice (1984)).

by firms listed on the NYSE. Of the 72 proposals, 45 involved no third-party equity participation, 23 were leveraged buyouts with outside equity investors, and four were withdrawn before the precise structure of the deal was announced.

In the median firm in our sample, management held 50.9 percent of the common stock, and there were a total of 1,890 stockholders. The median size of these companies was $70.9 million in annual revenues and $53 million book value of total assets. The median ratio of long-term debt to total assets was 12.6 percent. The median market value of the public stock interest totaled $6.3 million as of two months before the proposal.

This profile of companies proposing to go private suggests that they have generally been fairly small companies, with concentrated management ownership and low leverage ratios. But, while we have no systematic evidence, our general impression is that firms proposing to go private since 1980 have tended to be considerably larger on average, have had greater third-party participation, and have been financed with greater amounts of debt. (In the largest leveraged buyout bid to date, Esmark's management recently offered $2.4 billion to buy out its public stockholders.) Not surprisingly, companies proposing buyouts in recent years also appear to be characterized by smaller proportional management ownership than firms proposing to go private during 1973–1980.

To assess whether going private proposals tend to benefit public stockholders, we used open market stock prices as an index of stockholder welfare. Specifically, we examined the average stock price changes associated with two events: (1) initial proposals to go private made by the 72 firms in our sample and (2) withdrawals of the proposal by the 18 firms for which we could clearly identify a withdrawal announcement. Our statistical method isolates the impact of a management buyout proposal (or its withdrawal) on a particular stock's value by controlling for the effects of the time value of money, risk (or beta), and overall market movements.

Proposals to Go Private

Our empirical analysis indicates that, on average, initial proposals to go private are associated with substantial increases in stock prices. This finding holds at high levels of statistical significance using a variety of methods and time periods for measuring stockholder wealth changes. For example, the average company's share price increased 22.3 percent (net of risk-adjusted market movements) over the two days surrounding a proposal announcement. Furthermore, within this sample average, virtually all of the firms (68 of 72) experienced positive changes in share value.

The data also suggest that the market anticipates going private proposals. In the period immediately prior to formal announcement, the shares of many firms increase substantially in value. Anticipatory stock price runups also characterize other major corporate transactions, such as interfirm tender offers and mergers. Thus, if we measure the impact of the going private proposal over the two months immediately prior to and including the announcement, we are likely to obtain a more accurate assessment of the impact of the proposal on public stockholder wealth. This measure shows a 30.4 percent average rise in share price, after adjustment for general market movements. Again, almost all (65 to 72) sample firms experienced value increases in this two-month period.

These large price increases reflect the premiums over market value that managers offered public stockholders in going private proposals. We calculated offer premiums for the subsample of 57 proposals in which public stockholders were offered strictly cash compensation. These premiums averaged 56 percent when measured relative to the share price two months prior to the proposal announcement.

As mentioned earlier, going private transactions are usually viewed with suspicion because of the conflict of interest when management seeks to buy out the public stockholders. It is thus worth noting that going private offer premiums and stock value increases are comparable to those associated with arm's-length acquisition bids. For example, during roughly the same period that going private offer premiums were averaging around 56 percent, the average premiums in cash tender offers ranged from 49 to 56 percent, depending on the sample studied. Also, the 30.4 percent stock value increase associated with the average buyout offer is comparable to the 24 percent average increase in target firm value associated with merger announcements and the 40 percent increase for targets of tender offers.[2]

Insider Information Effects

Our evidence indicates, then, that public stockholders typically experience large wealth increases when managers propose to take a firm private. But does this evidence really mean that going private *per se* is the cause of this wealth increase? After all, wouldn't managers be most likely to seek to increase their ownership interest when they foresee better prospects for the company, *even as a public concern*, than those reflected in the pre-offer market price? And wouldn't an insider proposal to go private therefore reveal favorable, previously inside, information to outside market participants? If the answers to these two questions are yes, then the positive price impact may arise solely from the possibility, implicitly communicated by management's proposal, that the company's prospects are better than previously thought.

Further analysis suggests, however, that the price impact at the time of proposal is not due solely to the implicit release of favorable inside information. How did we determine this? We examined each firm's stock price *after* its proposal announcement—that is, after the market had the opportunity to capitalize the expected value of any inside information revealed by the fact that management wants to buy the firm. After announcement of the buyout proposal, one would expect the price to reflect roughly a weighted average of the values expected for the stock under

---

2. In all cases, the premium and stock value statistics mentioned in the text are measured relative to open market stock prices observed two months prior to announcement. The tender offer statistics are based on studies by Michael Bradley and by Gregg Jarrell and Michael Bradley. The merger returns are reported in a study by Peter Dodd.

two possible outcomes: (1) the going private offer succeeds, or (2) the offer fails and the stock continues to be publicly traded, at least for now.

For the offers that involved strictly cash compensation, the offer price exceeded the market price five days *after* the proposal announcement in 51 of the 57 cases, and by an average of approximately 14 percent. This price disparity suggests that the market considered the company worth more as a private than as a public enterprise. In other words, going private had a higher value to security holders than remaining public even *after* any favorable information implicit in the proposal announcement was capitalized into the stock price.

This 14 percent disparity reflects both the probability that the deal would not go through (which would harm public stockholders) and the expected delay in the receipt of the offer price. It is unlikely that the full 14 percent difference could be explained completely by the delay in payment. For our sample, the average delay was about 7.3 months (6.3 months median). It would take an unrealistically high 22 percent annual riskless interest rate to explain the price disparity solely on the basis of payment timing. Moreover, the 14 percent figure understates the true price disparity to the extent that the market anticipates that managers will raise the bid above the initial offer price. Such increases in the offer price are, in fact, quite common: 21 of the 57 cash bids in our sample were subsequently raised while only two were lowered.

Withdrawals of Going Private Proposals

For our sample of 18 proposal withdrawals, the announcement that managers were rescinding the offer was associated with a substantial reduction in stock prices. During the two-day period surrounding the withdrawal announcement, the open market stock price (net of market-wide effects) fell by an average of 8.9 percent. Regardless of the particular statistical method employed, we found the average wealth drop to be statistically significant at very high levels. In addition, a decline in stock price occurred for almost all (16 of 18) sample firms in which managers withdrew a going private offer, and the only two price increases were trivially small (less than 0.1 percent). Thus, according to the stock market's valuation, public stockholders would have been made better off had the going private proposal not been withdrawn.

The withdrawal price impact is smaller in percentage terms than the proposal price impact. This observation can be potentially explained by two factors. First, withdrawals are likely to be better anticipated by, and thus less surprising to, professional traders who closely watch firms with going private bids outstanding. A second reason is that withdrawal often signifies only a temporary removal of an offer. (We identified nine offers during the 1973–80 period that were revived from earlier offers in the same period.) The possibility that managers will renew the bid, perhaps at more favorable terms, should act to dampen the market's assessment of any loss in public stockholder wealth at withdrawal, as should the possibility that a competing bid will emerge.

Table 1. Public Stockholder Returns Associated with Going Private Proposals by 72 NYSE/AMEX Firms During 1973–1980.

	Percentage Rates of Return			
	Mean	Median	Maximum	Minimum
(1) Market value change in the two-day period surrounding initial proposal (72 firms)	22.27%	18.89%	89.94%	−22.12%
(2) Market value change over the 40 trading day period prior to and including initial proposal (72 firms)	30.40	28.62	137.53	−41.87
(3) Cash offer premium measured relative to the open market share price 40 trading days prior to proposal (57 firms)	56.31	50.00	200.00	−8.91
(4) Market value change in the two-day period surrounding proposal withdrawal (18 firms)	−8.88	−7.33	0.07	−28.58

Just as a going private proposal may reveal implicit good news about firm profitability, withdrawal of the bid may reveal bad news that is unrelated to the going private transaction itself. In other words, managers have an incentive to withdraw a proposal when they learn that the future prospects of the company (whether it remains public or goes private) are worse than they previously thought. Thus, a stock price decline at withdrawal could be primarily due to the implicit release of negative inside information about company profitability.

While we cannot rule out this possibility, two considerations suggest that implicit negative information is unlikely to explain the full stock price decline observed at withdrawal. First, managers have an incentive to disclose any "bad news" as it arrives (that is, while a proposal is outstanding) since it may lead public stockholders to view management's offer in a more favorable light. Second, as an empirical matter, we found no systematic indication of explicit negative information disclosure in the financial press reports of proposal withdrawals. In fact, we found several cases in which the withdrawal announcement was accompanied by explicit good news—for example, by competing bids or expressions of interest by other potential purchasers of the firm's shares.

Summary of the Evidence

Our data indicate that, on average, public stockholders experienced substantial stock value gains at the time of proposal to go private (see rows (1) and (2) of Table 1), were offered substantial premiums above market value in initial cash offers (see row (3)), and experienced substantial losses at proposal withdrawal (row (4)). Moreover, for almost every firm in the sample, the direction of change in value was the same as that of the sample average. Based on our statistical analysis of average wealth changes, it seems reasonable to conclude that, for our sample firms, the typical going private proposal made public stockholders better off.

III. The Role of Market Forces and the Legal/Regulatory System

What factors enable public stockholders to gain from these buyouts in which managers have an obvious incentive to pay as little as possible for publicly held shares? One factor is competition from other bidders. If managers of a given firm attempt to buy out public stockholders at a price perceived to be "too low," competing bids should emerge. And, indeed, we do observe them in at least some cases.

As an example, the management of Norton Simon recently proposed to buy out their public stockholders at $29.00 per share. This proposal was met by a series of competing bids by outside parties, and the firm was eventually acquired by Esmark at $35.50 per share. Esmark's own proposal to go private was just topped by an offer from Beatrice Foods. And when the management of Stokely Van Camp attempted to buy out their public stockholders at $50.00 per share, a number of competing bids emerged and the company was eventually acquired by Quaker Oats Company at 177.00 per share.

In many firms which seek to go private, managers already own a substantial block of stock. (As stated earlier, management's pre-offer ownership interest was 50.9 percent for the median company in our sample.) Such concentrated managerial holdings will deter some potential bidders from competing with management's proposal to go private. But even in this situation, stockholders are not powerless when faced with a management bid that is "too low," since they can challenge the proposal in a legal forum.

The rights accorded public stockholders under the current legal and regulatory system give them substantial bargaining power with managers seeking to take the firm private. Both the courts and the SEC provide strong incentives for management to waive its voting rights in going private transactions. Moreover, public stockholders can seek appraisal of their shares and can challenge the transaction in both state and federal courts. During our sample period (1973-1980), public stockholders in Delaware firms could challenge a going private transaction on a variety of grounds, including fraud and inadequate compensation. (A recent Delaware decision curtailed stockholder rights to sue in state courts on grounds of inadequate compensation, but expanded the scope of admissible arguments in an appraisal proceeding.)

The important implication is that the threat of private litigation to block or delay a buyout provides public stockholders with a significant bargaining tool— one that enables them to extract concessions from management. In fact, going private transactions typically meet serious legal challenge from public stockholders. According to Arthur Borden, a corporate lawyer, "almost every going private transaction to date has been met by a suit." In our sample, we found evidence of stockholder suit in 86 percent (31 to 36) of the going private proposals for which we had a relatively complete legal summary, and which did not involve third-party participation. Transactions with third-party participants were challenged by stockholders in only 12 percent (3 of 24) of the cases for which we had access to legal data. These observations suggest that third-party involvement in these buyouts may help avert legal challenge because such involvement mitigates the appearance of managerial "self-dealing."

A dramatic example of the role played by the legal system is provided by one of our sample firms that proposed to go private via cash merger. In this case, management owned sufficient stock to approve the merger unilaterally (under statutory voting rules for arm's-length acquisitions) and announced its intention to do so. The courts enjoined the transaction in the form proposed by management and the offer was subsequently withdrawn. The market price immediately prior to withdrawal was 217 percent above the offer price and remained well above after the withdrawal announcement. In this case, a successful buyout would have benefited management, but it would be difficult to argue that it would have benefited public stockholders at the specified offer price. As this example suggests, it would clearly be inappropriate to conclude from our analysis of sample averages that *every* buyout proposal benefits public stockholders.

IV. The Gains from Going Private

It seems reasonable to assume that managers benefit from the typical going private transaction since they voluntarily propose the buyout. If one accepts our evidence which suggests that public stockholders also benefit from the average transaction, it follows that going private must generate significantly real gains.[3] In other words, if public stockholders and managers both benefit from the typical going private deal, the size of the corporate "pie" must increase. This brings us back to the question we posed earlier: What are the expected benefits of this change in corporate ownership structure?

Savings in Stockholder-Servicing Costs

Because going private results in a substantial reduction in the number of stockholders, a clear potential source of gain is the avoidance of registration, listing, and other stockholder-servicing costs incurred by public companies. Such direct costs of public ownership include the additional legal and accounting fees necessary to satisfy SEC reporting requirements. Other direct costs include those associated with the preparation and mailing of annual reports and proxy statement materials, as well as stock exchange listing and registration fees. Public stock ownership also

---

3. An alternative explanation is that these gains simply represent wealth transfers from senior claimants. This latter explanation seems implausible since, for our sample, we found no evidence of systematic senior claimant litigation revealed in proxy disclosures and/or financial press reports. Moreover, one might expect, such wealth transfers to be relatively more important for publicly-traded senior claims, and only a handful of our companies had such issues.

entails additional salary expenditures for investor and public relations personnel—those people responsible for handling stockholder inquiries and related communications with the investment community and the financial press.

These direct costs of public ownership can be substantial. For example, in its 1976 proxy statement, Barbara Lynn Stores, Inc. estimated the annual cost of public ownership to be $100,000. When capitalized in perpetuity at a conservative real interest rate of 10 percent, this figure implies a total cost saving of $1 million from going private. When set against the market value of Barbara Lynn Stores' publicly held stock, which was roughly $1.4 million just before the announcement of management's proposal to go private, this capitalized cost saving appears to be substantial.

In a published guide for firms seeking to go public, Schneider, Manko, and Kant (1981) advise companies to expect the costs of public ownership to add up to $30,000 to $100,000 per year (not including management's time). Arthur Borden estimates that the direct costs of public ownership are "$75,000 to $200,000 annually for an average public company of AMEX size and considerably more if special problems should arise." These estimates, again, seem especially significant when translated into a capitalized cost saving and compared to $6.3 million, the total market value of publicly held shares for the median firm in our sample.

Although ignored in all of these cost estimates, the time required of top management can also represent a significant cost of maintain public ownership status. A recent news article explored this issue with Byron C. Radaker, CEO of Congoleum Corporation, a company that went private in 1980. According to the article, Mr. Radaker claims that as CEO of a private company, he is "the envy of fellow executives, who often wish they too could forgo meetings with securities analysts, hearings before government bureaucrats, and other time-consuming duties faced by heads of publicly traded corporations." According to Radaker, the avoidance of annual reports, SEC filings, and similar requirements enables employees to concentrate on more productive tasks and generates savings to Congoleum of between $6 and $8 million.[4]

The Effect on Managerial Incentives

Another potential source of gain from a change from public to private status comes from an improvement in the incentives faced by corporate management. Because increased ownership implies that managers stand to benefit more from their own effort, managerial productivity would be expected to increase when management's equity ownership in the firm increases. In cases where management acquires 100% stock ownership in the subsequent private firm, their equity ownership necessarily increases. Management's residual claim interest also typically increases following a transaction involving third-party investors, both through increased stock ownership and, indirectly, through employment agreements that tie managerial income more closely to firm profitability.

---

4. *Rochester Democrat and Chronicle*, November 7, 1982.

In general, productive gains from a pure organizational structure change can be expected when such a change enables managerial rewards to be more closely linked to managerial performance. For example, some profitable investment projects require a disproportionate effort by management and will therefore be undertaken only if management can capture a corresponding (disproportionate) share of the gains from these projects. In these cases, management compensation arrangements that deviate from strictly proportionate sharing of investment returns among all (public and management) stockholders can generate overall profitability increases. Such compensation schemes, however, are difficult to implement in public firms because outside stockholders may view them as "overly generous" to management, and can challenge their legality in the courts. For this reason, going private can generate productive gains to the extent that private ownership facilitates compensation arrangements that induce managers to undertake more of these profitable projects.

Casual empiricism does suggest that a return to private ownership enables managers to be compensated in ways that would be quite difficult to accomplish in a publicly-traded company. The July 24, 1976 proxy statement for the buyout of Big Bear Stores Company provides an example of such a managerial compensation scheme. This particular agreement covers a time period of 15 years, and provides for an incentive profit fund in addition to managerial salaries and fringe benefits. According to the proxy material, the incentive profit fund will be earned only to the extent that future operating earnings exceed a base earnings figure (specified to be approximately $12.7 million). The incentive profit fund will equal 100% of pre-tax earnings above $12.7 million, up to the point that pre-tax earnings total $15 million. Additionally, managers will receive 15% or earnings in excess of $15 million. Such a generous compensation plan would, of course, be exposed to possible legal challenge by outside stockholders if the company remained public. And yet, this and similar compensation agreements potentially yield material gains in managerial productivity, for at least some companies.[5]

The Role of Third-Party Investors

Another source of the value potentially created through leveraged buyouts comes from replacing a dispersed, largely passive public stockholder population with a small group of new investors who play a more active role in managing the firm. These third-party investors typically take a substantial equity position in the private firm and, therefore, have a greater incentive to monitor management (and allocate rewards appropriately) than do the typical stockholders of a public corporation. The new investors usually place representatives on the board of directors who oversee the operations of the private company following the buyout. The more active

---

5. Big Bear Stores is one of three sample firms that went private with third-party participants and have since returned to public ownership status. The observation that some firms subsequently go public suggests that the benefits of going private discussed here are not always permanent for all companies.

role taken by the new equity holders may therefore increase managerial productivity through increased monitoring of managerial decisions.

Third-party investors in leveraged buyouts must, of course, receive additional compensation to induce their active participation in the newly-private company. The realized returns to these investors have in fact been substantial. A recent *Fortune* article states that the leveraged buyout specialists Kohlberg, Kravis, Roberts, and Co., have earned an average annualized return of 62 percent on the equity invested in their deals.[6] And in the "Discussion" which immediately follows this article, Carl Ferenbach, another buyout specialist, states that his firm expects an annual return of 50 percent on their equity investments. Such returns include compensation not only for the commitment of equity capital, but also for the buyout specialists's role in arranging the initial financing and helping with financial management of the private firm. There is no reason to expect that equally high returns would (or should) have been earned by passive outside stockholders had the firm remained public.

Financial Leverage

Any additional financial leverage introduced by the transaction implies that equity holders in the newly private firm bear additional risks and, for this reason, should also expect to earn a higher rate of return than did the former public stockholders. An increase in leverage following the buyout may be made possible in part by changes in managerial incentives. For example, the private company's debt capacity can be greater due to the higher profits expected because managers own a greater residual claim interest or because their performance is now monitored by buyout specialists. This effect is reinforced by the increased borrowing itself to the extent that is provides managers with additional incentives to work harder in order to pay down the debt. Many newly private companies attempt to reduce their debt rapidly, which indicates that the initial borrowing is not introduced simply for its interest tax shield. Another explanation for the heavy leverage is that it is employed as a means of concentrating equity ownership when managers' personal wealth is small relative to the scale of operations.

Buyouts with third-party equity participants appear to be associated with a greater increase in financial leverage, perhaps because the value of the public stock interest tend to be larger in these deals (and managers' personal wealth is limited). For the small sample of firms for which we could obtain pro forma financial data, the increase in the debt-to-assets ratio was substantially more pronounced for those transactions involving third-party equity investors. For these buyouts, the median firm's debt-to-assets ratio increased from .11 under public ownership to a planned .86 under private ownership, which compares to an increase from .26 to .30 in transactions without third-party equity participation.

These figures suggest that the costs of debt financing may be lowered because third-party investors have long-term relationships with institutional lenders. Such

---

6. *Fortune*, January 23, 1984.

relationships would be jeopardized should the new equity holders take actions for a given firm that materially increase the credit risk borne by institutional lenders. Thus, these long-term relationships may serve as a form of collateral against potential damage to lenders and, consequently, may allow additional borrowing.

Corporate Tax Savings

Like cash acquisitons in general, going private transactions can yield income tax benefits at the corporate level, such as the additional depreciation deductions made possible by an asset value "write-up." In our sample, most going private transactions were structured as cash mergers with (or sales of assets to) a shell corporation, newly created and wholly owned by the incumbent management group. (Public stockholders received cash for their shares and the management group acquired full equity ownership of the operating company, or its assets, by virtue of its ownership of the acquiring shell corporation.) And, as mentioned above, the increase in interest deductions created by additional borrowing will provide corporate tax savings while the debt remains outstanding.

V. Summary

Our study offers empirical evidence about the impact of going private on public stockholder wealth. For our sample of 72 AMEX/NYSE firms that proposed to go private during 1973–1980, a variety of statistical methods and measures of average stockholder wealth changes indicates that the typical buyout proposal made public stockholders better off. Specifically, we find that public stockholder wealth increased approximately 30 percent, on average, upon the announcement of a going private proposal (when pre-proposal leakage of information is included in the return). We also find that public stockholder wealth decreased an average of 9 percent when managers withdrew a going private proposal. Managers offer substantial premiums (averaging about 56 percent for cash offers) to public stockholders in these buyouts.

Managers are willing to pay a premium over the value of the firm as a public company, presumably because going private transactions generate overall productive gains for these companies. Potential sources of these gains include improved managerial incentive arrangements, superior monitoring expertise provided by non-management stockholders in the subsequent private firm, savings in stockholder-servicing costs, and leverage-related benefits made possible by some buyouts. Public stockholders share in the gains from going private, presumably because of competition from other bidders and because, under the current legal/regulatory system, significant bargaining power is granted public stockholders in non-arm's-length acquisitions.

While our analysis suggests that the gain from going private may be substantial, it does not follow that all companies should be privately owned. We have emphasized the benefits of private ownership or, more precisely, the costs of public ownership that could be avoided by going private. But there are also important benefits to public ownership—most notably, the access to large amounts of equity capital on advantageous terms that reflect the benefits of risk reduction through diversification. For many, if not most, large companies the benefits of having access to public capital markets will remain the dominant factor in their decision to continue to operate as a public company. For other companies, including those we studied, the cost-benefit tradeoff apparently dictates a private ownership structure.

In principle, of course, companies should change from public to private ownership in response to changes in the underlying cost-benefit tradeoff. Unfortunately, we do not have the means of predicting such changes. (If we did, we would be heavily invested in going private candidates!) We can, however, offer one conjecture which might prove useful: namely, that companies will tend to find going private more attractive when they face a shrinkage of profitable growth opportunities which, in turn, reduces the value of access to the public capital markets. While we have no hard evidence to support (or refute) this speculation, it is worth noting the conventional wisdom that "dull," "stodgy," manufacturing companies make good buyout prospects.

VI. References

Bradley, Michael, "Interfirm Tender Offers and the Market for Corporate Control," *Journal of Business* (October, 1980), pp. 345–376.

Borden, Arthur M., "Going Private—Old Tort, New Tort or No Tort?" *49 New York University Law Review* (1974), pp. 987–1042.

DeAngelo, Harry, Linda DeAngelo and Edward M. Rice, "Going Private: Minority Freeze-outs and Stockholder Wealth," *Journal of Law and Economics* (October, 1984).

Dodd, Peter, "Merger Proposals, Management Discretion and Stockholder Wealth," *Journal of Financial Economics* (June, 1980), pp. 105–138.

Jarrell, Gregg and Michael Bradley, "The Economic Effects of Federal and State Regulations of Cash Tender Offers," *Journal of Law and Economics* (October, 1980), pp. 371–407.

Schneider, Carl W., Joseph M. Manko, and Robert S. Kant, "Going Public: Practice, Procedure and Consequences," *27 Villanova Law Review* (November, 1981), pp. 1–48 (reprinted by Packard Press, Philadelphia, PA).

12

Leveraged Buyouts:
A New Capital Market in Evolution

Carl Ferenbach
Berkshire Partners

The marketplace for leveraged buyouts is now a dynamic one, a capital market where constant innovation and evolution is ensuring further growth. There are at least ten funds representing approximately $2 billion of equity investment in leveraged buyouts. Since one dollar of equity supports about ten dollars of total investment in the average buyout, these funds support roughly $20 billion in investment—all from credible professionals with successful records of investment. There is also much more on the sidelines looking for ways to enter this market, and several so-called "mezzanine" funds are now in the market trying to raise junior capital in fund form.

Hence, the leveraged buyout is a growing phenomenon. W.T. Grimm, the keeper of acquisition statistics, reports that in 1982 13 percent of the 875 completed divestitures were accomplished by leveraged buyouts, as opposed to 6 percent five years earlier. During this period, the dollars expended on these transactions increased from $75 million to $1.36 billion. This is no passing fancy, but tangible evidence of a major trend toward decentralization in corporate America. It reflects the need of American industry to focus its resources on what its managers in any given environment know and do best. Also, there is a new activism on the part of managements to initiate buyouts and thus to become owners of their own firm. It reflects the attempt of entrepreneurial managers to manage financial risk creatively, applying their skills (and hard work and confidence) to earn very high returns in businesses which, for the most part, are mature, cash-generating businesses. My purpose today is to describe this new market and its trends, and to alert forward-looking management to the possibilities (and risks) it holds out.

More specifically, I'd like to talk a little about what leveraged buyouts are, why they are being done, what companies are best suited to them, who gets involved in them, very briefly how you do one, how you govern one once you've got it (because big changes come over these companies after a buyout), and whether we can expect to see more of them during the next few years. For purposes of illustration, I am going to use two actual cases. They're both well-known companies, but one of them I have to disguise. The first was a public company that was acquired through a buyout late last summer, a company called Signode Corporation. Signode was a $700 million a year company, earning about $35 million after taxes. It had virtually no debt, was a leading manufacturer of strapping systems. It had diversified to some extent, but it was essentially a packaging company. The other company I am going to call "Sneakers." Sneakers was a *division* of a major, publicly-owned, broadly-diversified company that didn't fit anymore. It was bought by its own management, together with an investor group.

I. The Motives

But first, let's look at leveraged buyouts and what's been driving them.

Leveraged buyouts are not new, they've been around for a long time. But they've become especially prominent in the last decade or so really, I think, for five key reasons. First, a large part of the U.S. industrial base has matured. This means that is hasn't been growing much, it hasn't been using much investment for new plant and equipment or new working capital. Consequently, some companies have started to generate a lot of cash. Second, particularly in the last several years, a lot of industry has begun to focus on the businesses they do best. There has been a broad corporate move toward decentralization. And, for some companies, this has meant shedding businesses. A third factor is high inflation, which was particularly important up to a year or so ago for several reasons. First of all, companies carrying fixed-rate debt benefited from inflation as long as their operating profits kept pace with it. On the other side of the equation, investors—especially traditional long-term lenders like the insurance companies—have been badly burned by inflation. Their traditional loan was a BAA, fixed-rate, 12½ year average life loan. In the 70s they got caught with lots of 8½, 9, 9½ percent paper to good credits when inflation rates were 10 percent or higher. They were getting clobbered, so they began to look for new ways to invest. And this brings me to a fourth factor behind the rise of leveraged buyouts: the development of new lending techniques and a new group of professionals capable of putting these deals together. A fifth reason was a poor stock market, which we had until last August [1982]. This meant that publicly-owned companies could be bought through the leveraged buyout process, which in turn has generated a lot of press and visibility.

As a general matter, you can look at recent buyouts as falling into three size categories. The large ones—over $100 million in value—have generally been financed through unsecured borrowings. They are generally very well-known, visible kinds of companies. Medium-size buyouts sometimes have unsecured debt, and often have a so-called "mezzanine" layer of debt or equity—that is, subordinated debt or preferred stock. Then, there are the small ones, which are generally done with secured debt combined with a little bit of equity, generally put up by the management group. The principal difference among these three groups is that the larger ones are more complex. They typically have a greater number of investor groups, and some of these investors will be major institutions.

II. The Leverage

Now, what does a leveraged buyout look like? Let's think of Signode, which was a typical industrial having roughly 10 percent debt to total capital. The buyout transaction basically turned the company's capital structure "upside down." Signode arranged for $320 million in revolving bank credits, and it had $70 million dollars of subordinated debt. In fact, $390 million out of the $450 million dollars of financing was debt of some kind. The resulting capital structure was thus nearly 90 percent debt. Furthermore, the equity base included $30 million of preferred stock as well as $30 million dollars of common stock. Thus, only about 7 percent of the acquisition price was common stock.

The Sneakers deal was financed with $70 million of bank debt, both revolving credit and a term loan, and $10 million (face value) of subordinated debt. And in this case, the seller took back paper. In addition to the subordinated debt, they took some preferred, and the preferred gave them the right to own some common stock. Thus, the seller still ended up owning 21 percent of the company. It had $10 million (face amount) of preferred and $10 million in common stock. So, only ten percent of the face amount of the purchase price of Sneakers was financed through common equity. That's the kind of leverage we're talking about.

Often the best companies for leveraged buyouts are really basically pretty dull companies. They're not growing much, they don't use much capital, they've been around for a while, they've got a long history of operation. They usually make things, which means they've got fixed assets. They're predictable because the things they make they've been making for a long time. So lenders and other potential investors can predict their future with reasonable confidence. (And those fixed assets, of course, can be written up to increase the depreciation tax shelter. Until recently, you could do partial liquidations and get very attractive depreciation rates on the stepped up assets. But these rules have changed a little bit.) Good leveraged buyout candidates also tend to be relatively debt free, and they generally have a good management team with an established track record.

III. The Participants and Their Incentives

Now let's talk about who gets involved in these buyouts and why. Returning to the Sneakers deal, recall that Sneakers was a division of a major company where it strategically didn't fit any longer. The parent company wanted focus, and they wanted to get out of that business. They looked around and said, "Who will pay the most?" For most big companies, until recently, the first person they thought of was somebody else in the business, or somebody in a related business. And almost always they find out that somebody in the related business probably doesn't want to pay as much for the company as they want for it. Now they consider a leveraged buyout, or perhaps the buyout is thrust upon them by an offer from subsidiary management.

But, even if a buyout may not seem like the first choice of divesting managements, the premiums paid to divesting companies in buyouts have been substantial. In fact, if you look at the evidence presented by Katherine Schipper this morning, the premiums in leveraged buyout deals tend to be higher than those in divestitures, spinoffs, and other going-private transactions. Consequently, the buyout market should not be considered as a market of "last resort." As with any purchaser, a buyout group must offer a price the seller feels is fair, and must make his price competitive otherwise someone else will outbid him. To be sure, buyout groups are somewhat restricted by their financing sources, and they do have a timing disadvantage relative to corporate purchasers. But there have been a number of cases where buyout bids have topped bids from corporate bidders.

Now, what about the other parties to the deal? One of the key changes in the leveraged buyout market, as I mentioned, is a new activism on the part of managements to initiate buyouts. The managements of undervalued companies may see an opportunity for ownership and profits in taking the firm private. The managements of unwanted divisions often see an opportunity to run their own businesses. And if the divesting or selling company will take some paper, as in the Sneakers' case, the selling company can both support its former divisional managers and profit from that management's success.

The banks who lend money to Sneakers, or in leveraged buyouts in general, see an opportunity to get a higher than normal rate on what they think is a reasonably safe loan. The loan is generally to a business they understand. They've been lending to businesses like this for a long time because such businesses have been around for a long time. And, in addition to earning these higher than normal rates of return, the banks earn fees for packaging the deal. Usually, at some point, the loan will be restructured and the banks will earn more fees. So they're attractive from the banks' point of view.

The packager, the people who put the deals together—usually investment bankers of some kind—also see something attractive in it. They earn a fee for doing the deal. They also usually invest in the deal. And if they've got a fund, they will generally earn the traditional venture capital override on funds invested if the new company is successful.

IV. How They Can Turn Out

The economics of the Sneakers deal make an interesting story. This is not necessarily the typical case, but it's a very attractive one. The investors, remember, put up $10 million in equity. Sneakers was a division generating about $160 million dollars of revenue, and about \$23 million of operating earnings. The fixed charges for its new debt, including both bank debt and the subordinated debt, were about \$10 million. So, after the buyout, they were earning about \$13 million on a pre-tax basis. After tax that's about \$7 million, and when you deduct the preferred dividend, that would leave about \$6.2 million available for the common stock.

If Sneakers were to grow by 20 percent, then the next year that operating number would go to \$27.6 million, those fixed charges remain the same, and after you've deducted financing charges, earnings available to common would have grown to \$8.7 million. And that would have been a 40 percent increase in distributable earnings.

Now if the stock market for some reason decides to get hot, which happened not long (maybe a year) after Sneakers became a private company, Sneakers could think about going public. And if they went public at, say, ten times earnings (Sneakers' leading competitor, it turns out, was selling in the market for about 13 times earnings), then that \$8.7 million of existing earnings would bring \$87 million dollars. Remember, a year and a half ago, we bought for \$10 million a company that now has put 8.7 dollars back in our pocket for every dollar that we put into it. Which is a pretty attractive return.

But you might say, "Well, in Silicon Valley, that's no big deal." That is, until you look at the down side on Sneakers. What do you think the odds are that that \$10 million was going to evaporate? Probably very small. Sneakers was founded in 1911. If Sneakers grew 5 percent instead of 20 percent, its operating earnings would have been \$24 million, and earnings available for the common would have dropped down to \$6.8 million. And even if you capitalize that at only six times earnings, the company is still worth \$40 million a year and a half after it's gone private. Now I don't know if anybody would pay you for it in that kind of market, but the value is still there, and that's an awfully good \$10 million investment.

Of course, they don't all work that way. Success stories like Gibson Greetings and Converse have been well publicized and are now well-known. And the allure of making from ten to thirty times your investment in one year is considerable. What has not been well publicized are stories of the buyouts that have not worked well. There are several stories of companies that have suffered severely from the combination of high leverage, high interest rates, and unprecedentedly low levels of operations during the recent recession. It is sometimes difficult for companies to recover from the kind of damage this experience can cause. But, these possibilities notwithstanding, the downside remains fairly limited relative to the size of the expected return.

So the motives for leveraged buyouts, then, are fairly clear. The stockholders of selling public companies get a price higher than the current market price. The lender/investors get better rates than they get lending to traditional industrials, but feel fairly safe because they understand the business. The common also provides a hedge to those lenders who want an equity stake in the upside potential. For example, if there were institutions in the Sneakers deal instead of the seller taking back paper, the institutions buying subordinated debt would have looked for an internal rate of return of about 30 percent. This includes both the rate they would get on their subordinated paper, and their expectation for the value of the stock five to seven years out (capitalizing the common stock at approximately 8 times earnings at that point).

And the packager gets his fee, puts it back in the deal, and has invested basically without putting up any of its capital. Also, the packager generally organizes a new board. In fact the other investors often look to the packager to stay on top of the deal, to be intimately involved, to report, and to make sure that management produces that rate of return.

Now the same principles, essentially, applied to Signode, except that in this case investors were buying out a publicly-owned company. Signode, however, faced a somewhat special set of circumstances. There was an interloper. Victor Posner had bought more than 8 percent of the stock and had stated his intention to buy as much as 25 percent. Now, there were several things that worried the Signode board about Posner. One was that Sharon Steel, which is a Posner company, was a competitor. Also, the history of Posner's dealings show that to date two-thirds of the companies in which he has bought an interest have had to do something: they've either ransomed the stock back, or they've merged, or Posner has basically acquired control. On top of that, Signode had a low market valuation—or at least it felt it was vulnerable to a takeover.

So the management and the board concluded that a change of control was inevitable. And once you've reached that conclusion and you still have some control over your own future, then one option is to do a leveraged buyout. But you have to be able to price the deal in the marketplace in such a way that it's fair to all the stockholders, it won't be topped by competition, and you can still finance it. And if you can meet those conditions, then you can accomplish the transaction.

V. The Mechanics

Now how do you do one of these? Well, here's a quick overview.

First, it is important to understand that within the buyout process, there is a set of tensions or conflicts associated with negotiating and financing the buyout. And once completed, the management process is governed by new owners—including the managers themselves—who have objectives quite different from those of the previous owners and management. Because different buyout groups—those who supply and/or arrange for the new capital—have different objectives and interests, it is obviously important to create a reasonable harmony of interests between management and the various investor groups.

Probably the greatest conflict of interest faces the management group which wishes to buy a division of a larger company. Unless they have accumulated significant personal wealth—most haven't—they will need the support of an investor group organized by a professional buyout group. Their first conflict comes in offering to buy themselves from their parent. By making the offer, they have given the parent company's management a problem. That is, can they stick with this group of divisional managers, or should they either replace them or in fact sell them the division? If the decision is made to sell, then a second conflict arises. Does parent company management have an obligation to solicit other offers and, if so, should the solicitation include other buyout groups? If the answer is yes, the subsidiary management has a problem. Should it elect to work with one group or should it await its parent's selection of a winner in the resulting auction? The issue, of course, is how much control over its own destiny management can reasonably expect to maintain. It is no less complex an issue if the target is a public company and the decision to sell rests on the shoulders of the non-affiliated board members and, ultimately, the shareholders.

The other investor groups considering the acquisition must also address this conflict. Can they proceed without the full support of the subsidiary's management? If so, how much will they really know about the business and what can they accurately represent to the lenders whom they will be asking to support the buyout?

These tensions often run beyond the buyer/seller relationship to the financial institution being asked to support the deal. With several buyout groups reviewing the acquisition, the same lenders may be called by one of several prospective acquirers. Because leveraged buyouts are financing instensive, having your financing committed, even preliminarily, is a significant advantage in the acquisition process. Banks and other lenders will be pressed, therefore, to make commitments quickly. Some, if not most, will refuse until the buyer has been designated if the transaction is competitive or even potentially competitive.

The pressure on lenders to commit can create several problems for the buyout itself. If they refuse to commit, the seller management or Board of Directors may decide that the sale is too risky or otherwise inappropriate. If they agree to commit, then the buyout group will be under pressure to come to terms quickly. In a financing-intensive acquisition, this is not an ideal environment for equity holders to protect their interests.

To cope with all this, it is essential to understand the price the business can support, and to approach lenders and obtain preliminary (even final) commitments. Management must know what it can invest and formulate a reasonable expectation of what it should earn. This means, of course, that a credible packager with equity funds available and strong institutional relationships is essential to a successful deal.

As an example of structural issues, negotiating the debt covenants is a big part, and a difficult part, of completing the deal. The working capital and net worth covenants are terribly important. The junior debt holders want fairly loose working capital/net worth covenants on the one hand. But the banks are ahead of them, and the banks would love to have tight covenants so that if they're triggered, they can do what they have to do to protect their claims. The junior debt doesn't want the banks in that position, they don't want the banks controlling the outcome of any problem that the company may have. So you have to reconcile those interests.

The shareholders' agreement governing who gets what and who can do what—that is, control—is a key, perhaps the key, document in a leveraged buyout. What rights a shareholder has in a private company and who can exercise control can be extremely tough points. And how all of these issues are worked out depends substantially on the artfulness of the packager or the investment banker that's involved in trying to put this all together.

VI. Management Compensation

You're also going to have to devise a new management compensation program. It it's been a publicly owned company or part of a publicly owned company, the compensation has probably been geared to something that was intended to maximize the value of the public equity. But, now that you're going private, you're focused on "cash" (as Al Rappaport loves to say), and you've got to deal with getting that debt down. (Also, because you're no longer a public company, your reporting systems have got to be geared to institutional investors.)

Some of the critical issues in designing a management compensation system are: How many members of management participate as equity holders, and to what extent? How should the company deal with a non-performing manager/shareholder? And how much stock (if any) should be reserved for future promotions? The extent of the participation depends a great deal on the size of the company, the stability and competence of senior management and higher-level middle management, the corporate culture, and the traditional organizational form. I have seen more than 20 participate and as few as two. Some borrowing is almost always necessary on the part of the management group. Forms of participation vary from direct purchase of various levels of promoted interest to forms of option plans. And it is important to structure the compensation plans so that they provide the proper incentives, rewards, and also the capacity to retire both corporate and personal debt.

Finally, you have to anticipate at the beginning what's going to happen at the end. Which is a recognition of the fact that at some point, everybody's going to want to have some liquidity for this basically illiquid private investment.

Another issue is governing one of these leveraged buyouts, particularly a large one. This can be a hard question to tackle because there are several models that have been used. One is to create a small board, with one or two managment members and one or two investors, including the packager. The packager basically becomes a part of the management team, and probably handles a great deal of the external financial needs of the company, interfacing with the various lenders and helping with general policy and strategy decisions. The other choice is to rely heavily on the management. Here, you would go for a larger, more traditional kind of board—the type you'd find in a public company. Outside directors would bring to the management their experience and advice on how to develop and grow the business. Which way you would go would depend on factors like management's ability and experience, their history and tradition, and the special abilities of the packager.

VII. The Effect of Management Incentives

Now what happens to these companies, in almost every one I've seen, is nearly an identical set of facts, set of results. It's an extraordinary transformation. Remember you have an established business, Sneakers has been in business since 1911, Signode was founded around 1915. There's an established culture there, they've been operating in a certain way for a long time. They're running their business in a certain way, and every management would have told you, particularly during the '81-'82 period, "Boy, we have really tightened down on our working capital requirements, we have really gotten our inventory down, we're running a tight ship."

But then the leveraged buyout occurs and, all of a sudden, an incredible amount of cash comes out of working capital—almost overnight. Once management has acquired the business, it must now focus a great portion of its time and energy on debt management. And they do get the debt down. I am continually surprised by how much working capital managers find they can do without once they enter a buyout environment. It's extraordinary what happens when a manager becomes a major stockholder.

Once having reduced their risk profile by controlling what they can control quickly, manager/shareholders then start focusing on the longer-term considerations: When do we want to start raising our investment levels again? Product and market development strategies become critical as the new equity holders become focused on the means to create additional value in their new company. Without resources to waste, strategies for new product development must be developed which are not capital intensive.

Sneakers, for example, eventually wanted to go public because they had a new line of clothing they wanted to bring into their product line. They saw a tremendous opportunity, but they couldn't risk doing it with that leveraged capital structure. By going public, by getting their debt ratios in line, and by giving up maybe some of the longer term upside, they could afford to do that.

VIII. The Future

Now what about the future for leveraged buyouts? The leveraged buyout market is steadily growing and evolving. Its growth reflects important trends toward decentralization in our society and in our business institutions. This decentralization of American industry, this "let's do what we do well" movement, is making properties available. There's an infrastructure of professionals that has grown up to handle and promote these deals. There are lenders who are geared up to do this, using new lending techniques. Insurance companies, of course, have learned to measure the tradeoff between risk and return on their equity investments, and they are looking for investments with a higher expected return. There's a venture capital community geared to investing in the preferreds in these deals. And the packagers have proliferated. There are a number of qualified packagers now, and of course those tend to be people who like to make things happen. So they're looking for deals, which means they're creating more deals. There have been books published about leveraged buyouts. I get a notice a week about some new conference on leveraged buyouts.

Also, entrepreneurs have gained a taste for this kind of success; they've read the stories and there are more and more businessmen who want to try to make it happen themselves.

Sellers have found it to be a market where they can get a better price and, more often now, they're thinging of the leveraged buyout as the preferred option, instead of as a last resort.

And finally, I guess, interest rates are normalizing. There's still a big inflation premium in the rate, but they've come down to a more workable, livable level. The trend is right. And even though the stock market has revalued American industry substantially in the last eight or nine months, there are still a lot of subsidiaries that don't belong, that are looking for a home. Therefore, we think the buyout has a bright future. It is a viable and interesting way to buy a business and to have some fun.

QUESTION: What percentage of these companies going private eventually become public again?

FERENBACH: Most, I think. They're basically indoctrinated with this idea: that it's either go public or sell out somewhere between year five and year ten, particularly if you have outside investors. That investor group is going to be pushing them that way. They want liquidity. The ones that have been done almost entirely by management may think about staying private. In fact, we differentiate among these deals: we use the term "going private" in the sense that if you're going private, you're going to stay private. But if you're going to do that and eventually pay out the shareholder-investor group, then you've got to think about things like dividends and other forms of payment which under current tax law have some significantly adverse effects on shareholders. So it's a difficult problem.

QUESTION: Why are investors or management willing to pay a premium over market to take these companies private? Are you saying they believe that these companies are undervalued? And if so, why are they undervalued?

FERENBACH: Interesting question. Most of these companies have matured. They have low growth rates and have not stated what they're going to do with their excess cash flow. They have not presented to their shareholder, or prospective shareholder base, an attractive prospect for investing excess cash flow. And thus management is looking at that kind of low valuation, and they then come forward and say, "We're going to do a buyout, and then invest our excess cash flow in a thoughtful effective way that will earn you a higher rate of return than you think you're going to get on the stock now." And this makes the new company worth more alone than as part of a conglomerate.

QUESTION: Why does the new company have such extraordinary debt capacity, so much greater than as part of the whole?

FERENBACH: Because they're mature businesses, because they're not growing. The combination of increasing the depreciation tax shelter and the greater general success of their operations will generate excess cash. You can't do a buyout if you don't have these conditions. The excess cash needs to go someplace. The purpose of a buyout is to apply that increase in excess cash to service and retire debt. Don't just accumulate it, or don't pour it down the sinkhole; don't reinvest it in the existing business if the existing business is earning relatively low rates of return. Pay down the debt.

QUESTION: Is the effect of changed management incentive really that dramatic?

FERENBACH: People wake up. If you're a subsidiary of a parent that's been milking you, that's been taking off your excess cash to put into somebody else's business, how exciting is your business? But if you wake up the next day and you're an owner and it's your cash and it's got to go to service debt, and if you don't pay the debt your money is going down the drain, your motivation is rather dramatically different. You get up a little earlier in the morning, and that's what happens.

13

The Shareholder Gains from Leveraged Cash-Outs:
Some Preliminary Evidence

Robert T. Kleiman
Babson College

In recent years, the market for corporate control has expanded at an astonishing rate. In 1986, for example, there were over 2,200 merger and acquisition transactions representing a total dollar volume in excess of $200 billion—a 20 percent increase over 1985.[1] As a result of this growth in takeover activity, corporate managers have devised a number of defensive strategies to preserve their independence. Academic research, however, strongly suggests that actions that reduce the possibility of takeover are generally harmful to the target firm's shareholders—especially those measures not submitted for shareholder approval.[2]

The purpose of this study is to analyze the stockholder consequences of a recently developed defensive strategy, the leveraged recapitalization (also known as a "leveraged cash-out"). The changes in capital structure and equity ownership

Dr. Kleiman wishes to acknowledge the partial financial support of Interactive Data Corporation and the helpful comments of Donald Chew, Editor of *The Continental Bank Journal of Applied Corporate Finance.*

1. The source of these statistics is *Mergers & Acquisitions*, September/October 1987.
2. A recent study by Gregg Jarrell, James Brickley, and Jeffrey Netter distinguishes between two broad categories of defensive measures—those receiving voting approval by shareholders and those adopted unilaterally by management without shareholder approval. On average, those defensive tactics which require shareholder approval do not harm shareholders. However, those defensive actions which are adopted unilaterally by management are in most cases harmful to target shareholders. For further details, see G. Jarrell, J. Brickley, and J. Netter, "The Market for Corporate Control: The Empirical Evidence Since 1980," forthcoming in the *Journal of Economic Perspectives.*

wrought by LCOs are similar to those brought about by leveraged buyouts (LBOs). In both cases, the firm significantly increases its financial leverage and management increases its proportional ownership of the company.

Recent research has shown that leveraged buyouts announcements are associated with material increases in shareholder wealth—on average, about 30 percent.[3] Because of the similarity of leveraged cashouts to LBOs, I begin with the hypothesis that leveraged cash-outs can be expected to produce stockholder gains of roughly the same order.

I. What are Leveraged Cash-Outs?

Although not originally conceived as such, leveraged cash-outs have become a popular defensive tactic that is used by target companies to ward off hostile takeovers. Such major recapitalizations provide existing shareholders with a large one-time payout in cash or debt securities while still allowing shareholders to maintain a significant equity interest in the restructured company. In these transactions, the firm replaces the majority of its equity (in fact, the *book* value of the firm's equity typically becomes negative) with a debt package consisting of both senior bank debt and subordinated debentures. The leveraging of the firm discourages corporate raiders who can no longer borrow against the assets of the target firm to finance an acquisition. Also, LCOs are often accompanied by a major restructuring in which the company, pressured by the debt, sells off assets and streamlines operations.

The most typical form of the LCO is that in which the company uses newly borrowed funds to pay its shareholders a large one-time dividend. There are variations on this formula (see Appendix A for three cases); but, in all varieties of LCOs, management-owned shares do not participate in the distribution, so that management's proportional ownership significantly rises. (In effect, leveraged recapitalizations are stock splits in which only the insiders' shares are split.)

The firm's outside shareholders either retain their existing shares or exchange their old shares for new shares, called "stubs." In the first leveraged cash-outs, Multimedia, FMC, Colt Industries, and Owens-Corning issued cash plus new stock to outside shareholders in exchange for their old stock. In later LCOs—such as those by Holiday Corp., Caesar's World, and Harcourt Brace Jovanovich—the firms took on substantial additional debt to finance the cash dividends, while management received new shares in place of the dividend. In either instance, however, the firm's shares continue to be publicly traded and, as a result, shareholders continue to have the opportunity to share in the future gains (or losses) of the firm.

---

3. See Harry DeAngelo, Linda DeAngelo, and Ed Rice, "Going Private," Chapter 11. See also Khalil Torabzadeh and William Bertin, "Leveraged Buyouts and Stockholder Wealth," *Journal of Financial Research*, (Winter 1987), pp. 313–321.

An Alternative to the LBO...

LCOs, as pointed out earlier, have several important features in common with leveraged buyouts. In both types of transactions, the firm changes from an equity- to a debt-dominated capital structure. In order to support the large amount of debt incurred in financing these transactions, management suspends dividend payments, thus conserving cash that would otherwise flow to the firm's shareholders. In this manner, non-tax deductible dividend payments are converted to interest payments which are fully tax-deductible; and, as a result, operating income for the next few years is almost entirely sheltered from taxation.

But possibly of greater benefit than the tax shields is the concentration of ownership in management's hands achieved by the use of leverage. In LBOs, management normally receives equity without making an investment. In LCOs, corporate managers' percentage ownerhsip increases by virtue of the fact that executives receive new shares of (roughly) equivalent value instead of cash (again, see the Appendix for the terms of exchange of three special cases). Shares in the newly recapitalized company (or, in the case of an LBO, the newly privatized company) may represent a significant portion of the wealth of the individual managers.

As in an LBO, the ownership structure that results from an LCO ties managerial rewards more closely to performance. Hence, LCOs, like LBOs, strengthen managerial incentives to operate efficiently through better management of working capital and smaller support staffs. Also, the high levels of financial leverage have a powerful disciplining effect since default or renegotiation of the debt can cost managers their independence and even their jobs. And finally, with discretionary cash flow dedicated to debt service requirements, management's temptation to reinvest corporate capital in low-return businesses (or, as potentially destructive, diversifying acquisitions) is largely removed.[4]

Given the strong similarities between LBOs and LCOs, then, it should come as no surprise that the best LCO candidates have much in common with LBO firms: namely, (1) a predictable earnings stream that can be used to service debt; (2) a "clean" balance sheet with little debt; (3) a strong market position in the firm's primary market; (4) mundane product lines not likely to become obsolete; (5) low requirements for future capital investment and research and development expenditures; (6) a heavy asset base which can be used as collateral for loans; (7) excess assets which can be sold off; and (8) experienced management with a proven track record. Companies undertaking these transactions are thus typically manufacturing companies having low levels of business risk.[5]

---

4. The argument for the control function of debt was first presented formally by Michael Jensen in "Agency Costs of Free Cash Flow, Corporate Finance, and Takeovers," *American Economic Review* (May 1986), pp. 326–329. Free cash flow is the cash flow in excess of that required to find positive net present value projects. For a less formal, but wider-ranging exposition of Jensen's "free cash flow" theory, see M. Jensen, "The Takeover Controversy: Analysis and Evidence," *Midland Corporate Journal* (Summer 1986), pp. 6–31.

5. The characteristics of leveraged buyouts described in this section are based on the discussion in DeAngelo and DeAngelo (1987).

But an Alternative with a Difference

Now that we have discussed the similarities, what are the critical differences between LBOs and LCOs? The most important—and indeed the factor which spawned the first LCO (in the case of Multimedia)—is that LCO firms remain publicly-traded companies and thus avoid the potential managerial conflict of interest associated with LBOs. Critics of LBOs argue that senior executives negotiating the sale of the company to themselves could be engaged in self-dealing—that is, profiting at the expense of their shareholders by buying shares at too low a price. Apologists for LBOs reply, however, that a company that proposes a management buyout at an inside price must conduct an auction and sell the company to the highest bidder. By announcing a buyout offer, management effectively puts the company "in play," thereby inviting higher bids from other would-be acquirers.

In contrast to an LBO, an LCO does not formally put the company "in play." Since the same group of shareholders remains in control after the leveraged recapitalization, management is not technically selling the company. It is, therefore, not compelled by law to respond to competing bids by virtue of the fact that an LCO does not actually establish an explicit value for the firm's shares. Rather, that value is equal to the per share amount of the shareholder distribution plus the ex-post trading value of the "stub shares." Hence, the appeal of LCOs as an anti-takeover strategy.

To be sure, LCO companies retain one of the disadvantages of public ownership which LBOs avoid: the costs of disseminating information to shareholders and satisfying SEC disclosure requirements. But continued public ownership also confers the benefit of access to the public capital markets with their attendant liquidity. This access to capital markets should enable LCO firms to raise capital on more attractive terms than private companies because investors are typically better able than private lenders to diversify away firm-specific risks. Also, whereas LBOs impose costs on managers by forcing them to hold poorly diversified and illiquid portfolios. LCOs can offer compensation packages that are better suited to the preferences of individual managers because of the marketability of the common stock. And, finally, since the public trading of a company's shares allows shareholders to readily sell their holdings if they disagree with corporate policies, there is less potential in LCOs for costly disagreements among stockholders.

II. Current Research on Defensive Tactics

According to most creditable research, anti-takeover actions typically impose significant losses on the target firm's shareholders. Much of this evidence is thus consistent with the "managerial entrenchment" hypothesis—the argument that actions which eliminate actual or potential takeover bids further managerial interests at the expense of shareholders.

For example, shareholders experience negative wealth effects from "greenmail" transactions—those in which a firm negotiates the repurchase of a block of its common stock at a significant premium above the market price in exchange for the blockholder's promise not to seek control of the firm.[6] Moreover, public stock-holders also experience significant losses in the following situations: when the managers of the target firm terminate merger negotiations;[7] when managers indicate their opposition to open market share accumulation;[8] when managers attempt to eliminate cumulative voting provisions (which enable outsiders to gain board representation);[9] when managers issue securities with poison pill provisions;[10] when the target firm and a substantial shareholder enter into a standstill agreement which limits the holdings of the shareholder to some maximum percentage for a specified number of years;[11] and when managers respond to hostile takeovers with defensive adjustments in their ownership and asset structures.[12] On the other hand, stockholders are typically not affected when managers bring litigation to stop or delay a tender offer or when firms adopt anti-takeover charter amendments.[13]

In contrast to most of the defensive tactics listed above, there are good reasons, as we have seen, to believe that leveraged cash-outs should work to increase share-holder wealth. Like some leveraged buyouts, LCOs can be viewed as defensive reactions to market pressures to change the corporate financial structure, while at the same time permitting incumbent management to remain in control. Like LBOs, because these transactions provide managers with greater equity ownership, organizational efficiency should improve. And, as in LBOs, the debt taken on in LCOs, besides providing valuable tax shields, effectively bonds managers' promises

---

6. For documentation of the negative stock market reaction to targeted share repurchases, see Larry Dann and Harry DeAngelo, "Standstill Agreements, Privately Negotiated Stock Repurchases, and the Market for Corporate Control," *Journal of Financial Economics* (April 1983), pp. 275–300; and Michael Bradley and L. Macdonald Wakeman, "The Wealth Effects of Targeted Share Repurchases," *Journal of Financial Economics*, April 1983, pp. 301–328.

7. For evidence on the rejection of takeover proposals, see Peter Dodd, "Merger Proposals, Management Discretion, and Shareholder Wealth," *Journal of Financial Economics* (June 1980), pp. 105–138.

8. On the market response to opposition to open market share accumulation, see Wayne Mikkelson and Richard Ruback, "An Empirical Analysis of the Inter-firm Equity Investment Process," *Journal of Financial Economics* (December 1985), pp. 523–553.

9. On the market response to the elimination of cumulative voting, see Sanjai Bhagat and James Brickley, "Cumulative Voting: The Value of Minority Shareholder Voting Rights," *Journal of Law and Economics* (October 1984), pp. 339–365.

10. See Paul Malatesta and Ralph Walking, "Poison Pill Securities: Stockholder Wealth, Profitability, and Ownership Structure," forthcoming in the *Journal of Financial Economics*, 1988; and Michael Ryngaert, "The Effect of Poison Pill Securities on Shareholder Wealth," *Journal of Financial Economics* (forthcoming 1988).

11. On standstill agreements, see Dann and DeAngelo (1983) cited in note 6.

12. On defensive adjustments in ownership and capital structure, see L. Dann and H. DeAngelo, "Corporate Financial Policy and Corporate Control: A Study of Defensive Adjustments in Asset and Ownership Structure," forthcoming in the *Journal of Financial Economics*, 1988.

13. On the market response to antitakeover charter amendments, see Harry DeAngelo and Ed Rice, "Antitakeover Charter Amendments and Shareholder Wealth," *Journal of Financial Economics* (April 1983), pp. 329–359; and Scott Linn and John McConnell, "An Empirical Investigation of the Impact of 'Antitakeover' Charter Amendments on Common Stock Prices," *Journal of Financial Economics* (April 1983), pp. 361–399.

Table 1. List of Leveraged Recapitalizations.

Firm	Date	$ Amount	Prior Hostile Bid
1. Multimedia	5/3/85	$890 million	YES
2. FMC	2/24/86	$1.8 billion	NO[c]
3. Colt	7/21/86	$1.5 billion	NO
4. Owens Corning	8/29/86	$1.5 billion	YES
5. Holiday Corp.	11/13/86	$2.7 billion	NO[d]
6. Harcourt Brace Jovanovich	5/27/87	$3.0 billion	YES
7. Caesar's World[a]	5/19/87	$960 million	YES
8. Allegis[b]	5/29/87	$3.0 billion	YES
Mean		$1.92 billion	

Source: The *Wall Street Journal*.

a. Recapitalization plan was subsequently rejected by the New Jersey Casino Commission.

b. Recapitalization was subsequently cancelled in favor of a restructuring proposal involving a special dividend paid from the proceeds of the sales of the firm's hotel and rental car units.

c. FMC was concerned about the emergence of an unfriendly suitor but no actual bid was announced in the *Wall Street Journal*.

d. There was speculation concerning a possible bid by Donald Trump, but no bid actually surfaced.

to pay out future free cash flows. In so doing, it reduces management's temptation to waste corporate capital on low-return projects and diversifying acquisitions.[14]

Finally, unlike most of the defensive strategies listed above, LCOs require shareholder approval, and it is unlikely that shareholders would consistently approve transactions contrary to their interests.[15]

III. Shareholder Gains From LCOs

In order to determine the shareholder consequences of leveraged recapitalizations, I examined the market reaction to announcements of LCOs by eight companies. These firms, the announcement dates, and the reported dollar value of the transactions are shown in Table 1. The average dollar value of the payouts to shareholders was close to $2 billion, a figure significantly greater than the level of the average management buyout.[16] In five of the eight cases, there was a previous announcement of a hostile takeover bid; and in one other case a *Wall Street Journal* article

14. Consistent with this line of reasoning, previous research has found that exchange offers of debt for common stock are associated with significant increases in common stock returns. See Ron Masulis, "The Impact of Capital Structure Change on Firm Value: Some Estimates," *Journal of Finance*, March 1983, pp. 107–126.

15. See note 2 earlier on the difference between the market's response to defensive transactions approved by management and those not so approved.

16. See Harry DeAngelo and Linda DeAngelo, "Management Buyouts of Publicly Traded Corporations," *Financial Analysts Journal*, May/June 1987, pp. 38–49, for evidence regarding the average size of management buyouts.

Table 2. Capital Structure Changes Resulting from the Leveraged Recapitalizations ($ Millions)

		Before Recapitalization	After Recapitalization
Multimedia	L-T Debt	73.2	877.7
	Net Worth	248.7	d576.4
	Book Value/Share	14.91	d52.4
FMC Corp.	L-T Debt	303.2	1787.3
	Net Worth	1123.1	d506.6
	Book Value/Share	7.54	d11.25
Colt Industries	L-T Debt	342.4	1643.1
	Net Worth	414.3	d1078
	Book Value/Share	2.55	d36.91
Owens Corning	L-T Debt	543.0	1645.2
	Net Worth	944.7	d1025
	Book Value/Share	31.70	d25.94
Holiday Corp.	L-T Debt	992.5	2500
	Net Worth	638.7	d850
	Book Value/Share	27.07	d31.15
Harcourt Brace Jovanovich	L-T Debt	790.3	2550
	Net Worth	531.5	d1050
	Book Value/Share	13.48	d21.00

Note: Deficit is denoted by "d." This table includes only those 6 companies that actually completed the leveraged recapitalizations.

indicated that management was concerned about the possibility of an unfriendly bid. Only in the cases of Colt Industries and FMC did there appear to be no public indication of a takeover threat.

Table 2 displays the changes in the firms' capital structures that resulted from these transactions. The increases in financial leverage are substantial and are even greater than those associated with leveraged buyouts. In each case, the firm has a *negative* net worth and book value per share upon completion of the recapitalization. Although the book value of the equity is negative, the market capitalization for each of the LCO firms remained substantially positive after completing the transaction. For example, FMC Corporation had a book value of negative $507 million and a market value in excess of $700 million just after completing its LCO.[17]

---

17. The large levels of financial leverage resulting from the leveraged recapitalization may have potentially offsetting negative valuation consequences. In particular, FMC Corp., Colt Industries, Caesar's World, and Allegis were placed on Standard & Poor's Credit Watch list for possible downgrading. Robert Holthausen and Richard Leftwich (in "The Effect of Bond Rating Changes on Common Stock Prices," *Journal of Financial Economics* 1986) have shown that firms which are added to the S&P Credit Watch list for possible downgrading experience significant negative abnormal returns. However, the results of this study indicate that these negative effects are overwhelmed by the positive benefits of the recapitalization.

Table 3. Changes in Share Ownership of Insiders for Firms Announcing Leveraged Recapitalizations.

Firm	Before Recapitalization	After Recapitalization
1. Multimedia	13%	43%
2. FMC Corp.	19%	40%
3. Colt Industries	7%	38%
4. Owens Corning	1%	16.2%
5. Holiday Corp.	1.5%	10%
6. Harcourt Brace Jovanovich	7%	30%
7. Caesar's World	1.5%	1.5%[a]
8. Allegis	1%	1%[a]
Mean	6.4%	29.5%

Sources: Proxy Statements and the Value Line Investment Survey.
a. Note that the percentage ownership of insiders for Caesar's World and Allegis does not change. In the case of Caesar's World, the New Jersey Casino Control Commission rejected the leveraged recapitalization after it had been approved by stockholders. In the case of Allegis, the leveraged recapitalization was subsequently cancelled in favor of a restructuring. Hence, the mean value for the "after recapitalization" column excludes these two companies.

Table 3 shows the changes in insider ownership that result from the LCOs. Prior to the transactions, management and employees, on average, owned only 6.4 percent of the company's common stock. (In comparison, previous research has found an average managerial ownership of 13.9 percent for the 30 companies that comprised the top, middle, and bottom ten of the Fortune 500 for 1975.)[18] However, after the completion of the LCOs, the average percentage of insider ownership increased to 29.5 percent. As argued earlier, the greater insider ownership stake (combined with the necessity of meeting the debt service requirements) can be expected to encourage greater organizational efficiency and value-maximizing behavior on the part of management.[19]

The Stock Market Response to LCO Announcements

One of the major implications of the efficient markets hypothesis is that stock prices respond rapidly and in an unbiased manner to the announcement of new

18. See Harold Demsetz, "The Structure of Ownership and the Theory of the Firm," *Journal of Law and Economics*, June 1983, pp. 375–390.

19. Randall Morck, Andres Shleifer, and Robert Vishny (in "Management Ownership and Corporate Performance: An Empirical Analysis," forthcoming in the *Journal of Financial Economics*) argue that performance declines as management's stake increases beyond the point where control challenges are effective. Clearly, this is the case with leveraged recapitalizations. However, with leveraged recapitalizations, the high levels of debt severely reduce managements discretion over the firm's free cash flows since the excess cash must be devoted to meeting the debt service requirements. Consequently, it is likely that management will follow value-maximizing behavior subsequent to the leveraged recapitalization.

Table 4. The Market Response to LCO Announcements.

	2-Day Returns	60-Day Returns
1. Multimedia	−1.2%	10.4%
2. FMC	8.0%[a]	21.0%
3. Colt	40.1%	28.5%
4. Owens Corning	−1.3%	37.7%
5. Holiday Corp.	0.0%	26.0%
6. Harcourt Brace Jovanovich	20.7%	55.6%
7. Caesar's World	6.5%	37.4%
8. Allegis	9.1%	50.0%
Mean	10.2%	33.3%
Mean (excluding Colt & FMC)	5.6%	—

a. The three-day return is 16.1%.

information. A large body of empirical evidence indicates that stock price changes provide the best estimate of the effect of a specific event on the value of the firm. Accordingly, this study compares the returns to companies announcing LCOs with the returns to the overall market over the same time period (adjusted for the risk of individual companies). The resulting market-adjusted returns may be interpreted as the stock market's assessment of the long-term value consequences of these recapitalizations.

Because five of the eight LCO companies had already received takeover bids (and one of the other three firms had publicly expressed awareness of an impending takeover bid), the market response to the announcement alone of an LCO would significantly understate the total gains to shareholders; a better measure would also incorporate the run-up caused by the possibility of takeover. I accordingly calculated the price changes both during the two-day period surrounding the announcement of the LCO and over a 60-day period prior to, as well as 40 days after, the day of announcement.

Consistent with previous merger studies, my study indicates that stock prices begin to rise approximately two months prior to the announcements of leveraged cashouts—primarily, in most cases, because of the presence of a hostile bidder. But even without including the substantial run-up in prices prior to the announcements, my results indicate that LCO announcements are associated with material increases in shareholder wealth. The average market-adjusted (or "abnormal") return on the day of announcement (day 0) was a positive 8 percent; and on day −1 the return was a positive 2.2 percent, amounting to a 2-day abnormal return of more than 10 percent. Over the 60-day period (−59,0) prior to and including announcement day, the eight LCO firms experienced an average positive return of 33.3 percent. And, as shown in Figures 1 and 2, there does not appear to have been any material change in the pattern of the abnormal returns in the 40 trading days following the announcements.

Figure 1. Plot of Daily Average Abnormal Returns.

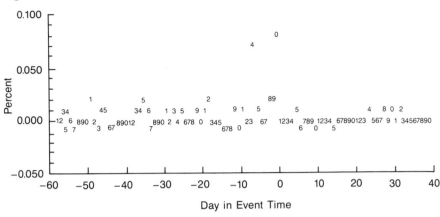

Figure 2. Plot of Cumulative Average Abnormal Returns.

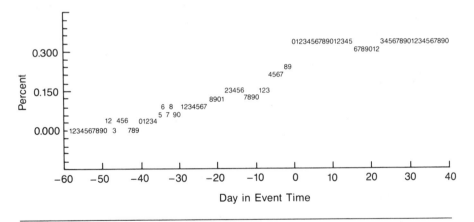

In analyzing the returns of the eight firms in the sample, it is useful to distinguish between "pre-emptive" LCOs (those cases in which there was no prior public indication of an outstanding or an expected takeover bid) and "defensive" ones. As indicated previously, the LCOs of Colt Industries and FMC can be viewed as pre-emptive, and the other six as defensive.

Of all the firms in the sample, Colt Industries achieved the largest positive market response during the two-day announcement period—roughly 40 percent. In the Colt case, there was no significant run-up in price prior to the announcement, and thus the immediate 40 percent price increase arguably reflects the *entire* capitalized value of the benefits expected from the recapitalization.

The case of FMC provides further evidence of the value of a largely, although perhaps not wholly, pre-emptive recapitalization. FMC's shareholders earned net-of-market of returns of 16 percent over the three-day period (−2 to 0) leading up to and including the announcement day. There had, however, been some run-up in FMC's price (on the order of 5 percent) in the two months prior to announcement of the LCO. Moreover, perhaps as if to explain this run-up, press accounts announcing the transaction contain statements by FMC's management that the recapitalization was motived in part by the general possibility of hostile takeover.

The other six LCOs, by contrast, may be characterized as unambiguously "defensive" recapitalizations. The two-day announcement returns ranged from −1.3 percent (in the Owens-Corning case) to a startling 20.7 percent for Harcourt-Brace-Jovanovich—surprising in that this 20 percent came on top of an earlier 35 percent stock price increase upon announcement of a takeover bid. The average two-day return to these six takeover targets was a positive 5.6 percent. Thus, in contrast to most other defensive maneuvers, leveraged cash-outs do not appear to harm shareholders. In fact, on average they appear to hold out benefits to shareholders that are commensurate with, if not greater than, those promised by takeover.

IV. Summing Up

This paper has examined the characteristics and valuation consequences of a recently developed anti-takeover defense—the leveraged cash-out. These transactions involve a recapitalization in which the company moves from an equity- to a debt-dominated capital structure. The firm uses the proceeds from the debt to make a large one-time distribution of cash to the firm's shareholders. Management-owned shares do not participate in the distribution, so that management's proportional ownership rises significantly.

In contrast to a leveraged buyout, the firm remains publicly traded and the firm's shareholders have the opportunity to share in future gains. Like leveraged buyouts, leveraged recapitalizations may be viewed as a response to market pressures to change the firm's financial structure while permitting incumbent management to remain in control. Management receives a substantial equity stake in the recapitalized companies, which raises their personal benefits from enhancing organizational efficiency. In addition, the substantial increase in financial leverage reduces management's discretion over the firm's free cash flow since the cash must be devoted to meeting the debt payments.

Consistent with the gains to shareholders in LBOs, this study finds significant positive abnormal returns around the announcements of eight leveraged recapitalization transactions. In contrast to many other anti-takeover devices, leveraged cash-outs appear to lead to a greater convergence of interests between managers and shareholders, thereby increasing shareholder wealth.

V. Appendix • Review of Terms of Exchange

1. FMC Corporation. There were three different parties to the transaction and three associated exchange offers:

1. Public shareholders—$70 + 1 new share
2. The thrift plan—$25 + 4 new shares
3. Management and the PAYSOP—$0 + 5-⅔ new shares

The share price of FMC 60 days prior to announcement of the LCO was roughly $70. The value of each of the three offers could be different, depending on the initial trading price of the new shares. If the new shares sold for $15, all three parties to the transaction would have held $85 in total value. After the transaction took place, the actual share price of the new shares was $16, thus giving shareholders $86 in total value and management over $90.

2. Colt Industries. In Colt's exchange offer, there were two parties—public shareholders and the Retirement Savings Plan; and the deal was structured so as to give both a claim of equal value immediately *after* the trading value of the new shares was established. Public shareholders received $85 in cash and one share of new Colt stock for each share held prior to the offering, whereas each share of stock held in the Colt Retirement Savings Plan received no cash and a number of new shares equal to one plus $85 divided by the initial trading price of the stub $(1 + 85/P_{stub})$. That price turned out to be $11.50, and thus the management group received 8.39 shares of the new Colt stock.

3. Owens-Corning. The outside shareholders in this recapitalization received $52 cash, $35 face amount (roughly $19 market value) of junior subordinated discount debentures, and one new share in exchange for each old share. Each of the common shares held by four of the company's employee benefit plans were converted into 7 new shares. Thus, as in the FMC deal, there is an implied value for the new shares ($11.80) at which the value of outsiders' and insiders' holdings would be equal.

14

Leveraged ESOPS and Corporate Restructuring

Robert F. Bruner
University of Virginia

The ESOP is treated as simply an employee benefit, but it is really a device to save the human race.

—Louis T. Kelso (founder of ESOPs)[1]

The American public is not too well-informed . . . these plans have been heralded as the basic solution for many of our economic ills. Specifically, one of our chief proponents . . . has said that widespread adoption of ESOPs will accomplish the following objectives: The restoration and acceleration of economic growth to unprecedented levels; create legitimate full employment for two or three decades; and lay the foundation for arresting inflation. I must confess that these are some claims. Certainly no one since I have been chairing this committee has come before us with any program that promises that much.

—Sen. Hubert Humphrey, Joint Economic Committee Hearing, 1975

The ESOP is first and foremost an employee benefit plan.

—Rosen, Klein, Young, 1986[2]

The author gratefully acknowledges the comments of Ronald J. Gilbert and Dennis Logue, the research assistance of Karl-Adam Bonnier, and the financial support of the Sponsors of the Darden Graduate School of Business.

1. As cited by H. Rosenberg, "Are ESOPs Headed for Trouble?" *Institutional Investor* 21 (August 1987), pp. 109–112.
2. C.M. Rosen, K.J. Klein, and K.M. Young, *Employee Ownership in America* (Lexington: D.C. Heath), 1986.

In the 13 years since sanctioned by Congress, leveraged employee stock ownership plans (leveraged ESOPs) have been the object of high-blown rhetoric. The debates over whether the ESOP is creating a more democratic capitalist system or whether it is a good employee benefit miss some significant insights about the real effects of ESOPs. I write neither to praise ESOPs nor to bury them but rather to suggest that the ESOP is first and foremost an instrument of corporate restructuring. Specifically, the ESOP is used to alter the design of equity claims and the structure of the equity clientele; and thus it belongs in a class with other equity restructuring tactics such as going public, going private, share repurchases, limited partnerships, franchising, split-outs, and hybrid securities.

Nearly 5,000 ESOPs are in existence today; about 20 percent of publicly traded corporations are believed to have them.[3] The corporate financial relevance of the leveraged ESOP to these and other firms is apparent in the principal conclusions of this paper;

- The ESOP can tap an unusual set of tax shields that can be of material value to shareholders.
- The ESOP may be useful to restructuring the firm's equity clientele and thus may facilitate, or discourage, changes in corporate control and align managers' motivations with those of shareholders.
- The ESOP may be used as a vehicle for managing the corporate capital structure and obtaining new equity capital—a particular problem for small or private companies.

The analysis also suggests that ESOP proposals should receive close scrutiny for the following reasons:

- The ability of an ESOP to exploit fully the potential benefits will depend on the larger financing, dividend, and investment strategy of the firm and on careful engineering of the various financial effects of the ESOP.
- There is conflicting evidence for an association between the establishment of an ESOP and wealth creation, or between the ESOP and higher employee motivation.
- Viewed strictly as a benefit from the employees' standpoint, better alternatives to the ESOP may exist.

What is an ESOP?

An employee stock ownership plan is formed by a company on behalf of its employees to receive retirement benefit payments and hold securities until the employees retire or separate from the company. Although the ERISA legislation passed

---

3. The Government Accounting Office estimated that there were 4,800 ESOPs in March 1986. The GAO also estimated that 7 million employees were included in ESOPs and that the aggregate amount of ESOP assets was $19 billion. See General Accounting Office. "Employee Stock Ownership Plans: Benefits and Costs of ESOP Tax Incentives for Broadening Stock Ownership," (December, 1986) Report Number GAO/PEMD-87-8.

Table 1. Legislative History of the ESOP.

Year	Law	Effect
1974	Employee Retirement Income Security Act (ERISA)	Sanctioned leveraged ESOP Permitted deduction by employers of both principal and interest payments on loans to ESOPs
1984	Deficit Reduction Act	Banks allowed to exclude from taxable income 50% of interest received on loans to ESOPs Permitted a tax-free rollover of proceeds from sale of a large block of stock to an ESOP if proceeds are reinvested in other securities within year Excluded dividends paid on stock held in ESOPs from corporate taxes, if paid in cash to participants Estate tax assumption—allows ESOP to assume the state tax liability of the former private company owner
1986	Tax Reform Act	Excluded 50% of gains on sales of stock to an ESOP by estates Allowed deduction of cash dividends that are used to repay ESOP loans Required independent appraisal of price paid by ESOP for securities Expanded 50% income exclusion for financial institutions receiving interest to mutual funds Expanded 50% exclusion to loans *to an employer* made in conjunction with the employer contributing stock to an ESOP (i.e., could contribute treasury stock and use loan proceeds for corporate purposes) Reduced maximum corporate tax rate to 34% from 46%

Note: In 1975 Congress created the TRASOP, which used a tax credit. In 1981 Congress phased out TRASOP and established PAYSOP which used other tax credits. In 1986 Congress ended PAYSOP. Also, legislation currently pending will limit the estate tax assumption to a maximum benefit of $750,000.

by Congress in 1974 first allowed ESOPs to borrow, Congress has continued to tinker actively with ESOP law, generally in the direction of more liberal provisions (see Table 1 for the legislative history of the ESOP).

All ESOPs consist of a defined-*contribution* type of pension-benefit program. Unlike a defined-*benefit* type of pension program, an ESOP does not provide guaranteed retirement income or annuities. An employer who establishes an ESOP simply agrees to make certain contributions into an ESOP trust fund to be used to purchase employer securities. As a result, the employee's retirement benefits depend not only on his or her compensation and length of participation in the pension program, but also on the investment performance of the ESOP employer's securities, and perhaps other securities in the trust.

ESOPs differ from plans such as pension, profit-sharing, and stock-purchase plans in three important ways. The first is that ESOPs have been exempted from the provisions of ERISA that require investment in a diversified portfolio of securities. Second, ESOPs are more separate from the employer. Unlike the situation of pension assets, a sponsoring corporation is unlikely to extinguish or revert the assets of an ESOP.[4] The reason is that, by definition, an ESOP is almost never over- or under-funded; an ESOP is not a defined-*benefit* plan and therefore has no test for the adequacy of funding.

The third and perhaps most important distinction of ESOPs from other plans is in the method of financing the plan. ESOPs may lever or not, as the designers of the plan may specify. In its 1986 report, the General Accounting Office (GAO) estimated that 2 percent of all participants covered by an ESOP and 8 percent of all assets under ESOPs were covered by leveraged ESOPs.[5] Another 4 percent of participants (8 percent of assets) are covered by ESOPs that were leverageable but not currently leveraged.[6] Because of their unusual corporate financial properties, this discussion will focus particularly on leveraged ESOPs.

When the ESOP is qualified by the Internal Revenue Service, the contributions to it by the employer are tax deductible. This provision includes dividends paid on shares of stock held by the ESOP (provided the dividends are used to repay a loan or are passed through as cash to the participants) and even contributions made in stock instead of cash (in which case the fair value of the stock is deductible). Moreover, the ESOP may borrow to purchase the employer's securities. A leveraged ESOP borrows from a lender to buy the common stock or convertible preferred stock of the employer.[7] The plan then services the loan from dividends and contributions that the employer pays to the plan.

There are two main differences between an unleveraged ESOP and a leveraged ESOP. First, an unleveraged ESOP or stock bonus plan can invest in a wider variety of corporate securities, including nonconvertible preferred stock and nonvoting common stock. The leveraged ESOP can invest only in those employer securities that are common stock or preferred stock convertible into common stock. The second main difference is that a leveraged ESOP is funded by a loan, whereas an unleveraged ESOP is funded with annual company contributions of stock or cash, which are then used to purchase stock. A leveraged ESOP can be used to

---

4. In practice, ESOPs, once created, are apparently virtually permanent institutions. No formal surveys of extinguished ESOPs exist, but one needs to look to a few extreme instances of bankruptcy and liquidation in order to identify any cases from public information. Interviews with ESOP specialists reveal that ESOPs are terminated very infrequently and far more infrequently than defined-benefit plans or profit-sharing plans.

5. GAO [1986], cited in note 3.

6. Nonleveraged ESOPs accounted for 3 percent of participants and 5 percent of assets, while tax credit-based plans, such as PAYSOPs and TRASOPs, which have been ended by recent tax legislation, accounted for 90 percent of participants and 79 percent of assets.

7. The securities held by the ESOP must carry dividends and voting rights as high as any other security of the same class.

acquire a large block of stock quickly; an unleveraged ESOP accumulates the stock in smaller increments over time.

In a leveraged ESOP, that portion of the contribution that is used to repay the principal amount of the ESOP debt is tax deductible up to 25 percent of eligible payroll. In addition, the portion of the company contribution that is used to pay interest is deductible without limitation, subject to certain nondiscriminatory tests.[8] For unleveraged ESOPs, the company may contribute cash or stock valued at up to 25 percent of eligible payroll per annum.

When the ESOP borrows, the debt is normally recorded as a liability on the employer's balance sheet.[9] The offsetting entry is a contra-equity account that indicates a reduction in shareholders' equity. As the loan is amortized, the liability and contra accounts are reduced symmetrically; and in calculating earnings per share, all shares of the ESOP are treated as outstanding.

As a result of these unusual features, the ESOP affords the opportunity to exploit unusual tax shields. First, principal is repaid in pretax dollars, because contributions to the leveraged ESOP are tax-deductible. This unusual tax shield may be augmented by making stock rather than cash contributions, which renders the noncash stock dividend tax deductible. This is a rare instance in which the issue of stock is deductible.

Second, tax regulations exclude 50 percent of the interest income to lenders from loans to ESOPs—the savings from which are often shared with the borrower.[10] At a 28 percent marginal corporate tax rate, the lender would be able to give as much as a 16.3 percent discount on the interest rate charged and still receive the same after-tax income on the loan to the ESOP as from an ordinary loan.[11] The National Center for Employee Ownership (NCEO) studied the magnitude of the discounts in interest rates on loans to ESOPs and revealed that banks reported discounts between 0 and 15 percent; companies reported discounts between 10 and 20 percent.[12] Because the ultimate borrower is the employer who must pay the benefit contributions that service the debt, and because the usual practice is for the employer to guarantee the debt of the ESOP, many view ESOP debt as a low-cost loan to the employer.

---

8. For instance, not more than one-third of the annual allocation can go to key employees.

9. The exception is when the debt of the ESOP is guaranteed by a third party. For instance, in about 20 percent of the instances in which a private company establishes a leveraged ESOP, the major shareholder will personally guarantee the debt. As another example, insurance companies often guarantee the debt of ESOPs used to transfer ownership of insurance agencies to key employees.

10. Tax Reduction Act of 1984, Sections 543 and 543.

11. The breakeven interest rate on an ESOP loan from a bank's standpoint is calculated as follows: $(i_0) \times (1-t) = [(i_0) \times .5] + [(i_n) \times .5 \times (1-t)]$ where i_0 = old interest rate (i.e., without benefit of the interest exclusion), and n = new interest rate, and t = marginal corporate tax rate. When the marginal tax rate is .28, this equation reduces to $(i_0) \times .837 = (i_n)$.

12. National Center for Employee Ownership, "Banks and Loans to ESOPs: Results of an NCEO Survey," *Employee Ownership* (December 1985).

II. Corporate Financial Applications of ESOPs

I argue that to view leveraged ESOPs strictly as employee benefits is to miss the significant restructuring effects these plans can have on firms. Before considering these effects, however, I will offer a brief description of how leveraged ESOPs have been applied (based, again, on the GAO survey of ESOPs established from 1979 to 1983).[13]

- *Buyouts:* Fifty-nine percent of leveraged ESOPs were used to buy out the owners of private companies. This largely reflects the owners' ability to roll over gains tax-free into a portfolio of securities when they sell to ESOPs. ESOPs have figured prominently in large public buyouts as well (for example, Amsted Industries, Parsons Corp.). Finally one observes ESOPs as the exit vehicle for investors in leveraged buyouts (Simplicity Manufacturing).
- *Divestitures:* Thirty-seven percent of leveraged ESOPs were used as divestiture vehicles. For instance, in the biggest ESOP deal to date, Hospital Corporation of America sold 104 of its 180 hospitals for $2.2 billion to HealthTrust, a new corporation owned by its employees' leveraged ESOP.
- *Rescue Operations:* Eight percent of leveraged ESOPs were used to save a failing company. The formation of Wierton Steel in 1983 is one of the more successful examples. Bankruptcies by Rath Packing, McLean Trucking, and Hyatt Clark Industries after such rescue attempts are reminders, however, of the risks involved.
- *Tax-Free Reversions of Excess Pension Assets:* The Tax Act of 1986 allows the tax-free reversion of excess pension assets if those assets are rolled over into an ESOP. Ashland Oil and Transco Energy Co. reverted $200 million and $120 million, respectively, into new ESOPs.
- *Takeover Defenses:* Six percent of leveraged ESOPs were formed to make the firms less vulnerable to hostile takeover. ESOPs were formed in response to takeover attempts of Phillips Petroleum in 1985, Dan River in 1983, and Harcourt Brace Jovanovich in 1987.
- *New Capital:* In eleven percent of the cases, ESOPs were used to raise new capital. Knowledgeable observers, however, doubt that the percentage is really that high. In any event, the sale of new shares of stock to an ESOP is infrequent.

III. Financial Effects of ESOPs

Establishing an ESOP, as suggested, is a restructuring transaction that can have several effects on the performance of the firm.

Changed Incentives

ESOPs may provide a sense of ownership (or self-determination) and monetary rewards that stimulate employee effort and align the interests of workers with those of the traditional equity owners of the firm more closely than previously. One

---

13. GAO [1986], cited in note 3.

study conducted in the late 70s reported that 41 percent of respondents in a survey cited the incentive effects on employees as the principal reason for establishing an ESOP.[14]

Restructuring the Equity Clientele

In effect, ESOPs add employees to the firm's equity clientele. The median rate of employee participation for all ESOPs is nearly 71 percent; and although the median percentage of stock owned by all ESOPs is 10 percent, the median is 20 percent for leveraged ESOPs (with 44 percent of leveraged ESOPs owning more than 25 percent of the stock).[15] This situation has several strategic implications.

First, it may induce employees to behave more like owners and could result in decreased labor unrest and perhaps a willingness by workers to give up forms of compensation or work rules that are relatively expensive to owners but less valuable to workers.

Second, the ESOP adds to the equity clientele a segment of investors who may value the company and its securities more highly than those investing at arm's length.[16] The application of ESOPs to restructurings of companies in financial distress (for example, Weirton Steel, Eastern Airlines, Rath Packing, McLean Trucking) illustrates that employees may be persuaded to buy securities on terms that objective investors would not. However, the ability of the company to exploit the employees' special interest may be limited by law.[17]

The third strategic clientele effect concerns voting control. Nearly 70 percent of ESOPs hold employer stock with voting rights. At the median, leveraged ESOPs account for 14 percent of the voting shares of their sponsoring companies.[18] Stock purchased by an ESOP is held initially in a suspense account, as the debt is paid off, the shares are allocated among the individual participants' accounts.

ESOP legislation allows trustees to vote unallocated shares. Plan trustees are usually appointed by management—and quite often they *are* management. Although

---

14. M. Conti and A. Tannenbaum "Employee Ownership," Report to the Economic Development Administration by the Survey Research Center, Institute for Social Research, University of Michigan (June, 1977).

15. GAO [1986], cited in note 3.

16. To the extent that capital markets are segmented, it will pay old shareholders to target the marketing of its securities toward those investor segments willing to pay the most. Aside from obvious segments based on personal tax rates and personal borrowing rates, pools of special interest can create unusual demand for certain types of securities, such as U.S. Savings Bonds and Israeli Bonds or project-financing participations (i.e., special interests based on the project's output). Employees may represent one such interested segment. The unusual features of an ESOP may assist the firm in accessing new capital when capital is difficult to obtain. Self-interest of employees may help explain the growing application of ESOP financings in leveraged buyouts as well as in distress situations, such as Weirton Steel, Rath Packing, and Eastern Airlines.

17. ESOP legislation requires that the ESOP pay no more than "adequate consideration," which is usually established as the market price of traded securities, or appraised value in the case of untraded securities.

18. GAO [1986], cited in note 3.

sponsors have the option to pass the voting rights of unallocated shares through to the plan participants, in 67 percent of all companies with leveraged ESOPs, participants do not have ordinary voting rights until their interest in the plan becomes allocated and the ESOP debt is amortized.[19] At Avis, for instance, workers will not have more than a 50 percent voting stake in the company until 10 years have passed. Even then they will vote only on major issues such as sale or liquidation of the company.

Because the ESOP can increase management control over common share votes, the ESOP is now a standard item on any menu of takeover defenses. There are limitations, however, on the use of ESOPs for corporate control purposes.[20] In particular, state laws regarding the fiduciary duty of managers to minority shareholders and the corporation may limit the use of ESOPs as a takeover defense.[21]

Tax Shields

Restructuring the firm with an ESOP may create value for shareholders simply by increasing the after-tax cash flows to shareholders.[22] Cash flows can increase

---

19. However, the Tax Reform Act of 1986 defines seven matters in which the vote *must* be passed along to the participants in ESOPs of private companies. These matters include sale or liquidation of the company.

20. For instance, ERISA requires plan fiduciaries to manage the ESOP (a) for the exclusive benefit of plan participants and (b) in a manner that a prudent man acting in a like capacity and familiar with such matters would use. Failure to do so would render the fiduciary personally liable to make good any losses that the plan suffered as a result of the breach. Certain other ERISA requirements are waived in the case of ESOPs.

21. Consider, for instance, the case of *Klaus vs. Hi-Shear Corp.* (528 F. 2nd 225 (9th Cir. 1975)), in which the plaintiff (the bidder) attempted to gain control of Hi-Shear Management responded with various defenses including the establishment of an ESOP. Voting of shares held by the ESOP was vested in an ESOP committee, which granted management an irrevocable proxy. The plaintiff requested injunctive relief alleging a breach of fiduciary duty to minority shareholders under California law. The courts found for the plaintiff, arguing that "the purpose of issuing stock to the ESOP was to dilute the plaintiff's voting strength." The court cited the need for a "compelling business purpose" whenever majority stockholders exercise control with a corresponding detriment (dilution of voting power in this instance) to minority stockholders. The court decided the harm to the minority stockholders outweighed the potential benefits from establishment of the ESOP. Case cited by H. F. Weyher and H. Knott, *The Employee Stock Ownership Plan* (Chicago, Ill: Commerce Clearing House, 1982), p. 141. A similar decision was reached in the case of *Podesta v. Calumet Industries, Inc* ([1978 Transfer Binder] Fed. Sec. L. Rep. (CCH) Para. 96,433 (N.D. Ill. 1978)).

22. The total value of the levered firm with a leveraged ESOP will be

$$V_L = V_u + tD + tE$$

where V_u is the value of the firm as if unlevered, E is the total current market value of the employer's contribution to the ESOP, t is the marginal corporate tax rate, and D is the market value of the employer's regular debt outstanding. This expression follows from the Modigliani-Miller equation for the value of the levered firm. (See J. K. Wamugi and J. McBride. "The Modigliani-Miller Leverage Equation and Optimal Capital Structure in Levered ESOP Firms," Ms. 1985, University of Wisconsin. Abstracted in *Proceedings of the Eastern Finance Association*, April 1985.)

Merton Miller has since presented a model wherein, at equilibrium, corporate savings from debt are partly, if not completely, offset by taxes paid by investors, implying smaller net tax benefits from leverage (see Merton Miller, "Debt and Taxes," *Journal of Finance*, [1977]).

for two reasons: (1) the reduction in the effective interest rate when lower cost ESOP debt is substituted for employer debt, and (2) the deductibility of payments to the ESOP, which in turn increases debt capacity. The 1986 GAO report estimated that, from 1977 to 1983, the tax incentives for ESOPs cost the U.S. Treasury $12.1 to $13.3 billion in lost tax revenue.

Economic Dilution

When they are not designed to replace but instead to supplement existing pension plans, ESOPs add to current employee benefits a new form of benefit, namely stock ownership. To the extent these benefits represent an additional cost to the firm (that is, costs net of any increase in the value of the firm resulting from improvement in incentives brought about by an ESOP), value is simply transferred from the non-ESOP shareholders to employees. This transfer is what I am calling economic dilution.

Investment bankers typically attempt to quantify this cost in terms of dilution of earnings per share—that is, in terms of the percentage increase in shares (if any) associated with the establishment of an ESOP. Not all ESOPs, however, are invested in new shares of the sponsor. And, in fact, the GAO reported that only 12 percent of leveraged ESOPs reported purchasing newly issued or treasury shares of stock. If the ESOP merely obtains previously outstanding shares from the other investors at fair (i.e., open-market) prices, there is no accounting dilution effect.[23]

Even in cases where there are no new shares and thus no accounting dilution, however, there is a real economic cost in the form of transferring from current shareholders to employees the benefits of leverage which might otherwise be available to the firm (I return to this later).

Benefit Substitution

If the ESOP replaces existing benefit programs, then the new debt-service payment is offset by a reduction in the old benefit expense. For instance, Ashland Oil's ESOP bought 20 percent of that company's stock in April 1986 as a takeover defense. Ashland later repaid the ESOP debt with excess assets from its pension fund and cut to 20 percent (from 70 percent) the matching contributions it would make to an employee savings plan. The GAO reports, however, that only 7 percent of ESOPs displace existing programs.

Financial Guarantee

As a matter of practice, banks require a guarantee of the ESOP's debt from the employer or a third party, which creates a contingent claim on the value of the firm.

---

23. The extent of economic dilution may depend on both a change in the number of shares and the price per share at which the ESOP buys from the firm. If the total number of shares remains constant but the ESOP buys at a below-market price, the other shareholders' wealth will be diluted.

IV. Two Hypothetical Examples

The size of the ESOP relative to the firm will determine the extent to which any of the effects listed in the previous section have much impact. To illustrate, the following two examples mirror prominent real-life applications of the ESOP: (1) the establishment of a small ESOP to displace a current defined-benefit pension plan; and (2) the use of a large ESOP in a leveraged recapitalization. The discussion in this section assumes that the ESOP is viewed as an integral part of the firm—consistent with the view of the FASB—though there are strong arguments to be made for the separationist view.[24]

A Relatively Small Leveraged ESOP

Suppose that a firm is considering establishing a leveraged ESOP in place of its current defined-benefit pension plan. The ESOP will borrow to purchase its shares on the open market (that is, the firm will sell no new shares in this transaction), as is the case in the vast majority of ESOPs. The firm proposes to service the ESOP's debts with dividends on its common stock.

---

24. The two views may be summarized as follows:

Integration of Entities. Much of the research on pension fund management presumes that the pension fund and the employer are really one entity and that any economic balance sheet should include the assets and liabilities of the pension trust. Current ESOP accounting conventions reflect this integrationist view: ESOP debt is considered a liability of the employer, and ESOP assets (i.e., the employer's own common stock) are carried in a contra-equity account.

Jack Treynor, for instance, has suggested that a balance sheet integrating the company and the pension fund best reflects economic reality (see J. Treynor, "The Principles of Corporate Pension Finance," *Journal of Finance* 32 (May 1977), pp. 627–38).

Separation of Entities. Other pension research suggests that pension assets and liabilities should be viewed as distinct from the employer. This research bases itself on arguments on the statutory, judicial, and regulatory protection of employees' claims to the assets of the pension fund. The ESOP may be considered even more separate from the firm than is the pension fund: (1) The employer only guarantees the ESOP's debt, not the retirement benefit associated with the ESOP; (2) Because ESOPs are defined-contribution plans, reversions of excess assets will, by definition, never occur; (3) The dissolution of an ESOP is a very rare event. The only datum available on dissolutions is a report by the GAO [1986] that, for 15 percent of its sample, the plans were not active at the time of the survey—which is not the same thing as dissolving the ESOP. Most of the reasons for terminating, converting, or discontinuing contributions to the ESOP had little to do with the plans themselves (e.g., business adversity, merger, liquidation, changes in legislation, burdens of ERISA). (4) The purchase of the sponsor's securities is not a strict requirement. In private companies the plan must offer employees over age 55 the opportunity to diversify their ESOP allocation among other firms' securities. Also, the trust is free to diversify its assets so long as at least 51 percent of the assets are committed to employer securities (otherwise the employer will lose the beneficial tax shields). And, finally (5) where the company's stock is not "liquid" (i.e., actively traded on an exchange), the company must give the ESOP participant a put option under which the company agrees to buy back the shares at fair market value determined by appraisal.

For examples of research taking this separationist view, see the following: See J. Bulow and M. Scholes, "Who Owns the Assets in a Defined Benefit Plan?," National Bureau of Economic Research Working Paper No. 924, July 1982; J. E. Pesando, "The Usefulness of the Wind-up Measure of Pension Liabilities: A Labor Market Perspective," *The Journal of Finance* 40 (July 1985); and M. Alderson and K. C. Chen, "Excess Asset Reversions and Shareholder Wealth." *Journal of Finance* 41, March, 1986.

Table 2. Comparative Operating Statements.

Line Number	Item	Pro Forma Results Without ESOP	Pro Forma Results With ESOP
1	EBIT[a]	50,000	50,000
2	Interest expense (old debt)[b]	(1,000)	(1,000)
3	Interest expense (ESOP)[c]	(0)	(900)
4	Principal repayment (ESOP)[c]	(0)	(1,000)
5	Displaced benefit[d]	0	1,900
6	Profit before tax	49,000	49,000
7	Taxes[e]	(16,660)	(16,660)
8	Profit after tax	32,340	32,340
9	Less: Principal (old debt)[b]	(500)	(500)
10	Plus: Dividend to ESOP[f]	0	1,900
11	Cash flow to all Equity holders	— 31,840	— 33,740
12	Number of shares[g]	10,000	10,000
13	Earnings per share	$3.23	$3.23
14	Cash flow per share	$3.18	$3.37

a. Earnings before interest and taxes are assumed to be invariant to the establishment of the ESOP. EBIT could vary if the ESOP enhances employee productivity. For conservatism, no productivity improvements are assumed.

b. The interest and principal on the regular debt are estimated assuming a coupon rate of 10%, an initial balance of $10,000, and equal annual principal payments of $500 over 20 years.

c. The interest and principal payments on the ESOP debt are estimated assuming a coupon rate of 9%, an initial balance of $10,000, and equal annual principal payments of $1,000 over 10 years. The assumption that ESOP debt carries a lower interest rate than regular debt is consistent with the discussion in Section 1 concerning the 50% interest exclusion for lenders.

d. The "displaced benefit" item is an adjustment to EBIT reflecting the assumption that the ESOP displaces a pension plan requiring annual contributions of $1,900. The contribution to the employee is assumed to be the same under the ESOP as under the pension plan.

e. A marginal corporate tax rate of 34% is used.

f. The ESOP interest and principal (lines 3 and 4) are actually paid as a dividend from the company to the ESOP. Thus, in computing the cash flow to all shareholders, this dividend must be added back.

g. It is assumed that no new shares are issued.

Assume the firm earns $50,000 before interest and taxes and, prior to the formation of the ESOP, has $10,000 in outstanding debt bearing a 10 percent interest rate. It intends to raise an additional $10,000 of debt (carrying a lower 9 percent rate, to reflect the tax exclusion for lenders) to purchase shares on the open market. Assume also, for the sake of simplicity, that the ESOP simply replaces a pension plan which required annual contributions of $1,900.

The firm's comparative operating statements, both with and without the ESOP, are shown in Table 2. The statements show that cash flow per share to equityholders (line 14) is higher under the ESOP than without it. This result reflects the combined effects of the tax shields, the fact that the debt is actually serviced with dividend payments, and the displacement of the pension expense by the ESOP contribution. Despite these benefits, the increase in cash flow per share is relatively small—consistent with the basic assumption that the ESOP contribution is small relative to EBIT.

A Leveraged Recapitalization with an ESOP

Now consider the financial effect of a relatively large leveraged ESOP. Large ESOP transactions have occurred in divestitures, major recapitalizations, and leveraged buyouts. Here the ESOP becomes a major equity claimant on the firm as well as the funnel for significant flows of debt capital and debt service.

To illustrate these effects, suppose that a firm decides that it will restructure and must choose among three fairly dramatic transactions: (1) a leveraged ESOP; (2) a leveraged recapitalization involving payment of a large special dividend; and (3) a leveraged stock repurchase.

In this comparison, assume that the firm earns $100,000 before interest and taxes and, prior to restructuring (as in the earlier case), has $10,000 in outstanding debt with a 10 percent interest rate. Assume also that the book value of the firm's equity is equal to $490,000, thus giving the firm a 2 percent debt-to-capital ratio.

More specifically, assume management is faced with the following alternatives:

1. establish an ESOP to buy shares on the open market, to be financed by $500,152 in new debt bearing an interest rate of 8 percent (lower than 10 percent to reflect the 50 percent tax exclusion to the lender). Equal annual principal payments of $51,000 will retire the total debt of $510,152 in 10 years.
2. pay an extraordinary dividend of $355,097 to shareholders, to be financed completely by a third-party loan, carrying a 10-percent interest rate and requiring equal amortization of principal over ten years, and
3. repurchase $355,097 worth of equity (6,788 shares at $53.79 a share), to be financed in the same manner as the special dividend in proposal 2 above.

In each of the three cases, the resulting debt service coverage ratio (EBIT divided by after-tax interest expense plus principal payment) falls to 1.65 times. This coverage constraint together with the assumed level of EBIT and coupon rates determines the amount of borrowing. I also assume that the firm is not growing and that depreciation expense just equals the new annual investment necessary to maintain the firm. Finally, in all of these cases, it is assumed that the ESOP does not displace, but is simply added to, existing pension contributions.

Table 3 represents the hypothetical firm restructured under these three scenarios. The table reveals that *total* cash flow (line 11) and cash flow per share (line 14) are materially higher for the ESOP case. This result reflects the implicit deductibility of principal payments—which, along with a lower coupon, are the chief benefits distinguishing it from the straight debt restructuring.

Consistent with the cash flow results, the total value of the firm—debt plus the market value of the equity—is also highest (line 26) under ESOP financing. The source of this increase is the present value of the new tax shield created under

Table 3. Large Restructuring Example Comparative Financial Statements.

Line Number	Item	Pro Forma Without New Structure	Pro Forma Dividend Restructuring Without ESOP	Pro Forma Restructuring With ESOP	Pro Forma Repurchase Restructuring Without ESOP
1	EBIT	100,000	100,000	100,000	100,000
2	Interest expense (regular)	($1,000)	($36,510)	($0)	($36,510)
3	Interest expense (ESOP)	($0)	($0)	($40,812)	($0)
4	Principal repayment (ESOP)	($0)	($0)	($51,015)	($0)
5	Displaced benefit	$0	$0	$0	$0
6	Profit before tax	$99,000	$63,490	$8,173	$63,490
7	Taxes	($33,660)	($21,587)	($2,779)	($21,587)
8	Profit after tax	$65,340	$41,904	$5,394	$41,904
9	Less: Principal (reg. debt)	($500)	($36,510)	($0)	($36,510)
10	Plus: Dividend to ESOP	$0	$0	$91,827	$0
11	Cash flow to all equity holders	— $64,840	— $5,394	— $97,221	— $5,394
	Per share data				
12	Number of shares	10,000	10,000	10,000	3,212
13	Earnings per share	$6.53	$4.19	$0.54	$13.05
14	Cash flow per share	$6.48	$0.54	$9.72	$1.68
15	Pro Forma balance sheet data (beginning of year)				
16	Debt (book value)	$10,000	$365,097	$510,152	$365,097
17	Equity (book value)	$490,000	$134,903	($10,152)	$134,903
18	Total capital	$500,000	$500,000	$500,000	$500,000
	Market value balance sheets: assuming integration of entities				
19	Real assets	$500,000	$500,000	$500,000	$500,000
	Present value of tax shields				
20	Debt regular	$2,336	$47,859	$0	$47,859
21	ESOP debt	$0	$0	$173,452	$0
22	Total assets	$502,336	$547,859	$673,452	$547,859
23	Debt (regular)	$10,000	$365,097	$0	$365,097
24	Debt (ESOP)	$0	$0	$510,152	$0
25	Equity	$492,336	$182,762	$163,300	$182,782
26	Total capital	$502,336	$547,859	$673,452	$547,859

a. Earnings before interest and taxes are assumed to be invariant to the restructuring. EBIT could vary if the ESOP enhances employee productivity. For conservatism, no productivity improvements are assumed, which is consistent with the research surveyed.

b. The interest and principal on the regular debt are estimated assuming a coupon rate of 10%, an initial balance of $365,097, and equal annual principal payments over 10 years. The interest and principal payments on the ESOP debt are estimated assuming a coupon rate of 8% (reflecting the interest exclusion for lenders), an initial balance of $510,152, and equal annual principal payments over 10 years. In estimating the initial debt balances in all three cases, it is assumed that the firm can sustain a ratio of EBIT to after-tax debt service of 1.65X.

c. In this example, assume that the existing pension contribution is not displaced by the ESOP contribution, although in some restructurings displacement occurs.

d. A marginal corporate tax rate of 34% is used.

e. The ESOP interest and principal (lines 3 and 4) are actually paid as a dividend from the company to the ESOP. Thus, in computing the cash flow to all shareholders, this dividend must be added back (line 10).

f. No new shares are assumed issued in the ESOP restructuring, i.e., the ESOP borows and buys shares in the open market). Under the share repurchase restructuring the reduction in shares is calculated by solving for deltaN in the following equation:

$$P_1 = MV_1/(N_0 - deltaN)$$

Where P_1 is the share price *ex post*, MV_1 is the total market value of equity *ex post*, N_0 is the original number of shares, and deltaN is the number of shares repurchased.

the ESOP financing (line 21), which in turn is reflected in the higher market value of the equity (line 25).

These tax savings allow greater borrowing capacity for ESOPs ($500,000 of new debt as opposed to $355,000 under other restructuring alternatives, again holding debt service constant), which in turn leads to larger cash flows for non-ESOP shareholders.

As these two examples are meant to suggest, the magnitude of the ESOP's effect on value will be determined by the size of the ESOP and the amount of debt relative to the value of the firm. But, as these examples also suggest, and as will become clearer in the next section, ESOPs are not for all companies; in fact the potential benefits depend on particular circumstances that may not pertain to most firms.

V. The Financial Engineering Challenge of the ESOP Restructuring

Exploiting the potential benefits of the ESOP is not a straightforward task. In practice, the restructuring designer must work with five constraints:

- The amount of cash flow available for debt service;
- the size of the firm's payroll;
- the debt-amortization terms the firm can obtain (in practice usually straight-line over 7–10 years);
- the firm's dividend policy; and
- economic dilution.

It is also important, of course, that the firm have a large, reliably positive tax exposure. These constraints can be modeled individually, but the joint effect of several slightly binding constraints may be to limit severely the possible application of ESOP financing.

Cash Flow Available for Debt Service, Payroll, Amortization

The following constraints dictate the maximum volume of ESOP debt: (1) the firm must be able to service the ESOP debt; and (2) the payroll must be large enough such that, within the 25 percent of payroll limit, the principal of the debt may be amortized. While debt amortization can be tailored to the size of the firm's payroll, we can use a rough rule of thumb for estimating the maximum amount of debt assuming equal amortization.

$$\text{Payroll} \times .25 \times \text{Amortization in Years} = \text{Maximum ESOP debt}$$

The minimum operating cash flow required to service this amount of debt is

$$\text{EBIT} = (i + (1/N)P$$

where i is the interest rate on the debt, N is the number of years necessary for the debt to amortize on a straight-line basis, and P is the principal amount of the debt.

In our example of the large recapitalization in Table 3, the maximum amount of ESOP debt available would be $550,000 (based on a payroll of $220,000). In this example, however, the ESOP is *able* to borrow only $510,000 while still maintaining a coverage ratio of 1.65 times (which we assume, however arbitrarily, is the minimum acceptable).

Dividend Policy

As the principal on an ESOP loan is repaid, the shares held in escrow are allocated to eligible employees. The contributions to pay principal are tax deductible to a limit of 25 percent of employee compensation *except* when the contribution is in the form of a dividend. Dividends on unallocated shares used to pay principal do not count against the 25 percent limitation. Practically speaking, this exception allows the firm to (a) assume even more ESOP debt and/or (b) amortize the debt more rapidly than the payroll limitation would allow.

Under the exception for dividends, the firm's main constraint on the extent of ESOP borrowing is the magnitude of its cash flow. In the examples presented in Tables 2 and 3, I have assumed that the ESOP payment is entirely covered by a common dividend. A second possible constraint is that firms are not allowed to discriminate against non-ESOP security holders, who receive a *pro rata* share of total dividends paid. This may reduce slightly the amount of total cash flow that the firm may pay as a dividend to an ESOP. And finally, firms may want to evaluate possible adverse equity signalling effects if a dividend initially set high to cover ESOP principal payments is later reduced (after the loan is repaid) to funnel cash to other uses.

Economic Dilution

ESOP transactions are potentially dilutive insofar as they effect a transfer of shareholders' wealth to employees. The wealth transfer takes two main routes. First, most ESOPs are formed as a benefit *in addition* to the employees' existing pension, profit-sharing and other plans. To the extent that the ESOP contribution is not offset by a reduction in other benefit plans, the employees will have received a real gain in wealth at the expense of the residual owners. Second, the ESOP (i.e., employees) makes use of a resource that actually belongs to the original shareholders—namely, the unused debt capacity of the firm. To the extent that the employees do not compensate the original owners for the use of this resource, the employees gain at the owners' expense.

How much economic dilution is acceptable in an ESOP restructuring? Economic dilution is perhaps the most severe constraint one will confront in designing ESOP transactions.[25] In evaluating the extent of potential dilution, the fundamental

---

25. Nonetheless, Eric Gleacher, head of Morgan Stanley's mergers and acquisitions group has told me that ESOPs remain relatively rare features of leveraged acquisitions because of the severe dilution they usually impose.

Table 4. Value Delivered to Public Shareholders

Alternative	Cash Payment	Stub Value	Total Value To Public
No Restructuring	$00.00	$492,336	$492,336
Share price after		$49.23	
Shares held by public		10,000	
Restructuring via			
Dividend	$355,097	$182,762	$537,859
Share price after		$18.28	
Shares held by public		10,000	
Restructuring via			
Stock repurchase at $53.79/share	$355,097	$182,762	$537,859
Share price after		$53.79	
Shares held by public		3,212	
Restructuring via ESOP			
1. ESOP Pays $66.35/share	$500,152	$40,203	$540,355
Share price after		$16.33	
Shares held by public		2,462	
2. ESOP pays $65.03/share	$500,152	$37,707	$537,859
Share price after		$16.33	
Shares held by public		2,309	
3. ESOP pays $53.79/share	$500,152	$11,448	$511,600
Share price after		$16.33	
Shares held by public		701	

question to ask is whether shareholders are better off under the ESOP restructuring both (1) than they were before and, probably more relevant, (2) than they would be under other restructuring proposals. Putting the issue in this perspective focuses attention on the total value paid to shareholders: cash flows in the form of dividends or shares repurchased plus the market value of any remaining equity held. (Simply comparing the firm's stock price after each of the three transactions is meaningless.)

An example of this kind of analysis is presented in Table 4, which is based on the large restructuring simulations of tax benefits shown in Table 3. First, one observes that the dividend and share repurchase alternatives are identical in terms of value delivered to shareholders ($537,859, which equals the sum of the $355,097 payout plus the market value of the public's remaining shares (the "stub"), $187,762). Thus, although the resulting stock prices are different, the market value of the stub equity is identical.

In the lower half of the table, I show that the relative value of the ESOP restructuring to shareholders depends critically on the price at which the ESOP buys its shares. Holding the amount of ESOP borrowing constant at roughly $500,000, we see that the price at which the ESOP is permitted to purchase the shares determines the *number* of shares it can purchase, and thus the number of shares remaining in the public's hands.

For example, if the ESOP buys $500,000 worth of shares from the public at a price of $53.79 (the same price as in the proposed stock repurchase), the ESOP ends up owning about 93 percent of the firm's remaining shares; and the public receives only about $511,600 in total value (the $500,152 payout plus a stub worth $11,448 ($701 \times $16.33)), as opposed to $537,859 in the alternative restructuring plans.

The breakeven stock price to the ESOP in this case would be $65.03. At that price, the public shareholders would be indifferent between the ESOP and the other restructuring alternatives because they would receive the same total value: in the ESOP case, the $500,152 payout plus a remaining 23 percent ownership worth roughly $38,000.

On the other hand, if the ESOP were made to pay a price as high as $66.35 per share, shareholders would continue to own roughly 25 percent of the firm's stock (valued at roughly $40,000), and thus receive a total value of $663,452. At $66.35 a share, the ESOP is in effect paying the full marginal value for its shares (that is, the sum of the market value of all the stub equity ($163,300) plus the new debt ($500,152) equals $663,452 which, when divided by 10,000 shares, is $66.35). In this case, shareholders are receiving all of the added value from the leverage and other ESOP-related tax benefits.

The price of $66.35 would be appropriate if shareholders could produce on their own all the tax benefits of an ESOP without actually having to sell their shares. But, in fact, the leveraged share repurchase alternative more closely approximates what the firm could do on its own with conventional financing.

As this example is meant to illustrate, then, raising the share price to the ESOP is the main lever by which the negative effects of dilution can be regulated. In practice, however, there is no theory or rule of thumb to dictate what the price to the ESOP *ought* to be. It is determined rather in a process of sharp bargaining—although it is important to keep in mind that the Department of Labor has been known to disallow ESOPs because of disadvantageous terms of sale.[26]

Differential Equity Claims

Other methods of dealing with the dilution constraint involve the use of cumulative preferred stock and dual-class common stock. Preferreds have been used in leveraged partial dispositions of subsidiaries or divisions of public companies. Though the new company may be unable to pay dividends in the first few years, the eventual payment of the cumulative obligation to the former owner effectively raises the price at which the ESOP bought its equity stake.

In the instance of dual-class common, the ESOP explicitly pays a higher price for its shares in consideration for the seniority of its dividend. For instance, Dan

---

26. Note that, in the ESOP examples discussed in Table 4, the real value of the shares is $16.33 (market value of equity divided by 10,000 shares). By comparison, share prices of the range $53 to $66 suggest that the ESOP is vastly overpaying. This, however, is illusory because the $16.00 is a gift from shareholders to employees (unless other benefits have been given up). The biggest loser in this process is the U.S. Treasury.

River, Inc. went private with an ESOP in 1983 to avoid takeover by Carl Icahn. The ESOP acquired 70 percent of the company with an investment of $110 million in Class A common stock at a price of $22.50 per share. Managers and an institutional investor invested $4.3 million to buy 30 percent of the company in Class B common stock at $2.06 per share. The Class B common is indexed to float at $22 per share less than the Class A common and is junior to the Class A in liquidation. The Class A common has limited voting rights, however, which can be exercised only upon a proposed merger or sale of the company. And until allocated, the ESOP stock will be voted by the trustee as directed by management. The voting rights of Class B stock are unrestricted.

VI. ESOPs and Corporate Performance

The GAO reported that the most often cited reason for leveraged ESOP formation (88 percent of cases) was to provide an employee benefit. Indeed, ESOP proponents argue that this benefit links the worker to the performance of the firm.[27] Although ESOPs have been the subject of relatively few rigorous studies, the limited evidence reveals at best a weak association between ESOPs and enhanced corporate performance based on either fundamental[28] or capital market[29] measures. The largest and

---

27. The GAO reports that, in 73 percent of its cases, respondents said that improved productivity was a key reason for ESOP formation.

28. Some studies consider the fundamental determinants of stock price performance such as productivity, growth, and profitability. Long [1980] studied the impact of employee ownership on job attitudes in three firms and concluded that the positive impact was greatest when the amount owned was highest and participation was strongest (see R. Long, "Job Attitudes and Organizational Performance under Employee Ownership," *Academy of Management Journal* 23 (December 1980)). Rosen, Klein, and Young [1986], cited in note 2, offer mixed statistical evidence: ESOPs are not strictly motivating; motivation depends on whether the size of the ESOP contribution is large, whether the ESOP is a key part of managerial philosophy, and whether there are "strong communications." Kraus [1984] concludes that the hypothesis that ESOPs cause employees to work harder is weakly supported. He notes that productivity improvement follows a trend beginning at the same time as the ESOP is formed, although the improvement may be a result of other, coincidence changes (e.g., new management). He concludes that "the evidence casts serious doubt" on employee ownership as a stimulus to increased motivation and decreased labor/management conflict: "It is clear that an ESOP is not sufficient to substantially increase motivation." (D. Krause, *Employee Ownership and Employee Attitudes: Two Case Studies* (Norwood, PA: Norwood Editions, 1984), p. 144)

Regarding other performance measures, Wagner and Rosen [1980] find that 13 publicly traded firms that had ESOPs featured growth and profitability above the median of a large sample of companies, although they conducted no statistical tests of the difference. The mean percentile rankings of the ESOP firms was 71 percent on sales growth rate, 62.8 percent on gross profit margin, 69 percent on return on equity, and 75 percent on growth in book value per share. It is difficult to know what to conclude from this comparison without knowing more about the distribution (particularly the variance) of the two samples.

Rosen and Quarry [1987] report that 45 firms with ESOPs had growth rates of sales and employment greater than a matched sample of non-ESOP firms by 5 percentage points (see C.M. Rosen and M. Quarry, "How Well is Employee Ownership Working?," *Harvard Business Review* 65 (September–October 1986)).

However, Bloom [1985] found in a study of 610 firms using Tax Credit ESOPs that the differences in productivity and profit ability disappeared when he controlled for differences in inventory changes,

Table 5. Comparison of Wealth Effects of ESOPs, Profit-Sharing, and ERISA Plans (Averages for 1980–84)

	Contribution As Percent of Payroll	Gain in Value Before Contribution	Total Gain
ESOPs	10.1	11.5%	21.6%
Profit sharing	8.9	n.a.	n.a.
ERISA Plans[a]	6.0	12.6%	18.6%

Source: *Employee Ownership*, Washington: National Center for Employee Ownership, December 1985.
a. Defined-benefit pension plans.

most recent study (done by the General Accounting Office (1987)) found no evidence that ESOPs improve corporate economic performance.[30]

One explanation for the lack of a measurable change in motivation is that most ESOPs provide limited monetary incentives. One study estimated that, if all the dividends paid in 1976 to ESOPs were divided equally among all workers, the individual would receive only an additional $341.76 per year.[31]

Moreover, there *are* alternative methods for supplying employee incentives and providing for their retirement. Table 5 presents a comparison of the wealth effects of ESOPs, profit-sharing plans, and ERISA pension plans. Superficially the results show that ESOPs result in larger employer contributions and slightly underperform other plans in terms of investment performance. These results, however, fail to adjust for the fact that the ESOP has a portfolio that is largely, if not completely, concentrated in the same firm in which the employee has his or her human capital invested. In other words, we should expect to see higher contribution and investment performance to compensate employees for the lack of diversification. General evidence has yet to be presented that, on a risk-adjusted basis, ESOPs offer incentives superior to other type plans.

gross plant per employee, and performance of the company before it adopted its ESOP. He concludes that economic analysis of ESOPs without necessary scientific controls will mistakenly show better performance (see S.M. Bloom (1985) *Employee Ownership and Firm Performance*, Doctoral Dissertation presented to the Harvard University Economics Department, Cambridge, MA. Ann Arbor, MI, University Microfilms International, 1986 No. GAX 86–08722).

29. Wagner and Rosen [1980] averaged the total return to shareholders (price change plus dividends) for the year in which the ESOP was established over 13 ESOP firms. They found that average hit the 48th to 51st percentile of a large sample of other firms. This preliminary evidence does not support an association between ESOP formation and stock prices.

30. The GAO drew 111 firms from a sample of 1100 firms and compared their median after-tax return on assets to a matched sample of non-ESOP firms for a period from 2 years before the founding of the ESOP to 3 years after. The change in profitability for ESOP firms was not significantly different from the non-ESOP sample.

31. C. Burck, "There's More to ESOP Than Meets the Eye." *Fortune* (March 1976).

Conclusions

Leveraged ESOPs deserve careful consideration as equity restructuring tactics. They may be used to restructure the equity clientele of the firm, and have the potential to create significant equity value. This benefit may be offset, however, by the economic dilution that results from an uncompensated transfer of value from shareholders to employees. Also, the ability to take full advantage of the tax benefits of ESOPs may, in many cases, be limited by the height of market prices, the size of the firm's payroll, and dividend payout. The constraints probably exclude many firms from the potential pool of material ESOP restructurings.

Nevertheless, we will probably witness a growing use of ESOPs in corporate restructurings. The rush by investment banks and large commercial banks to set up special departments for structuring ESOP-related transactions implies a growing demand in the marketplace.[32] And the developing market for ESOP debt securities, with the resulting decline in interest costs, suggests broadening acceptance on the part of investors and issuers alike.[33] The extent to which managerial expectations of the ESOP are fulfilled will depend on the appropriateness of design and implementation. As yet, though, the jury remains out on whether the ESOP will realize the grander promises of its founders.

---

32. Large banks now advertise their ability to employ ESOP financing as an element of corporate restructuring programs on behalf of their customers. Bankers Trust structured the Health Trust sale for HCA; and Irving Trust structured the ESOP financing for Avis. See E. T. O'Toole, "The Best Deals in 1987," *Barron's*, January 18, 1988.
33. The ESOP loan paper typically consists of floating rate notes securitized and/or backed by letters of credit sold to investors with an appetite for the 50 percent tax break for lenders. Drexel Burnham Lambert is trying to build a secondary market in ESOP paper.

15

Beyond the Tax Effects of ESOP Financing

Andrew H. Chen
Southern Methodist University

John W. Kensinger
University of Texas at Austin

The tax incentives for Employee Stock Ownership Plan (ESOP) financing cost the federal government about $2.5 billion in fiscal 1986, and are projected to reach $4.4 billion in 1990 if current trends continue.[1] ESOPs were created by a series of legislative acts written into law from 1974 to 1986, and arose out of the theories of Louis Kelso, who established the first ESOP at a California newspaper some thirty years ago. He found a powerful political ally in the chairman of the Senate Finance Committee, Russell Long of Louisiana. Senator Long retired in 1986, however, and a new ally with his combination of commitment and clout will be hard to find. In future deliberations, legislators are likely to be very demanding as they decide whether to maintain the incentive structure that now exists.

In 1975 there were only about 1,200 corporations with ESOPs. Now there are approximately 8,000, with almost 8 million employees participating.[2] That works out to an average of about 1,000 employees per plan, but this number is deceptively high—distorted by a few very large plans. Most of these corporations are small, and only a handful of them have ever been publicly traded. In a recent survey of 188 large companies conducted by Towers Perrin, moreover, it was found that 75 percent lack ESOPs. Most don't want them, the survey found, and only 12 percent of those with ESOPs reported taking full advantage of the tax benefits.[3]

---

1. Source: U.S. Office of Management and Budget.
2. National Center for Employee Ownership, July 1987.
3. *Wall Street Journal*, October 27, 1987, p. 1.

At first it seems surprising that more corporate giants have not taken advantage of the ESOP incentives, but there may be good reasons for their wariness. If taxpayers aren't getting their money's worth the incentives will be taken away, and those who jumped on the band wagon too hastily may be left high and dry. Besides, it is questionable wisdom to make a major change for tax reasons only, unless there is good economic justification as well.

So what else is there to recommend ESOP financing? There are two potential non-tax pluses for ESOP financing, one well-known and one below the surface. The first is the potential for enhanced productivity through better employee motivation. The second is enhanced market control over reinvestment of corporate cash flows. Besides giving employees a chance for an ownership stake in their companies, ESOPs put cash into the hands of stockholders, who from then on make the reinvestment decisions themselves. For several years after that, leveraged ESOPs commit the firm's cash flows to debt retirement, and divert the funds from cash cows into the marketplace where they can nourish the highest-valued new ventures.

On the negative side, there are some potentially damaging problems due to lack of diversification. Unfortunately, too, there are those who would use ESOPs to "save" dying operations, thwart takeovers, or entrench privileged groups.

I. Some ESOPs Work, But Some Don't

Consider the following "optimistic" scenario: Employees who have labored long and hard are offered the chance to emulate great capitalists by borrowing the money to buy their employer and pledging the cash flows of the company as collateral for the loan. Working for themselves now, instead of a faceless group of shareholders, they work harder than ever before. They pay off the loan in a few years, and then prosper.

The optimistic scenario has a real life counter-part in the very successful employee ownership plan at W.L. Gore & Associates Inc. of Newark, Delaware. Gore makes Teflon-based materials for vascular grafts, as well as Gore-tex, the advanced insulating fabric used in linings for NASA spacesuits and top-of-the-line ski clothing. Employees are called "associates," senior employees are called "group leaders" or "area leaders" rather than supervisors, and it is said that a family atmosphere pervades the workplace. Some workers with 15 years of service have accumulated $100,000 or more in the plan.[4]

The O & O supermarket chain in Philadelphia is another such story. The chain, which was formerly a money-losing division of A&P, has made a turnaround which is attributed to the incentives of employee ownership. National Steel's Weirton plant was saved from closing by an ESOP in January 1984, and since then has shown profits for the past ten quarters. Likewise, employee ownership transformed troubled Bridgeport Brass (Connecticut) into the successful Seymour Specialty Wire Co.

---

4. John Hoerr, "A Company Where Everybody is the Boss," *Business Week*, April 15, 1985, p. 98.

The optimistic scenario is appealing, yet essentially assumes that there are no limits to the potential payoff from hard work and industriousness, regardless of the object upon which they are focused. But, consider an alternative "pessimistic" scenario: An aging company operating a dingy, red-brick factory has employed townspeople from the surrounding communities for generations. Over the years, the employees' union has won a middle-class lifestyle for its members, but now the employees fear for the future. Foreign competitors, with cheap labor, are undercutting prices and taking market share. The price of the company's stock has plunged and corporate raiders are on the prowl, threatening to liquidate the company. In an effort to save their jobs, employees put up their pension assets and borrow heavily in order to buy the stock in their company. Market forces prove impossible to thwart, however, and the company continues to wither in the face of competition. In the end, the employees still lose their jobs, and the government has to bail out their pension plan.

There have been many attempts to use ESOP financing as a bailout for dying enterprises.[5] In the troubled steel industry, for example, there have been several ESOP rescue attempts. In exchange for wage concessions, an ESOP saved McLouth Steel Corp. from bankruptcy liquidation. Likewise, LTV arranged to sell its Gadsden, Alabama plant to employees. In a related industry, Kaiser Aluminum & Chemical Corp. sold a group of 1200 workers a plant that makes refractory bricks (which are used to line blast furnaces, and thus face declining demand). Laid-off workers have even entertained the hope of buying and reopening U.S. Steel's Diquesne Works, despite conditions that were eloquently described by one observer as follows:

> The blast furnace stands rusting among overgrown railroad tracks. Pigeons roost in the top of the steelmaking shop. The plant would need a $200 million continuous caster. And nothing can ever be done to remedy its location, hemmed in by the Monongehela River Valley far from deep-water ports.[6]

The tax preferences of ESOP financing, as attractive as they are, cannot overcome the tremendous cost disadvantage that antiquated steel mills face in competition from foreign producers and modern U.S. mills. Such bailouts can do no more than prolong the agony of reducing capacity in overcrowded industries, and hold back the stronger operations in the process.

Some bailouts, moreover, have already gone to the end of the line. In 1979, for example, employees got 60 percent control of Rath Packing Company's aging, inefficient, five-story main plant in Waterloo, Iowa, in exchange for wage concessions. Although worker ownership was credited with remarkable improvements in productivity, worker absenteeism, and grievances, the plant was still compelled by inexorable market forces to close its doors in 1984.

---

5. An estimate of seventy such bailouts was given in John Hoerr, Gelvin Stevenson, and James Norman, "ESOPs: Revolution or Ripoff?" *Business Week*, April 15, 1985, pp. 94–7.
6. Douglas R. Sease, "ESOPs Weren't Meant to be Bailouts," *Wall Street Journal*, December 2, 1985.

II. When is Employee Ownership Most Beneficial?

Employee ownership is not a panacea, and shouldn't be prescribed indiscriminately. Selling all or part of the company to the employees works only when it resolves conflicts that otherwise would exist between the owners and employees in such a way that both groups are better off.

Employee ownership is certainly not a new thing, but is the norm in many sectors of the economy. In the legal and medical professions, for example, the sole proprietorship and the professional partnership are the predominant organizational forms.[7] This is natural because such large proportion of productivity is attributable to human capital, which is inherently non-marketable. Sole proprietorship is also commonplace in agriculture, where, despite the extensive use of capital equipment, productivity ultimately depends upon the farmer's willingness and ability to work long, hard hours, even when sick, as well as the grit to fight the forces of raw nature if need be—and that can't easily be bought for wages. With the wave of venture capital financing, employee ownership is also becoming wide-spread in high-tech research, where human capital is again a key component.

ESOPs Don't Always Create Improved Incentives

Advocates of employee ownership argue that it provides improved motivation, leading to greater effort and less waste. The value of extra effort varies greatly, however. For a star research scientist, the right incentives may make the difference which leads to a great discovery. For a sales representative, incentives may make the difference between a so-so performance and high-quality customer service—which can be worth a lot of money. For a janitor, however, the potential is considerably less. Thus, careful focus is called for in making the most of any incentive package, and ESOPs do not facilitate such focus. Attempts to do so, in fact, have been squelched by the U.S. Labor Department, which regulates ESOPs.

Even when highly-developed human capital is not involved, however, on-the-job consumption of perks could be reduced by employee ownership. This works more effectively in small organizations than in large ones, though. Such savings occur only when the active participants in the business are willing to forgo direct compensation and accept an increased equity value instead. If, for example, an employee derives $20 worth of satisfaction from consuming something that costs the employer $100 to provide, such consumption is inefficient. If the employee had a 25 percent ownership stake and so could realize a $25 increase in his share of profits from eliminating the perk, he would opt for more efficient consumption. If the employee had only a 1/1,000th share, however, there would be little incentive to voluntarily forgo on-the-job consumption.

---

7. For an in-depth analysis, see Eugene Fama and Michael Jensen, "Organizational Forms and Investment Decisions," *Journal of Financial Economics* (June 1985).

To the extent that employee ownership resolves other conflicts of interest between employees and owners it has potential to enhance value.[8] But there are limits. Since employees depend upon their employer for the bulk of their livelihood, they cannot help having a different set of priorities than outside owners, for whom the fate of the company affects only a small portion of their total wealth. Take the case when, for example, there is a compelling need to reduce excess capacity in an overcrowded industry. It is hard for an increase in the value of one's stake in an ESOP to offset the loss of a union job.

Another factor is the strength of the labor unions representing the employees. Consider a capital-intensive firm which has made a heavy investment in production equipment, so that the marginal product of financial capital is large relative to the marginal product of human capital. A problem would arise for such a firm if the workers were able to gain a strong bargaining position and take some of the marginal product of financial capital for themselves in the form of higher wages, benefits, or on-the-job consumption. If anticipated by the capital market, the prospect of such seizures would depress stock values and reduce the inflow of capital into the company. In such a case, an ESOP could help resolve the conflict between owners and labor.

ESOPs Lack Diversificaiton

The inherent problem in employee ownership is that it does not permit portfolio diversification. A given amount would be more valuable if contributed to a diversified pension plan portfolio rather than an ESOP.[9] Of course, the problem would be much less severe in the case of a large, diversified employer, corporation than in the case of a small, technology-intensive firm.

The ability to diversify a portfolio across a broad range of stocks from different companies and industries has generated considerable social benefits by making efficient risk-sharing possible. In drilling for oil, for example, putting all of one's wealth into a single well is very risky, whereas spreading that wealth over several wells is much more prudent. Likewise in R&D, committing all of one's wealth to a single research project is much more risky than spreading the wealth over a pool of projects. With diversifiable risks neutralized in portfolios, it is possible to mobilize capital for enterprises which otherwise would not be underwritten.

Adding to the disincentives, there is reason to believe that having an ESOP will increase the tendency to underinvest in new expansion projects. Corporate management in general may be less willing to take on risky ventures than outside shareholders would prefer. This is because the consequences of failure that are suffered by the managers are more severe than those suffered by the diversified outside shareholders.[10] This difference in risk exposure may cause managers to

---

8. See, for example, James Brickley, Ron Lease, and Clifford Smith, "Ownership Structure and Firm Value," University of Rochester Finance Department Working Paper (February 1987).

9. A. Marcus, "Risk-Sharing and the Theory of the Firm," *Bell Journal of Economics* (1982).

10. The outside shareholders can diversify away firm-specific risk in their portfolios, whereas the managers cannot.

avoid ventures that seem too risky from their own undiversified viewpoint, but which are attractive from the diversified viewpoint of outside shareholders.[11]

A corporation with an ESOP has decision-makers whose financial well-being is bound even more tightly to the health of their employer—in which they have tied up not only their human capital, but also their financial capital. Unable to remove any of their wealth from the employer corporation, they are even more prone to underinvest in new growth opportunities or new technologies than their counterparts in non-ESOP firms (who can diversify at least their financial capital).

Since the market value of a firm reflects not only the present value of cash flows from established operations, but also the present value of growth opportunities,[12] this tendency to underinvest could depress the value of a firm with a large proportion of employee ownership. The underinvestment factor is far less significant, however, for firms in mature industries with relatively few growth opportunities than for companies in young industries where there are many opportunities for growth and assimilation of new technologies.

Based on consideration of this underinvestment problem alone then, mature, leverageable companies with strong labor unions and few investment opportunities would seem to offer the best candidates for ESOP financing. On the other hand, the incentive benefits provided by employee ownership are likely to be greatest in smaller, human-capital-intensive corporations—that is, high-growth, perhaps high-tech operations where individual initiative is most critical. But such companies can hardly support the debt necessary to secure the tax benefits of ESOP financing.

So now we need to examine the structure of ESOP financing to see how it can increase the value of large companies in mature, slow-growth industries.

III. ESOP Financing Fundamentally Alters Corporate Control

ESOPs Divert Cash Flows Into the Marketplace

The basic arrangement of an ESOP is summarized in Figure 1. The reality of ESOP financing is that it transfers control to the marketplace. A closer inspection reveals how. When the ESOP buys stock from existing shareholders, they are immediately free to redeploy the funds into any other ventures they find attractive, choosing from the full array of opportunities in the capital market. When the employer has guaranteed the loan, the net effect is an immediate return of capital to outside shareholders, with the company's future cash flows impounded to repay the resulting

---

11. This prediction is based upon the current understanding of the principal/agent relationship that exists between the corporation's owners and its managers, and the tendency to pass up good investment opportunities is referred to as a "residual agency cost." For the classic theoretical formulation of the "agency cost" concept, see M. Jensen and W. Meckling, "Theory of the Firm, Managerial Behavior, Agency Costs and Ownership Structure," *Journal of Financial Economics* (1976). For an explanation of the corporate underinvestment problem accompanying a highly levered capital structure, see also Stewart Myers, "Determinants of Corporate Borrowing," *Journal of Financial Economics* (1977).

12. See Stewart Myers, "Determinants of Corporate Borrowing," *Journal of Financial Economics* (1977).

Figure 1. How ESOP Financing Works.

debt. And as the debt service payments are made, *the lender* decides how to reinvest them. Thus cash is forced out of the employer corporation by the ESOP financing.

Besides this diversion of capital into the marketplace, the tax incentives work in a further way to divert the cash flow out of the company. With the ESOP tax privileges the corporation can eliminate income tax completely and, in the case of 100 percent ESOP ownership, make its entire pre-tax cash flow available to retire the trust's debt. Only if such a corporation retained earnings for new investment would there be any need to pay income tax—which is a significant change.[13] Traditionally, income tax laws have kept cash inside a company, since paying dividends resulted in double taxation. In the case of a buyout by a leveraged ESOP under current tax rules, the tax penalty is instead levied against retention of earnings for reinvestment. It is therefore better for an ESOP-owned corporation to raise expansion capital by selling new stock to the ESOP rather than retaining earnings; and when this requires the ESOP trust to go to the market for a loan, the growth plans must meet outside scrutiny.

When a mature or declining firm throws off large sums of cash, but has few attractive internally-generated growth opportunities, stockholders may fear that managers will squander free cash flows on ill-advised attempts to expand the firm into areas in which it lacks experience, expertise, and competitive advantage.[14] When this concern is strong, shareholders will value any arrangement which commits management to pay out the free cash flows to investors. With creditors to

---

13. Even if the ESOP held only a portion of the stock, there would still be a strong incentive to pay out all earnings. Suppose, for example, the ESOP owned 50% of the stock in the employer corporation. Then, half of every dollar paid in dividends would be deductible, whereas all of a dollar retained would be taxed. If the corporation earned $10 million, it could pay out as much as $8.3 million in dividends at one extreme (100% payout), or retain $6.60 million for reinvestment at the other extreme (100% retention). Starting from so far behind, the corporation would need a significant advantage to be able to reinvest its earnings more profitably than the stockholders could do on their own.

14. The "free cash flow" of a firm is the excess over what is needed to finance the economically-sound expansion projects available to the firm.

appease, the cash flows become committed to interest and debt retirement for a significant period into the future. New projects would have to compete for external funding, rather than be sustained by the employer's cash flows. If there is and danger that management might not be as demanding as the marketplace in scrutinizing internal investments, this change increases the probability that the cash flows will find their way to the highest-valued uses—thus enhancing economic efficiency.[15]

IV. ESOPs Aren't Meant to Protect Managers from Unhappy Stockholders

Attempts have been made to use ESOP financing to create a protective barrier against raiders, by selling a significant block of stock to employees. Using ESOP financing as an anti-takeover defense may prove ineffective, however, since the ESOP's shares are held in trust until they are allocated to the employees as the loan is repaid. The trustee (even one appointed by management) has a fiduciary responsibility to the employees, and is personally liable for decisions.

After raids by Boone Pickens and Carl Icahn, for example, Phillips Petroleum announced plans to form an ESOP that would buy over 30 percent of its common stock (for $1.5 billion).[16] Under ERISA, the trustee's primary responsibility is for the retirement income of the employees, but there is leeway to consider the employees' job security. Phillips management, therefore, sought Labor Department approval for a plan that would require the trustee to vote in accordance with the wishes of a majority of participating employees, hoping that they would vote against any future takeover attempt for fear of losing their jobs. This novel request became moot, however, when Phillips settled with Icahn and tabled the proposed ESOP.

Just as managers could make defensive use of an ESOP, however, a raider could use an ESOP as an ally. A successful takeover, moreover, is not the only way for an outsider to force a change upon management. The recent saga of UAL Corporation (now known as Allegis) is a familiar example. Last year United Airlines' parent corporation faced some unusual problems with its own pilots, as well as rumored raids. Mr. Richard Ferris, UAL Chairman, had worked long and hard to realize his dream of creating a full-range travel services company, building a conglomerate whose separate operating divisions included United Airlines, Hertz, Hilton Hotels and Westin Hotels—with the airline's computerized reservation system at its heart. Much to his dismay, however, the pilots' union arranged an offer to buy the airline, with the reservations system included. An ESOP would pay $4.5 billion.

The pilots made their offer on April 5. To put this offer in perspective, the total market value of equity in the whole UAL conglomerate on March 27, 1987 was just under $3 billion ($59 per share). After the offer, the stock commenced

---

15. This idea was first developed in Michael C. Jensen, "Agency Costs of Free Cash Flow, Corporate Finance and Takeovers," *American Economic Review* (May 1986).

16. "Firms Find New Role for Stock Plans," *The Dallas Morning News*, January 13, 1985.

a strong upward movement. The board of directors rejected the bid, however, and the pilots began looking for an ally who would take over the parent company and sell them the airline.

The pilots found their friend in Coniston Partners. With the proposed ESOP as a potential buyer for United Airlines, as well as other prospective buyers for Hertz and the corporate hotel properties, Coniston Partners had the leverage they needed to influence the board of directors. Though holding far less than a controlling interest, they threatened a proxy fight. This threat persuaded the board to repudiate Ferris' strategy, forcing his resignation in June. The stock then edged toward $90 per share, a 50 percent gain in about two months.[17]

V. ESOPs Aren't Meant to Protect Any Privileged Group From Market Forces

The proposed United Airlines ESOP helped overthrow Ferris, allowing investors (and particularly Coniston Partners) to realize a significant increase in value. At the same time, however, it contained a potent recipe for disappointment. The core of the problem is that privileged employees were seeking to resist the forces of the marketplace. Ultimately, not even the tax subsidies of ESOP financing can prevail in such a quest; and, as of this writing, the proposed ESOP has not come together, although United Airlines is shedding its hotel and rental car holdings.

The UAL pilots and flight attendants were highly paid by industry standards. The head of the pilots' union, moreover, has been quoted as saying, "We have to control the company from which we draw our salary."[18] Presumably, the object of seeking control is to protect the payroll, and entrench against the marketplace.

Yet, the machinists' union were being paid at market levels, and they balked at the deal. The deal could not be struck without their willing participation, and the union lacked confidence in employee ownership as a result of their disappointing experience with it at Eastern Airlines. (There, despite 25 percent employee-ownership, the company was taken over by an archly anti-union rival.)

There was another more subtle cause for concern on their part, too. Dollars which should be labeled as profits and shared among all employees would instead go to a select few in the form of inflated paychecks. And if the pilots and flight attendants were able to go on earning more than the industry standard, the airline would be hard-pressed to compete, thus threatening job security for all employees.

---

17. See the following for more details: 1. Judith Valente and Scott Kilman, "Pilots May Seek Partner to Buy Parent of United," *Wall Street Journal*, April 27, 1987, p. 6; James Ellis and Chuck Hawkins, "The Unraveling of an Idea," *Business Week*, June 22, 1987, pp. 42–43; and 2. Kenneth Labich, "How Dick Ferris Blew It," *Fortune*, July 6, 1987, pp. 42–44, 46.

18. Quoted in Robert L. Rose, "United Pilots Leader Stays on Course," *Wall Street Journal*, July 17, 1987, p. 21.

VI. ESOPs Aren't Supposed to Be Tax-Privileged Management Buyouts

In order to gain management cooperation, several recent ESOPs have given top executives a significantly more attractive deal than the other employees received. The Dan River ESOP is a case in point. Guided by Kelso & Co. (an investment banking firm specializing in ESOPs) the employees took over the company as a defense against a raid by Carl Icahn in 1983, and in the process created two classes of common stock. A group of top managers put up a relatively small proportion of the total price, yet got not only a disproportionately large stake in the company but also a relatively rich share of the upside potential.[19]

Carl Icahn went away, but workers still had little say in running the company, and labor union members continued to be laid off in response to unrelenting pressure from imports. Although Dan River avoided the takeover, control of its cash flow was returned to the marketplace, and the necessity of servicing the debt from the employee buyout closed the cash spigot for further investment in the company. This outcome was not palatable to many employees, as reflected in "a near-unanimous feeling that majority ownership has not produced even token democracy in the workplace."[20]

The problem at Dan River, however, was really too much for any sort of "employee entrepreneurship" or "workplace democracy" to solve. Dan River was a mature company which could not compete in world markets because, in a labor-intensive industry, its costs far exceeded those of foreign competitors.

Dan River was not the only situation in which top management received a disproportionate share of equity. In another case, Raymond Industries terminated its pension plan in order to finance an employee buyout, with the loan to be repaid by what would otherwise have been pension fund contributions. A small management group got half as many shares as all the other employees, for about a twentieth as much investment, along with a disproportionate share of upside potential.[21] It's little wonder that some employees felt they got a raw deal. The Blue Bell ESOP,

---

19. The ESOP acquired 70% of the company with a $110 million investment in Class A common stock at a price of $22.50 per share. A group consisting of a Kelso investment fund, plus twenty-six members of top management, paid $4.3 million for 30% of the company, mostly in the form of Class B common stock valued at $2.06 per share. Since the buyout there is no longer any market in the stock, so a periodic valuation will be made by an independent appraiser. According to the rules, the Class A stock will always be worth about $22 per share more than the Class B, but the disparity in the initial values gives management a disproportionate share of the upside. If Class A stock rose to $26, for instance. Class B would rise to about $4—which would be a 100% gain for Class B, compared to only 16% for Class A.

20. Pete Engardio, "At Dan River, 'A Lot of Us Feel That We Got Took,'" *Business Week*, April 15, 1985, p. 97.

21. A group of Kelso & Co. investors and twenty-eight Raymond managers paid $5.4 million in cash, stock, and stock options for Class B common stock at $1.09 per share. The ESOP borrowed $100 million in order to buy Class A common stock at $10 per share. The Class B stock, pegged at a price $10 below Class A, gives management a disproportionate share of the upside potential. If Class A went up 50% to $15, for example, Class B would increase nearly five-fold.

also arranged by Kelso & Co., is yet another example of the same. Finally, in July 1985 the Labor Department blocked a similar deal at Scott & Fetzer Co., a Cleveland manufacturer, setting a precedent which stood for two years.

In mid-1987, however, Hospital Corporation of America (HCA) proposed a successful combination of an ESOP buyout and a leveraged management buyout (LBO). This deal is the biggest ESOP yet. Despite criticism labeling it an explicit attempt to create a tax-privileged management buyout, it overcame the stigma of prior two-tiered deals by creating just one class of stock and promising that all classes of owners will be given identical treatment.[22] HCA earmarked 104 of its less-profitable hospitals for sale to 25,000 employees. For $1.8 billion the ESOP gets 51 percent of the new company. The rest goes to the management group.

The rub is that HCA keeps the best hospitals, while the employee-owned company gets smaller, undiversified facilities that account for 35 percent of HCA's current revenues but only 20 percent of profits. The projected cash flow of the new company, furthermore, barely covers the $200 million annual debt support payments. With hospitals under intense pressure from cost-containment efforts by the insurance and the federal government, there could be problems.

VII. The Debate Over ESOP Financing

Despite his firm's uneven treatment of labor and management in several of the ESOPs it helped arrange, Louis Kelso (the "father" of the ESOP) has expressed his desire to reform the economic order. He aims, he says, at "expanding America's ownership base—democratizing its economic power."[23] ESOP financing, in Kelso's vision, is designed to enable people who possess little or no capital to borrow the price of an ownership stake in their employer corporation, on the strength of the employer's cash flows. Kelso makes it plain that the heart of his vision is a redistribution of capital in favor of "economic democracy," and that the means for this redistribution is financial leverage combined with tax subsidies. Kelso and his political allies have devised a system of tax preferences which disperse ownership claims to people who might otherwise not be able to accumulate capital quickly.

A more conservative view of economic democracy, in contrast, is concerned simply with ensuring that owners receive the full benefits of their property rights, and that no one is made better off at the cost of another. Kelso's plan, on the other hand, aims to accomplish a fundamental redistribution of those property rights, using the taxing authority to convince the reluctant.[24]

Surprisingly, ESOP financing stirs controversy at the other end of the ideological spectrum as well. Some workplace reformers are concerned because nothing in the structure of an ESOP trust requires that labor be given a voice in management. In his *Business Week* column, for example, Robert Kuttner voiced the concern

22. Gary Weiss, "HCA May Breathe New Life into ESOPs," *Business Week*, June 15, 1987, p. 94.
23. Louis O. and Patricia H. Kelso, *Democracy and Economic Power*, Ballinger Publishing Company, Cambridge, Mass., 1986, p. xi.
24. The taxpayers, after all, get the bill for the "gift" of employee ownership.

that, too often, employee ownership plans do not give workers voting rights and therefore lack a "philosophical commitment to democratize" the workplace.[25] Steven L. Dawson, Executive Director of the Industrial Cooperative Association, a lobbying organization for employee ownership, reinforced Kuttner's points by arguing that ESOPs give workers a kind of "second-class" ownership: workers get a share of profits, but not the control that comes with "first-class" ownership.[26]

The real issue, however, is not employees versus owners or managers versus workers, but rather entrenchment of any kind against the forces of the marketplace. It is our contention that freedom of the marketplace, more than worker control of the enterprise, is at the heart of economic democracy, and that difficulties may arise if any group gains excessive bargaining power. History is replete not only with instances of owners taking unfair advantage of workers, but also labor unions, guilds, or management groups entrenching themselves against the forces of the marketplace. Such entrenchment leads to inefficient resource allocation—hence fewer goods, higher prices, and a diminished standard of living for everyone.

VIII. Concluding Remarks

Too little employee representation in the circle of owners may result in missed opportunities for cost reduction and increased productivity, yet too much may result in slower long-term growth potential for the company. Choosing the best mix of employee and outside ownership means seeking a delicate balance, which may differ greatly from one enterprise to another. The greatest potential gains from employee ownership can be expected to be in those enterprises which depend heavily upon human capital for their productivity. Such enterprises, unfortunately, are typically smaller, high-growth companies that lack the debt capacity required for large, leveraged ESOPs. Small, high-growth firms also generally do not need ESOPs to strengthen the incentives of management, or even employees, to perform. These workers have already achieved for themselves, by virtue of their choice of employer, a high-risk, presumably high-reward profile that should be its own motivator.

ESOPs also hold out significant benefits to capital-intensive companies which must contend with powerful labor unions; while the lowest costs, in terms of foregone investment opportunities caused by high leverage, occur in those companies with limited potential for future growth.

By encouraging an increased proportion of employee ownership across the board, however, the ESOP tax preferences could create mischief in two ways. The tax preferences can keep a dying enterprise limping along, creating an imbalance in its industry which holds back the stronger competitors and so creates economic inefficiency. Perhaps even more damaging in the long run, these preferences may discourage valuable investment in new technologies and other growth opportunities

---

25. See, for example, Robert Kuttner, "Worker Ownership: A Commitment That's More Often a Con," *Business Week*, July 6, 1987, p. 16.
26. In a letter to the editor in *Business Week*, August 3, 1987.

by fostering an overly cautious attitude brought on by inefficient diversification of employees' capital.

The marketplace has shown a remarkable ability to find areas where employee ownership is important, and without the encouragement of tax preferences. There are some who suppose that the marketplace is too slow in making necessary changes and therefore needs a boost in the form of tax incentives. The market, however, has time and again proved its remarkable resiliency and adaptability, and the lessons of history suggest that we interfere with it at our peril. Where the benefits of employee ownership exceed the costs, the marketplace can be expected to seek them out on its own.

When multi-billion dollar tax incentives are lavished, however, we are in danger of serious distortions. ESOP financing brings large rewards at the expense of the tax collector, but to one and all it brings a significant change in the way investments in new technology are evaluated and financed. This may in some cases help shareholders wrest control over free cash flows from reluctant management, and so accomplish a much-needed reallocation of resources to higher-valued uses. But it may also hold resources longer than necessary in low-valued uses, or hamper the growth of an enterprise which would otherwise have higher potential.

Finding the best balance of employee ownership for a given enterprise is tied intimately with the problem of allocating the providers of labor and capital with their fair share of output. Mature, diversified corporations with strong labor unions and few growth opportunities, on balance, are likely to be the best candidates for ESOP financing. Such companies, however, can be harnessed effectively by other highly-leveraged financing arrangements such as LBOs, leveraged recapitalizations, and takeovers. These arrangements also substantially reduce the tax payments made by the company, and commit the cash flows to debt support payments.

16

An Economic Analysis of R&D Limited Partnerships

John D. Martin
University of Texas at Austin

John W. Kensinger
University of Texas at Austin

Research and Development Limited Partnerships (RDLPs) represent a relatively recent innovation in business organizational form, as well as a potentially major change in the role of financial intermediaries. RDLPs, which are used to raise capital for research and development expenditures, have experienced rapid growth during the 1980s. During the 3½-year period between January 1981 and June 1984, more than 200 RDLPs were created for the purpose of financing over $2.3 billion in R&D.

The RDLP represents an alternative to more traditional ways of financing R&D expenditures. By using an RDLP, a company obtains the needed research without having to resort to internal equity financing, the sale of new equity, or added borrowing. Very briefly, an RDLP involves a triangular relationship among three parties, the corporation seeking the research, the general partner (frequently the firm seeking the R&D), and the limited partners. The general partner manages the business and assumes unlimited liability for all debts of the partnership. The limited partners provide the bulk of the funds to the RDLP in return for an interest in whatever monies the R&D effort produces.

A major factor underlying the creation and growing popularity of RDLPs is the tax treatment accorded the limited partners. In a landmark Supreme Court

We wish to thank several people for valuable comments and assistance. Dr. Jack Williams of the U.S. Department of Commerce and Dr. Robert Curry of Merrill Lynch R&D Management Company have participated in very informative discussions. Elizabeth Robertson of the U.S. Department of Commerce commented on an earlier version and was very generous with data.

decision in 1974, the court ruled that R&D expenses could be deducted even if the taxpayer were not carrying on a trade or business.[1] Prior to this time such deductions only were allowed if the taxpayer were currently engaged in a related business activity. Tax advantages, however, constitute only one of many factors we identify as major potential motivating forces behind the formation of RDLPs.

The hefty tax incentives make RDLP financing look a lot like a direct government grant for research. In fact, one might wonder what difference there is between a Federal program that encourages research at the expense of tax revenues and one that pays out grant money after the tax collectors have done their work. There is a key difference. With the RDLP approach it is the market, as opposed to the bureaucracy of government, that decides which research projects get funding. Furthermore, when RDLP financing is used, those investors who bear the risk of the project's failure are the ones who receive the rewards of success. In the case of a direct grant, by contrast, the principals of the recipient firm bear no risk, yet stand to gain if the research is successful.

In a very recent development, some of the major investment banking firms in the United States have set up R&D management subsidiaries to serve as the general partner for several R&D projects. Such direct involvement in the management of ongoing enterprises represents a major change in the role of investment bankers (in the context of recent history). The general model is for the investment to raise a block of funds through a "blind-pool RDLP," and then serve as general partner (GP). The funds are subsequently allocated to specific projects at the discretion of the GP. When the funds are exhausted, a new pool may be formed.

The GP plays a very significant role in such a blind pool, being responsible for project selection as well as for ongoing project management. At the time they put up their money, the limited partners may not know what projects they will

---

1. In the landmark Supreme Court case involving Snow vs. Commissioner in 1974, the court ruled that Research and Development expenditures *could* be deducted even if the taxpayer were not carrying on a related trade or business. Previously such deductions were allowed only if the taxpayer were currently engaged in a related business activity. Section 174(a)(1) of the tax code provides that "A taxpayer may treat research or experimental expenditures which are paid or incurred by him during the taxable year in connection with his trade or business as expenses which are not chargeable to capital account. The expenditures so treated shall be allowed as a deduction." The Snow vs. Commissioner case effectively lifted the "in connection with his trade or business" requirement such that a new limited partnership organized for the purpose of developing a new process or product is nonetheless entitled to deduct research and experimentation expenses.

This point was clarified in the 1984 case of Green vs. Commissioner (No. 29477-83, 83 T.C. No. 37, 11/5/84), in which the court found that the R&D deductions can't be taken when the agreements of the partnership preclude ever entering into a trade or business. Lasala Lmt., the partnership in question, acquired rights to a technology from the inventors and simultaneously licensed another company not only the base technology but also any technology resulting from the research. Furthermore, the agreements gave Lasala no right to control the research done by the contractor. Because Lasala had in effect sold any patent rights it might acquire from the research before research began, it was deemed to be incapable of ever entering into a trade or business. This pitfall can be avoided by preselling rights or options to purchase rights for production of a specific final product, rather than for the whole technology. The crucial issue is whether the RDLP retains an active interest in the research.

help finance, but must go on faith in the abilities of the GP. In addition to the pools offered by the public, funds have also been raised through private placements of blind pools, in which the limited partners include corporations, pension funds, and other institutional investors.

The implications of private placements of RDLP pools could be important. In this type of arrangement, money from institutional investors is put into exploratory investments that are directly managed by subsidiaries of other financial institutions. This represents a potentially significant concentration of power at the financial centers of the economy. Officials at the U.S. Department of Commerce have even proposed the development of limited partnerships to purchase the successful results of these RDLP pools for the purpose of manufacturing and marketing them. All this, then, suggests the possibility that a significant amount of future business activity might be conducted under the direct management of financial institutions.

Although RDLPs provide an important source of financing to U.S. corporations, they have received little attention in the finance literature. Our objective in the present paper is to review the background of RDLPs and discuss the economic implications of their use. In our discussion we will pay significant attention to non-tax-related motives for RDLPs, as well as to the considerable, but more obvious, tax incentives. The paper is structured as follows: In Section 1 we discuss the organization of an RDLP, including the roles of each of the participants involved. Section 2 provides a deeper analysis of the economic advantages of the RDLP organizational form. Section 3 discusses the potential *disadvantages* of RDLPs, and the use of RDLPs in the context of the choice of an optimal organizational form. Section 4 gives a brief discussion of the problems to be dealt with in structuring contracts (and an Appendix summarizes the use of RDLPs to date).

I. The Organizational Form of an RDLP[2]

The organizational form of an RDLP is governed by a partnership agreement which specifies the rights and duties of the two classes of participants (that is, the general and limited partners). The general partner can be either a single or multiple parties who manage the business affairs of the partnership. The limited partners, on the other hand, are investors in the business who provide *no* active management participation. They provide capital to the RDLP in return for the tax benefits they derive and the expectation of any payments derived from the commercialization of the results of the R&D effort. Because they have no voice in management, the limited partners' liability is limited to the amount invested. In addition to the general and limited partners, the formation of an RDLP will frequently involve the efforts of a number of other parties. These include the following: a) an *R&D contractor(s)*, which provides the actual research effort; b) the *investment broker*, who provides

---

2. This section relies heavily upon the discussion by R.B. Ellert and M.R. Rubin in "Information and Steps Necessary to Form Research and Development Limited Partnerships," Mimeo, Office of Productivity, Technology and Innovation, U.S. Department of Commerce, December 31, 1983.

assistance in selling the limited partnership units to investors; c) the *manufacturer/ marketer* firm, which actually brings new products resulting from the R&D effort to the market, and d) the *end user* individual or firm, which makes use of the new technology or product.

The most obvious advantage of the use of an RDLP relates to the tax treatment of partnership income and losses (which will be discussed later in more detail). In a partnership, tax consequences flow through directly to the investors. Unlike the corporation, the partnership does not represent a separate taxable entity, so the partnership incurs no tax liability as an entity separate and apart from the investors. The RDLP thus can offer a firm seeking R&D funding a means of forming a mutually-beneficial association with high-tax-bracket individuals, for whom the ability to expense R&D costs is more valuable. In the past, the limited partners in an RDLP have sometimes been able to recover from 60 to 90 percent of their investment in the year in which the RDLP was formed. Since the end of 1984, however, it is no longer possible for the partners simply to deduct R&D expenses in the year payments are made to the contractors. Instead, the expenses can now be deducted only as the funds are actually used up in the research effort.

The most significant tax advantage of the RDLP, however, is the opportunity it provides to avoid the corporate level of taxation. Investors who own shares of common stock in a corporation are effectively subjected to two levels of taxation (corporate and personal), whereas the revenues and expenses of a partnership flow through directly to the partners without an intervening level of firm taxation.

Compelling as the tax advantages are, even more interesting economic considerations arise from the potential of RDLP arrangements to change the way industrial research efforts are organized. Within traditional financial arrangements, one firm fulfills all the roles of sponsor, research contractor, and manufacturer/marketer. With RDLPs, there is the possibility to distribute these roles in a variety of potentially more efficient ways.

The limited partnership is a very flexible organizational form which admits many possible manifestations. Most RDLPs to date, however, have conformed reasonably well to one of two patterns: 1) one firm seeking R&D for its own benefit, or 2) an entrepreneur which conducts R&D for one or more firms with which it may have no previous ties or connections. Although it has not been used so far, a third distinct possibility is for an RDLP to be used as the vehicle for a joint venture undertaken by several related companies.

One Firm Financing R&D for its Own Use

In this case the general partner is also both the R&D contractor and the manufacturer/marketer. There is, however, a very important, potentially disastrous flaw in this form of organization: namely, the potential conflict of interest between the general partner and the limited partners. As the R&D contractor, the GP has an incentive to maximize the costs charged to the partnership. As manufacturer/ marketer, the GP has an incentive to minimize payments for rights to the technology developed.

A good example of these incentives at work is what happened at Storage Technology two years ago. Storage Tech put together two limited partnerships in order to raise funding for development of a high-performance IBM compatible mainframe computer. Storage Tech served as general partner and spent $70 million, of which over 80 percent came from limited partners. The last increment of $10.6 million was raised from 181 limited partners in September 1983 amid promises that the project was on schedule and on budget. In January 1984, however, the financially troubled Storage Tech cancelled the project, citing technical difficulties and cost overruns. The partners were advised that they had suffered a total loss. In the aftermath, a class action suit was filed by an infuriated limited partner on behalf of the 181 investors who had come on board just four months before. The suit sought return of the $10.6 million invested, plus $20 million in punitive damages. Furthermore, it sought treble damages for alleged securities fraud and racketeering. This suit also named Smith, Barney, Harris Upham & Company, which sold the partnership units. The basis of the suit was the allegation that Storage Tech, as general partner, did not act in good faith toward the limited partners, to whom it owed a fiduciary responsibility.

Another example is the case of Xebec Corporation, a San Jose, California-based maker of computer data storage devices. In a suit filed in November 1985, the limited partners are seeking actual damages of more than $15 million and punitive damages of more than $25 million. The suit alleges that Xebec, as general partner, incurred unwarranted expenses and improperly subcontracted work to its own affiliates. Furthermore, the suit alleges tha Xebec unfairly produced new products that compete with the partnership's products.[3]

This has nevertheless been the most widely used form of RDLP. Its principal advantage relative to the other forms to be discussed is the fact that the firm seeking the research, by virtue of becoming the general partner in the RDLP, retains control over the research just as if it had taken place within the firm. This could be of particular importance if the firm seeking the R&D is closely held, since the sale of equity funds may bring with it a new group of shareholders (e.g., a venture capitalist), who might seek an active role in controlling the firm's R&D activities. In this regard an RDLP can be viewed as an alternative to the use of venture capital financing. A startup firm, for example, may find it possible to use an RDLP to raise the funds needed to produce and market a fully-developed product, building upon a previously developed base technology. The RDLP could accomplish this while placing little or no liabilities on the firm's books.

Furthermore, inclusion of a purchase option in the RDLP (which allows the sponsor to buy out the interests of the partnership at a specified price) provides the sponsoring firm/general partner with a *potential* means for retaining the profits derived from successful research. Of course, because the limited partners will

---

3. For press accounts of the Storage Technology case, see *Wall Street Journal*, 2/9/84, p. 36, *Computer World*, 2/13/84, p. 1, and *MIS Week*, 2/15/84, p. 1. For an account of the Xebec case see *Wall Street Journal*, 11/27/85, p. 14.

want to protect their right to share in these profits, the value of the call option to the firm/general partner will depend upon the terms of the call option and the limited partners' willingness to accept them. The inclusion of this option, incidentally, is a clear instance where the interests of the firm/general partner would be at odds with those of the limited partners, a point to which we will return later when we analyze the advantages and disadvantages of RDLPs.

The Independent Entrepreneur General Partner RDLP

In this type of RDLP organization the general partner has *no* affiliation with the firms for which R&D is undertaken, avoiding the conflicts of interest noted earlier. The general partner seeks out the technologies which it will then contract to have developed and marketed. Furthermore, the R&D contractor may be independent of the manufacturer/marketer. Under this category of organizations we find "mutual fund"-like RDLPs, which raise large sums of money through the formation of a single RDLP; the latter then invests those funds in a portfolio of R&D projects. With this type of arrangement the limited partners invest in a set of projects and thus the returns they realize reflect the benefits derived from diversification.

Recently, investment bankers have begun offering pooled RDLPs to the public, partly in response to promotional efforts by the U.S. Department of Commerce. A typical example is the ML *Research & Development Partners 1*, registered in June 1984 by Merrill Lynch, which offered $100 million of limited partnership units to the public with a minimum investment of $10,000. The general partner was the ML R&D Management Company. The funds were earmarked for a variety of projects to be done for several sponsoring companies. In addition, the registration allowed the pool to invest up to 35 percent of its funds in other RDLPs.

Morgan Stanley, in the summer of 1984, set up Morgan Stanley Ventures, Inc. to be general partner for another $100 million pooled RDLP to be offered to institutional investors. It also aimed to invest in a variety of projects for several different sponsors.

Unlike those RDLPs in which the sponsor also serves as the general partner which raise just enough funds to finance a single well-defined project or group of pre-specified, related projects, pooled RDLPs raise large, arbitrary sums to be placed by the general partner in projects to be selected later, for a group of different sponsors. The research work may be contracted out to independent laboratories, or be done by the sponsor under the supervision of the investment banker's R&D subsidiary. The job of the general partner in such a pool is clearly different from that of the general partner in an ordinary RDLP. In the pooled arrangement the general partner must first of all exercise discretion in the selection of projects. In the case of a single project RDLP, that selection is done by the limited partners. The general partner in a pooled RDLP subsequently bears responsibility for management of research efforts by several different contractors, and must negotiate favorable contracts with the many different manufacturer/marketer sponsors. As if the task were not sufficiently complicated, the projects may be in several different and unrelated technologies.

If the management and technical skills of the general partner are up to the challenge (which is no mean assumption), the pooled RDLP offers limited partners the tax advantages of single-project RDLPs, with the further advantages of a relatively low minimum investment and diversification over several research projects in different technologies. Furthermore, such arrangements allow the research work to be done by the best laboratories available in the world, with specialized tasks done by the most capable institutions.[4]

Multi-Sponsor RDLPs

This particular organizational form has not yet been used, but it is a possibility worth noting. It involves a joint venture R&D sponsored by a consortium of several firms via a single RDLP. One of the sponsors, a jointly-owned subsidiary, or an independent party may serve as general partner. The actual research may be contracted to individual sponsors, or to independent laboratories (e.g., university research laboratories). Since multiple firms are involved in cooperative R&D efforts in a joint venture type agreement, there arises the specter of anti-trust prosecution. Properly structured, however, such RDLPs provide a potential means for financing large-scale exploratory efforts which are beyond the means of any single firm acting alone.[5]

Restrictions to the Widespread Use of RDLP Financing

First of all, state "blue-sky" laws limit the pool of qualified investors. Beyond this, two of the major drawbacks to investing in RDLPs as a limited partner are the large minimum investment currently required and the lack of liquidity. The first of these is being solved by the pools. In 1985 Merrill Lynch raised $70 million dollars in a partnership whose units sold for $5,000 each. The liquidity problem might be solved if the partnership units could be traded publicly.

Public trading of partnership units is indeed possible. For example, the units of Apache Petroleum Company are currently traded on the New York Stock Exchange. No small fry, it recently paid $402 million for the oil properties of Dow Chemical, and subsequently issued $43 million worth of new units with warrants to help pay off the resulting debt. May Energy Partners, a spinoff of May Energy, is another example of a publicly-traded partnership. Moreover, the units need not be traded on an exchange. The institutions forming pools could make a secondary market in the units of partnerships under their management.

---

4. Merrill Lynch R&D Company is an example of the high degree of development that has already been achieved. The president comes from an investment banking background, but two vice-presidents come from research backgrounds. One has a Ph.D. in chemistry and the other in electrical engineering. The technical advisory board includes a former head of the National Academy of Sciences, along with several other top scientists.

5. Antitrust considerations arise where joint R&D is organized via a RDLP. There are no rigid rules of illegality applied to joint research via a RDLP. Instead, the Justice Department has taken a "rule of reason" approach and evaluates each joint venture on a case by case basis.

The primary concern about the public trading of RDLP units is that such activity might jeopardize the favorable tax treatment that accounts for much of their attractiveness. That is, public trading of units increases the risk that the IRS might treat the RDLP as a corporation for tax purposes. Treasury regulations set forth four criteria for determining the tax status of a partnership. These criteria are in the form of questions, and if the answer is "yes" to more than two of them, then the partnership is taxed as a corporation. The questions are as follows:

1. Does the partnership have continuity of life?
2. Is there centralization of management in the partnership?
3. Is there limited liability for members of the partnership?
4. Is there free transferability of partnership interests? (see 26CFR 301.7701-2)

If partnership units were traded publicly, the answer to the last question might be "yes." Public trading of limited partnership units, however, might not necessarily be a cause for considering the partnership to have the corporate attribute of "free transferability." Treasury regulations state that a partnership possesses that attribute if each partner "has the power, without consent of the others, to substitute for himself, in the same organization, a person who is not a member of the organization." (26 CFR 201.7701-2(e)(1)) If only the limited partners have the power of substitution, but not the general partner, the attribute of free transferability might not be judged to be present. Furthermore, even if the answer to the last question were "yes", an answer of "no" to at least two others would preserve favorable (i.e., partnership) tax treatment.

II. Motives for RDLP Financing

A variety of economic issues arise with respect to the use of limited partnerships to finance a firm's research and development. The fundamental economic issue is this: *Why do firms select an RDLP as opposed to organizing their R&D efforts under the corporate umbrella?* Our fundamental response to this issue will be based upon a Coasian "efficiency" argument.[6] We argue that the RDLP form of organization is chosen because it is the most efficient form of organization to perform the task. That is, the RDLP minimizes the transaction costs associated with organizing, funding, and carrying out the R&D activity. In this regard we will identify some basic economic advantages which may be tapped by RDLPs. These include tax arbitrage, increased completeness of the capital market, improved risk sharing, and market (as opposed to firm) firm control of R&D expenditures.

Tax Arbitrage Using RDLPs

To illustrate the tax arbitrage opportunities made available through the use of RDLPs, let's look at some examples of the after-tax return from a successful

---

6. The classic formulation of this argument by R.H. Coase appeared in Coase's article, "The Nature of the Firm," *Econometrica*, (November 1937), pp. 386-405.

research project under different organizational forms. The "facts of the case" are fairly simple. HiTech Company had developed a base technology and was ready to refine it into the first commercial product. In 1984, they invested $100 million in the development of the new product, Audions. The development effort was successful, producing a patent. One year after making the investment, HiTech sold the patent for Audions to another company, Jumbo, Inc., for $125 million. The pre-tax rate of return realized on the project was therefore 25 percent.

Of course, we are more interested in the after-tax return, which we'll now calculate. First, we'll assume that HiTech is a profitable corporation that is paying income tax at the 46 percent marginal rate for ordinary income, and that it pays the 28 percent alternative tax rate on capital gains. We'll also assume that all of the investment was deductible in 1984, while the taxes paid on the gains fell in 1985. Then, we'll assume that HiTech does not qualify for the Sec. 30 tax credits on increased investment in research.[7] Finally, we'll assume that the sale of the patent to Jumbo qualifies for capital gains treatment under Sec. 1235 of the Tax Code.

Under these assumptions, the original investment on an after-tax basis was $100 million $\times (1 - 46) = $54 million. The after-tax payoff at the end of the year was $72 million,[8] and the after-tax rate of return on the project was thus 33 percent. However, we have only considered corporate tax. Eventually, the stockholders will pay additional tax on this gain when they receive dividends or sell their stock for a capital gain.

Suppose that instead of being a corporation, HiTech was organized as a partnership. Then gains and losses would pass directly to the partners and be taxed at the rates which apply to individuals. Let's assume the worst, namely that all the partners are in the top individual income tax bracket, paying 50 percent on ordinary income and 20 percent on capital gains. The after-tax payoff would have been $70 million.[9] The rate of return realized from the investment in this case is 40 percent after tax. Not only is this higher than the rate of return realized under the corporate form of organization, but also there is no further tax liability for the investors.

Why is the after-tax yield superior under the partnership form of organization? First, the ordinary income tax rate is higher for individuals than for corporations, so the deduction of research expenses is worth more to individuals. Second, the maximum tax rate on capital gains is significantly lower for individuals than it is for corporations, so the gain from the sale of the patent is also worth more to individuals.

---

7. This could be so if HiTech made relatively large investments in research over the previous three years.

8. The $100 million that was written off the year before was recaptured under Sec. 1245 of the Tax Code as ordinary income. The remaining $25 million profit was taxed as a capital gain at the 28% alternative tax rate. Thus the payoff after tax was $125M − .46($100M) − .28($25) = $72M.

9. The $100M that was written off the year before was recaptured under Sec. 1245 of the tax code as ordinary income. The remaining $25M was taxed as a something else.

Clearly, the after-tax return is more attractive in the partnership case. The purpose of the next example is to illustrate how a corporation might gain some of the advantages of the partnership by financing the Audion development project with an RDLP. Suppose HiTech Corp. had organized the Audion RDLP to raise money for the project instead of funding it internally. In this example, HiTech serves as general partner in the RDLP, taking a 20 percent share of expenses and income. The limited partners take an 80 percent share. Following common practice, HiTech licenses the basic technology to the partnership. The fee agreed to by the partners is $2.5 million.[10] Then the total amount to be raised by the RDLP would be $102.5 million ($100 million for the research plus $2.5 million for the rights to the base technology). The limited partners' share in that is $82 million, and HiTech's share is $20.5 million. Of course, after receiving the payments for the rights, HiTech's contribution is $18 million.

After taxes, the investment made by the limited partners would be $82M×(1−.5) = $41M. The payoff after tax would be $100M−.5($82)−(.2($18M) = $55.4M. The rate of return realized by the limited partners after tax would be 35 percent. This is better than the rate of return in the pure corporate case, and is free of any further individual tax liabilities. Furthermore, the limited partners enjoy limited liability, just as shareholders of a corporation do.

The after-tax investment by HiTech in 1984 would be ($20.5M×(1−.46))−($2.5M×(1−.46)) = $9.72M. The after-tax payoff in 1985 would be $25M−.46($20.5M)−.28($4.5M) = $14.31M, and the after-tax rate of return realized by HiTech would be 47 percent. Both HiTech and the limited partners are able to realize a higher rate of return than HiTech could on its own from the same project.

In order to keep our examples simple, we assumed outright sale of the patent rights for a lump sum. In many cases, though, RDLPs receive royalty payments over a number of years from a successful project, rather than a single lump sum. In such cases it is possible for the royalties to be treated as capital gains by the partners in an RDLP, while they are deducted against ordinary income by the corporation paying them. Each $100 paid in royalties represents an after-tax cost of $54 to the payer, but an $80 after-tax receipt by the highest-bracket individual partner. Whenever $54 can be transformed instantly into $80 or more, lucrative arbitrage opportunities are present.

RDLPs and "Off-Balance Sheet" Financing

Some have suggested that the need to form a separate entity relates to the potential benefits derived from off-balance sheet financing. The financial economist, however, would argue that in an efficient market—one in which investors are intelligent enough to see through the paper transaction—the benefits derived from off-balance sheet financing are trivial or nonexistent. At least one study, however,

---

10. We'll assume that HiTech transfers only part of the rights to the basic technology, so the income from the licensing agreement is treated as ordinary income (see Sec. 1235 of the IRC).

suggests that firms sometimes behave as if off-balance sheet financing were important. Horowitz and Kolodny found that the requirement for firms to expense rather than capitalize their R&D expenditures led to a significant decline in R&D expenditures made by smaller firms.[11] They concluded that this decline resulted from a desire to avoid sharp reductions in reported accounting earnings.[12] Thus, although financial markets *may* see through the form of the transaction, it is not clear that managers (especially of smaller firms) are convinced that this is the case. The RDLP alternative neutralizes the adverse impact of R&D on the income statement, and could make R&D more attractive to such managers.

Besides the issue of managerial perceptions, Horowitz and Kolodny pointed out several "imperfections" in the capital market which might make off-balance sheet financing relevant, at least for smaller firms. Listing requirements of the various stock exchanges include a minimum reported earnings requirement. U.S. government regulations concerning the determination of a firm's acceptability as a government contractor include a number of accounting ratios which must be within acceptable ranges. Banks and other institutional lenders may also place undue emphasis on accounting numbers as opposed to the economic reality of the firm's financial condition. Therefore, a firm (particularly a smaller one) may find that RDLP financing provides the means to conduct necessary research while preserving the accounting data necessary to allow it to have its stock listed, gain federal contracts, and enjoy good relations with banks and other financial intermediaries. At this point, however, we must recognize that the existence of any benefits to be derived from off-balance sheet financing is an empirical issue which may or may not be testable.[13]

Improved Risk Sharing via RDLPs

Another reason for forming an RDLP relates to the prospects for risk sharing.[14] RDLPs enable a firm to finance its R&D without having to underwrite the investment needed to fund that effort, thus it shares the risk of failure with the partners in the RDLP. The basic economic issue here is whether the firm could gain the same benefits of risk sharing by internalizing the R&D activity within the firm. In other words, is it really necessary to form a separate entity in order for the benefits of risk-sharing to be captured? For example, it might be argued that all

---

11. In 1975 the Financial Accounting Standard Board and the Securities and Exchange Commission banned the use of deferral, or capitalization, method of accounting for R&D expenditures and required expensing by all firms.

12. See B. Horowitz and R. Kolodny, "The FASB, the SEC, and R&D," *Bell Journal of Economics* (Spring 1981), pp. 249–62.

13. A first approximation might involve assessing the R&D expenditures made by firms that have entered into RDLPs to determine whether the overall level of R&D by those firms has been impacted by the use of the RDLP. In addition, an event type study of the market value impact of the formation of the RDLP may shed some light on the market's evaluation to the use of RDLPs.

14. The argument was made by Ellert and Rubin [1983], cited earlier.

of the available risk-sharing benefits can be obtained through shareholder diversi-fication in their personal investment portfolios. The problem with this argument, however, is that the managers who make the decisions have much at stake in their employer corporation; and they cannot so easily diversify away the risk created by a major R&D project. RDLPs provide a way to remove much of this risk burden from managers, allowing them to make decisions on the same basis as would be done by diversified shareholders.

Stated in more technical terms, RDLPs provide a means to reduce what finan-cial economists now call "residual agency costs."[15] By this we mean the principal/agent relationship that exists between the corporation's shareholders and the man-agement of the firm. The basic agency problem that concerns us here is that cor-porate management may be less willing to take on risky ventures than shareholders want them to be. This is because the consequences of failure that are suffered by the managers are more severe than those suffered by the owners. Corporate management cannot diversify as completely as the shareholders can, due to manage-ment's inability to diversify its human capital. Stated somewhat differently, the value of management's human capital is tied very closely to the success or failure of a particular corporation. Thus, the firm-specific risk of the corporation will affect the value of management's human capital and correspondingly enter into its decision calculus. On the other hand, the shareholders can completely diversify away firm-specific risk in their individual portfolios. This difference in the risk exposure of the owners versus the managers could provide an incentive for manage-ment to avoid risky ventures which offer a high probability of an unfavorable im-pact on the value of their human capital.

The RDLP offers an organizational solution to this principal/agent problem by removing the R&D investment from the corporation while maintaining corporate control over the research activity.

Market Versus Management Control Over R&D Via RDLPs

One might argue that a significant difference exists between R&D undertaken within the confines of the corporation seeking the research and that which is financed using an RDLP. In the latter case the financial market has the opportunity to value the R&D effort directly, whereas in the former instance the decision to undertake the R&D effort is under the control of the firm's management and for practical purposes, is outside the immediate purview of the market. In effect the use of an RDLP represents a move by the corporation to spin off a part of its investment activities while retaining certain rights to any benefits derived from the R&D effort. In a sense the decision by corporate management to use an RDLP is tantamount to "unforming" a part of the firm.

---

15. For the classic theoretical formulation of the "agency cost" argument, see M. Jensen and W. Meckling, "Theory of the Firm: Managerial Behavior, Agency Costs and Ownership Structure," *Journal of Financial Economics* (1976).

In the context of the modern theory of the firm, a firm can be thought of as a collection of resources that have been removed from the "market arena" through discretionary contracts and placed under the control of the firm's management.[16] Therefore, the decision to use an RDLP to organize, manage, and finance a firm's R&D is synonymous with a decision *not* to include those activities within the corporation. Instead, as in a spinoff, it subjects the R&D investment directly to the discipline of the marketplace.

Completing the Capital Market: The Scarcity Value of RDLPs

When the R&D efforts of a corporation are financed entirely within the corporate umbrella, an investor has a limited array of choices relative to the situation in which an RDLP is used. If the investor wants to underwrite a company's research, he or she must buy a piece of the firm's entire portfolio of activities, including on-line projects as well as the full array of R&D activities. There is a limited opportunity for the investor to change the portfolio weights of individual projects.

When R&D projects are packaged in an RDLP, the investor's opportunity set is expanded. The investor can pick and choose those R&D projects or pools which mesh best with his existing portfolio of investments. Using Stewart Myers's terminology, RDLP financing allows investors the opportunity to invest in a firm's "growth possibilities" separately and apart from its "assets in place."[17] This increase in the investor's opportunity set provides investment choices which were previously not available. Investors may be willing to pay significantly more for investment opportunities that are scarce. Furthermore, by adding to the set of existing investment opportunities, RDLPs make capital markets "more complete," if you will, and this process of "completing" the capital market improves its ability to allocate resources to their highest-valued use.

III. Why RDLP Financing May Not be for Everyone

The tax incentives for the use of RDLP financing seem to be very substantial, so we naturally wonder why there hasn't been a stampede of major proportions in their direction. The financial theory of agency offers some insights that are helpful in explaining why RDLP financing might not be universally appealing. Earlier we made reference to a problem which Jensen and Meckling referred to

---

16. See A.M. Spence, "The Economics of Internal Organization: An Introduction," *The Bell Journal of Economics* (Spring 1975), pp. 163–72. Spence refers therein to a firm as a "mini-capital market" in which the allocation of contracted resources is guided by the firm's management. In the case of the RDLP we see that the R&D is "sold" in the market, thus granting the market more control over the firm's investment decisions. Hence, the decision to use an RDLP constitutes a decision to "unform" a part of the firm's activities or remove them from under the corporate umbrella. Thus, one way to approach the decision to form a RDLP is to consider the same factors which are relied upon on the theory of the firm literature, i.e., transactions (contracting) costs and uncertainty.

17. See S. Myers, "Determinants of Corporate Borrowing," *Journal of Financial Economics* (November 1977), pp. 147–76.

as "residual" agency costs,[18] and we noted that the use of RDLP financing provides one possible solution to this particular agency problem. There is another agency problem, however, which can in fact be aggravated by the use of RDLP financing.

The financial theory of agency also recognizes a problem which arises when managers possess valuable information which is not available to the market.[19] Financial economists refer to this as the "informational assymetry" problem, but, however formidable its name, the essence of the problem can be explained fairly simply. The problem can arise with any form of external financing. Managers often possess valuable information about new projects which cannot be communicated unambiguously to the capital market. One potential barrier to communication is the need to keep competitors in the dark in order to maintain the competitive advantage which makes the project potentially profitable. Whenever such an informational assymetry exists, managers face a problem. If new claims against the firm are sold in the capital market, they will be undervalued due to the lack of complete information. That is, their market value will be less than their fair value, and this difference constitutes a kind of agency cost. Different forms of financing produce different informational asymmetry costs. It is management's job to find ways to finance new projects which minimize the informational asymmetry costs borne by existing stockholders.

Given the potential conflicts of interest that are inherent in RDLP financings, it is necessary to provide a great deal of unambiguous information about the research project in order to obtain a fair price for the partnership units sold in the capital market. Earlier we noted that when a single firm uses RDLP financing to fund research for its own use, there are serious potential conflicts of interest between the general partner and the limited partners. In such an arrangement the corporation which sponsors the research serves simultaneously as general partner in the RDLP, R&D contractor, and manufacturer/marketer of the resulting product. The managers of the sponsoring corporation have a responsibility to their stockholders to maximize the payments received from the partnership for the conduct of the research, and to minimize the amount paid out to the partnership to obtain licensing rights. The managers have exactly the opposite set of responsibilities to the limited partners in the RDLP. If the potential limited partners are rational, they will expect that managers' loyalties will be with their stockholders. Potential limited partners will compensate by reducing the amount they are willing to pay for a given claim against the outcome of a research effort. The more information they are given, and the stronger their contractual protection, the more they will

---

18. Such costs arise when managers have a substantial firm-specific investment of human capital in their employer corporation, which they stand to lose if the employer corporation fails. When managers are unable to diversify away such risk, they may have an incentive to avoid making investments which are in fact attractive from the diversified viewpoint enjoyed by stockholders. The reduction in the value of the firm which results from such a propensity to be unduly cautious is an agency cost.

19. The argument has been explored by Hayne Leland and David Pyle in "Informational Asymmetries, Financial Structure, and Financial Intermediation," *Journal of Finance* 32 (May 1977), pp. 371–187.

be willing to pay. However, making significant information about the firm's research program public could seriously undermine the corporation's competitive position.

The informational asymmetry costs associated with debt financing are much less of a problem than is the case with an RDLP. The payments promised under a debt contract are not linked solely to the outcome of a specific research project. Therefore the details of that effort do not need to be revealed as fully as would be the case with an RDLP financing. Internal equity financing of research efforts would further reduce the informational asymmetry problem. In summary, the maintenance of a competitive advantage may be so valuable that it renders the tax advantage associated with RDLP financing unattractive.

Firms in established industries where competition is intense could find the informational asymmetry costs of RDLP financing particularly burdensome. Therefore, corporations such as General Motors or IBM, which have gone to considerable lengths to cultivate technological leadership, could be extremely reluctant to use RDLP financing arrangements in which they themselves serve as general partner. On the other hand, a firm in an emerging industry, where competitive relationships have not become established, might find it less onerous to make a full disclosure of the information about its research program.

The development of blind-pool RDLP financing could significantly increase the desirability of RDLP financing in industries where competitive advantage is important. When an independent general partner is involved, as in the case with investment bankers' R&D subsidiaries, the conflict of interest between the general partner and the limited partners is resolved. When the managers of the sponsoring corporation have confidence in the discretion of the investment banking firm, they will be less reluctant to reveal information necessary for a fair valuation of the partnership claims on the sponsoring corporation. As a result, informational asymmetry costs may be reduced to a level below the value of the tax advantage, thereby making RDLP financing attractive.

As the R&D management subsidiaries mature and establish track records, potential limited partners will be increasingly confident about having faith in their judgment, in the absence of specific information about the projects to be undertaken. If they can simultaneously inspire confidence that the sponsoring corporations are receiving a fair price for the claims against them, and that the limited partners are being treated fairly, the R&D subsidiaries will provide a potentially very valuable service. They will make available the advantages of RDLP financing while resolving (at least partially) the informational asymmetry problem that attends the raising of external funds.

IV. Sharing Rules and Optimal Contracting in RDLPs

The formation of an RDLP offers a myriad of contracting problems for the participants. These problems arise with respect to the sharing of the research efforts among the corporations seeking the research, the general partner (if different than the corporation seeking R&D), and the limited partners. Subject to negotiation are the distribution of R&D expenses during the formative years of the RDLP between the general partner(s) and the limited partners, the amount paid to license the base technology, the sharing rule for royalties derived from the R&D effort should it be successful,[20] and the terms of any buyout option (should it be included) between the firm seeking the R&D and the RDLP.[21]

In addition to these "contract formation" items there exists a second set of problems associated with carrying out the terms of the limited partnership agreement. This set of issues is generally referred to under the rubric of the principal/agent problem. In the context of an RDLP, a principal/agent problem can arise any time that the general partner's best interests are at odds with those of the limited partners because the general partner has full operating control over the activities of the RDLP. Conflicts of interest are particularly of concern in the case where the sponsor of the research is the general partner. In the absence of detailed contractual protection in such a case, it is to be expected that the limited partners would substantially reduce the amount they would be willing to pay for a given promised set of benefits.

V. Concluding Remarks

Since RDLP financing is a relatively recent phenomenon and still new to the academic finance literature, we have provided a broad overview of the subject. Our intent has been to identify the primary finance issues that arise in the use of this type of financing arrangement. It is our hope that this work will be a stimulus for indepth study of the many important financial problems which RDLPs bring forward.

Virtually unheard of five years ago, R&D Limited Partnership financing has grown into a multi-billion dollar source of funds for a critically important type of investment activity. It has proven to be useful not only for small firms, but also for companies such as Cummins Engine, Control Data, and Emerson Electric. Of particular importance is the very recent (within the last two years) surge of

---

20. The rules for distributing losses and income between the general and limited partners is set forth in the partnership agreement and can treat the two classes of participants differently. For example, the distribution of losses might be as follows:

> Until the limited partners as a group have been allocated an amount of losses equal to the aggregate amount of their capital contributions in the partnership, only 1% of the losses will be allocated to the general partner and the remaining 99% to the limited partners. Thereafter, losses will be distributed 99% to the general partner and 1% to the limited partners. Allocations to the individual partners then reflect their proportionate investment in the partnership.

21. The corporation seeking the R&D may include an option to purchase a license to develop and exploit the technology developed by the RDLP. The "call" option on the license agreement will include an exercise price equal to the "fair market value of the license" at the time of exercise as determined by an impartial third party. The exercise price to the corporation can include both a fee paid at the time of exercise and a royalty agreement between the corporation *and* the limited partners.

growth in the formation of blind pools of R&D projects managed by major investment banking firms such as Merrill Lynch and Morgan Stanley. These pools, which already raise as much as $100 million at a crack, represent a significant new undertaking for investment bankers. As the general partner, the R&D management subsidiary is responsible not only for project selection, but also for project oversight from start to finish. This may include selection of research facilities to do the work, scheduling of the tasks involved in the research effort, and monitoring of the efforts of the researchers. These responsibilities require skills not previously associated with investment banking. The R&D subsidiaries which have been formed in the last two years are pioneers, developing new organizational and financial structures for the conduct of fundamentally important productive activity. The investment bankers' R&D subsidiaries represent an advance into territory previously left exclusively to non-financial firms and may be the vanguard for a fundamental expansion of the role of financial institutions.

VI. Appendix: Trends in RDLP Financing, 1978–84

The attached tables reveal the major trends in RDLP financing over the brief period of their existence. The first RDLP recorded by the U.S. Department of Commerce was a $20 million partnership sponsored by the now-defunct Delorean Motor Company in 1978. Following this RDLP the Commerce Department recorded only two RDLPs prior to 1980. In 1980, four RDLPs involving only $2.5 million were formed. In the following year, activity picked up markedly, with the formation of twenty-two partnerships accounting for $205.5 million in R&D financing. In 1982, the total financing with RDLPs more than tripled, and has continued at about that level through 1984.

One of the most apparent trends is the rapid rise of RDLP pools in the period 1982–84. Pools sought to raise $65 million in 1982. That more than doubled to $138 million in 1983, and subsequently more than tripled in 1984, to $454.4 million. To summarize the growth in importance of RDLP pools we note that in 1982 they accounted for only 9% of the total funds raised by RDLPs and by 1984 they accounted for 73%. In addition, the average size of each pool in 1984 was $35 million, and there were several $100 million pools in the planning stage. In fact, the increased size of the pooled RDLPs in conjunction with their increased frequency of use resulted in a doubling of the average size of RDLPs, in general, from 1983 to 1984.

Yet another trend worth noting is the significant increase in the size of the largest individual partnerships. In the '70s and early '80s there were very few RDLPs which were larger than $20 million. By 1984, Morgan Stanley Research Ventures set out to raise $110 million in one partnership. However, even this pool is dwarfed by the $220 million DCTech partnership now being planned to finance the development of automated manufacturing technology.

Table 1. A Partial Listing of RDLPs Formed During the Period 1978–84.[a]

Sponsor Company	Date of Offer	Funding	Project Type
Delorean Motors	3/23/78	$ 18.75m	Automobile
Trilogy Limited	8/6/81	55.00m	Semiconductors
Agrinetics Corp.	11/2/81	55.00m	Genetic engineering
Anacomp	4/28/82	21.15m	Computer software
Ventrex Laboratories	6/30/82	15.00m	Medicine
Control Data Corp.	7/19/82	30.00m	Computer hardware
BEHR Technology	9/21/82	16.65m	Multiple projects
Calif. Biotechnology	10/20/82	24.00m	Genetic engineering
Syntex Corporation	11/8/82	23.50m	Medicine
ALZA Corporation	2/11/83	16.00m	Multiple projects
Cetus Corporation	5/16/83	75.00m	Medicine
Cummins Engine	8/12/83	19.00m	Diesel engine
Technology Funding Inc.	8/31/83	20.00m	Computer software
ALZA Corporation	9/12/83	30.00m	Drugs
PRC Technology	9/20/83	25.60m	Electronics
Policy Mgmt. Systems	10/24/83	10.85m	Computer software
Xebec	11/7/83	18.00m	Computer software
Orbital Research Corp.	11/10/83	26.00m	Space technology
Emerson Electric Corp.	11/12/83	19.60m	Public utility
BEHR Venture Group	11/17/83	32.23m	Multiple projects
R&D Funding Corp.	12/15/83	100.00m	Multiple projects
NPI	1/18/84	12.88m	Agriculture
Hybritech, Inc.	2/9/84	70.00m	Medicine
Paco Pharmaceutical	3/13/84	19.00m	Drugs and medicine
HL R&D Co.	6/28/84	100.00m	Multiple projects
DCTech	Planned	220.00m	Manufacturing
Innovation Investors	NA	24.00m	Pool (medicine)
Hybritech Clinical Partners	NA	80.00m	Medical
CommTech Technology	NA	25.00m	Private pool
Crosspoint Venture	NA	40.00m	Blind pool
Biogen N.V.	NA	25.00m	Medical
A-C Enertech, L.P.	NA	18.75m	Energy

Source: Industrial Technology Partnerships Program, Office of Productivity, Technology and Innovation, U.S. Department of Commerce, Washington, D.C., December 1984. This is a partial listing. According to the Commerce Department, no complete listing of RDLPs is available.

a. This partial list consists of those RDLPs which involved a minimum of $10 million in funding and is based upon information from the U.S. Commerce Department. According to that source no *complete* listing of RDLPs is available.

Table 2. RDLP Funding by Year, 1981–84.

Year	Number of RDLPs	Total Funding
1984	27	$ 662,995,000
1983	81	806,126,000
1982	72	709,723,000
1981	22	205,449,000
		Total: $2,344,293,000

Source: Industrial Technology Partnerships Program, Office of Productivity, Technology and Innovation U.S. Department of Commerce, Washington, D.C., December 1984. This is a partial listing. According to the Commerce Department, no complete listing of RDLPs is available.

Figure 1. Funds Raised by RDLPs 1980–84.

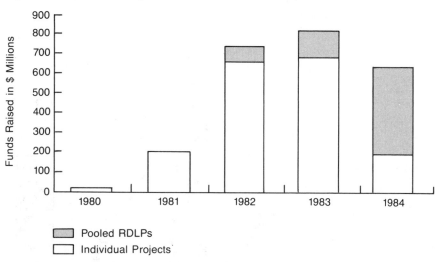

Pooled RDLPs
Individual Projects

Figure 2. Relative Importance of Pooled RDLPs.

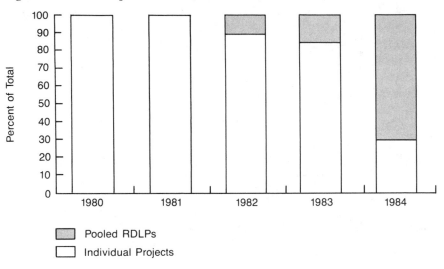

Figure 3. Average Size of RDLPs.

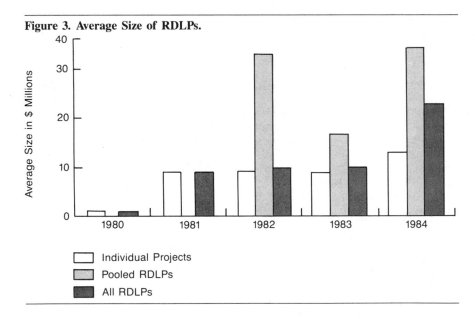

PART III
Executive Compensation

17

Executive Compensation, Corporate Decision-Making and Shareholder Wealth:
A Review of the Evidence

Richard A. Lambert
Northwestern University

David F. Larcker
University of Pennsylvania

I. Introduction

In recent years the compensation of corporate management has become the focus of a major controversy. The level of executive pay and its relationship to corporate performance are now central issues in a generally heated debate among legislators, corporate directors, economists, financial journalists, and compensation professionals.

As a sampling of the rhetoric generated by this controversy, consider this pronouncement in Carol Loomis's widely cited *Fortune* article entitled (provocatively, if not very judiciously) "The Madness of Executive Compensation":

> In a totally rational world, top executives would get paid handsomely for first-class performance, and would lose out when they flopped. But to an extraordinary extent, those who flop still get paid handsomely.

Moreover, Loomis continues,

We would like to thank John Balkcom, Donald Chew, Alfred Rappaport, Lawrence Revsine, and Mark Ubelhart for helpful comments on earlier drafts.

> It is widely believed that many compensation committees are rubber stamps, unwilling to be hard-nosed about the pay of top executives, particularly those chaps who are fellow members of the board.[1]

Or consider this more forceful expression of dissatisfaction with corporate compensation committees, which appeared in a recent *Wall Street Journal* editorial:

> Boards of directors, individual shareholders, and large institutions have got to clean up their own acts with respect to corporations that have poor performance and then make that performance even poorer by offering outrageous amounts of compensation to demonstrably incompetent executives.[2]

Finally, in another recent *Wall Street Journal* editorial, entitled "Reform Executive Pay or Congress Will," Peter Drucker calls for executives to limit their compensation to a multiple of the compensation earned by the "rank and file."[3] And, perhaps taking its cue from Drucker's moralistic tone, the American Law Institute has added to the general furor by proposing amendments to the Business Judgment Rule which would change the composition of corporate boards of directors, further restrict the autonomy of corporate managements, and regulate executive compensation.[4]

Executive compensation consultants, while predictably far less hostile, have also been strongly critical of conventional compensation practices. But here the discussion has focused not on the appropriate *level* of executive pay, but rather on the proper criteria, the ideal "scorecard," for evaluating managerial performance and awarding bonuses. The widespread use of short-term, accounting-oriented measures like EPS and EPS growth has come under attack, and a number of alternatives have been proposed to strengthen the unity of interest between management and stockholders. Some consultants have proposed real, or inflation-adjusted, returns on stockholders' equity (that is, the return on equity minus the cost of equity capital) as the ideal basis for incentive compensation.[5] Others have argued that discounted cash flow is the performance measure which corresponds most strongly to the process by which investors price corporate shares.[6]

Meanwhile, as the controversy rages on in political and business circles, academics have begun to explore some of the issues raised above. In contrast to the morass of baseless charge and countercharge in which the public debate has become

---

1. *Fortune* (July 12, 1982).

2. Graef Crystal, "Congress Thinks It Knows Best About Executive Compensation," *The Wall Street Journal* (July 30, 1984).

3. "Reform Executive Pay or Congress Will," *The Wall Street Journal* (April 24, 1984).

4. On other fronts, although generally only in isolated cases, shareholder activists have levelled charges of "excessive" compensation in attempts to oust incumbent directors in proxy fights. See, for example, the proxy fight discussions regarding Pantry Pride Inc. in the *Wall Street Journal*, Proxy Contest Announcement (November 21, 1984), p. 45.

5. Louis J. Brindisi, "Creating Shareholder Value: A New Mission for Executive Compensation," Chapter 19, and Jude Rich and Ennius Bergsma, "Pay Executives to Create Wealth," *Chief Executive* (1982).

6. See, for example, Alfred Rappaport, "How to Design Value-Contributing Executive Incentives," *Journal of Business Strategy* 4 (1983).

enmired, researchers in the fields of economics, finance, and accounting have established the beginnings of a scientific inquiry into questions of managerial economics. The result to date has been a small, but rapidly growing body of empirical studies providing insights into matters like the following:

- What are the consequences of the separation of ownership from control in the large public corporation? How effective are compensation contracts in overcoming conflicts of interest between management and stockholders?
- What are the pros and cons of various "scorecards" for evaluating managerial performance and awarding executive bonuses? What is the optimal "mix" of components—stock options, annual cash bonuses, long-term performance payments, etc.—in the total compensation package?
- Do compensation contracts "really matter" to executives? That is, do managers respond differently to different compensation plans?
- To what extent is annual executive compensation related (and, furthermore, to what extent *should* it be related) to year-to-year corporate performance and stockholder returns?
- How effective is the labor market for executives—that market which sets a manager's "opportunity wage"—in curbing management's natural tendency to pursue its self-interest at the expense of stockholders?

Our purpose in this article is to review the academic literature on executive compensation. We also discuss some of the more innovative incentive plans introduced by compensation professionals in recent years.

II. A Framework For Examining Executive Compensation

A recent development in the theory of corporate organization, known as "agency theory," has focused attention on the separation of ownership from control in large public corporations. In the context of this theory, management incentive compensation plans are viewed as one of several important means of reducing potential conflicts of interest between management and shareholders. (The others are the existence of a market for corporate control, which disciplines inefficient managers through the threat of takeover, and a market for executive labor, which in theory weighs an executive's past service to shareholders when determining his or her opportunities for alternative employment.) To the extent the separation of ownership from control is a serious problem in the large public corporation (and the recent proliferation of leveraged buyouts can be construed as evidence in support of this supposition), an effective compensation program can add value to the firm by improving the alignment of management incentives with stockholder interests.

There are three principal kinds of conflicts discussed in the agency literature. First, and most obviously, whereas shareholders' primary interest is in having a management team which maximizes their financial return, executives may derive "nonpecuniary" benefits ("perks," in the vernacular) from their control over corporate resources. They may authorize purchase of superfluous corporate jets. Or, with far more serious consequences, they may seek to build a corporate empire through a series of large acquisitions at costly premiums which penalize their own shareholders.[7] (It is important to note that in this context "perk" means any expenditure which has a higher value to management than to shareholders. Thus, "perks" have a potential value much larger than the sum of costs for club memberships, first class air travel, etc.)

Second, management and shareholders can differ sharply in their attitudes toward the risk of potential investment strategies. Whereas shareholders can diversify their wealth by spreading it among different assets, a large portion of a manager's wealth (human capital, compensation earned, and stock in the firm) is tied to the fortunes of the company. Therefore, we would expect managers to be more risk averse than shareholders. Too great a difference in risk aversion might cause a manager to turn down a project that would benefit shareholders because the perceived personal risks are too high.

Third, there is a potential conflict between the decision-making time horizons of executives and shareholders. For example, an executive's investment decisions may be evaluated by the compensation committee over a shorter time period than shareholders use in assessing the eventual outcome of the same investment decisions. This pressure may in turn cause a manager to evaluate projects based on their immediate impact on profits, rather than according to the present value of cash flows over the life of the investment. A foreshortened decision-making horizon thus may motivate management to turn down profitable long-term investments.

From the perspective of agency theory, then, executive compensation contracts are *not* simply a tax-efficient vehicle for delivering pay to executives (although taxes offer at least a partial explanation for some features of compensation plans).[8] The primary function of incentive compensation plans is to control the kinds of conflicts of interest between management and shareholders described above. And, as we hope to show in the next section, the ability of the agency framework to identify the sources of conflicts between stockholders and executives is useful in determining the "optimal" design of a compensation plan.

---

7. For example, it is sometimes argued that founders of firms (e.g., Henry Ford) place such a high value on power and maintaining control over the operations of the firm that these actions decrease their personal wealth and the wealth of the shareholders. In this context, perquisite consumption can be very costly to shareholders. Similarly, the announcement of a "bad" corporate acquisition can decrease the total market value of the acquiring firm's stock by millions of dollars.

8. For some additional discussion of tax/incentive aspects of compensation contracts, see G. Hite and M. Long, "Taxes and Executive Stock Options," *Journal of Accounting and Economics* 4 (1982), M. Miller and M. Scholes, "Executive Compensation, Taxes and Incentives," in W. Sharpe and C. Cootner (eds.), *Financial Economics Essays in Honor of Paul Cootner* (1982), C. Smith and R. Watts, "Incentive and Tax Effects of U. S. Executive Compensation Plans," *Australian Management Journal* (1983), R. Lambert and D. Larcker, "Stock Options and Managerial Incentives," working paper, Northwestern University (1984), and M. Scholes and M. Wolfson, "Employee Compensation and Taxes: Links with Incentives and With Investment and Financing Decisions," working paper, Stanford University (1984).

III. Compensation "Scorecards" and Contract Design

How then, are current compensation plans designed to control such conflicts of interest between management and stockholders? And, furthermore, how effective are they in accomplishing this end? In this section, we discuss the implications of the agency issues discussed above for choosing the appropriate performance measure, as well as the structure and components of the compensation package.

Before considering specific contract designs, it is useful to point out some of the difficulties that arise in evaluating managerial performance. For one thing, the separation between ownership and management prevents shareholders from directly observing much of management's activity. Also, because shareholders almost never possess management's familiarity with the operations of the firm, they may not be able to evaluate the consequences of those actions they can observe. As a result, they must often rely on reported *results* (on an accountant's periodic measure of net income, for example, or share price performance) as the basis for evaluating management's performance. Unfortunately, these results are likely to reflect the effects of a large number of factors which are not under management's control. This may make it difficult to determine whether poor results are due to "bad luck" or to poor decisions on the part of management.

Another problem is that the consequences of management's current decisions may extend over many years, and it is often difficult to foresee today their effects on the value of the firm in *future* periods. These difficulties suggest that compensation contracts (or any other disciplinary mechanism) can never be fully successful in resolving agency problems. But, given such limitations, let's see how the contracts are designed to deal with these management-shareholder conflicts.

Executive Expenditures and Risky Investments

One objective of a good compensation scheme is to motivate managers to make expenditure decisions that benefit shareholders. To approach this problem, consider the extreme (and improbable) case of an executive whose compensation is totally independent of his performance. An example would be a manager whose compensation consisted entirely of a *fixed* salary—one which, say, in real terms remained unchanged from year to year. Such a manager would have no incentive to increase shareholder wealth because he does not share in any of the resulting gains. He would be much more likely than other executives to avail himself of perquisites of all varieties, at the expense of his shareholders.

This incentive problem—one which all companies with outside stockholders face to at least some degree—can be reduced by making part of an executive's compensation depend upon the financial performance of the firm. By allowing managers to share in the company's gains, a compensation plan provides them some incentive to develop strategies that will increase shareholder wealth. Also, since the executive now bears some of the costs of "perk" consumption, he will be less likely to evaluate corporate expenditures according to the personal satisfaction—and perhaps, in the case of some major investment decisions, the sense of power or prestige—they offer him.

Given this concern, it may seem that the optimal compensation scheme will bind executive compensation as tightly as possible to changes in the stock price of the firm. The problem with this solution, however, is that stock prices are often affected by factors beyond management's influence. This means that tying management's compensation very closely to the firm's stock price will greatly increase executives' individual exposure to risk. And imposing large personal risks on management can actually *reduce* shareholder wealth—in two ways. First, an increase in management's exposure to market risk will make the compensation scheme less attractive, all other things equal; and in return for bearing additional risk, executives collectively will require an increase in the general level of their compensation.[9] Second, increasing an executive's exposure to risk may cause him to become more conservative in his investment strategy. He may turn down risky projects which promise high expected returns to shareholders and accept only "safe" projects offering stable, but substandard returns.

How can the compensation package be designed to give executives the incentive to increase profits and control expenditures, or "perks," while at the same time encouraging them to pursue risky, though profitable investment strategies? One possibility is to supplement stock price movements with other measures of firm performance, thereby providing compensation committees (and shareholders generally) with additional information that makes it easier to separate the effect of executives' actions from other factors that influence the firm's profits. In this way, an executive can be shielded from the "exogenous" or uncontrollable variables that affect the firm's profits, and his individual contribution can be more easily identified and evaluated.

To be effective, however, such measures must reflect the effectiveness of management more clearly than do stock prices; or, at a minimum, they must provide information about managerial performance that stock prices do not. For example, if stock prices were always a fixed multiple of accounting earnings, there would be no benefit to basing executive compensation on both earnings and share price—because both measures would be providing the same information about management's performance. But because stock prices are not fixed multiples of EPS, this means that stock prices and accounting earnings provide somewhat different (although certainly not unrelated) indications of management's effectiveness. By combining several different measures of performance, some of the "noise" contained in each individual measure can be removed, offering a better assessment of managerial performance.[10]

---

9. A recent study by Rick Antle and Abbie Smith has, in fact, shown that the average level of total compensation (salary plus bonus plus change in the value of stock holdings) is positively related to the riskiness of total compensation. See R. Antle and A. Smith, "Measuring Executive Compensation: Methods and An Application," working paper, University of Chicago (1984).

10. It is, of course, common to observe companies using multiple performance criteria in their compensation contracts. For example, Libbey-Owens-Ford Co. has a performance plan tied to increases in return on net assets and increases in sales. In similar manner, Sears, Roebuck, and Co. bases their annual bonus payments on a combination of return on equity, growth in total revenues, net sales, gross

An alternative is to weigh corporate performance against the performance of other comparable companies. In such *relative* performance schemes, executive compensation is set according to how well the company performs relative to a comparison or peer group.[11] The implicit assumption underlying this approach is that the construction of a peer group allows general market or macroeconomic influences and industry-specific influences to be removed from the performance measure, thereby providing a better measure of an executive's distinctive contribution to the firm's profitability. The biggest difficulty in implementing such an approach is finding an appropriate peer group, especially for companies that have many different products. But, for many firms operating in well-defined industries, such as banking, paper, and oil, relative performance measures are becoming commonplace features of the compensation plan.

Another way to encourage managers to take risks, while still controlling "perks," is to structure their compensation in such a manner as to offset their risk aversion. Consider a project that shareholders perceive to be a worthwhile risk (that is, the investment has a positive net present value after discounting at the required rate of return). As suggested, when a manger is more risk averse than shareholders, he may turn down a positive net present value project because he perceives the adverse consequences *to him* if the project performs poorly to dominate the favorable personal consequences if the project succeeds. The manager's risk aversion can be partially offset if his compensation contract is designed to make the adverse consequences associated with the "downside" less severe, or to make the favorable consequences of the "upside" more attractive. Properly designed stock options, or accounting-based option contracts, may be the answer to neutralizing a manager's risk aversion. Options may be effective in encouraging management to invest in riskier projects because, while they carry no additional downside risk, their value generally increases as the volatility of the company's stock price rises, and they allow managers to share in the upside potential of the firm.

In general, then, agency theory implies that it is desirable to compensate executives on the basis of share price in order to give them incentives to control their expenditures and develop strategies that increase shareholder wealth. But, the choice of how closely to tie management's compensation to share price must also consider the effect of exposing executives to greater market risk. The degree to which the executive's compensation should be tied to share price will therefore depend on the relative importance of these two incentive problems in the particular firm.

---

profit, and growth in net premiums earned. The subset of performance criteria used by Sears for specific executives varies depending upon the business unit and executive level.

11. For additional discussion of relative performance contracts, see Mark Ubelhart, "A New Look at Executive Compensation Plan," *Cash Flow* (1981), and R. Antle and A. Smith, "An Empirical Investigation into the Relative Performance Evaluation of Corporate Executives," working paper, University of Chicago (1984).

Decision-Making Horizon

The agency problem that results from differences in the decision-making time horizon of shareholders and executives can be partially resolved by changing either the "scorecard" or the payoff structure of compensation. The compensation "scorecard" can be changed from a measure with a "short-term" focus (such as yearly accounting earnings) to a measure which has an inherently "long-term" focus (for example, the market price of the common stock).[12]

Consider, for example, the situation where a manager is contemplating a capital investment with a positive expected net present value, but an adverse impact on accounting earnings in the early years of the project. An executive compensated primarily on the basis of yearly accounting earnings may reject this project because of its effect on his "short-term" compensation. If the executive is instead compensated on the basis of share price (through, say, stock or stock options), he will be more likely to accept the project because he expects it to have a favorable impact on his compensation. The implicit assumption of this approach, of course, is that executives believe that the "long-term" performance measure (that is, the stock price) will eventually, if not immediately, reward him by reflecting the "long-term" consequences of his investment decisions.[13]

An alternative, or perhaps complimentary, way to lengthen the executive's decision-making horizon is to defer the payoff earned by the executive to some future point in time. Some corporations defer part of an executive's yearly bonus and require that the deferred compensation be paid in common stock. Since the executive's compensation is explicitly tied to the performance of the corporation in subsequent years, this type of bonus deferral will tend to lengthen his decision-making horizon.

In a similar manner, many corporations have also adopted compensation contracts known as "performance plans."[14] These contracts provide payoffs to executives if the growth in specified accounting numbers (generally earnings per share or return on equity) over a three- to five-year performance period exceeds some target. One important feature of performance plans is that the compensation earned from this contract is deferred until the end of this period. Nothing is earned if the executive leaves or is terminated during the term of the performance plan. And this stipulation, of course, could extend a manager's time horizon through at least the duration of the performance period.

---

12. Throughout the analysis, we assume that the share price is the present value of the expected future cash flows that accrue to equity holders discounted at the appropriate risk-adjusted rate of return. Therefore, share price has an inherently "long-term" focus.

13. For some evidence that the stock price impounds the consequences of unexpected changes in "long-term" investments, see J. McConnell and C. Muscarella, "Capitalized Value, Growth Opportunities, and Corporate Expenditure Announcements," working paper, Purdue University (1983).

14. For example, 54 of the *Fortune* 100 have performance plans as of 1983. See Towers, Perrin, Forester, and Crosby, *1983 Executive Total Compensation Study*, New York: Towers, Perrin, Forester, and Crosby (1983).

Figure 1. Typical Short-Term Bonus Contract.

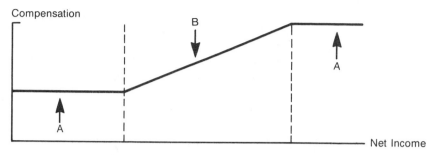

IV. Do Compensation Contracts Really Matter?

The next question we want to examine concerns whether executives really respond to the incentives provided by their compensation contracts. If the agency framework is useful in analyzing compensation questions, we should observe that executives compensated with different contracts will exhibit differences in their decision-making. We now turn to a review of the empirical evidence on this question.

Academic research has recently begun to examine the incentive effects of compensations contracts. This research is typically conducted in one of two ways. First, researchers look for changes in executive decision-making after a *new* compensation contract is adopted. For example, do managers compensated by a new "long-term" contract undertake more "long-term" investment? Second, studies attempt to ascertain whether the variation in existing compensation contracts across firms is associated with differences in executive decision-making. For example, do managers receiving a substantial portion of their compensation from a bonus contract make different decisions than managers receiving only a modest bonus? The results of this set of studies provide some insights into agency problems related to executive expenditure decisions, risk aversion, and decision-making horizon.

Executive Expenditure Decisions

A typical funding formula for establishing the yearly bonus pool for executives is diagrammed in Figure 1. There is generally a threshold level of net income which must be surpassed before any bonus is paid (for example, net income must exceed five percent of total capital employed). Most proxy statement disclosures indicate that when net income exceeds this minimum standard, the bonus pool is computed as some percentage of net income above the threshold. The bonus pool also often has an explicit ceiling. For example, in some compensation plans, the bonus may not exceed total cash dividends paid or, perhaps, some target percentage of the total salaries of the executives participating in the bonus plan.

A recent study by Paul Healy has attempted to determine how executives actually respond to the incentives inherent in these kinds of net income-based contracts.[15] Specifically, the question posed by Healy's study is this: Do executives adjust their expenditure decisions in order to increase the payoff from their yearly bonus contract?

The hypotheses of Healy's study can be illustrated using Figure 1. Consider the case where an executive expects net income to be on the "flat" portion of the contract (denoted as A in Figure 1). In this case, a manager would have an incentive to accelerate accounting recognition of expenses (say, maintenance) and defer recognition of revenues (for example, by delaying sale of goods until after the fiscal year is closed). Such accrual or deferral decisions would have no effect on the executive's bonus in the present year, but would increase the probability of obtaining a bonus in subsequent periods. By contrast, an executive who expects net income to fall in the "sloped" portion of the contract (denoted as "B" in Figure 1) faces the opposite set of incentives. His or her bonus for the current period can be increased by accelerating the recognition of revenues and deferring the recognition of expenses.[16]

The results of Healy's study confirm our expectations. As predicted, managers who expect reported net income to fall below the bonus threshold appear to decrease revenues and increase expenses. The opposite pattern of behavior is observed when executives expect net income to fall between the bonus threshold and the ceiling.

A study conducted by Mark Wolfson examines the effects of bonus contracts on the behavior of executives in oil and gas partnerships.[17] Many of these partnerships are organized such that limited partners contribute capital to the enterprise and a drilling agent performs the exploration and development activity. The contracts specifying how the costs and revenues are shared are often designed to take advantage of tax code regulations. In one common sharing arrangement, the limited partners bear all of the drilling costs. After discovery of oil and gas, the drilling agent bears all of the costs necessary to complete the well. The limited partners and the drilling agent then share the revenues earned from the sale of oil or gas.

The arrangement ideally should be structured such that the drilling agent has an incentive to complete every well where the total revenues accruing to *both* parties are expected to exceed his costs to complete the well. An "agency" problem arises, however, because the drilling agent receives only part of the revenues associated with completion while bearing all of the costs. The drilling agent thus has an incentive to complete only those wells for which his share of the revenues exceeds the cost of completion. Thus he is not likely to complete all of the wells that would benefit the limited partners.

---

15. P. Healy "Evidence on the Effect of Bonus Schemes on Accounting Procedure and Accrual Decisions," *Journal of Accounting and Economics* (forthcoming).

16. The hypotheses of Healy's study are similar to those developed and empirically examined in D. Larcker and L. Revsine, "The Oil and Gas Accounting Controversy: An Analysis of Economic Consequences," *The Accounting Review* (1983).

17. M. Wolfson, "Empirical Evidence of Incentive Problems and Their Mitigation in Oil and Gas Tax Shelter Programs," in J. Pratt and R Zeckhauser: *Asymmetric Information, the Agency Problem, and Modern Business*, Harvard University Press (forthcoming).

If the limited partners view this agency problem to be serious, they will be less willing to invest funds in such partnerships. The drilling agent therefore has an incentive to devise a means of reducing this conflict of interest. One way to counteract this "noncompletion" incentive is to select only highly risky drilling programs, those whose expected outcome is highly variable. In this way, the wells are likely to be "so good" or "so bad" that the interests and objectives of the limited partners and the drilling agent are brought together. In such extreme cases, the fortunes of the drilling agent and limited partners are virtually identical: either they both "win big" or they lose the initial investment by the limited partner.

Wolfson tested this hypothesis, and his results suggest that partnerships with contracts like those described above engage in significantly more risky (exploratory) drilling than partnerships that operate under different sharing arrangements.

A study by one of the present authors examines changes in the level of "perks" associated with the adoption of bonus contracts by major commercial banks.[18] In this study "perks" are defined as occupancy, furniture, and salary expenditures, as well as the number of bank employees. (It is assumed that bank managers prefer to have more expensive working conditions and larger staffs than the level of expenditures desired by shareholders.)

This study determines specifically whether the ratio of management's expenditures on "perks" (as defined above) to operating revenue decreases following the adoption of an annual bonus contract. (This hypothesis follows, of course, from our earlier discussion: a manager compensated with a bonus contract bears part of the cost of expenditures on "perks," whereas a manager with only a fixed salary does not.) The results indicate that banks without bonus contracts had a significantly higher ratio of "perks" to operating revenue than similar banks with bonus contracts. Moreover, there is some evidence that the ratio of nonpecuniary expenditures to revenue decreases following the adoption of the bonus plan. Thus it appears that bonus contracts influence the expenditure decisions of bank managers.

Risk Aversion

Some evidence on the issue of whether executives behave as though they are more risk-averse than shareholders has been provided by Yakov Amihud and Baruch Lev.[19] Their study examines executive motives in conglomerate mergers.

Finance theory maintains that mergers undertaken *solely* for corporate diversification do not benefit stockholders because they can costlessly duplicate such diversification by holding different securities. Executives, however, benefit from corporate diversification because they hold partially "undiversifiable" portfolios, consisting of their compensation claims on the firm and their human capital. The authors hypothesize that because executives are more risk-averse than shareholders,

18. D. Larcker, "Short-Term Compensation Contracts, Executive Expenditure Decisions, and Corporate Performance: The Case of Commercial Banks," working paper, Northwestern University (1984).
19. Y. Amihud and B. Lev, "Risk Reduction as a Managerial Motive for Conglomerate Mergers," *Bell Journal of Economics* 12 (1981).

executives undertake conglomerate mergers to decrease the variability of the value of the firm. By decreasing firm variability through conglomerate-type acquisitions, managers can effectively diversify—and thus increase the value of—their own "undiversifiable" portfolios."

Amihud and Lev find in fact that companies with broadly dispersed stock ownership—those in which there is no dominant shareholder to monitor corporate decisions—are more likely to engage in conglomerate or diversifying mergers than firms with concentrated ownership interests.[20]

In a somewhat more direct analysis of the ability of compensation contracts to affect executive risk aversion, we examined changes in firm variability associated with the *initial* adoption of stock option plans.[21] We attempted to determine whether the adoption of a stock option contract motivates managers to increase the variability in equity returns.

Two possibilities are considered in this study. First, standard option pricing models suggest that the value of an option increases as the variability of stock prices increases. This suggests that the adoption of stock options will counteract executives' risk aversion and motivate them to increase firm variability. A second possibility is that standard option pricing models are not applicable to *executive* stock options. Executives cannot sell their options to other investors. Nor can they short their own stock, making it difficult to construct the riskless hedge required for option pricing models to work. In fact, under certain circumstances, stock options may actually *increase* the risk aversion of a manager, thereby motivating him to decrease firm variability.

An explanation of why the standard option pricing formulas may not be appropriate in valuing executive stock options is as follows: Consider the behavior of a risk averse manager who cannot diversify or hedge the risk associated with the option's payoff. If he expects the options to finish far "in the money" (which is likely because options are usually granted with an exercise price equal to or below the stock price at the date of the grant), he may want to "bank" the value of that option by *decreasing* the variability of the firm's stock price, thus increasing the odds that the options will finish "in the money."

If, however, an executive's options are expected to finish "out of the money," then a manager may have an incentive to increase the variance of the firm's stock price in order to increase the probability that they will become valuable. This suggests that granting options that are initially "out of the money" may be the solution to overcoming managers' risk aversion.

---

20. For additional discussion of managerial incentives in acquisitions, see B. Lev, "Observations on the Merger Phenomenon and a Review of the Evidence," *Midland Corporate Finance Journal* 1 (1983), D. Larcker, "Managerial Incentives in Mergers and Their Impacts on Shareholder Wealth," Chapter 18, and R. Lambert and D. Larcker, "Golden Parachutes, Executive Decision-Making, and Shareholder Wealth," *Journal of Accounting and Economics* (forthcoming).

21. R. Lambert and D. Larcker, "Stock Options and Managerial Incentives," working paper, Northwestern University (1984).

The results of our study indicate that firms whose options are expected to finish "out of the money" tend to exhibit increasing stock price variability following the adoption of stock option plans. In contrast, companies whose options are expected to finish "in the money" tend to exhibit decreases in stock price variability.

Decision-Making Horizon

As discussed earlier, if the decision-making horizon of management is significantly shorter than that of shareholders, this can lead to "underinvestment" by the corporation. For example, if an executive is being evaluated solely according to near-term accounting performance and a profitable investment project under consideration is expected to have an adverse impact on earnings in early years, he will have an incentive to reject that investment.

One possible way to mitigate this problem is to adopt a compensation contract designed to lengthen executives' decision-making horizon. This presumes, of course, that compensation contracts can actually motivate a manager to lengthen his decision-making horizon. Although this issue cannot be examined directly, it is possible to determine whether the investment behavior of executives changes after a contractual change.

In a study published in 1983, one of the present authors examined whether the adoption of "long-term" compensation contracts was associated with increases in "long-term" investment.[22] The specific focus of this study was the adoption of "performance plans," those contracts which provide deferred compensation when certain "long-term" (generally ranging over a three- to six-year period) goals are met. The relative amount of capital investment of companies adopting performance plans was compared to the investment of similar firms without performance plans. The results of the study indicated that firms adopting performance plans had substantial increases in capital investment after the contractual change relative to similar firms without performance plans.

Stockholder Response to New Compensation Plans

The research on whether compensation contracts "really matter" suggest that the design of such contracts influences executive decision-making. But how does this influence translate into shareholder wealth? Furthermore, how do investors respond to the adoption of new compensation plans?

Several studies have, in fact, documented that stock prices rise when companies announce the adoption of "long-term" compensation contracts.[23] These studies

---

22. D. Larcker, "The Association Between Performance Plan Adoption and Corporate Capital Investment," *Journal of Accounting and Economics* 5 (1983).

23. For an analysis of the security market response to the adoption of "long-term" compensation contracts, see D. Larcker, "The Association Between Performance Plan Adoption and Corporate Capital Investment," *Journal of Accounting and Economics* 5 (1983) and J. Brickley, S. Bhagat, and R. Lease, "The Impact of Long-Range Managerial Compensation Plans on Shareholder Wealth," *Journal of Accounting and Economics* (forthcoming). It is important to note that the market reaction to the disclosure

find that "long-term" contracts are associated with an approximately one to two percent increase in shareholder wealth. (Although these percentages might seem small in absolute terms, it is important to remember that the firms making these contractual changes are extremely large, and these percentages translate into millions of dollars of increases in shareholder value.) In short, compensation contracts do "appear to matter"—to investors as well as management.

V. The Relationship Between Pay and Performance

To this point, we have suggested that agency theory provides a framework for analyzing issues in executive compensation. We have also presented evidence that the theory is useful in predicting the "incentive effects" of different compensation contracts. In this section, we bring the theory to bear on the available evidence regarding the relationship between executive compensation and corporate performance.

Much of the controversy surrounding executive compensation tends to focus on whether executive compensation is related to corporate performance. That is, are current compensation contracts really designed to "pay for performance?" Criticism of executive compensation in the financial press is based almost entirely upon intuition and personal observation—what financial economists call "anecdotal" evidence.[24] Although no formal statistical analysis is done, these articles generally conclude that there is little or no relationship between executive compensation and corporate performance or shareholder wealth. Corporate compensation practices are then pronounced "irrational," failing to distinguish between good and bad performance.

Two academic studies presented at the University of Rochester's recent Conference on Managerial Compensation and The Managerial Labor Market address this issue more systematically.[25] Both of these studies examine the correlation between changes in compensation and changes in *shareholder wealth* for large samples of major U.S. corporations; and both show a positive, statistically significant correlation between executive compensation and shareholder wealth. This empirical evidence is, of course, inconsistent with the charges often made in the financial press.

---

of a new compensation plan will reflect not only the market's assessment of the desirability of the compensation scheme, but also the market's assessment of any new strategy changes that are being introduced at the same time.

24. One of the few attempts in the financial press to document its case more carefully is the *Fortune* article by Carol Loomis, which graphed executive compensation (defined as salary plus bonus) versus a single accounting measure of corporate performance. As discussed in more detail shortly, there are two problems with this study. First, instead of the change in shareholder wealth, return on equity is used as the measure of firm performance. Second, the analysis ignores the stock options and shares owned by the executive, the value of which are of course, directly related to shareholder wealth.

25. K. Murphy, "Corporate Performance and Managerial Remuneration." *Journal of Accounting and Economics* (forthcoming) and A. Coughlin and R. Schmidt, "Executive Compensation, Management Turnover, and Firm Performance: An Empirical Investigation," *Journal of Accounting and Economics* (forthcoming).

Such findings, however, should not be taken to imply that American corporations have attained the optimum in incentive compensation. In fact, the coefficients measuring the correlation between compensation and shareholder returns, although statistically significant, are rather small. Also, rather modest changes in compensation occur for large changes in shareholder wealth. For example, Kevin Murphy reports that a ten percent change in the equity value of the firm is associated with only about a two percent increase in total executive compensation. Therefore, although there is a statistical association between executive compensation and shareholder wealth, it is difficult to predict changes in executive compensation from changes in shareholder wealth. The correlation results, nevertheless, do suggest that executive compensation in American corporations is not total "madness."

One problem in interpreting these studies is that they typically exclude changes in the value of the executives' stock holdings and stock options from their measure of compensation. Obviously, these components of executive wealth are tied *directly* to changes in shareholder wealth; executives with large holdings in their company's stock are clearly rewarded for good performance and penalized for bad performance through the change in value of their personal stock holdings. And, as other studies show, the stock holdings of top executives in their own companies often constitute a significant portion of their wealth. This suggests that financial press "studies" correlating only annual salary and bonus with accounting profitability measures may seriously understate the real relationship between corporate performance and total compensation.[26]

How Should Compensation Correlate with Shareholder Returns?

Given that a significant portion of the wealth of top executives is already directly tied to stock price performance, we are led to ask: In the best of all possible compensation plans, how *should* the non-stock components of compensation like salary, yearly bonus, and performance plans be related to annual stock price changes?

As suggested earlier, one implication of agency theory is that it may be desirable to base compensation on other measures of the firm's performance in order to "filter out" the effects of random events on stock prices. The "noise" in stock prices may impose too much risk on executives, exposing too much of their compensation to factors beyond their control. Such risks may in turn cause them to become excessively conservative in their investment policy. Therefore, in designing compensation plans, companies can find it necessary to use criteria other than stock price—accounting earnings, return on equity, cash flow, sales, comparisons with industry-average rates of return—to supplement the direct dependence of an

---

26. For some additional evidence on the importance of equity holdings to managerial decision-making, see G. Benston, "The Self-Serving Management Hypothesis: Some Evidence," *Journal of Accounting and Economics*, (forthcoming), R. Walkling, and M. Long, "Agency Theory, Managerial Welfare, and Takeover Bid Resistance," *Rand Journal of Economics* 15 (1984), and W. Lewellen, C. Loderer and A. Rosenfeld, "Merger Decisions and Executive Stock Ownership," *Journal of Accounting and Economics* (forthcoming).

executive's stock-related compensation on stock prices. In this sense, the absence of a strong relationship between firm performance and contemporaneous salary and bonus need not be an indication of the irrationality of corporate compensation practices.

To summarize, then, the positive statistical correlations detected in these studies suggest that executive compensation is not total "madness." However, without additional information about the seriousness of "agency" problems resulting from managerial risk aversion in specific firms, it is difficult to determine what the correlation would be between the "optional" compensation package and shareholder returns. Small positive correlations may represent an "optimal" contract for managers in highly cyclical industries, and thus exposed to some large risks they cannot control. Alternatively, in cases where risk aversion is not a serious concern, the same small positive correlations may imply that current compensation plans fail seriously in motivating management to act in the interest of its shareholders.

VI. The Labor Market for Executives

The fact that changes in compensation are correlated with changes in shareholder wealth also tells us little about whether the *level* of executive compensation is correct. Large positive correlations between changes in compensation and shareholder wealth can exist at the same time as executives are being "overpaid" or, for that matter, seriously "underpaid." The level of executive compensation is determined, in theory at least, by the operation of a labor market for executive services. Moreover, to the extent that it effectively determines the relationship between executive performance and *future* levels of executive compensation, this labor market can provide an important means of motivating executives to serve their shareholders.

There are two important aspects of the labor market. First, the labor market sets the executive's opportunity wage, and this provides a lower bound on the amount of total compensation which must be paid to retain him. At the same time, the availability of other executives of comparable experience and ability at this opportunity wage provides some constraint on the level of compensation demanded by executives in their current jobs. This tells us, for example, that executives cannot simply pay themselves any compensation level they desire.

Second, the labor market has the potential to control agency problems.[27] When an executive makes decisions which harm stockholders, the labor market should lower the executive's current opportunity wage (as well as all future period levels of compensation). To the extent executives are penalized in this way for poor decisions, they have less incentive to behave in a manner which benefits themselves at the expense of their shareholders. (This disciplining effect of the labor market assumes, of course, that the labor market has good information about the shareholder consequences of an executive's decisions.)

---

27. For additional discussion of this point, see Eugene Fama, "Agency Problems and the Theory of the Firm," *Journal of Political Economy* 88 (1980).

There have been several empirical studies which have examined aspects of the labor market for corporate executives.

We recently completed a study examining the effects of large corporate acquisitions on subsequent executive pay in an attempt to determine whether the labor market seems to reflect the consequences of executive decisions on shareholder wealth.[28] Specifically, we analyzed the change in real executive compensation (relative to industry standards for firms of a similar size and industry) in the period surrounding the completion of a large acquisition.

Two possibilities were considered. First, there is a strong positive relationship between the level of executive compensation and firm size. This suggests that an executive can increase his compensation simply by increasing firm size, regardless of the impact of this size increase on shareholder wealth. Second, the labor market value of executives should reflect *both* the change in firm size and the effect on profitability caused by an acquisition. If the labor market takes into account changes in shareholder wealth in setting an executive's opportunity wage, we should observe increases in executive compensation only for those acquisitions producing increases in shareholder wealth.

The preliminary results of our study suggest that *real* (inflation-adjusted) executive compensation (relative to industry and size standards) increased following a substantial increase in firm size via acquisition. As predicted, however, virtually all of this increase went to executives making acquisitions which increased shareholder wealth. The managements of companies making acquisitions which reduced their share prices saw no increase in the relative level of their real compensation.

Another study presenting evidence of a rational labor market was performed by Anne Coughlan and Ron Schmidt. They attempted to determine whether changes in shareholder wealth are a good predictor of executive terminations.[29] (To be fired is, of course, to face the most extreme form of labor market discipline, especially when it makes it difficult to obtain another comparable job.) The study finds that terminations are more likely to occur after decreases in shareholder wealth.

A third study of the executive labor market focuses on changes in shareholder wealth at the time of an "unexpected" death of a chief executive officer (CEO).[30] The market's response to the announcement of the "unexpected" death of a CEO offers an ideal test of the value of a top executive to a firm. Assuming the search costs of obtaining a new CEO are small relative to the market value of the firm, the effect of an "unexpected" CEO death on shareholder wealth will depend on the stock market's assessment of the value of the former CEO relative to the expected value of the new CEO. From the shareholders' perspective, the value of a CEO

---

28. R. Lambert and D. Larcker, "Executive Compensation Effects of Large Corporate Acquisitions," working paper, Northwestern University (1984).
29. A. Coughlan and R. Schmidt, "Executive Compensation, Management Turnover, and Firm Performance: An Empirical Investigation," *Journal of Accounting and Economics* (forthcoming).
30. W. Johnson, R. Magee, N. Nagarajan, and H. Newman, "An Analysis of the Stock Price Reaction to Sudden Executive Deaths: Implications for the Managerial Labor Market," *Journal of Accounting and Economics* (forthcoming).

is the capitalized value of the CEO's expected future contributions to the value of the firm minus the capitalized value of the CEO's expected future compensation.

If CEO's, as is often alleged by the financial press, have the power to control boards of directors, one would expect the strength of a CEO's control to increase with his seniority. This implies, of course, that the former CEO would have more control over the board than the CEO expected to succeed him. And if such is the case, the former CEO should be paid more (relative to his contribution to the firm's value) than the expected payments to the new CEO. If the relatively "overpaid" CEO dies unexpectedly, the announcement of the death should be accompanied by a positive security market reaction.

The results of the study, however, show a pronounced *negative* security market reaction—at least to the deaths of those CEOs who were not the founders of their companies.[31] This result suggests that CEOs are not overpaid relative to their contribution to shareholder wealth (not at least when compared to alternative managers available in the labor market).[32]

VII. Innovations in Compensation Design

The evidence on executive compensation and the market for managerial labor suggests that current executive compensation practices are not total "madness." This discussion should not be construed, however, to imply there is no room for improvement in the design of compensation contracts. In fact, it is interesting to examine some of the recent innovations in compensation contract designs proposed (generally) by compensation consultants and, in some cases, adopted by corporations. Most of these innovative contracts seem designed primarily to deal with the kinds of "agency" problems we have been discussing throughout.

In 1983, for example, Johnson Controls, Inc. developed a unique seven-year performance plan for two of their most senior-level executives (both of whom were then about 60 years of age). In each of the seven years, the base amount of the plan (consisting of $300,000 and $100,000 for the two executives, respectively) is multiplied by a percentage that varies between zero and 150 percent. The determination of each percentage is based upon the *ratio* of the average annual total shareholder return for Johnson Controls (over the ten-year period ending with the current year) to the average total shareholder return for a peer group of Fortune

---

31. However, the study does find a significant positive reaction to the announcement of the unexpected death of an executive who was the corporate founder. This is consistent with the hypothesis that corporate founders, who often own a substantial portion of the firm's stock, are able to exercise control over the board of directors that enables them to be paid more relative to their contribution to firm value than their successors.

32. It is important to realize that the security market reaction to a CEO death is more complex than simply the difference in capitalized value of the compensation paid to the new CEO relative to the old CEO. The magnitude of the change in shareholder wealth depends upon the new CEO's contribution to firm value minus compensation paid (in technical terms, the CEO's marginal product) relative to the old CEO's contribution to the firm value minus compensation.

500 companies over the same period.[33] Each of the yearly awards is then invested in a hypothetical portfolio consisting of the stock of Johnson Controls. The payment of the total value of this hypothetical portfolio is deferred until the end of the seven-year performance period.

There are several interesting aspects of this performance plan. First, the term of the contract extends approximately three years beyond the retirement of the two executives. This feature appears to be an attempt to lengthen the decision-making horizons of executives—especially in the case of those near retirement age. This contract explicitly motivates the executives to consider the impact of their decisions on the company after they leave the corporation.

Second, the "scorecard" for the annual changes in the value of the performance plan is formally tied to changes in shareholder wealth over the prior ten years. This is unusual because performance plans are typically based upon earnings per share or return on equity growth rates. One explanation for the choice of changes in shareholder wealth is that the board of directors is attempting to lengthen the executive's decision-making horizon by selecting a scorecard that has a longer performance evaluation horizon than yearly accounting numbers.

Finally, the performance plan is based on *relative* changes in shareholder wealth. This appears to be an attempt to isolate that portion of changes in shareholder wealth that is under management's control from economy- and industry-wide effects. The choice of a ten-year period for assessing the performance of the company may be an attempt to "wash out" other random elements that affect performance in a single year.

Another example of an innovative compensation scheme is the performance unit plan adopted by TRW in 1983 for 28 of its key executives. Under this plan, the value of each performance unit varies according to how TRW ranks relative to 98 peer companies. More interesting, performance is measured using the ratio of the market value of the firm (equity plus debt) to the *inflation-adjusted* value of net assets (typically referred to as the "q ratio"). The key feature of the TRW contract is that the impact of inflation on accounting measures is explicitly considered. This is important because inflation can severely distort historical accounting measures of corporate performance. For example, corporations (or divisions within corporations) with "old" assets will produce a higher return on assets than otherwise similar corporations (or divisions) with "newer" assets. Since asset age and changes in price level are explicitly considered in the TRW approach, this should produce a more reasonable accounting-based comparison between TRW and peer companies and among the divisions of TRW as well.

A more general, conceptual innovation in compensation design has been proposed by Booz•Allen and Hamilton Inc. The consulting firm's compensation specialists have developed what they call a "Strategic Reward Map" (see Figure 2).

33. Notice that this contract is similar to the market-indexed option suggested by Mark Ubelhart later in this issue. See "Business Strategy, Performance Measurement, and Compensation," and also an earlier article, "A New Look at Executive Compensation Plans," *Cash Flow* (1981). Relative shareholder value compensation contracts have also been adopted by Clevepak Corp. and U.S. West.

Figure 2. Strategic Reward Map (Booz•Allen & Hamilton).

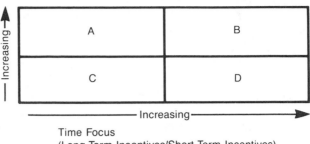

The Strategic Reward Map has two dimensions. The first is called "risk posture." It is measured by the ratio of contingent compensation (i.e., the sum of yearly bonus, stock options, SAR's, performance plans, restricted stock, and phantom stock) to yearly salary. This dimension attempts to capture the degree to which an executive's compensation is "at risk." The second dimension is called "time focus." It is measured by the ratio of long-term compensation (i.e., the sum of stock options, SAR's, performance plans, restricted stock, and phantom stock) to the annual bonus. This dimension attempts to capture the degree to which an executive's compensation is obtained from long-term (multi-year) performance measures versus short-term (single-year) performance measures. In terms of the agency theory framework, the risk posture and time focus variables are measures of the (1) potentially non-diversifiable risk imposed upon the executive and (2) the executive's decision-making horizon.

The Strategic Reward Map has several potential applications. First, it provides a simple way to synthesize the critical elements and compare compensation practices within a sample of firms. Second, it provides a convenient way to track changes in the "mix" of compensation components over time. Also, it may be possible to develop recommendations regarding contractual design in various portions of the map. For example, consider a firm which has a large market share in a profitable industry with substantial barriers to entry, but where product or service innovation is unlikely to be profitable. For this type of company, it may be desirable to motivate managers to be conservative in their decision-making and to be most concerned with the short-term impact of their actions (that is, make few changes and simply manage the existing customer relationships). The executive compensation contracts would accordingly produce a risk posture and time focus in the quadrant labeled C in Figure 2. By contrast, if the profitability of the firm depends upon executives undertaking risky investments with long-term payoffs, then the compensation plan should be structured according so as to fall in quadrant B.[34]

---

34. One must be careful, however, not to impose so much risk on the manager that he becomes too conservative in his decision-making.

Another approach deserving mention—one that has been widely popularized by executive compensation and management consulting firms—is to measure corporate performance by the "spread" between return on equity (ROE) and the equity cost of capital.[35] One can justify the use of ROE "spread," just as one can justify the use of many financial surrogates, by arguing that this measure provides additional information about managerial actions not contained in stock price changes. But this measure is typically cited as the appropriate scorecard for compensation purposes because of its strong positive correlation with the ratio of the market value of equity to historical book value. This empirical correlation is then used to justify the statement that the most direct way to create shareholder value is to increase the spread between ROE and the equity cost of capital.

There are a number of serious flaws with this argument for using ROE "spread," at least as the sole basis for evaluating managerial performance. For one thing, ROE is an *accounting* measure, one which has all of the inherent problems associated with the historical cost accounting system (e.g., inflation distortions and arbitrary cost allocations). The equity cost of capital, however, is a *market-determined* required rate of return for investing capital in risky projects; and it is at best unclear how the cost of capital related to the ROE. Moreover, all of the empirical analysis supporting "spread" uses the ratio of market to book as the primary measure of management's success in creating shareholder value. But it is not obvious that shareholders' primary interest is served by managements intent on maximizing their company's price-to-book ratio. The most direct measure of interest to shareholders is the rate of return on their shares. And we are aware of no evidence that indicates that "spread" is directly associated with total shareholder return (or, better yet, with the rate of shareholder return in excess of the normal rate of return given the company's risk).

In fact, it is easy to illustrate that managers compensated on the basis of ROE "spread" may be motivated to decrease shareholder wealth. For example, assume that a manager is considering the adoption of two investment projects, both of which are expected to have a return which exceeds the firm's cost of capital. Assume the ROE "spread" for project A exceeds the "spread" for project B. If the manager is compensated on the basis of ROE "spread" *alone*, he can maximize the "spread" and his compensation by selecting only project A. In this example, the use of "spread" (or any rate of return measure) can have the unfortunate effect of motivating the manager to reject projects which would increase shareholder wealth.[36]

---

35. See Louis Brindisi, "Creating Shareholder Value: A New Mission for Executive Compensation," Chapter 19; and J. Rich and J. Larson, "Why Some Long-Term Incentives Fail," *Compensation Review* (1984) for a discussion of "spread" in a compensation context. Once case of adoption of this approach is First Tennessee Corp.'s executive compensation plan.

36. One solution to this problem is to change the compensation contract from one based upon rate of return to one based upon residual income. See C. Horngren, *Cost Accounting: A Managerial Emphasis*. Prentice-Hall (1982), Chapter 20 for some additional discussion of this point.

Given this potential problem of "underinvestment" (as well as the potential for manipulating accounting-based measures in general), we recommend caution in using the ROE "spread" as the principal measure of corporate success and as the "scorecard" for computing management incentive awards.

VIII. Summary

Our review of the academic research has provided an analysis of a variety of issues concerning executive compensation. We began by using agency theory as an economic framework to identify potential conflicts of interest between management and shareholders. Viewed in this context, the primary function of a corporate compensation plan is to reduce such conflicts by providing management with the strongest possible incentives to maximize shareholder value.

The framework enables us to offer some specific suggestions for reducing management-stockholder conflict through the design of compensation contracts. Empirical tests in the agency literature show that executives respond predictably to the incentives built into compensation contracts. Furthermore, *changes* in compensation plans affect executive decision-making in ways consistent with our theory of corporate managers as self-interested economic agents.

The available evidence on the relationship between executive pay and corporate performance documents a positive relationship between senior executives' annual incomes and annual shareholder returns. The correlation becomes especially clear when changes in the value of executive holdings in their own company's stock and stock options (which are often quite substantial) are included in the calculation of income.

The labor market of executives also plays a critical role in curbing management's tendency to pursue its own self-interest at the expense of its stockholders. Research bearing on the executive labor market suggests that an executive's opportunity wage—and, in fact, the ability to retain his job—is related to the effect of his decisions on his shareholders. Also, research showing negative market responses to unexpected deaths of CEO's suggests that most executives are not able to exercise enough control over boards of directors to pay themselves more (relative to their contribution to the firm's profits) than the compensation required by alternative managers.

In general the emerging body of research on the economic consequences of executive compensation suggests, contrary to most discussions in the popular press, that executive compensation is not total "madness." This, of course, does not imply that the conflicts are totally resolved, or that all companies are equally proficient at controlling these conflicts.[37]

---

37. It is important to note that our focus has been primarily directed to the use of compensation contracts and external labor markets to motivate managers to work in shareholders' interests. We have not discussed the disciplining effects of competition within the internal labor market and the market for corporate control. Obviously, the role that compensation contracts play in motivating managers is influenced by the ability of these other mechanisms to discipline managers into selecting actions which increase shareholder wealth.

The recent trend of corporate reorganizations (spin-offs, leveraged buyouts, and so forth) may also reflect attempts by executives and shareholders to control management incentive problems.[38] One of the more plausible arguments why management groups and investors are paying substantial premiums over market to take firms private is the radical improvement in management incentives. Taking the firm private greatly reduces and, in some cases, eliminates the separation of ownership and control that characterizes most large public corporations. Corporate spin-offs also promise improvements in management incentives. By separating operating units that were previously combined, spin-offs allow the performance of the individual operating units to be evaluated more accurately, thereby improving the ability of the parent company to reward and thus motivate divisional operating managers.

---

38. For additional discussion of these issues, see G. Hite and J. Owners, "The Restructuring of Corporate America: An Overview," Chapter 4, K. Schipper and A. Smith, "The Corporate Spin-Off Phenomenon," Chapter 9, and H. DeAngelo, L. DeAngelo and E. Rice, "Going Private: The Effects of Change in Corporate Ownership Structure," Chapter 11.

18

Managerial Incentives in Mergers and Their Effect on Shareholder Wealth

David F. Larcker
University of Pennsylvania

We have been talking a lot today about redistributions of wealth among security holders in mergers: who wins, who loses. But we have talked relatively little about why managers undertake mergers, and whether they win or lose. In my presentation, I will provide some analysis of management incentives in mergers and the effect of incentive compensation contracts on managerial decisions and, ultimately, on shareholder value.

By way of outline, I will first provide a very general framework for looking at some of the managerial motives for mergers. It's a framework that has become popular in the literature of accounting and financial economics, and is typically referred to as the "agency" model. Next I'll consider the question: Do compensation contracts really matter? That is, does the existence and design of these kinds of contracts influence corporate investment in general and merger decisions in particular? And how does this influence translate into changes in shareholder wealth? Then I'll look specifically at managerial incentives on both sides of the merger. First, I'll consider the managers of the buying firms—those executives making the major investment decisions—to determine whether certain kinds of compensation contracts are associated with the characteristics of these mergers (including the expected profitability, as reflected in the market's reaction to the deal). Finally, I'll look at the managers of selling firms, focusing primarily on anti-takeover amendments and golden parachutes.

I. Agency Theory

The basic premise of agency theory is rather simple: managers and owners, that is, shareholders, have potentially contradictory motivations. Managers, one could argue, are interested primarily in maximizing the utility derived from their compensation and non-pecuniary items, whereas owners are primarily interested in maximizing stock price. Consequently, the decisions of managers can diverge from stockholder interests in several respects. For example, because managers can leave the firm or be fired (or because they may be evaluated according to short-term performance), managers may have a shorter-term decision-making horizon than shareholders. To the extent that stock prices (and thus shareholder value) reflect the longer-term prospects of corporations, shareholders are likely to have a stronger interest in the longer-term outlook and the longer-term expected profitability of investments made by managers.

Agency theory, then, concerns the potential conflicts of interest between managers and stockholders. It also concerns itself with corporate practices which have been designed to overcome, or at least mitigate, such "agency" problems. One development aimed specifically at this problem is the widespread use of incentive compensation contracts, especially at the senior level within the corporation. The most common of these are bonus contracts, which are generally based on annual performance. Another common form of incentive compensation is stock options, which of course are tied directly to stockholder value. The purpose of such contracts is to reduce so-called "agency" costs by aligning, as closely as possible, the interests of management with those of shareholders.

Over the past few years, the financial press has taken a rather dim view of corporate investment policies. Management has been repeatedly chastized for taking a short-term view of the world, and much of the blame has been directed at corporate compensation practices. It has also been charged that prevailing incentive plans have influenced managers to undertake "unproductive" mergers rather than "productive" long-term capital investment. Also, the resistance to acquisition proposals by managers of target firms, together with the proliferating adoption of "porcupine amendments" and golden parachutes, has caused many to question management's service to its shareholders.

But whether, or to what extent, management pursues its own interest to the detriment of shareholders is really an empirical question, one that we don't as yet have enough evidence to answer with confidence. However, we do have some evidence, and I will be discussing that part of this body of evidence which bears of the effectiveness of compensation contracts in bringing together the interests of management and stockholders.

II. Do Compensation Contracts Matter?

The main focus of my presentation, then, will be on the questions: Do different compensation contracts seem to induce different choices by the managers involved in mergers? And do these choices have any significant, systematic effect on share-holder wealth?

But before I attempt to address this issue, I want to review some evidence which suggests that compensation contracts affect corporate decisions *in general*. I would like to talk about two studies I've done which ask very generally: When companies make major changes in compensation contracts with their managers, do we see changes in managerial decisions—particularly in investment or expenditure patterns? Furthermore, do we see any systematic market response to announcements of such changes in compensation programs?

In the first of these studies, I examined the adoption of long-term contracts, typically referred to as "performance plans." These performance plans generally defer a fairly certain amount of compensation sometime into the future, and this amount is tied to accounting-based yardsticks like growth in EPS and return on shareholders' equity. The important aspect of these contracts is that the compensation is deferred into the future, and the manager receives payment only if certain longer-run targets are met.

In this paper, I argue that if a manager has an important deferred compensation contract, this may lengthen his or her decision-making horizon. Since capital investments typically have negative earnings and cash flows in "early" time periods and positive earnings and cash flows in "later" periods, capital investment will be most desirable to a manager who evaluates the financial consequences of the investment over a "long" decision-making horizon. Therefore, my expectation was that capital investment would increase for those firms adopting such perform-ance plans. The results indicate that there are substantial changes in the level of corporate investment for the set of firms adopting these longer-range incentive contracts relative to a set of firms not using performance plans.

I also examined the stock market response to corporate announcements of performance plan adoption. Using a methodology very similar to the one we've been talking about throughout the day, I found there was a significant positive stock market reaction to the *announcement* of the contractual change. It was on the order of one percent.

A second study I did looked at expenditure decisions by bank executives when their banks introduced short-term accounting-based compensation contracts. These contracts were in effect profit-sharing arrangements. I reasoned that these execu-tives, because they were now getting part of the profits, would be less willing to make expenditures which would not increase the profits of the firm. And in fact, I find that when banks adopt such short-term incentive plans, the level of expen-ditures on "discretionary" (non-pecuniary) items tends to decrease.

Thus, the results of these two studies tend to confirm our suspicion that com-pensation contracts do affect managerial investment decisions. Furthermore, the market even seems to anticipate the beneficial effects of deferred compensation contracts by responding favorably to the announcement of such long-term incen-tive plans.

III. Management Incentives in Mergers

Now, however, we want to ask a more specific question: Do compensation contracts also explain some of the results we observe with mergers? There has been relatively little work done with respect to mergers. Baruch Lev, the chairman of this session, performed a study which attempted to determine whether the reduction of the risk associated with the managers' human capital and "fixed" compensation claims was really an important motive for mergers. Baruch's hypothesis was that if managers are risk-averse, then holding other things constant, they will prefer investments which reduce firm risk and, in so doing, reduce the risk associated with their own future compensation. To the extent a manager is compensated through salary alone, he has fixed claims on the firm which are very similar to those of a bondholder. Viewed in this light, it makes sense for managers to choose the same kind of investments as those which would benefit the firm's bondholders. That is, if the manager has substantial fixed claims on the firm, we'd expect to see him take on investments which decrease cash flow variability. Of course, one of the most obvious variance-reducing investments is a conglomerate type of acquisition.

Baruch's study reasoned that this kind of agency problem—that is, the problem of management undertaking investments which are inconsistent with shareholder objectives—will occur most frequently in companies where managers don't own much of the stock, and where there are no large blocks of stock outstanding such that a few large investors would have the incentive to closely monitor and control the actions of management. Such companies are typically referred to as "manager-controlled" firms. Baruch's hypothesis was that managers are more likely to seek conglomerate mergers (and thus diversify their human capital and the various fixed claims that they hold on the firm) in manager-controlled than in owner-controlled firms.

The empirical results of this study provide support for the operation of this risk reduction motive in corporate mergers. Baruch finds that the operations of manager-controlled firms are more diversified than those of owner-controlled firms, and that manager-controlled firms engage in more conglomerate type of acquisitions—that is, those acquisitions which tend to be diversifying investments. To the extent that these acquiring firms have paid large premiums over market simply to diversify (that is, when there are no expected synergies), this diversification strategy may account for much of the adverse market reaction to announcements of mergers.

I've also taken a look at this issue in a little bit more detail. Some of the questions I attempted to answer in one of my own studies were these: Do compensation contracts or performance "scorecards" faced by managers seem to influence merger activities and shareholders' wealth? In particular, does the structure of the merger deal appear to be related in any way to the provisions of the buying firm's management compensation contracts? For example, is there any relation between the compensation contract and the effect of the merger upon proforma EPS?

The second major question I consider is: Does the market respond differently to announcements of acquisitions by companies with different compensation contracts? For example, if we have a merger undertaken by a management compensated largely by stock options, do we find a different market reaction than the reaction to acquiring companies whose managers are compensated largely in terms of salary and annual bonus?

I looked at 43 merger proposals, both successful and unsuccessful, that occurred between 1976 and 1979. (About 70 percent of these deals were successful.) In each of these mergers, the board of directors of the bidding company owned less than 5 percent of the outstanding shares, so I would tend to classify them all as *manager-controlled* firms. As I suggested, if there's an agency problem related to mergers as diversifying investments, it will tend to be most pronounced when the management or directors don't own much of the outstanding equity.

I also restricted my sample to those mergers in which there was only a single bidder for the target firm. These were all basically friendly deals. I wanted to abstract away from the multiple bidder problem. The average acquisition premium paid by this sample of bidding companies was about 60 percent. Also, all the acquired firms were either traded on the New York or American Stock Exchange. The average size of the acquisition was about 16 percent of the market value of the buyer. Thus, these were fairly substantial acquisitions.

Well, to add to some of the controversy we discussed this morning, I came up with results very similar to Peter Dodd's negative findings on mergers. I found that the cumulative abnormal return to bidding companies was a negative one percent over the period extending from roughly two days before until three days after the merger announcement. This result, together with the negative results of Dodd's study of the 1971–1977 period, leads me to believe that the mergers that have been done in the 70s are fundamentally different from the mergers done in the 60s. I think that if we looked at the *Wall Street Journal* over the 70s and 80s, most of the *big* mergers have been greeted with a negative share price reaction.

One other point: I discovered from reading *Wall Street Journal* articles about these bidding firms that announcements of dividend and earnings increases sometimes come on the same day in which mergers are announced. In fact, in my sample of 43 bidding firms, there were four firms that announced fairly substantial dividend increases along with the announcement of an impending merger. If I remove those four firms from the sample, the negative response to the bidders is much larger than that reported here. The winners and losers among these firms appear to be split fairly equally. But, on average, the losers lost far more than the winners won.

IV. The Effects of Differences in Compensation Contracts

Let's now turn to the more specific questions about how compensation contracts seem to influence the kinds of mergers we see, and how the market responds to these deals. I have adopted the following framework for classifying compensation contracts: (1) whether they were short term—that is, paying off on a yearly basis—or deferred; and (2) whether they were based on accounting or market measures of performance. Short-term, accounting-based forms of compensation include things like yearly bonus plans, profit sharing plans, and dividend units (although these are not very common). Typical long-term, market-oriented contracts are stock options, stock appreciation rights (which are just like stock options except you don't have to exercise the option to get the appreciation), and restricted stock, which are simply stock grants. Finally, the one that's really new are the long-term accounting-based measures, typically referred to as "performance units" or "performance shares." There are some important contracts I ignore in this study, and some of them are potentially important. They include employment contracts guaranteeing executives a specified salary, golden parachutes (which we'll talk about a little later), pension plans, consulting arrangements, and various perquisites. However, I think the contracts I do consider encompass enough of management compensation to make my results meaningful.

In terms of data collection, I went through about 200 proxy statements to obtain information about the compensation plans of my sample of 43 bidding firms, and found what I think are some rather surprising results. First of all, I found that almost all the compensation of the executives of these firms was based on short-term, accounting measures. Although the ratio of short-term, accounting compensation to total compensation ranged anywhere from 50 percent all the way up to 100 percent, the average for this sample of firms was 90 percent. However, there is an upward bias to these percentages because I valued the stock options at their theoretical *lower* bound (as opposed to a value obtained from an option pricing model). The important point is that there is not much longer-term, market-based incentive provided for the managements engaged in these large M & A deals.

V. Some Results

Let's look at the preliminary results of my study. The research hypotheses were admittedly somewhat exploratory. It's hard to build very rigorous models to handle these kinds of questions. The first thing I attempted to answer was whether the characteristics of the merger are related in someway to the compensation contract. For example, I would expect that managers would be more likely to understand mergers which increase pro-forma EPS when most of their remuneration comes from accounting-based sources. I also predicted that as the percentage of remuneration tied to accounting measures goes up, the stock market's reaction to the merger would be more adverse. I base this expectation on the fact that there are a lot of ways to increase earnings without benefiting—and, in some cases, while even penalizing—shareholders. This is the well-known incompatibility between earnings and the cash flows of interest to shareholders. And I think as we move more to an accounting-based type of contract, we may be motivating the manager to take investment projects that are less consistent with maximizing shareholder value.

One result of my study is that the percentage of accounting-based compensation increases, managers are more likely to use cash in doing the deal than managers with more market-oriented compensation contracts. However, the most interesting result is that the more accounting-oriented the compensation plan, the more negative, on average, the market's reaction to the merger.

These results suggest that, at least for this specific decision, this sample of firms, and this time period, the management incentive contracts may not be consistent with the objectives of the owners of the corporation. This is not to say that such contracts are globally inappropriate—because, after all, we're only looking at one specific decision made by the manager. Such accounting-based contracts may be great for other decisions, but they don't appear to be great for mergers.

The implication of this I think is clear. The type of contract used to compensate managers seems to be associated with the characteristics of mergers, and also with changes in the wealth of buyer companies' shareholders that result from these deals. I would thus argue that managerial motives arising from the structure of compensation contracts appear to be an important explanatory variable for understanding merger activity.

VI. The Sellers

Let's move now to the other side of the merger transaction, to the incentives and responses of the target companies' management. Here I'm going to confine my comments to studies of "anti-takeover" amendments and golden parachutes.

Anti-takeover charter amendments, also known as "shark repellents," are shareholder-approved changes in the corporate charter, including things like supermajority voting and staggered election of boards of directors. There is a study recently published by Harry DeAngelo and Ed Rice which attempts to explain why these anti-takeover amendments are introduced, and what effect they have on the wealth of target shareholders. One of their hypotheses is the so-called managerial entrenchment hypothesis. They argue that managers propose anti-takeover amendments in order to increase their expected job security and compensation. If that's the case, then we would expect the market to respond negatively to these amendments because they can be used to shelter inefficient managers from the discipline of the takeover market.

DeAngelo and Rice find about a one percent negative stock market reaction in the period surrounding the proxy release disclosing that there's going to be a vote on the adoption of anti-takeover amendments. I don't think this result is statistically significant, although it's hard to tell from their study. However, it provides at least weak support for the managerial entrenchment hypothesis. I think the interesting question, here, is: If these anti-takeover amendments are associated with adverse changes in the wealth of shareholders, then why do target shareholders vote for them? In fact, a recent study by John McConnell and Scott Linn suggests that anti-takeover amendments are associated with an increase in shareholder wealth. Thus, the shareholder wealth effects of anti-takeover amendments certainly deserve further study.

VII. Golden Parachutes

I want to move on to "golden parachutes," the compensation contracts that have recently been chastized by the financial press. Golden parachutes are simply employment contracts, or changes to the existing employment contracts, that provide substantial compensation to executives in the event their firm undergoes some type of change of control. If you read the proxy statements, they're about that nebulous in stating the triggering mechanism and payout provisions.

My colleague, Rick Lambert, and I have examined the market's reaction to the adoption of golden parachutes by a sample of 90 companies. These were basically Fortune 1000 firms—some OTC firms, but for the most part New York and American Stock Exchange companies. The golden parachutes that we observed were *not* approved by shareholders; they simply show up in the proxy statements. Golden parachutes, furthermore, are not necessarily trivial in dollar magnitude. On average, they are about 2 percent of the market value of the firm's equity (as calculated when the golden parachutes go in). In some cases, however, they're over 10 percent of the market value of the firm. In a typical golden parachute, 10 executives are covered. However, this number ranges anywhere from one up to the 250 executives covered by the much publicized Beneficial Corporation contract.

The traditional view of golden parachutes in the financial press is that they're bad news for stockholders since they deter potential buyers. In defense of golden parachutes, it has been argued that these compensation contracts strengthen the incentives for target management to act in the interest of stockholders (by relinquishing control) when faced with an acquisition proposal. So, at first glance, it isn't clear whether or not this realignment of management incentives is worth more to shareholders than the deterrent to takeover provided by golden parachutes.

Our study of the market's response to announcements of golden parachutes are "good news" for the firm. For our sample of 90, we find that the share price goes up 2 percent on average. (We excluded from this sample firms like Bendix and Martin Marietta, where they put these contracts in during the acquisition period. Obviously that would drive up the share price artificially.) Using a "cleaned-up" sample (which made adjustments for earnings and dividend announcements and unusual proposals in the proxy statements) of about 60 firms, we find the market response to be a little over 3 percent.

The interesting issue concerns whether it is possible to discriminate among those firms where the market goes up, those firms where it doesn't go up at all, and those firms where it actually goes down. So, we attempted to determine whether there was some way of segregating our sample of firms to explain why the market responded favorably to some golden parachutes and unfavorably to others.

We began this attempt to classify the firms by considering three different explanations why companies might adopt golden parachutes. First, we hypothesized that, in some cases, golden parachutes are put in as part of an overall anti-takeover package. In fact, this is explicitly stated in about 10 percent of the proxies in our sample. In such cases, where the motive is to fight off a takeover and entrench the incumbent management, we would expect the effect of golden parachutes on shareholder wealth to be negative.

Second, we considered a kind of managerial risk-sharing or insurance argument. This has a sort of ambiguous effect on the value of the firm. By insuring a manager's compensation against the loss which he would incur if his firm was taken over and he were subsequently fired, golden parachutes may stop the manager from doing things to make the firm unattractive to potential bidders. (And we have seen these "scorch the earth" policies.) To the extent that golden parachutes prevent this kind of behavior, or otherwise strengthen the incentive of taget management to act in stockholder interests, golden parachutes may be good news for the firm and thus have a positive effect on shareholder wealth.

The other side of this argument, however, is that once we insure the target manager's compensation, we also decrease the ability of the market to discipline the target manager. In that case, the protected manager may over-consume perks or discretionary expenditures, or whatever. And that can have a negative effect on the value of the firm.

A third possibility is that golden parachutes may signal to the market that a takeover is likely. The argument is that when managers attempt to protect their compensation in this way, this may convey some private information to the market that the probability of a takeover has increased. To the extent the market bids up the price of the firm in anticipation of a large acquisition premium, we would expect this effect of golden parachutes to be positive.

So, given these three possible effects, we attempted to separate our sample of firms into three groups, according to which of these three effects would be expected to prevail. We started by establishing some measures of "takeover risk" designated to distinguish likely from less likely takeover candidates. The variables we used as proxies for takeover risk were the size of the firm (the larger the firm, the lower the risk of takeover), large block holdings of a company's stock by another corporation (as evidenced in 13-D filings), past acquisition bids, and recent substandard performance (losses). We then reasoned that, for those firms with higher takeover risk, the adoption of a golden parachute would be more likely to convey positive information to the market. In fact, we found that there is a positive correlation between higher takeover risk and the size of the market's positive response to golden parachute, but the relationship was not statistically significant. So there's no strong support for the explanation that the positive market response to these contracts is related to the information released about the possibility of takeover.

However, we do find that when it's mentioned that these golden parachutes are part of an anti-takeover package, there is a significantly *negative* market reaction to the announcement of the golden parachute. This is consistent with the managerial entrenchment hypothesis.

At the same time, we also find that the "managerial insurance" or "risk-sharing" hypothesis has the most statistical explanatory power. We reasoned that this risk-sharing effect would be strongest in cases where the golden parachutes are largest (relative to the market value of the firm and relative to the number of executives covered). We find that as takeover risk goes up, management tends to put in bigger golden parachutes—that is, offer managers more insurance; and as we insure the manager more, we find that the security price reaction is more favorable.

To summarize our study on golden parachutes, then, we find that golden parachutes are associated with a positive, statistically significant security market reaction. We also find that differences in the market's reaction to the adoption of these contracts can be partially explained by differences in variables which proxy for different motives. Specifically, in those cases where resistance to takeover is explicitly stated as the motive, the market responds negatively to this evidence of managerial entrenchment. But, in those cases where the contracts seem designed to provide management with the incentive to act in shareholder interest in the event of a takeover bid, the market response is significantly positive.

QUESTION: Isn't there some sort of settling up in the labor market when these executives put in large compensation contracts to protect themselves against dismissal?

LARCKER: That's something we don't know very much about. We don't know much about compensation contracts in general, but we know even less about the labor market for top managers. If we believe that there's going to be some kind of settling up to give managers their just deserts, then it's going to tend to reduce the conflicts of interest between managers and stockholders. This should also help to solve the problem—to the extent that this is really a problem—of overly aggressive managers building conglomerate empires at the expense of their stockholders.

QUESTION: Don't you think that some of the differences in these contracts might reflect differences among firms as to how much of a manager's human capital is tied to the firm, and how much is transferable?

LARCKER: Yes, I think you're right. The story that I've often heard is that firms tend to underpay their managers relative to their marginal product in the early years, and then overpay them in later years. It's kind of an implicit contract. So these golden parachutes may essentially be giving managers what they're entitled to by these implicit compensation contracts that have been built up over the years. This is certainly consistent with sort of the insurance effect that the evidence seems to support.

VIII. Summing Up

In closing, I would like to just run through what are probably the most important findings of our work attempting to trace the effects of incentive compensation on managerial decisions (including mergers, of course) and on shareholder value. Although it's probably a little premature, I will venture the following statements.

First, the structure of compensation contracts—that is, whether short- or long-term, accounting- or market-oriented—appears to affect managerial decision-making. For example, those managers compensated on a deferred basis appear to choose to undertake more investment. Furthermore, the market seems to have acknowledged this because it responds favorably to contractual switches to deferred compensation policies.

Second, we find that diversifying or conglomerate acquisitions are much more prevalent among large, manager-controlled firms (those with broadly dispersed stock ownership) than owner-or shareholder-controlled firms. This suggests that the managers of acquiring or bidding firms in M & A act as if they desire to decrease the total cash flow variability, although it is by no means clear that such variance reduction benefits shareholders. In fact, to the extent companies acquire other firms simply to diversify their risks (and pay a large premium to do so), they may be penalizing their stockholders. The greater use of stock options, or some other market-based compensation scheme, might be useful in overcoming the risk aversion of management which may be driving much of this unprofitable diversification.

Third, compensation contracts appear to influence some of the characteristics of the merger, For example, managers of firms whose compensation is more accounting-oriented tend to engage in cash transactions.

Fourth, and perhaps most important, the stock market's response to the acquisitions by accounting-oriented firms has been significantly less favorable than to acquistions by firms whose managers are compensated according to longer-term, market-based incentive plans. Thus, the adoption of more market-oriented compensation plans may furnish management with better incentives with respect to merger decisions.

Finally, anti-takeover charter amendments seem to have a slight negative impact on the wealth of target shareholders. This provides at least some support for the argument that these measures entrench existing management at the expense of shareholders. But, golden parachutes, except when adopted as part of an explicit anti-takeover package, seem to have a positive impact on the wealth of target shareholders.

19

Creating Shareholder Value:
A New Mission for Executive Compensation

Louis J. Brindisi, Jr.
American Compensation Systems, Inc.

I. Introduction

Historically, the mission of the business enterprise has been to provide a return on investment. Today, that basic principle necessarily is expressed in more complex and compelling terms where the publicly held corporation is concerned; The ultimate corporate objective is to create shareholder value—value, that is, as measured by the sum of common stock appreciation and dividends paid to shareholders. To do this, top executives must develop and implement successful corporate and business-unit strategies. Executive compensation is critical to this process in two ways: first, by supporting the strategies, management processes, organization approaches, and culture critical to creating shareholder value; and second, by paying directly for the value created.

II. The Growing Pay/Performance Gap

The need to view executive compensation from this perspective is all the more urgent given the growing disparity between CEO pay and corporate performance as measured by shareholder-value creation (Figure 1).

Our study revealed that in the early sixties, significant shareholder value was created as the result of truly strong corporate performance. During the period 1960–1965, shareholder value for the S&P 400 grew at an average annual rate of

Figure 1. The Emerging Pay/Performance Gap.

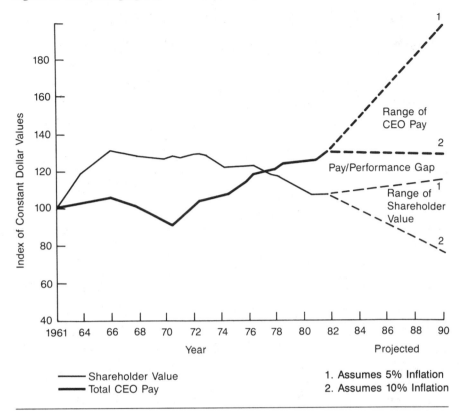

Sources: Shareholder Value — S&P 400; Compensation — Proxies and surveys of 80 companies in S&P 400.

9.1 percent, closely tracking the 9.4 percent average annual real growth in return on equity (ROE). Executive pay, however, while increasing, did not keep up with this pace (as also shown in Figure 2).

This trend began to reverse itself in the latter half of the decade. From 1966 to 1970, corporate performance and shareholder value began to decline. And, since 1970, shareholder value has drifted steadily downward, while executive compensation has climbed ever higher. In light of the prospects that the trend of rising CEO pay will continue, it is particularly inappropriate for companies to continue operating compensation systems in which executive rewards bear little relation to corporate performance. Such programs provide no support for the shareholder-value creation process and thus have the potential to greatly exacerbate the pay/performance gap that has emerged.

While academicians and economists have been principally responsible for articulating in the public forum the concern over shareholder-value creation, a quiet but potentially noisy revolution has been brewing among institutional investors.

Traditionally, this group of shareholders has endorsed management policies as a matter of course. More recently, however, large investors have begun casting their lot with dissident shareholders critical of poor management performance and consequent weak shareholder returns. These critics sometimes go even further than simply questioning high executive rewards in the face of poor performance, at the extreme challenging incumbent management to justify its tenure under such conditions. While the fact that executive compensation increases are outpacing shareholder-value creation is in itself a matter of concern, more important is the underlying cause of the phenomenon: Most of today's executive reward systems have only weak links—and sometimes none at all—to the creation of shareholder value.

The concern over this pay/performance gap is not diminished by the bull market that began in mid-1982, which resulted in substantial new shareholder wealth. This recent upsurge reflected anticipated lower cost of capital and therefore the increased spread in real ROE. For the most part, the upturn took place across the board, with companies' relative positions remaining essentially the same. Those companies with higher ROEs, however, generated more shareholder value than those with lower ROEs.

Top management of some of the real winners in this market have been handsomely and justly rewarded through stock incentives. In other cases, however, lesser (but not modest) gains resulting from the exercise of options granted years earlier have been only *coincidental* with shareholder-value creation during this period, and not the result of effective competitive positioning and strategic management. In the absence of a *direct relationship* between such reward opportunities and effective strategic management, shareholder value created under these circumstances seems destined to be serendipitous, short-lived, and inconsistent with long-term prospects.

How did we arrive at this predicament? Answering that question requires, first, an understanding of the performance/reward relationship that characterized the 1960s; second, an appreciation of the factors affecting corporate performance during the 1970s; and finally, an evaluation of executive pay systems as they have evolved over the past ten years.

In the following pages we analyze trends in corporate performance and executive pay over the last two decades and show how and why the pay/performance gap has developed. In addition, we offer approaches for restructuring compensation systems so that they provide both effective incentives and true rewards for achievement of the strategic and financial objectives that result in shareholder-value creation.

III. Pay and Performance Over Two Decades

The early 1960s provided a dramatically different environment from that in which business operates today. Postwar expansion continued and the business environment was, by and large, dynamic and predictable. Corporate results were strong; earnings, return on equity, stock prices, and shareholder value all grew substantially.

Executive reward systems were remarkably simple, straightforward, and effective in rewarding shareholder-value creation, since the principal components were base salary and stock options. Fewer than half of America's major corporations had annual bonus plans in 1960. This compensation element was relatively new at the time and, compared to today, small and highly variable. Options, by contrast, were not only commonplace but sizeable in most cases and, because of strong corporate performance, valuable. In fact the largest segment of variable compensation for executives during this period came in the form of option gains. In short, substantial executive rewards depended heavily on shareholder-value creation.

This harmony among executive pay, real corporate performance, and shareholder rewards began to dissipate with a series of environmental shocks in the late 1960s and early 1970s. Tax law changes represented the first wave of disruptive influences beyond executives' control. Qualified stock options, introduced by the Revenue Act of 1964, became less attractive with the introduction of a minimum tax on option gains in 1969 and were finally eliminated altogether in 1976. While they were eventually replaced by nonqualified options, other forms of variable compensation, such as annual and long-term bonuses in particular, were also introduced. These other pay elements, while a substitute for options, were not contingent on shareholder-value creation and in most cases were inimical to it.

Performance in the Seventies

The second major environmental shock of the 1970s was, of course, the tenfold rise in crude oil prices and the consequent surge in worldwide inflation, which translated at the corporate level into a dramatic rise in the cost of capital. It was at this point that the performance side of the equation began to go sour, as real returns failed to match the cost of equity capital (Figure 2). Pinned in on both sides by depressed markets, and the higher cost of new productive investment, most companies could find little rationale for pursuing long-term investment strategies. It was perhaps no surprise, then, that both shareholder value and the average market value of common stock declined in real terms, by 10.5 percent and 36 percent respectively (Figure 3). All these signals of weakened corporate performance implicitly boosted the attractiveness of alternative investments to common stock, such as treasury bills, money markets, and oil and gas ventures.

Executives who ascribed the plunging value of their companies' stocks to "vagaries of the marketplace" and held up their earnings growth as a defense were apparently unaware that for listed companies, in general, real (deflated) ROE— not EPS growth—has all along been the principal performance factor determining market-to-book ratios. Growth alone did not ensure premium market values. However, those companies whose equity and assets grew at high ROEs were awarded premiums in market-to-book values, while companies whose equity and assets grew at low returns were penalized in terms of those values.

This relationship between ROE and market value was, to be sure, somewhat obscured by the fact that real earnings in the 1956 to 1972 period moved roughly in the same direction as deflated ROE and the price/book ratio, although often

Figure 2. The High Cost of Doing Business.

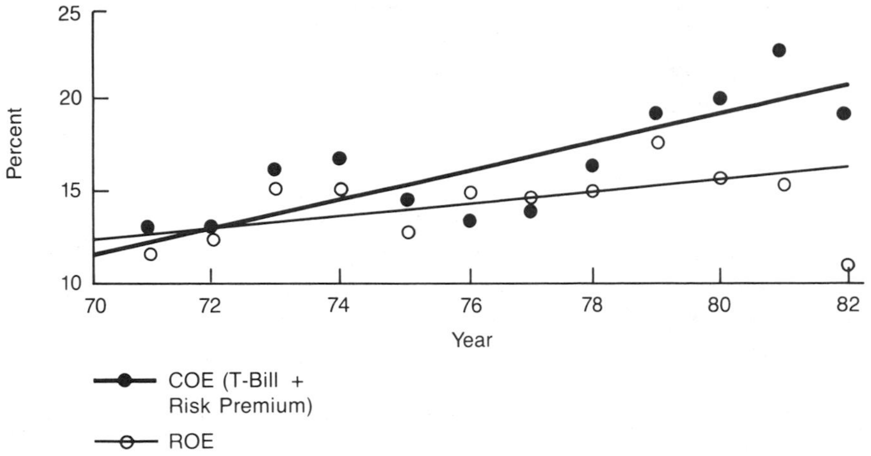

Sources: S&P 400; U.S. Dept. of Commerce Statistics.

Figure 3. Shareholder Value and Market Price Trends.

Sources: S&P 400; GNP Deflator.

at different rates (Figure 4). In 1973, however, the coincident movement of earnings and price/book ratios came to an abrupt halt, while the parallel movement of market-to-book values and ROE continued.

The validity of this empirical relationship between ROE and market/book is seen in the various industry segments examined in the Booz•Allen study; two examples in Figure 5. Among major communications companies and pharmaceuticals producers, the correlation between market/book and ROE has been significant, while the correlation between market/book and earnings per share growth has

Figure 4. Market Value Indicators: ROE vs. EPS.

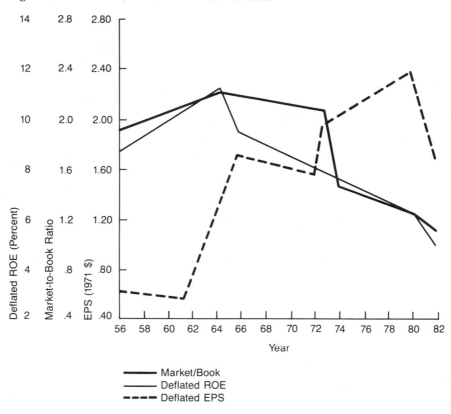

been practically nil. The additional message of Figure 5 is the value of ROE as an intra-industry, comparative measure of performance: Companies above the line benefit from significant market premiums related to long-term ROE performance, while the stock of companies below the line sells at a discount.

Compensation Responses in the 1970s

An executive compensation system has four principal dimensions:

1. *Size of awards*—the number and type of pay plans available and the (potential) dollar amount of each;
2. *Risk entailed*—the portion of pay in the total package that depends on real corporate performance and resulting shareholder-value creation;
3. *Performance required*—the use of shareholder-value-related strategic and financial measures to set performance goals that reflect the cost of equity and competitive realities; and
4. *Time*—the relative emphasis on short-term versus long-term performance and the precise time horizon used for measurement.

Figure 5. Performance and Valuation Patterns in Key Industries.

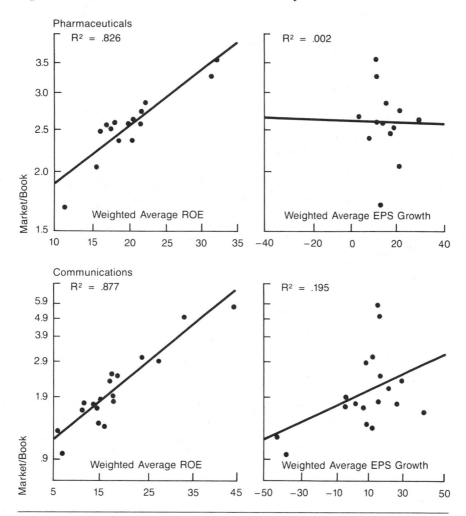

Note: ROE and EPS Numbers are geometrically weighted as follows: 1982—16; 1981—8; 1980—4; 1979—2; 1978—1.

By emphasizing the first component and paying lip service to the second, many companies have ended up with "pay delivery" systems whose effect is simply to deliver dollars to executives.

This is exactly what happened in the seventies. Corporations focused on controlling pay delivery—increasing award size and reducing risk. At the same time, popular wisdom held that corporations could not control stock price, hence the increasing importance of long-term bonuses in the executive pay package. These two factors, along with corporate-performance goals expressed in such terms as

Figure 6. Performance Measures Used for CEO Bonuses.

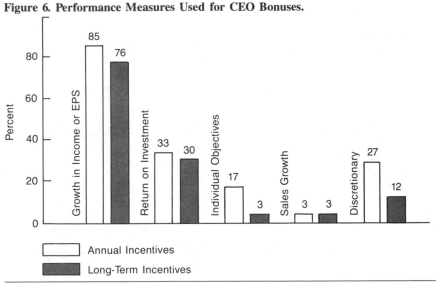

Source: 80-Company Study.

nominal EPS, resulted in significant increases in executive pay and a severe weakening of performance reward linkages.

By far the most significant development in the executive pay package during the 1970s was implementation of short- and long-term bonus plans, which built up the total pay package substantially. Today, more than 95 percent of the S&P 400 companies have annual executive bonus plans, whereas in 1971 the proportion was 50 percent. Moreover, annual bonuses are much more important today averaging nearly 70 percent of salary now versus less than 40 percent a decade ago.

For the most part, these bonuses have rewarded performance as measured by short-term criteria such as earnings per share (Figure 6). The pitfalls of this approach were not so evident in the high-inflation environment of the 1970s, when EPS was climbing steadily. Yet companies were in effect mistaking accounting symbolism for economic reality, ignoring the dynamic environment in which they competed and failing to ensure that corporate returns exceeded the cost of capital.

At their worst, bonus plans based on measures such as growth in earnings per share lead to the establishment of goals that have little or nothing to do with shareholder-value creation. They provide the temptation to pump up short-term earnings through strategies that may be detrimental to sustained high relative performance and the consequent creation of shareholder value. For example, the arbitrary reduction of R&D spending, postponement of investment in more efficient plant and equipment, and the continued support of marginal operations are all telltale signs of short-sighted management. Not surprisingly, bonus plans that reward these tactics also tend to discourage management from making the investment, portfolio, and asset-redeployment decisions required to enhance long-term ROE.

Figure 7. Changing Patterns in CEO Compensation.

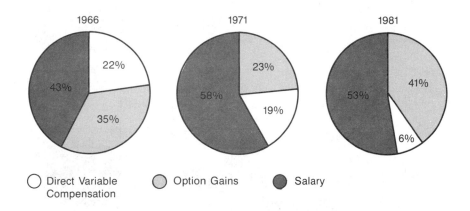

The proliferation of bonus plans was, in retrospect, not surprising, given the decline in the attractiveness of options due to changes in the tax laws and diminished opportunities for significant gains. By 1981, option gains—the most direct link to shareholder value—had dwindled to represent a very small part of actual compensation for the top echelon of management, a dramatic contrast to the mid-1960s, when options produced one-third of CEO rewards (Figure 7).

The significance of the decline in option gains is further underscored by the fact that there was no trade-off between option grants and direct variable compensation. Rather, new pay plans were added to existing programs. The possible effects of these multi-layered compensation programs became apparent by mid-1983, when the benefits of the bull market that had begun barely a year previously were toted up. Option grants that had lain dormant for several years were finally ripe for exercise, making it possible for many executives to take home their share of the personal wealth created by the strongest market surge since the Depression. Meanwhile, companies continued paying short- and long-term bonuses for achievement of the wrong performance goals.

IV. Executive Pay In The Eighties

By focusing on pay delivery instead of shareholder value creation in the 1970s, America's major corporations set the stage for a significant pay surge in the 1980s. A large number of today's executive pay packages insulate CEOs from the consequences of weak performance and low market valuation of their stock, while positioning them to benefit from any positive results that occur, as we are now witnessing.

Figure 8. Actual and Projected CEO Compensation.

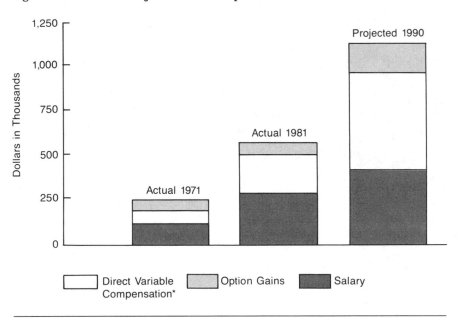

*Includes annual and long-term bonus.
Source: 80-Company Study.

How high might executive pay rise? If we extrapolate past pay practices and assume 5 percent inflation in the 1980s, then the *average* pay for CEOs in the S&P 400 companies would be about $1.1 million by 1990, as seen in the following pay profiles (Figure 8). Still a rarity today, the million-dollar annual paycheck will become commonplace and highly visible by the end of the decade.

Given the current trends in shareholder-value creation, the Dow Jones Industrial Average would have to be in the 1600–2100 range to justify this level of CEO pay. In other words, sizeable executive rewards will be accompanied by a growing pay/performance gap unless corporations adjust their present incentive plans dramatically. This means turning away from traditional accounting performance measures that discourage shareholder-value creation and toward the strategic, financial, and operating factors that drive premium market valuations.

Creating shareholder value in this decade will be a daunting task for American industry in general, but not an impossible one. Companies that are able to produce ROEs above their cost of capital and in excess of returns available from other investments, as well as sustained real growth in corporate assets or equity, will be those that create shareholder value. And it is those companies that will be able to justify truly high executive rewards. Once executive compensation packages are reconstituted to reflect the shareholder-value concept, the CEOs of winning companies will be paid like winners, while the losers will be paid like losers.

Understanding the empirical relationship between corporate ROE and price/ book ratios is the critical starting point both for establishing strategic objectives

Figure 9. The Strategic Approach to Executive Compensation.

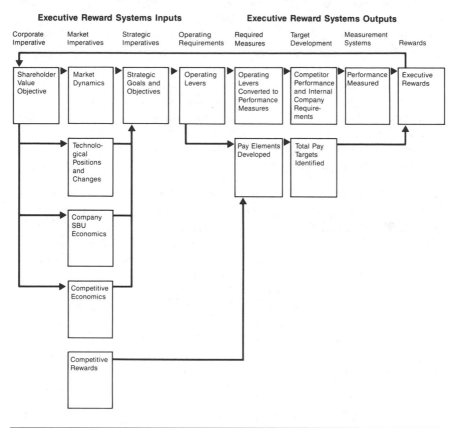

Sources: S&P 400; U.S. Dept. of Commerce Statistics.

of improving real corporate performance and for developing executive reward systems appropriate to such strategic management. Implicit in this approach, of course, is the ability of management, first, at the top level of the organization, to confront the major issues of portfolio and asset management and, second, at the business-unit level, to determine the strategic and operating factors that produce competitive advantage and therefore support corporate objectives and shareholder-value creation.

The process for translating shareholder-value objectives into performance requirements and reward programs is shown graphically in Figure 9 and explained on the following pages.

1. Establish a Competitively Based Shareholder-Value Target. As part of the corporation's regular strategy and financial planning process, top management must develop quantified shareholder-value targets which take into account the company's cost of equity and present competitive position.

To express a shareholder-value objective simply as an absolute figure, however, may miss the point. As a basis for performance measurement and reward, a company's objectives must be related both to its own recent performance and, even more important, to the expected performance of competitors in the marketplace. In fact, the shareholder-value concept has meaning *only* in a competitive context, since the market's valuation measures one investment opportunity against others. From a management perspective, those investment options are defined as companies competing in the same industry or in the same market segments. Given the commonality of the external challenges—be they economic, regulatory or technological—that such competitors face, the winners that emerge will be those companies whose executives successfully pursue and achieve strategies that take full account of these environmental variables.

2. Establish Real ROE Goals. Since market-to-book premiums are largely determined by the ratio of return on equity to cost of equity, it is critical that the corporation establish real ROE goals. This objective can serve as a basis for both long- and short-term performance awards. In addition it will allow management to simulate stock price appreciation and shareholder-value creation, so that the potential option gain to executives can be determined and established as a real, not illusory, reward opportunity.

The real ROE goal required to achieve a shareholder-value objective can be either positive or negative, depending upon the company's profitability position and, in the case of derived-demand industries such as oil and gas, the industry's position on the demand curve. In establishing these goals, weak companies should be required to improve their negative real ROEs, while high-performing companies should strive to maintain or, better still, to improve their positive ROEs.

3. Determine ROE Derivatives; Set Business-Unit Objectives. Corporate ROE objectives acquire true meaning only when they are translated into specific performance targets and strategies within the company's different business units. These will vary considerably (particularly in diversified firms) depending on the economics of the business, its mission, competitive factors in the market, and the relevant investment horizon. Furthermore, balancing strategic and financial goals and weighting the contribution that each of these factors is expected to make to shareholder-value creation in the case of each business unit is, by definition, a difficult task for top management. It is a necessary one, however, if the corporate ROE objective is to be met. The secondary benefit of this exercise is that it fosters acceptance of shareholder-value objectives among business-unit heads and, in doing so, sets the stage for business-unit specific executive compensation programs. Finally, it encourages business-unit management to pursue cash-generation goals instead of sheer growth, where appropriate.

4. Determine the Mix of Pay Elements. Once shareholder-value targets have been established and management processes adjusted to reflect a fuller understanding of the market-valuation process and resulting performance requirements, the mix of pay elements can be established, taking into account the various roles of corporate-level and business-unit executives. Under no circumstances should the mix of salary, annual bonus, long-term bonus and stock options be determined simply by competitive, industry-based surveys.

The actual profile of *corporate-level* executives' reward opportunities should reflect an emphasis on long-term tasks and results. Salary, a long-term or "career achievement" pay element related to asset-management responsibility (and not revenue size), should constitute a larger percentage of the reward package than is currently the case in most companies. The implication: a higher base salary for the CEO, as appropriate to this top executive's long-term role and responsibility for shareholder-value creation.

Design of both *short- and long-term incentives* is even more critical to supporting the achievement of strategic objectives. In general, *annual bonuses* for CEOs should be proportionally smaller than they are now. In addition, they should be designed to reward strategic milestones, rather than simply short-term financial results, and should be granted only after a strategic assessment by the board.

At the same time, long-term incentives should be emphasized more heavily at the top level. *Long-term bonuses* are appropriate if they are based on ROE and its derivatives—the performance factors that drive improvements in price-to-book ratios and shareholder value. Long-term incentives should be provided also for business-unit management. In general, more managers should be eligible for long-term incentives than is now the case.

5. Reemphasize and Revitalize Stock Options.   Stock options granted as long-term incentives are essential to top management's role in achieving corporate objectives. Options provide the most direct link between shareholder-value creation and executive rewards. This principle is the heart of our study findings: *The market is rational and predictable in rewarding or penalizing company performance in terms of market-to-book ratios; it reacts quickly to both positive and negative changes in real performance; and it maintains premium market-to-book ratios for companies expected to sustain relative high performance.*

Therefore, a new stock-option strategy is called for in the eighties. It will include very large option grants—"super" option plans—to those relatively few corporate and business-unit executives who can induce strategic performance, and the use of "junior" common stock plans that reward achievement of ROE and growth goals.

6. Unbundle Program Design; Construct Business-Unit Reward Programs.   The process of reconstructing inventive awards should be carried out for both corporate and business-unit management. The reward opportunity mix that is appropriate for a CEO of a particular company, however, should not be considered a model for executive pay throughout that company.

On the contrary, reward programs for business-unit executives should generally avoid reliance on "global" measures of performance such as earnings, ROE, or equity growth because such measures may not accurately reflect a particular business unit's mission. Effective rewards programs are based, rather, on specific measures critical to the strategic success of the business concerned, e.g., market share, product/technological developments, growth, cash generation, and cost position. Once rewards are focused on business-unit results, management can more effectively achieve its mission.

Within a *diversified company*, executives responsible for growth businesses should expect to see a major portion of their incentive rewards in the form of long-term pay elements based on those units' performance. For a business in a *turn-around situation*, a large short-term annual reward is appropriate: the business objective is, by definition, focused on a short-term horizon, and management's success or failure will be made obvious during that time frame. Finally, a mixed approach is usually appropriate for *mature businesses*.

The rationale for varying the pay mix from one business unit to another becomes even clearer when the time factor is taken into account. The length of the pay measurement period in each case should reflect a unit's performance cycle or investment/results horizon. For example, a company whose basic business is forest products found that matching its performance period to the industry's three-year cycle was an excellent basis for establishing the time horizon for its paper-board unit's long-term incentive program. In its power generation subsidiary, however, performance over the unit's five-year plan became the natural time element in the design of executive rewards.

7. Recognize Organizational Interdependencies. One word of caution: In some companies, organization interdependence is critical, desirable, and efficient. Unbundling compensation programs in these cases may be effective only if this strategy supports the ability of each business to meet its mission and the corporation's ability to reach overall objectives. Where synergies exist—for example, share costs, management experience, marketing strategies and distribution channels—unbundling must be accomplished without the loss of the real advantages that scale provides. In many companies, consumer products firms, and information industry companies are all typical of this phenomenon—the organization's decision-making processes, support systems, and culture all may affect the corporate-level target-setting process once particular objectives have been set for the business units. In any event, organizational interdependencies, which naturally affect implementation of overall strategy, must be understood and factored into the executive compensation program design.

8. Avoid Punitive Compensation Practices. Effective incentive/reward programs are typically found in corporate "winners," companies that have records of consistently outperforming their peers and whose objectives reflect a commitment to maintaining superior ROE performance or even enhancing relative position. Adoption of such programs is of at least equal importance among the "aspirers," companies whose performance is at the middle or toward the bottom of the scale, but

Figure 10. Results of a Performance-Based CEO Incentive Compensation System.

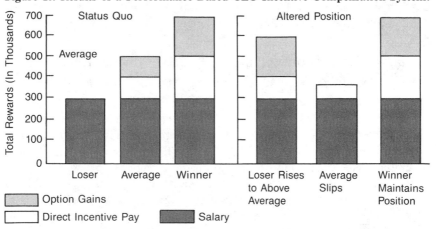

whose current goals reflect a commitment to improve performance and relative position. Even the "loser" has the opportunity to move up the ladder—if the company can meet the formidable challenge of, first, setting ambitious targets and, second, integrating strategic management and reward opportunities that provide incentive for attainment of these new goals. If it fails on either count, it will most likely remain a loser, just as the winners and aspirers run the risk of losing competitive position if incentive compensation and business objectives are not mutually supportive.

A graphic representation of the dynamic nature of such compensation programs is shown in Figure 10. Taking the status quo, we see that the CEO of a winner company earns more than twice as much as the CEO of a loser company, even though the base salary is the same for both. The pay differential is accounted for by incentives linked to true high relative performance.

In the altered profile shown in Figure 10, the loser has adopted effective strategies and adjusted pay opportunities accordingly. As a result, the rewards for this company's CEO now exceed the average. Meanwhile, the average company has slipped in performance, and executive pay here has fallen dramatically, as it should, given the link of rewards to performance. Finally, the winner has been able to maintain its position. Its strategies have continued to ensure its competitive edge, returns have remained in place, the company has rewarded its CEO, and the stock market has rewarded the shareholders.

There is a difference, however, between letting the losers lose big—as in cases where performance falls short of goals, or where those goals are unambitious in the first place—and designing a system that embodies more disincentive than incentive. To implement punitive pay cuts as a retort to weak short-term performance, for example, or simply to raise performance hurdles without establishing commensurate incentive opportunities will inevitably prove self-defeating. Competent management cannot be motivated nor shareholder interests furthered through such obvious disincentives. On the contrary, shareholder interests are best protected when strategic management practices are reinforced and when executives are rewarded for improving corporate performance.

V. Shareholders and Executives: A Common Goal in Shareholder-Value Creation

These guidelines for the eighties can be effectively applied in a variety of situations, regardless of the industry concerned or the company's competitive position. It is that latter factor that underlies our thesis that appropriately constructed executive incentive rewards, while not *sufficient* for shareholder-value creation, are certainly *necessary* and *critical* to this ultimate measure of strategic success.

Given the strategic targets to aim for, senior executives certainly should have the opportunity to realize financial gain in harmony with real benefits accrued to shareholders. Once commitment to such targets is confirmed, then inertia or criticism on the issue of executive compensation is no longer justified. Curiously, despite the recent trend of significant nominal pay increases for CEOs, companies have in fact historically been just as reluctant to pay high performers well—really well—as they have been to let the losers suffer the appropriate consequences. Winners should be paid like winners. In the pay-delivery environment that we have inherited, it will take considerable courage on the part of corporate boards and compensation committees in particular to establish such programs. But this is the only way in which shareholders and executives alike will come out ahead.

20

Performance Measurement and Management Incentive Compensation

G. Bennett Stewart III
Stern Stewart & Co.

Incentive compensation plans should be designed to build morale, retain good managers, and promote decisions that will benefit shareholders. Only seldom does this really happen. All too frequently investors get shortchanged by compensation plans that encourage management to achieve short-term, accounting-oriented goals having no direct bearing on companies' values. The framework we have developed is intended to reward management only when value is created for investors.

A wide body of research has demonstrated that the primary determinant of stock prices is the adequacy of the corporate return on total capital in relation to the cost of obtaining that capital. While other factors are important, and should be considered in any comprehensive evaluation of performance, management's compensation should be based in large part on the relationship between the corporate return and investors' demanded return. This helps to ensure that management wins the competition for capital, not just the competition for business. Growth adds to the value of shareholders' investment only when an adequate standard of profitability is met as well.

Stern Stewart & Co. has developed a combined measure of profitability and high-quality growth that we call "Economic Value Added," or "EVA." As the basis for incentive compensation, it focuses management's attention on the critical problem of allocating and managing capital. In our society, where savings rates are low relative to those in countries like Japan and Germany, and where real interest rates may be kept high by the prospect of large government deficits, efficiency in utilizing scarce capital becomes all the more important. EVA-based compensation plans thus help to achieve both a favorable allocation of resources and high stock prices for investors.

Another problem with most incentive compensation plans is that management gets shortchanged when the value of sound operating decisions and long run strategies is temporarily distorted by fluctuations in economic conditions. Simply stated, most plans today compensate the business cycle, not management. It is no wonder that management loses incentive, avoids taking risks necessary to remain competitive, and even seeks employment elsewhere. Our approach avoids this shortcoming by considering the stage of the business cycle and the performance of competitors in appraising performance.

Briefly, it involves a statistical procedure to analyze the effect of broad-based economic and industry conditions on the profitability of the company over, say, the last 10 years. This produces a simple formula that can be used to separate the performance reported in any given year into components attributable to: 1) general economic conditions, 2) industry-specific factors, and 3) the distinctive contribution of management. By so isolating management's performance, such a compensation plan is not only fairer to management, it also benefits investors by encouraging managers to adopt a longer time horizon for creating value. The practicality of the approach is indicated by the fact that in recent years it has been adopted by numerous companies in industries as diverse as airlines, soft drink bottling, and oil service.

Before discussing the major features of the plan, however, we look at the shortcomings of some of the most common management compensation standards now employed. The benefits of adopting an incentive plan based on the cash flow measures incorporated in EVA should be clarified by this discussion.

I. The Problems with Common Measures of Performance

The most widely used standards of performance are earnings, earnings-per-share, return on equity, and growth in sales or profits. From the point of view of the shareholder, all of these measures are seriously flawed. Management can achieve any one of these goals without necessarily increasing the value of shareholders' investment.

Accounting Measures Mix Finance with Business

For example, bottom-line earnings and earnings-per-share (EPS) are both subject to criticism because they reflect the outcome of financing as well as operating decisions. Managers can increase earnings through financial leverage created with preferred stock or debt financing. Such increases do not necessarily benefit common shareholders.

Consider that any company can use debt to increase earnings as long as the after-tax rate of return on investment exceeds the after-tax cost of borrowing money. Today high-grade corporate bonds may cost as little as 6 percent after taxes. Thus corporate investments, including acquisitions, that yield more than 6 percent will increase bottom-line earnings if financed with debt. This is hardly tantamount to meeting an acceptable standard of profitability.

The reason such leveraged earnings do not benefit stockholders is simple. Investors will not ignore the additional financial risk they bear. Bottom-line earnings will vary more over a business cycle, and hence will be riskier, due to the contractual obligation to meet fixed interest payments each year. The lower P/E multiple that investors will assign due to greater risk will more than offset any increase in earnings, and the company's share price will fall. Only if profits from the investment cover the full cost of debt and equity financing will investors benefit.

The Problem with Return on Equity

Like earnings per share, a return on equity (ROE) standard can also be manipulated through leverage. It should be the intent of senior management to compensate officers for operating decisions that add value to the company and not for financial actions having no effect on shareholder values. Another problem, unique to the ROE standard, applies to companies with convertible securities outstanding. As the company's stock price moves about the exercise price of the convertible, there will be a point at which it will be in the interests of the common shareholders to call the convertible and force conversion. In fact, it is a source of controversy as to why so few convertibles are actually called when this point is reached. One reason may be that the conversion to common stock will increase the book value of the equity, thus reducing the calculated return on equity. Again, if ROE is the primary standard of performance, the interests of managers and shareholders may be at odds.

Accounting Fails to Represent Cash Flow

A still more serious flaw of accounting measures of performance is their failure to reflect cash flow. This can result in decisions which, while boosting EPS, harm shareholders. Just two examples are the LIFO/FIFO decision and the amortization of goodwill in acquisitions. As is well known, LIFO inventory accounting results in lower earnings (relative to FIFO) but lower taxes as well. Thus, rewarding management according to earnings, rather than a cash flow standard, encourages management to pay higher taxes—this despite an impressive body of evidence showing that investors respond favorably to changes from FIFO to LIFO inventory accounting.

Many companies also regard amortization of goodwill as an important issue in undertaking acquisitions. In fact, some companies refuse to undertake acquisitions if pooling of interest accounting cannot be applied. But since amortization of goodwill represents neither a cash cost nor a tax shield, shareholders are neutral towards this expense.

There is compelling evidence that what matters most to investors is how much is paid for an acquisition relative to the (cash-flow) benefits realized, and not how the acquisition is subsequently recorded. Managers, however, may be biased against even strategically sensible acquisitions if their compensation is based on achieving an earnings target.

Accounting Misses Value

Accounting measures are especially misleading when earnings and value go in opposite directions. For example, under present accounting procedures, outlays for product development, market-building, and research are expensed in the year in which they are incurred. Accountants insist these outlays should be expensed because their future returns are uncertain. Businessmen, however, know that such outlays create value and therefore should be capitalized.

It is true that these expenditures are among the most risky that a company makes and that, in many instances, individual outlays do not pay off. In the aggregate, though, it is these outlays that provide the foundation for the future value of corporate America. Investors do not require every expenditure to pay off, but only that there be enough winners creating enough value to cover the cost of the losers.

To compute the return on their investment, investors relate the cash benefits realized in future years to their initial cash outlay. To be consistent in measuring performance, management should adopt the same "full cost" accounting procedure employed by investors. R&D and market-building expenditures should be capitalized, not expensed as accountants prescribe.

Using EPS as a corporate yardstick encourages management to shy away from the risks associated with new investment. It causes management's decision-making to focus on the near-term costs of value-creating expenditures without considering the longer-term benefits they may bring. The time horizon for payback thus narrows considerably, putting American managers at a disadvantage to their more patient foreign competitors. To remedy this problem, incentive compensation plans should encourage managers to focus on the determinants of long-run value, not on short-run earnings.

Accounting Misleading in Acquisitions

An even more serious shortcoming of EPS arises when evaluating acquisitions consummated through an exchange of shares. EPS will *always* increase following a merger with a company bearing a lower P/E ratio; it will *always* decrease after a merger with a higher P/E ratio company. Is it therefore logical to conclude that the acquisition of companies with lower P/E ratios will always benefit investors, whereas the acquisition of higher P/E ratio companies will always be harmful? Stated differently, can an acquisition be judged "good" or "bad" without knowing whether there are any operating synergies to be realized or if the premium paid is excessive? Instinctively we know the answer is "no," but why is our intuition right?

The answer lies in the fact that P/E ratios change in the wake of acquisitions to reflect either an improvement or a deterioration in the overall *quality* of earnings.

The dilution in EPS following the acquisition of a higher multiple company can be offset by an increase in the P/E multiple, so that the stock price need not be adversely affected. The multiple will rise because higher quality earnings are added to lower quality earnings. Add high octane gas to low octane gas, and the rating will increase. The same is true of earnings.

The opposite happens with the acquisition of a lower multiple company. It is true that EPS will increase, but it is possible that the dilution in the multiple will more than offset it, leading to a lower stock price. Investors care about *both* the quality and the quantity of earnings in setting stock prices. EPS represents only one-half of a two-part equation.

In conclusion, EPS is misleading as a basis for judging the merits of undertaking an acquisition with an exchange of shares. Companies that currently sell at high P/E ratios can make acquisitions that harm shareholders while at the same time increasing EPS. By diluting their P/E ratio, such companies mortgage their future in order to show higher per share earnings today. Equally questionable is the reluctance of the management of companies selling at modest P/E ratios to acquire attractive candidates just because of potential earnings dilution. This would happen less frequently if management incentive compensation plans focused on the real determinants of share value.

Growth Misleading

Operating managers frequently are preoccupied with increasing sales, both absolutely and relative to their competitors. Their motivation is to be the biggest and the best in order to win against their business competitors. Unfortunately, managers with a single-minded determination to compete for business may wind up losing the competition for capital that drives stock prices. Without considering the additional resources required to achieve growth, management may fail to provide an adequate return on shareholders' investment. Thus, rewarding sales growth may give management incentives inconsistent with investors' objectives. Stock price may suffer as a result.

Growth in earnings also is a tempting objective. Many of the most successful companies in America today have long, uninterrupted records of rapid earnings growth. Their impressive performance has earned them stock price multiples that are the envy of business men everywhere. It seems only sensible to conclude that rapid growth in earnings should be the first priority of management. However, it is the *quality* of growth, not the quantity, that is of overriding concern to investors. Growth without adequate *profitability* will reduce stock price.

A brief illustration will make this point. Assume that all we know about two companies, "A" and "B," is that they are expected to grow at the same rate of, say, 10 percent a year. At this stage, it is a silly question to ask which company, "A" or "B," is more valuable. Obviously, we expect them both to sell at the same price.

With a single additional piece of information, we can conclude that "B" is more valuable than "A." Suppose we are told that "B" requires relatively little investment in new capital to sustain its growth, whereas "A" requires a substantial amount of new investment each year to keep its earnings growing. "B" sells at the higher price and P/E because it requires less capital to produce the same stream of earnings as "A." Stated differently, "B" sells at a higher price because it is able to earn a higher rate of return on capital than "A."

The Return on Total Capital

The best indicator of the investment quality of any company, then, is its rate of return on total capital. This answers the first question influential investors ask of management: "What am I getting out of the business relative to what has been put in over time?" The more successful a company is at earning high returns on capital, measured in relevant cash-flow terms, the greater will be the value of its shares.

In addition, by calculating the return on the *total* amount of debt and equity capital employed, this procedure eliminates biases introduced by changes in the financial structure of the company or by changes in interest rates. And by reversing non-cash charges to earnings, and by capitalizing all value-building expenditures, this measure of performance will be unaffected by goodwill amortization or by accounting expenses for R&D and marketing.

By comparing the return on capital with the cost of capital, management can determine whether it has been successful in adding value to shareholders' investment. The cost of capital can be interpreted as the *total* return that debt and equity investors collectively require for accepting the (operating and financial) risk inherent in the company's securities. Management should be responsible for earning at least this return because investors expect to do just as well by investing in a diversified portfolio of other companies' securities having similar risk.

II. Economic Value Added

Because the spread between the return on capital and the cost of capital is a major determinant of share prices, our recommended incentive compensation system uses this as the primary indicator of management's performance. Our compensation framework also encourages management to grow the company, but not by sacrificing required profitability. This is done by calculating a measure called "Economic Value Added," a procedure that involves multiplying the spread between the return on capital and the cost of capital by the amount of capital management has investment in the business.

Economic Value Added is equal to the difference between the level of earnings management achieves and the level of earnings investors require as compensation for bearing risk. More formally, it is calculated as follows:

$$\text{EVA} = (\text{Return on Capital} - \text{Cost of Capital}) \times \text{Average Total Capital}$$

If the return on total capital is less than the cost of capital, EVA will be negative, providing an indication that the capital could have been more productively deployed elsewhere. If the return is greater than the cost of capital, EVA will be positive.

This means that management has been able to create value for investors by satisfying customers' needs more efficiently and creatively than their competitors.

There is a direct link between EVA and share price. Investors will bid share prices to a premium or discount to the value of capital employed that is equal to the present value of anticipated future EVA. Companies like Hewlett-Packard, Johnson & Johnson, and Procter & Gamble sell at premium prices because their managements have demonstrated an ability to invest funds to earn attractive rewards for investors. On the other hand, steel companies justifiably sell at discounts to the replacement value of assets employed because management is incapable of earning a sufficient return. EVA and share prices thus go hand-in-hand to motivate the proper allocation and management of capital.

To be more specific, management is provided with three important incentives when the goal is to increase EVA. These are: 1) to improve the efficiency of existing capital employed, 2) to commit new capital to projects where the rate of return exceeds the cost of capital, and 3) to liquidate and redeploy capital from underperforming operations. These important incentives are missing, in large part, from all of the more commonly-employed techniques for evaluating management performance.

It may appear that strategic objectives such as the attainment of a high market share, or the development of high quality products, are not recognized in EVA. In fact, these achievements will be rewarded through EVA provided their returns outweigh their costs. In our framework, goals relating to the competition for business are not ends in and of themselves, but are subordinate to the generation of value—that is, the competition for capital. Consequently, management is provided with an incentive to formulate strategic plans that will be highly regarded by the investment community.

Turnaround Situations

In the application of these principles there are special cases that will require additional adjustments. As an example, consider a "turnaround situation"—one which is characterized by low profitability, not just at the present time, but for several years prior. In this case, a straightforward calculation of EVA will always result in a judgement of inadequate performance, and a low or perhaps non-existent bonus for several years. Under such conditions, the question becomes how to motivate a talented manager to take on the challenge of bringing an underperforming division up to an adequate standard of profitability.

The best method of compensation in "turnaround" situations is to reward managers on the basis of the *change* in EVA over a pre-determined period of time. Thus, if the current year's EVA is negative, but is less negative than the prior year's, this constitutes an improvement in performance that should be rewarded. In this way, new management is not penalized for inheriting the problems created by past decisions, and is compensated for achieving progress towards reaching the benchmark standard (the cost of capital). In addition, the manager can be required to break even in EVA within, say, five years.

Compensation based on the change in EVA is also appropriate for an overperforming division. In this case, the present manager should not be rewarded for benefits derived from prior decisions, but only for *additional* value created for investors in future years. Last, for the more normal situation, where a division or company is earning a return just about equal to its cost of capital, the unadjusted measure of EVA would be the appropriate measure for setting incentive compensation awards.

III. The Effect of Factors Beyond Management's Control

In reviewing the adequacy of EVA it may also be important to give consideration to prevailing conditions, both in the economy and in the company's industry. To the extent that these conditions are beyond management's control, management should not be penalized (or rewarded) for returns due specifically to such external factors. Instead, management should be required to perform better in good years, so as to offset the inevitable shortfall incurred during poor years. Only in this way will incentive compensation reward good performance, not good luck.

A major shortcoming of almost all incentive plans we have reviewed is that they require the attainment of some fixed standard. On an annual basis the standard generally is established in a budget prepared before the year has begun. In today's volatile economic climate there is no guarantee that the economic conditions contemplated in the budget will materialize. Variance from budget then measures the accuracy of management's budget forecast rather than the quality of management per se. If the economy sours midway into a year, management is apt to lose all motivation once they realize their bonus is unattainable for reasons beyond their control. Most managers will simply write the entire year off, while the truly outstanding ones may be inclined to seek employment elsewhere.

Even when the bonus is tied to the attainment of strategic objectives stretching out over several years, there is no assurance that the time span will begin and end with comparable business conditions. For example, a five-year incentive plan that expired in 1982 would have begun in the expansionary year of 1977 and ended in a recession year. Any improvement in the company's strategic condition over that period would have been buried in the business cycle. (In fact the vice chairman of a major electrical equipment manufacturer told us that this turn of events was creating a severe morale problem among senior operating managers who received no long-range incentive bonus in the previous year, even though they had unquestionably contributed to the company's success over the past five years.) With the great uncertainty over where interest rates, inflation, and economic growth are heading, it becomes even more crucial to design long-range incentive plans that are flexible enough to accommodate unforeseeable changes in business conditions.

21

The Motives and Methods of Corporate Restructuring

G. Bennett Stewart III
Stern Stewart & Co.

David M. Glassman
Stern Stewart & Co.

There can be no doubt that the restructuring boom has richly rewarded the deal-makers. But, just as many investors rightly ask their stockbrokers—"but where are our yachts?"—you may be wondering whether the restructurings of the past decade have benefited our economy, shareholders, management and employees.

Do corporate "raiders," as the label suggests, pillage companies for their personal enrichment, leaving a weakened economy in their wake? Or do they instead promote improvements in corporate performance and increases in market values for all to share? If raiders are a force for good, can we learn from them any lessons about how to structure your company more effectively? You may be concerned, for example, that your company's "breakup" value exceeds its current stock price. If so, you may ask why does the discount exist, and could you do anything to close this worrisome gap?

These and other questions prompted us to undertake a review of some 300 financial restructuring transactions completed in the past decade. Our single most important discovery was that, in the vast majority of cases, corporate restructurings have led to sustained increases in both market values and operating performance.

While initially skeptical of such financial alchemy, and even more reluctant to embrace the explanations proffered by most investment bankers, we eventually became convinced that there were "real" economic explanations for the impressive increases in value and performance accompanying restructurings. Among the most important restructuring "motives" are these:

This article was previously published by, and is reprinted with the permission of *Cash Flow* magazine.

- Strengthening incentives;
- Achieving a better business fit;
- Sharpening management focus;
- Creating pure-plays that have unique investment appeal;
- Curtailing an unproductive reinvestment of cash flow;
- Eliminating subsidies for underperforming businesses;
- Achieving a higher-valued use for assets;
- Increasing debt capacity; and
- Saving taxes.

Our explanations are fundamentally different from those of most investment bankers, who seem to think that restructurings lift stock prices merely by raising the market's *awareness* of the intrinsic value of a company, without any fundamental change in operating efficiency. In view of the strong evidence of market sophistication, and based upon our own evaluations of restructuring transactions, we are convinced that restructuring does indeed change the way corporations are run.

Our research has uncovered some 20 or so recurring methods of restructuring. For convenience, we divide the restructuring methods into three categories:

1. *Asset restructurings* are techniques that change the ownership of the assets that support a business. These methods include the use of partnerships or trusts to save taxes, discharge surplus cash flow, and split companies into more productive business units.
2. *Business unit restructurings* can increase value in three ways: (a) by promoting growth through acquisitions, joint ventures, or offering a subsidiary's shares to the public; (b) by separating a business unit from the firm through a sale, spin-off, split-off or partial liquidation; and (c) by undertaking an internal leveraged recapitalization (a transaction which we will describe later).
3. *Corporate restructurings* change the ownership structure of the parent company through (1) issues of a new form of debt, preferred stock, or common stock; (2) share repurchases; (3) leveraged ESOPs; (4) leveraged cash-outs or leveraged buyouts; or, most radically, (5) complete sales, liquidations or split-ups of the firm.

To introduce our restructuring framework, let's start with what is perhaps the most controversial method of restructuring: increasing leverage.

I. Why Leverage Matters

The leverage ratios of many American companies have increased dramatically over the past decade, as the result of leveraged buyouts, share repurchases, recapitalizations, debt-financed acquisitions, and the proliferation of junk bonds. Has this leveraging strengthened or sapped the competitiveness of American companies? Felix Rohatyn, senior partner at Lazard Frères, articulates the naysayers' viewpoint:

> This [the high degree of leverage in LBOs] has two consequences, both highly speculative. First, it bets the company on a combination of continued growth

and lower interest rates, with no margin for error. Second, it substitutes debt for permanent capital, which is exactly the opposite of what our national investment objectives ought to be.[1]

While increased leverage has probably raised the level of expected corporate bankruptcies, we also believe that there are three reasons why the aggressive use of debt has been a positive force for the economy as a whole, a catalyst for many American companies to increase their productivity and value:

- Debt is cheaper than equity because interest payments are tax-deductible.
- A debt-financed recapitalization, by concentrating the ownership of equity, can strengthen incentives for investors to monitor their investment, and for management and employees to perform.
- To retire debt, a company may be forced to forgo unprofitable investment and to sell underperforming or unrelated assets or businesses to more productive owners; in general, the need to repay debt creates a compulsion to improve efficiency.

II. Tax Benefits

First of all, debt is a less expensive form of financing than equity because interest expense is tax-deductible while dividend payments are not. Start with the notion that all capital has a cost—if nothing else, an opportunity cost—equal to the rate of return investors would expect to earn by owning other securities of similar risk.

By substituting debt for equity, you will not change the overall amount of capital used in a business, nor the total rate of return needed to compensate investors for bearing business risk. But the implicit cost of equity has been replaced, at least partially, by the explicit tax-deductible cash cost of debt. Substituting debt for equity within prudent limits increases a company's intrinsic market value because debt shelters operating profits from being fully taxed.

This can be true even when the interest rate rises that must be paid on the debt. However high the rate on debt may be, the implied interest rate on the equity it replaces must be higher still because equity is riskier to own, and its cost is not subsidized by a corporate tax savings. Junk bonds, in other words, should not be thought of as expensive debt financing. Junk bonds are rather an inexpensive, because tax-deductible, form of equity.

Corporate raiders know well debt's value as a tax shelter. By highly leveraging their targets, they are able to capitalize the value of pre-tax instead of after-tax profits:

'Accountants just assume taxes have to be paid,' says Mario J. Gabelli, a money manager, buyout specialist, and aficionado of cash flow analysis long before it was fashionable. 'But you don't have to pay taxes . . . Remember you're an owner-investor, not a passive shareholder, and you have control of the cash. You don't care about profit. So you take on a bundle of debt and devote the

---

1. "On a Buyout Binge and a Takeover Tear," *The Wall Street Journal* (May 18, 1984).

cash flow more towards servicing the debt than to producing taxable profits. And as you pay down the debt, your equity in the company automatically grows.'[2]

We frequently encounter chief financial officers who, though they acknowledge the tax advantage of debt, argue against its use because they do not "need" to borrow money. They point out that their companies already generate more cash than they can productively invest; so, for them, borrowing money is unnecessary. We think this view is mistaken. In order to take full advantage of the tax benefit of debt, a company should borrow if it is able to, not because it needs to. In fact, *the less a company needs to raise capital to finance expansion, the more money it should borrow.*

Instead, it is those companies that need to raise new capital that should shun debt, preferring equity to preserve financing flexibility. For Apple Computer, for example, the need to fund technological innovation and market expansion is so much more important than saving taxes that the company quite rightly borrows no money whatsoever: equity supports Apple's growth. It is ironic but true that the more a company needs money to finance a wealth of attractive new investment opportunities, the less money it should borrow.

But when a company has surplus cash flow, making it easy to service debt, new debt should be raised to take advantage of the tax shelter it provides. Raising debt is advisable in these circumstances even if the proceeds are used just to retire common shares.

A leveraged buyout carries this premise to its logical extreme. The classic LBO candidate is eminently bankable precisely because it generates a steady steam of cash to repay debt. Will Rogers apparently was right in observing that "bankers lend money to their friends, and to those who don't need it." Our recommendation, then, is to borrow money if you can, not because you must. Neglecting debt's tax benefit is one sure way for a strong cash generator to attract the attention of the raiders.

But while we are on the subject of saving taxes, why not convert to a partnership to avoid paying corporate income taxes entirely? As a flow-through vehicle, a partnership incurs no tax liability. Instead, the investors in a partnership are taxed as individuals on their share of partnership income. With the personal tax rate now beneath the corporate tax rate for the first time in memory, the logic of housing income-producing assets in a partnership is compelling. Why put assets in a corporation where earnings are taxed once at 34 percent and twice if distributed, when the same assets put in a partnership would have their earnings taxed just once at 28 percent?

There is a problem, however. Moving assets already housed in a corporation into a partnership triggers a corporate tax on the difference between the current value of the assets and their tax basis. Depending on how the conversion is accomplished, it may require shareholders to pay a tax. A decision to convert an existing

---

2. "The Savviest Investors Are Going With The (Cash) Flow," *Business Week* (September 7, 1987).

corporation to a partnership thus becomes a straightforward capital budgeting exercise, weighing the up-front tax costs against an ongoing tax savings.

Unfortunately, the tax code may be revised to tax certain limited partnerships as corporations, thereby subjecting them to double taxation. The value of the ongoing tax benefit must be discounted for this uncertainty, further tipping the present value calculation against conversion. But help is on its way. We can dress up a corporation and make it behave like a partnership. Here's how. What two essential economic attributes distinguish a partnership from a corporation? Partnerships are not taxed and generally distribute all cash flow to investors. The answer, then, is to lever up a corporation and use the proceeds to retire equity. The corporation is thereby effectively converted into a partnership while avoiding any up-front corporate tax! Interest expense now largely shelters the company's operating profits from corporate income tax. The operating profits instead mostly flow through as interest income to be taxed to the holders of the company's bonds.

Moreover, paying interest and principal on the debt raised causes the company's cash flow to be discharged, again much as it would be in a partnership. The equity investors that survive the recapitalization, like the general partners in a partnership, still have control of the firm. And yet, unlike general partners, the liability of these shareholders is limited.

In short, a highly-leveraged corporation can match the desirable tax and cash flow attributes of a partnership, while retaining the corporate advantages of limited liability and trading liquidity—truly the best of both worlds.

But, however important taxes are in making debt more attractive than equity, the tax benefit alone cannot account for the great increase in leverage in recent years. If anything, the reduction in the corporate tax rate would reduce the incentive to use debt as a tax shelter. The raiders have taught us that there are at least four more reasons to use debt aggressively.

III. Cash Disgorgement

A good reason to borrow money is to repay it! When a company incurs debt, the obligation to pay it back it removes from management the temptation to reinvest surplus cash in substandard projects or overpriced acquisitions. Like Ulysses lashed to the mast, management's hands are tied by its debts. Then, though the siren calls of investment opportunities may beckon, the company ship rows assuredly onward, avoiding the fate of the failed projects that litter the shore. Repaying debt need not entirely preclude growth, but with the cash flow that a company internally generates dedicated to retiring debt, expansion must be financed with new capital, subjecting management's investment plans to the discipline of a market test.

The Standard Oil Company of Ohio ("SOHIO") provides a good example of the "reinvestment risk" that corporations impose on their stockholders. SOHIO for many years was a sleepy regional refiner and marketer of oil. After finding extensive oil reserves on the Alaskan north slope, it became an enormously profitable cash cow. Curiously, SOHIO sold for a depressed price-to-earnings ratio, even though it earned a very high return on equity and sold for the highest price-to-book ratio of any of the major oil companies.

How do we account for that? The high return on equity and price-to-book ratio resulted from SOHIO's successful investments. Value had unquestionably been added to the capital that SOHIO had invested in Alaska. The low price-to-earnings ratio signalled the market's lack of confidence in SOHIO's future profitability. In fact, it resulted from a downright fear that the flood of cash from the North Slope would be wasted in SOHIO's basic businesses or in unjustifiable premiums for acquisitions.

SOHIO justified investors' fears by choosing both downhill paths. Management splurged on costly oil forays (of which the dry-as-a-prune Mukluk well is but one prominent example), bought extensive mining reserves at inflated prices, and made the exceedingly expensive ($1.77 billion) and highly suspect acquisition of Kennecott, the copper company. The results of SOHIO's capital investments were so bad that British Petroleum, SOHIO's part owner, let go SOHIO's chairman and brought in a new team to reverse the company's misfortunes.

But why single out SOHIO when almost all the major oil companies have made similar blunders (Exxon with it office systems venture and Reliance Electric acquisition, Mobil with Montgomery Ward, ARCO with Anaconda, and so on)? It's just human nature to spend money when you get your hands on it.

Nevertheless, it is a fundamental tenet of corporate finance that the wisdom of making an investment does *not* depend on whether funding comes from inside or outside the company. Even if internal cash flow finances growth, those funds could just as well have been repatriated to investors and then explicitly raised. Internalizing the cost of capital does not avoid it. In practice, however, the inclination to invest is more highly related to the availability of cash than to the presence of attractive uses.

Why is this textbook lesson so widely ignored? The answer lies in reasons of great importance to senior management and of grave concern to investors. A large and growing company is more powerful and prestigious (and, in the past, was less vulnerable to takeover before junk bond financing became available) than a small, contracting one. Moreover, a diversified company is more stable than one reliant on a single business, and can justify a corporate bureaucracy with no direct operating responsibility or accountability. And, as Professor Michael Jensen has observed, middle level managers also are inclined to root for expansion if it creates new senior management positions to be filled.[3] For all these reasons, most companies prefer to reinvest cash flow rather than to pay it out.

Consider the case of Ford, which (at the time of this writing), after two years of record profits, now sits on top of over $9 billion in cash and securities.

---

3. "How to Detect a Prime Takeover Target," *The New York Times* (March 9, 1986).

Where will Ford pounce? The stock markets buzz almost daily with rumors about takeover plays by Ford, which openly says it wants to buy companies to offset the auto industry's cyclical swings. In recent months, Boeing, Lockheed, and Singer have been rumored targets.[4]

While it is easy to see the benefits diversification may bring to Ford's senior managers and employees (to say nothing of its investment bankers), is diversification in the best interest of its shareholders and our economy? Was it not the company's dependence upon the auto market that forced management to streamline production and to innovate in order to survive—and that is thus the cause of their present success?

By making survival less dependent on Ford's ability to compete in the auto industry, diversification will dampen the company's drive to make painful, necessary adjustments should hard times come again. Perhaps Ford can justify buying an electronics or aerospace company to obtain technology. But would it not be more efficient to license the technology, or form a joint venture, if that is the motivation? Most fundamentally, would an acquisition be made if Ford had to raise the cash, or is the mere availability of cash prompting its use?

Warren Buffet, Chairman of Berkshire Hathaway, states the problem in typically eloquent and witty style in his 1984 Annual Report:

> Many corporations that show consistently good returns have, indeed, employed a large portion of their retained earnings on an economically unattractive, even disastrous, basis. Their marvelous core businesses camouflage repeated failures in capital allocation elsewhere (usually involving high-priced acquisitions). The managers at fault periodically report on the lessons they have learned from the latest disappointment. They then usually seek out future lessons. (Failure seems to go to their heads.)

> In such cases, shareholders would be far better off if the earnings were retained to expand only the high-return business, with the balance paid in dividends or used to repurchase stock (an action that increases the owner's interest in the sub-par businesses). Managers of high-return businesses who consistently employ much of the cash thrown off by those businesses in other ventures with low returns should be held to account for those allocation decisions, regardless of how profitable the overall enterprise is.

Are we suggesting, then, that senior managers are tempted by self-interest to sometimes make decisions contrary to their shareholders' welfare? Yes, we are. Reinvestment of cash flow without shareholder approval is the corporate equivalent of taxation without representation. Just as our founding fathers understood that no single body of men could be entrusted to serve the public interest and created a system of checks and balances, so do many financial restructurings take away from management the power to reinvest a company's cash flow and restore that power to the shareholders. Management, in such cases, is then forced to appeal to investors to vote for its investment plans by contributing new capital.

---

4. "Can Ford Stay on Top?" *Business Week* (September 28, 1987).

Are we also saying that the market is more astute than management in making investment decisions? Yes, again. How, for example, can executives of oil companies know that drilling for more oil is the most productive present use of society's scarce resources? Impossible, obviously. The resources freed up by not drilling for oil would be invested in activities where oil company executives have no relevant experience—for example, developing the next generation of supercomputer, or in biotechnology. Yet such resource allocation tradeoffs are decided by portfolio managers every day when they choose which companies' shares to buy and which to sell. Moreover, the advent of powerful microcomputers, extensive financial databases and a growing body of business school graduates well-versed in powerful analytical methods has enhanced the market's ability to make accurate and rapid-fire evaluations.

Corporate managements, on the other hand, labor under an inflated sense of the importance of their products or industry relative to competing alternatives. They maintain a dogmatic optimism in the face of justifiable market skepticism and, perhaps most important, persist in ignoring the strong evidence showing that stock prices tend to be an accurate barometer of a company's intrinsic value (meaning that the upside potential is offset by an honest assessment of the downside risk).

For all these reasons, we are convinced that *the current wave of restructurings has much to do with the increasing sophistication of capital markets worldwide, and not the alleged lack of it.*

There are five ways that responsible management—or, failing that, a corporate raider—can return control of discretionary cash flow to the market and eliminate the discount on value caused by the market's perception of reinvestment risk. All five can be illustrated with examples drawn from the oil industry.

Repurchase Shares

The most flexible method is to discharge surplus cash voluntarily by repurchasing common shares in the open market over time. Exxon did this. Responding aggressively to overcapacity in the oil industry, Exxon cut its employment, refinery capacity, and service stations by a third from 1980 to 1986. It then used the cash generated by this move to buy back common stock on the open market, over $7 billion worth from June, 1983, earning it the following accolades from *Business Week*:

> In effect, Exxon has sent a message to its stockholders and the public: "Our industry is shrinking, at least for the present, and we think we should shrink a bit along with it. So we are returning some capital to our shareholders. They, not Exxon management, will decide how this money should be reinvested in the U.S. economy." That is good for the economy.[5]

Exxon's share return (dividend and price appreciation) since the buyback plan was first announced has bettered the share return produced by both Unocal and Phillips, where restructuring was forced upon management by a raider. Both of

---

5. *Business Week*, (August 19, 1985).

those companies had announced aggressive expansion plans despite declining fundamentals in the oil business, an approach guaranteed to put them directly "in harm's way."

Leveraged Share Repurchases

The second way to cure reinvestment risk, then, is to buy back stock aggressively and finance the purchase with debt. In such cases, the retirement of stock that may have taken place voluntarily over time is forcefully discounted to the present. Boone Pickens' threats prodded Unocal and Phillips to use corporate debt and leveraged ESOPs to finance a wholesale stock buyback, thus forcing recalcitrant management to discharge cash they otherwise would have used for unrewarding drilling projects or costly diversification.

Such leverage admittedly leaves Unocal and Phillips less able to withstand or capitalize on changing fortunes in the oil industry—one reason why companies that voluntarily restructure almost always outperform those forced to give in to a raider. *Business Week* concurs:

> Exxon's program of stock buyback makes a lot more sense than scrambling around to buy new properties. If the oil business comes back, Exxon, tighter and richer, will be in far better shape to benefit than many oil companies now overloaded with debt.[6]

Partnerships

The third means to give investors control over the reinvestment of cash flow is to house assets in a partnership. We previously noted that a partnership can benefit investors by avoiding double taxation of earnings. Partnerships can cure reinvestment risk as well. By law, the investors in a partnership must include in taxable income their share of the partnership's earnings, whether distributed or not. Because there is no additional tax liability, investors usually insist that partnerships distribute all available cash flow.

On August 25, 1985, the board of Mesa Petroleum announced a plan to convert the corporation to a partnership, explaining the rationale for this move in a shareholders' prospectus:

> Historically, the Company has paid out little of its cash flow as dividends and has been committed to a policy of replacing its annual product of oil and gas reserves through exploration and development and through acquisitions. The Company has paid relatively low amounts of federal income taxes because of deductions resulting from its expenditures. In recent years, however, the Company has significantly reduced its exploration and development expenditures in response to industry conditions, which will result in the Company's paying substantial federal income taxes if it continues its business as presently conducted.

---

6. Ibid.

> In view of the limited reinvestment opportunities available to the Company, the Board of Directors believes that the interests of stockholders will be better served if a substantial portion of its available cash flow is distributed directly to its owners. To distribute substantially greater cash flow more efficiently, the Board of Directors believes that the partnership form is preferrable to the corporate form.

Mesa's stock price soared from $14 to $18 over the period surrounding the announcement. Although the voice of the market is all that really matters, analysts also saw the wisdom of the change and applauded it. A DLJ research bulletin responded as follows:

> Properties appear to be worth full value in partnership form because the owners have control of the reinvestment as the partnership pays out most of its cash flow. Avoidance of the corporate tax and a higher basis for cost depletion add to the appeal of newly formed partnerships.[7]

Or, as an L.F. Rothschild analysis put it,

> We anticipate that future capital expenditures, while rather limited, will have a relatively high rate of return because of the selectivity available to management.[8]

Although partnerships normally pay out all available cash flow, this does not preclude them from expanding. Indeed, since becoming a partnership, Mesa has aggressively sought acquisitions, starting with Diamond Shamrock, usually by offering to swap new partnership units for a target's outstanding shares. Such expansion is not precluded, therefore, but must pass a market test.

Leveraged Acquisitions

Michael Jensen, cited earlier, has noted that debt-financed mergers also can assure investors that future cash flow will not be wasted. After a highly-leveraged acquisition is completed, the consolidated entity must dedicate the cash flows of both companies to repay debt. The result is much the same as if both firms independently had borrowed to buy back their own stock and then agreed to merge through a stock-for-stock swap.[9] A highly-leveraged merger milks two cash cows with one stroke.

SOCAL's acquisition of Gulf provides a good example, with Boone Pickens again playing the protagonist. Mr. Pickens' threats to acquire Gulf and convert it to a royalty trust prompted management to seek out a white knight. SOCAL answered their plea, paying $13.2 billion, all financed with debt, to acquire Gulf. Before the merger, SOCAL's leverage ratio (total debt-to-total debt and equity

7. Donaldson Lufkin & Jenrette, *Securities Corporation Research Bulletin* (September 30, 1985).
8. I.F. Rothschild, Underburg, Towbin, Company Research (September 25, 1985).
9. M. Jensen, "The Takeover Controversy: Analysis and Evidence," Chapter 1, pp. 6–31.

capital) was 10 percent and Gulf's was 20 percent. Afterwards, SOCAL and Gulf emerged with a consolidated leverage ratio of 40 percent, a debt burden still being paid off.

Our calculations show that in the period surrounding the takeover, the combined market value of SOCAL and Gulf rose over $5 billion, compared to a portfolio of oil stocks. This remarkable increase in value is attributable to three things:

- first, the value of operating synergies—the textbook benefits derived from consolidation, rationalization, economies of scale, etc.;
- second, the tax benefit of the new debt; and
- third, the elimination of a discount for reinvestment risk that had been placed on the value of both companies. Investors would be more inclined to fully value the future cash generated by both companies knowing it would be used to retire debt.

Dividends

The last method that commits a company to disgorge cash is to pay or increase dividends. Because most companies' boards are reluctant to cut dividends once they have been raised, an increase in dividends usually is interpreted by the market as a lasting commitment to pay out future cash flows to shareholders.

Arco, for example, increased dividends as part of an overall restructuring announced in May, 1985. Capital spending was cut 25 percent, annual operating expenses were reduced $500 million, and refining and marketing operations east of the Mississippi were put up for sale, freeing up cash for Arco to buy back 25 percent of its stock for $4 billion and to increase the dividend by 33 percent. Although Arco also took a $1.3 billion writedown of its eastern assets, investors reacted favorably, sending Arco's stock price rocketing from about $50 to $62.50, a gain in market value of $2.8 billion.

Although we have just demonstrated how increasing dividends increased market value as part of an overall restructuring, increasing dividends is usually a less desirable method for distributing cash. For one thing, it is not tax effective. From the company's viewpoint, dividends are less attractive than interest payments because they are not tax deductible. Investors also generally prefer a share repurchase program to receiving dividends for the following reasons: receiving dividends is compulsory but selling shares is voluntary; a capital gain from a stock sale can be offset by capital losses, and while dividends are taxed entirely, the gain to be taxed on repurchased shares is reduced by the investor's tax basis. Perhaps most important, though, the obligation a company incurs to pay dividends is not as compelling as servicing debt with its threat of bankruptcy (a topic we return to later).

Partial Public Offerings

Offering the public stock of a subsidiary unit stands in contrast to the methods that force the disgorgement of cash. A partial public offering binds the *use* of cash. Investors know that the cash from such a public sale will be used by the unit they have chosen to invest in, unlike an offering by the parent, where the funds raised must flow through a pachinko machine of competing internal uses with no assurance they will ever reach the most promising ventures.

Consider the case of McKesson Corporation, a $6 billion distributor of drugs, beverages, and chemicals that last year sold to the public a 16.7 percent stake in its Armour All subsidiary. Although Armour All accounted for only $90 million in sales (less than 2 percent of total revenues), McKesson's stock increased by 10 percent (from $60 to $66 a share) upon the announcement of the intended offering.

Armour All, however, is a rapidly growing (20% annually, compared to 10% for McKesson), highly profitable unit that McKesson could use to launch an expansion into consumer products. Able now to access capital directly, Armour All is more likely to reach its full growth. A public market for Armour All stock also helps establish a separate identity and sense of autonomy for employees, and enables the unit to attract and retain key executives through stock options, an important consideration in a heavily marketing-oriented and entrepreneurially-driven businesses.

Goodbye, Boston Consulting

These restructuring examples refute a planning paradigm popularized many years ago by The Boston Consulting Group wherein a company's mature "cash cows" were supposed to fund the growth of promising businesses ("question marks") into highly-performing "stars." By making a company self-funding and self-perpetuating, the BCG approach appealed to corporate managers because it circumvented the monitoring processes of the capital markets. In reality, the poorly-performing "dogs" ate the cash, while the "question marks" either were starved, overmanaged, or were acquired for obscene premiums.

Our analysis of stock prices has demonstrated that severing the link between mature cash cows and promising growth opportunities creates value. Let the "cows" pass their cash directly to investors. And let the "question marks" depend directly on the markets. Such a roundabout route is the most direct way to assure that value is created.

IV. Incentives

A debt-financed recapitalization can dramatically strengthen incentives. Raising debt to retire equity concentrates the remaining common shares in fewer hands. This increases the incentive for shareholders to monitor their investment closely and for management and employees, if they are given equity or an equity-like stake, to perform well.

Investor Incentives

The reason why concentrating equity benefits investors is first cousin to the theory that won James Buchanan the Nobel prize in economics. Mr. Buchanan wanted to understand why Congress passed laws that did not meet with general approval. The reason, he speculated, was that special interest groups successfully lobbied legislators to pass laws to benefit them at the expense of all taxpayers. When benefits are concentrated and costs are diffused, he believed, our democratic system of government lacks a safeguard to stop a minority from exploiting the majority.

A similar conflict exists in large, broadly-capitalized firms, this time between management and shareholders. Suppose that in an understandable search for job security, prestige, stability, and so forth, management made decisions that failed to maximize shareholders' wealth. While all shareholders would benefit from better management, the costs of waging a proxy fight or otherwise rallying investors would be borne selectively. Given the uneven distribution of costs and benefits, it may not make sense for an investor of small group of investors to shoulder the costs of opposing management.

But if debt were raised to retire shares, the equity of the firm would be concentrated in fewer investors' hands. With the cost of the value lost through mismanagement now more forcefully registered on each share, shareholders have greater motive to monitor the company's performance, giving management a greater incentive to perform.

To illustrate, suppose that a company starts with 10 million common shares selling at $10 each for a total market value of $100 million, and no debt. Assume that misguided management reduces value by $20 million, or $2 a share, so that the shares would trade for $12 if the company were properly managed.

Even this 20 percent discount might not lead shareholders to rebel. But if management could be induced, for example, to borrow $50 million to retire 5 million common shares in the open market, the $20 million of lost value would be spread over only 5 million remaining shares. The result—a $4 a share discount— would now be a full 40 percent of value, a gap which might indeed incite a shareholder revolt. Management, alert to the greater incentive that investors have to monitor their performance, would have to be more attentive to creating value for shareholders and less preoccupied with pursuing their own agenda.

For example, shortly after Sir James Goldsmith prompted Goodyear to buy back 48 percent of its stock, Robert E. Mercer, chairman and chief executive officer, said that Goodyear "will be more attuned to the stock price than before."[10] Goodyear reversed its wasteful diversification program, selling its aerospace unit to Loral and its oil reserves to Exxon for hefty premiums. Goodyear now concentrates on improving the value of its core tire and rubber operations.

A leveraged buyout carries even further the benefit of investor concentration. In these transactions, a broad herd of equity investors is replaced by a small group of "lead steers"—sophisticated debt and equity players—who act quickly and surely to restructure liabilities or replace management if such action is warranted. An LBO realigns management's interests with those of investors.

---

10. "Goodyear Tire and Rubber Sees Proceeds From Asset Sales Exceeding $3 Billion," *Wall Street Journal* (January 19, 1987).

Figure 1. Compensation Risk Map.

Debt-like					Equity-like
Wage	Lower Wage	Lower Wage	Lower Wage	Lower Wage	X
Defined Benefit Pension	X	X	X	X	X
		Interest Expense (Creditors)			
	Profit Sharing	Profit Sharing	Profit Sharing	Profit Sharing	X
		ESOP	ESOP	ESOP	X
			Leveraged Equity Purchase Plan	Leveraged Equity Purchase Plan	Leveraged Equity Purchase Plan
				Leveraged Cash-Out	

Incentives for Management and Employees

If, in the process of recapitalizing the company, management and employees receive an equity stake, the motivational benefits of equity concentration are further amplified. The accompanying "Compensation Risk Map" shows how restructuring incentives—moving left to right, from low risk to high risk—can create value.

No Guts—No Glory

The most secure, debt-like approach to compensation (on the far left of the chart) would be to pay a wage and provide a defined-benefit pension, a "no guts and no glory" scheme that clearly separates compensation from the success of the business. Employees are treated as bondholders and naturally they adopt the risk-averse mentality of creditors as they go about their appointed tasks. Worse yet, employees effectively become senior creditors because wages and pension payments are paid even before debt is serviced and, in the event of a bankruptcy, are senior to unsecured creditors. Such a compensation scheme robs a company of its capacity to raise debt.

Profit-Sharing

Let's move one notch to the right on the risk map and reduce wages (if not immediately, then over time), eliminate the defined-benefit pension, and introduce a very special sort of profit-sharing plan. This sort of compensation mix works more like a convertible security; one part provides the employee with the fixed return of a bond, while the other, like equity, is tied to the success of the firm.

Restructuring compensation this way accomplishes two things in one fell swoop:

- Incentives for employees are created for the first time and
- Debt capacity is augmented

What should concern lenders is where they stand in line for payout on a company's income statement (or, to be more precise, on the cash flow statement), not their alleged priority on the balance sheet. Conventional accounting statements mistakenly show profit-sharing distributions as an expense that is senior to the payment of interest when, in fact, profits are shared only after interest expense has been covered. Because lenders are in line for payout before profits are shared, but after wages are paid, introducing a profit-sharing plan in lieu of wages increases debt capacity. It is unfortunate that most widely-followed leverage statistics fail to capture the substitution of income statement equity for balance sheet leverage that takes place as many companies restructure compensation.

To the greatest extent possible, bonuses should be based on the profits earned at a decentralized level—activity-by-activity, plant-by-plant, business unit-by-business unit—and not according to the results achieved by the company overall. Only that will forge a direct link between performance and compensation. If bonuses are based on general corporate profits the link between pay and performance is so weak that profit-sharing has little value as an incentive.

Worthington Industries is one of a handful of large American companies that use profit-sharing to account for a major portion of employee compensation—at least 25 percent and in some cases as high as 50 percent. Management insists that its profit-sharing arrangement provides strong productivity incentives to workers. Moreover, by substituting variable for fixed costs, it virtually eliminates the need for layoffs and stabilizes profits in economic downturns.

ESOPs

Let's turn the compensation amplifier up another notch by introducing an Employee Stock Ownership Plan ("ESOP"), possibly in exchange for an even further reduction in wages. Providing employees with common stock in the firm through an ESOP accomplishes four things beyond sharing profits.

First, common stock represents a share in current and *future* profits. employees are given the incentive to consider the long-term consequences of their actions.

Second, ESOP incentives accumulate the number of shares an employee owns increases with each year's allocation, making their monetary and emotional stake in the firm grow over time. Profit-sharing incentives are unchanging. Nothing carries over from one year to the next.

Third, an ESOP can build up a company's debt capacity more effectively than can a profit-sharing plan because it is self-financing. By law, the cash a company contributes to an ESOP must be applied to purchase common shares in the sponsoring corporation (even if a company chooses to contribute common shares directly to the ESOP, the result is the same as if cash first was contributed to the ESOP and then used to buy company stock). An ESOP makes cash boomerang, carrying it out the front door as compensation and returning with it through the back door as new equity.

With profit-sharing, what goes out, stays out. Profit-sharing distributions, though calculated after interest expense is paid, need to be financed and may not necessarily be financed with company equity. Such financing risks are of concern to lenders and may limit a company from attaining its full debt capacity. ESOP contributions, however, are automatically equity-financed, a distinctive benefit that expands a company's debt capacity in a way that most conventional leverage ratios fail to acknowledge.

Fourth, Congress has granted ESOPs a number of special tax breaks that are not applicable to profit-sharing plans. For example, a commercial bank may exclude from its taxable income one-half of the interest received on a loan made to an ESOP. Because of this, ESOPs can borrow at favorable rates (usually less than 85% of prime) to prepurchase shares in the sponsoring corporation (a "leveraged ESOP"). The ESOP trustee applies subsequent cash contributions from the company to pay down the ESOP loan and allocates inventoried shares of equivalent value to the employees (with vesting over a three-to-seven year period of plan participation). Even with such a leveraged ESOP, it still is true that contributions to the ESOP are equity financed. The equity financing simply takes place in advance.

Accounting for the formation of a leveraged ESOP is identical to a share repurchase: the company's debt goes up (by the amount of the ESOP loan) and its equity goes down (by the cost of the shares the ESOP purchases). The ESOP loan is considered a company liability because the company guarantees the loan and the loan must be repaid with cash contributed from the company. It is what happens afterwards that makes a leveraged ESOP different from a share repurchase.

As the company makes future cash contributions to the ESOP, its debt goes down and its equity goes up, a double-barreled reduction in leverage that is unique to ESOPs. Company debt declines as the ESOP loan is repaid. Equity is written up by the value of the common shares allocated to employees—a value that matches the debt retired. A share repurchase, by contrast, is followed by just a single-barreled blast at leverage: debt goes down as it is repaid, but equity does not automatically accrue. The two-fisted unleveraging of a leveraged ESOP is perhaps its greatest advantage as a tool of corporate finance: a company's ability to recover quickly from a debt-financed share repurchase dramatically increases with its use.

Having just sung the praises of leveraged ESOPs, we hasten to add that their benefits often are exaggerated by overzealous proponents. For example, much has been made of the fact that, whereas corporate debt must be amortized from a company's after-tax cash flow, ESOP debt is repaid from cash contributions that are tax-deductible. The alleged benefit arises from confusing an operating expense and a financing flow. . . . (See the Appendix for a more detailed account, and qualification, of the tax benefits of ESOP financing.)

The bottom line on ESOPs is that incentive, debt capacity and tax benefits team up to make them an attractive compensation restructuring device for many companies. A careful evaluation of an ESOP's real advantages is advisable, however, before taking action.

Leveraged Equity Purchase Plans

Now, let's turn the heat up yet several more degrees and make management sweat. While there are many ways to provide key managers with incentives to create value, one of the most exciting new concepts is the "leveraged equity purchase plan," a method popularized by the Henley Group.

Henley was formed in early 1986 as the spinoff of 35 poorly performing units from Allied-Signal. It floated to an initial market value of $1.2 billion, a remarkably lofty value considering that the businesses comprising Henley collectively lost $27 million the year before. To what can we attribute this impressive market value placed upon Henley? To Chairman Michael Dingman, his management team, and the expectation of very strong incentives for management to create value.

Henley unveiled an incentive scheme so powerful that we expect it to be widely imitated. On October 10, 1986, twenty of Henley's top executives bought, at a slight premium to market value, freshly issued shares in Henley amounting to about 5 percent of the company's common equity capitalization. The executive team financed the $108 million price tag for the 5.1 million with (1) a $97 million non-recourse loan from Henley that was secured by the shares and (2) with $11 million of their own capital. Not only is this a boon for management, it also benefits the company's investors. Here's why.

Should Henley's share value fall after the plan in initiated, the executives may tender their shares to Henley in satisfaction of the loan and without recourse to their personal assets. Granted, management can lose *only* their $11 million investment. But are the other shareholders hurt because the loan is non-recourse? Not in our opinion. An additional $11 million will be in the corporate coffers and no additional shares will be outstanding.

Should Henley perform well, it is true shareholders face a 5 percent dilution in upside value. But remember two things. First, Henley executives fully paid for the *initial* market value of the shares by incurring debt (which must be repaid before the shares could be sold) and by contributing capital. Shareholders are diluted only on the *increase* in value.

And second, management now has a dramatically heightened incentive to create value. Does it not make sense to offer the baker a piece of the pie if, as a result, he is apt to bake a much larger one for all to share?

Some may ask what separates the Henley incentive plan from ones where management simply is paid to increase value or proxies for value. In theory, nothing; in practice, everything.

First, no matter how good are the measures used to determine cash bonuses, there is no substitute for a traded stock price as an indicator of value. Most performance measures, for example, capture the results of a single period, while stock prices capitalize the value of good management decisions over the life of the business.

To illustrate this crucial difference, suppose that sound management leads to competitive advantage, one improving operating profits after taxes by $20 million a year. If management is awarded a 5% share of the profits, the bonus pool would rise $1 million.

The share value of the company, however, is apt to capitalize the value of the annual profit improvement. If, for example, the cost of capital is 10 percent for our hypothetical company, value would rise $200 million ($20 million/.10). If management had obtained 5% of the shares through a leveraged equity purchase plan, the value of their stake would increase $10 million, or 10 times what they might expect from a profit-sharing plan. Owning equity amplifies the reward for good management decisions—and the penalties for poor ones.

There is, in addition, a crucial accounting difference between a cash bonus payment and a share ownership scheme. Cash bonus payments are recorded as an expense; an appreciation in the value of shares held by management is not. This remarkable inconsistency in accounting treatment is one reason, we believe, why many boards of directors feel uncomfortable about providing unlimited cash bonuses even in circumstances where management clearly deserves them. The preoccupation with maximizing reported earnings stands in the way of paying people what they are worth.

Another reason cash bonus payments often are limited is that they must be financed by the company whereas share appreciation is financed by the market. Though either selling shares or borrowing against them can compensate the manager who owns stock, neither drains financial resources directly from the firm. So, much like an ESOP, the compensation managers receive by participating in a leveraged equity purchase plan is automatically equity financed. This augments debt capacity, while cash compensation payments use it up.

Besides providing a powerful incentive to management, the Henley scheme also is an effective form of financial communication. Just by announcing their participation in such a plan, management issues a strong statement about their confidence in and commitment to the value of the company. When we encounter senior management groups who claim that their company is undervalued, we suggest it would be an opportune time to introduce a leveraged equity purchase plan. "Well, we are not *that* undervalued," they say.

The Henley plan assures more than just equity investors of management's commitment to creating value. It provides important safeguards for creditors as well. Lenders know that there is no surer way to guarantee the value of their debt than to provide management with an incentive to increase the value of the equity that stands beneath it. And, in a downturn, creditors must be comforted knowing of management's desire to recoup the $11 million of equity they contributed to the business. Again, published statistics on leverage fail to account for the crucial distinction between equity provided by management and equity provided by the market.

Chairman Michael Dingman explains his intentions:

> We believe that substantial borrowing and equity risk taking by key executives
> will create the entrepreneurial conditions that are critical to Henley's success.[11]

Dignman also commented that the leveraged equity purchase program was modelled
on the way executives participate in a leveraged buyout and was better than a stock
option plan because executives make an up-front investment and can watch the
value of that investment fluctuate with the stock price.

Henley is so pleased with the plan that it is making the same offer to key
executives of its subsidiary business units. For example, after a stake in Fischer
Scientific, a medical products subsidiary, was distributed to shareholders and began
to trade, top executives there were able to purchase stock in the unit under a similar
leveraged purchase plan. Henley's restructuring suggests that decentralized pay-
for-performance compensation schemes are coming into vogue for management
as well as for the rank and file.

Where does corporate leverage fit into a leveraged equity purchase plan? Corporate leverage can make it easier for management to acquire a significant stake
in the assets underlying the equity, an important consideration because managers
really manage assets, not equity.

To illustrate, suppose that senior management was willing to invest $1 million
to purchase equity in a company that had $100 million of assets. If the company
were financed entirely with equity, management could acquire a mere 1% interest.
If, however, the company borrowed $80 million to retire common shares, manage-
ment could obtain a full 5% stake in the remaining $20 million of equity.

Such a recapitalization makes it possible for management to invest an amount
equal to just 1% of the assets and to reap 5% of the payoff from improved asset
management. Corporate leverage, by amplifying the benefit derived from a more
productive use of resources, will multiply management's incentive to perform.
This suggests that combining corporate leverage with a leveraged equity stake for
management may be an extremely potent formula for creating value. The next
step forward along our compensation risk path does just that.

The Empire Strikes Back: Leveraged Cash-Outs

The next step out, actually something of a great leap, takes us to the "leveraged
cash-out," a powerful financial restructuring method that uses corporate leverage
to amplify the incentive that owning equity provides to management and employees.
Leveraged cash-outs have promoted such dramatic increases in market values that
they have proven very effective in warding off hostile takeover bids.

With the value generated by the recapitalization as an ace up its sleeve, management can up the ante to the point where raiders usually decide to fold their cards

---

11. "Henley Group Says 20 Officials to Buy 51 Million Shares in Unusual Program," *Wall Street Journal*
(October 10, 1986).

Figure 2. FMC Exchange Offers.

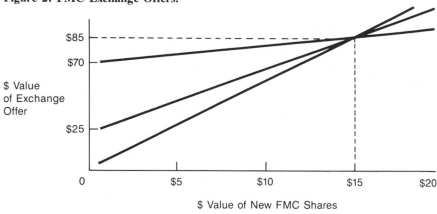

or not enter the bidding at all. Then, instead of a raider, a company's own stake-holders—its management, employees, customers and shareholders—walk away with a pot of added value.

The management of FMC Corporation, for example, sensing the company's vulnerability to an unsolicited offer, initiated a leveraged cash-out. As a pre-emptive strike to deter a raider, their restructuring following the masochist's creed: be the first to do unto yourself as others would do unto you. No competing offer was forth-coming, and today FMC operates very successfully as an independent, publicly-traded entity. Let's see why.

On February 20, 1986, FMC proposed to exchange a package of cash and new shares for each common share held. At that time, FMC's shares were selling for about $70. There were three parties to the transaction, and three exchange offers:

- The "public" received $70 and 1 new share
- The thrift plan received $25 and 4 new shares
- Management and PAYSOP received no cash and 5⅔ new shares

By accepting less cash but more new shares than the public, insiders increased their ownership in FMC from 14% to 41%. The recapitalization thus served to concentrate equity in the hands of management and employees, dramatically strengthening their incentive to perform (and to sell the company, should an attrac-tive offer be made). The heightened incentives may be illustrated by plotting the exchange offers.

The horizontal axis represents the value of the new FMC shares, and the ver-tical axis is the corresponding value of the proposed exchange offer to the three parties. The points of intersection on the vertical axis are the cash portions of the offers: $70 for the public, to fully cash out the current market value of their shares, $25 for the thrift, and nothing for the management. The slope of the lines drawn from those points simply adds the value of the new shares on top of the cash portion (1 share for the public, 4 for the thrift, and 5⅔ for management).

All three intersect at a common point reflecting the "intrinsic" value of the transaction. Note that, should the new shares sell for $15, all three parties would hold $85 of value. The public, at one extreme, has $70 of cash and one new share worth $15. Management, at the other end, holds 5⅔ shares also worth $85.

Should the new shares sell for more than $15 each, management (and the PAYSOP) would be the greatest beneficiary. For example, if the new shares sold for $20, management's 5⅔ new shares would be worth $113.33, while the public's combination of $70 plus 1 new share would sum to a value of just $90. Should the new shares sell for less than $15 each, management would be the greatest loser. This aggressive payoff schedule indicated that, after the recapitalization, management would hold a Henley-like leveraged equity stake in FMC. FMC's message to investors sounds a lot like Henley's, too. By voluntarily taking on a leveraged equity stake, management is expressing its commitment to and confidence in creating at least $85 worth of share value out of a company that was selling for just $70 a share at the time of recapitalization.

The message was heeded by the market: FMC's shares rose from a price of $70 to just over $85 as the recapitalization was first announced. Before the deal was sealed, however, FMC's shares nearly touched $100. Apparently Ivan Boesky, as a result of sound financial analysis (and some inside information), was buying FMC shares. To mollify the public and turn back Boesky's threat, management subsequently had to increase the public's cash portion to $80.

With nearly 25 million shares outstanding, the recapitalization increased FMC's total market value by $750 million ($30 price increase × 25 million shares), an increase in value that is net of $60 million in costs incurred and fees paid to professional advisors.

This remarkable appreciation in value can be attributed largely to the benefits of debt financing.

- Operating profits for the foreseeable future will be sheltered almost entirely from corporate taxation;
- With discretionary cash flow dedicated to debt service the risk of an unproductive reinvestment has been eliminated;
- Management and employees have greater incentives to perform, and more obvious penalties for failure.

Just how much debt financing was used? Gulp!! To finance the cash payments, FMC became *very* highly leveraged. In fact, debt initially increased from 25 percent to over 125 percent of combined debt and equity capital. Because the cash paid to investors handily exceeded the book value of FMC's common shares, the company emerged from the recapitalization with a negative accounting net worth. (Not to worry, however, because market capitalization exceeded $700 million.) How is it possible that such astounding leverage could be serviced?

First, FMC announced that the new shares would not pay dividends. By conserving cash that otherwise would flow to its shareholders, FMC augmented its ability to retire debt. Non-tax-deductible dividends were converted to fully-deductible interest payments. But far more important than dividend retention is the fact that every important measure of corporate health, except growth, improved after the recapitalization.

The carrot of incentives and the stick of potential bankruptcy spurred FMC's management and employees to exceptional performances. Widening profit margins and a more efficient management of working capital improved profitability. Free Cash Flow, the single best indicator of ability to service debt, exploded. The combination of slower growth and improved profitability opened the floodgates on the discretionary cash generated to pay down debt. The money that FMC disgorged will pour back into our economy to be investment in promising ventures.

An additional appeal of leveraged cash-out is that they avoid many of the ethical complications of LBOs. In a leveraged buyout, management benefits richly if the value of the company can be increased beyond the price offered to buy out the public shareholders. This creates a conflict between management's responsibility to shareholders and its self-interest. There is no way to get around the suspicion that management steals the company from the public shareholders in an LBO that subsequently performs well.

With a leveraged cash-out, however, investors participate in the value created after the recapitalization because they retain shares in the sponsoring company. Moreover, a shareholder could, if he wished, duplicate management's stake. In the FMC transaction, for example, the $70 of cash that a public shareholder received could be used to purchase 4 and ⅔ new shares (at the intrinsic share price of $15). When those new shares are added to the one new share issued in the exchange, the public shareholder, like the insiders, would hold 5⅔ new shares.

A public shareholder also could reverse the recapitalization. By using the cash received from the exchange offer to buy a representative slice of the debt issued by FMC to finance the exchange offer, a shareholder could restore the claim that shareholders held on FMC's earnings before the recapitalization. Now, however, FMC's original common equity is divided into a lower risk-for-lower expected reward, interest-earning claim (the junk debt) and a higher risk-for-higher expected reward, non-dividend-paying claim (the new FMC shares). Such a financial restructuring cannot change the risk in the underlying assets, nor can it force a shareholder, or society at large, to bear more risk.

The benefit of hindsight indicates that joining management, and thus maximizing one's equity stake in FMC, would have been a wise decision. Since the recapitalization, the new FMC shares have sold for as much as $60, giving the 5⅔ new shares a peak value of $540, certainly not a bad return for a stock that sold for $70 before the recapitalization was announced.

FMC did not escape the October, 1987 market meltdown, however, FMC's common shares by late 1987 were selling for approximately $30 each, at roughly half their $60 peak. The S&P 500 had dropped a mere 30% during that interval. Does this disparity challenge the wisdom of FMC's leveraged cash-out? Not at all.

FMC's shares fell further in value than the S&P 500 because of their greater financial risk, making the comparison grossly unfair. Investment risk must be the same in order to meaningfully compare return outcomes. To properly compare

Table 1. Summary of FMC's Performance ($ Millions).

	Before Recap	After Recap	
	1981–1985[a]	1986	1987 (6 mo.)
Revenue growth	(1)%	(8)%	3%
EBIT/capital	13%	18%	23%
EBIT/sales	7%	10%	12%
Working capital/sales	13%	3%	5%
Free cash flow[b]	$250	$320	$500
Total debt/total capital	20%	100%	90%
EBIT/interest	6.6×	2.2×	1.5×
Stock price appreciation	17%	62%	35%

a. Average over 5-year period.
b. Cash flow from operations, after taxes but before financing charges, net of new investment in working capital and fixed assets.

how well FMC's public shareholders would have done with and without the leveraged cash-out, we must assume that the cash proceeds received in the exchanged offer were used to purchase FMC's junk debt. Comparing the return on $70 worth of FMC junk debt (actually $80 worth with the revised offer) and one new FMC share with the S&P 500 is a fair measure of the wisdom of the leveraged cash-out. Because FMC's debt declined in value only modestly after the market crash, the risk-adjusted performance of FMC actually was better than the S&P 500—an endorsement of the leveraged cash-out.

That is all well and good for the fortunate public shareholders. But what about management who, by design of the exchange offer, were forced to hold just new shares in FMC? Of course the crash hurt them more than shareholders who could place the cash proceeds from the exchange offer into lower risk investments. But do not weep for management. Even the marked-down $30 value for the new shares they hold is 50% more than their initial $20 value. Moreover, the 5⅔ shares given to management in the recapitalization are still worth nearly $170, a 140 percent gain over the original $70 value.

The Ultimate Incentive

The most equity-like compensation on the risk map provides no wage, pension, profit sharing or ESOP. Indeed, the last step is the Lee Iaccoca plan: a $1 salary combined with a load of stock options. Terrific incentive, Lee. How one eats before your ship comes in we can only surmise.

V. Appendix: Qualifying the Tax Benefits of ESOPs

An ESOP is much the same as compensating employees with cash and then requiring them to purchase an equivalent value of company common shares (all without imposing a current tax on the employee, a benefit common to all qualified retirement plans). A company's contributions to an ESOP are tax-deductible because they are a real compensation expense of the firm. The fact that the compensation is converted into company stock does not diminish its cost, nor does the fact that the company's liability to repurchase those shares may be deferred until the distant future. The expected present value cost to repurchase shares allocated to employees, no matter how far off, is, by definition, the current value of those shares.

A leveraged ESOP is just an ordinary ESOP coupled with an up-front, debt-financed share repurchase. A leveraged ESOP entails much the same thing as:

- first, compensating employees with cash (a tax deductible expense);
- next, requiring them to use the cash to buy company common shares of an equivalent value from the ESOP; and
- lastly, making the ESOP apply the proceeds from the stock sale to pay down its debt (a non-tax-deductible financial event).

By sleight of hand, many ESOP peddlers would have their clients erroneously associate the benefit of deducting the ESOP contribution with the repayment of the debt when in fact, the tax-deduction arises from incurring a compensation expense—the granting of shares to employees. Despite appearances, it simply is not cheaper to amortize debt through an ESOP than it is through the company itself.

In truth, the benefits of a leveraged ESOP over an ordinary one are that money can be borrowed at a lower interest rate (but not that principal can be serviced more cheaply), it permits the company to contribute to the ESOP each year up to $60,000 per employee instead of $30,000, and maybe one more thing.

In the Tax Reform Act of 1986, Congress enacted a change in the treatment of dividends that many leveraged ESOP boosters claim is a sure-fire benefit. In fact, it may or may not be helpful, depending upon the circumstances.

A company can now deduct from its taxable income dividends that it pays on common shares held by an ESOP, but only if the ESOP trustee uses those dividends to repay an ESOP loan, an action that frees-up additional shares to be allocated to employees.

If the dividends used to repay the ESOP loan come from shares that the ESOP already had allocated to employees, there is a real benefit. In such a case, the company gets a tax-deduction without incurring an additional expense and without harm to the plan participants. The cash dividends that would have credited to the participant's accounts are simply transformed into company common shares of equivalent value. No harm done, but the company gets a tax-deduction merely for effecting this bit of financial alchemy.

If, however, the dividends used to repay the ESOP loan come from shares held in escrow—that is, not yet allocated by the ESOP to plan participants—there is an offsetting cost. In such a case, the shares allocated to employees represent additional compensation. The tax deduction the company receives on the dividend is only consistent with the expense incurred in granting employees new shares to which they would not otherwise be entitled. Unless the added expense is offset by the benefits arising from improved employee incentive, or from reductions in other forms of compensation, using such dividends to repay the ESOP loan may turn out to be an expensive way for a company to amortize debt.

Another problem many ESOP afficionados gloss over is that, no matter which of the preceding cases applies, tax-deductible dividends can lead to one of life's most unpleasant experiences—a minimum tax liability. By law, one-half of the difference between taxable income (after certain adjustments) and reported income is a tax preference item subject to a minimum tax of 20%. Deductible for tax but not book purposes, ESOP dividend payments give rise to just such a tax preference, and a potential minimum tax assessment. The Lord giveth and the Lord taketh away.

The IRS reserves one of the most generous of an ESOP's tax benefits for the owners of private companies. They are entitled to sell shares to an ESOP and to defer paying a tax on any gain (provided that the proceeds are reinvested in domestic companies and the ESOP owns at least 30% of the company stock after the sale). This tax code provision enables the owners of private corporations to cash-out and diversify their accumulated wealth without incurring a current tax, while providing for the eventual transfer of the shares to company employees, a nifty benefit to be sure.

In addition, private companies can establish ESOPs for employees of individual business units within the overall company, a benefit that generally is denied to public firms. Under such a plan, the ESOP trustee uses cash contributed by a subsidiary to acquire the subsidiary's shares (either existing shares held by the parent or new shares issued by the sub) and allocates those shares to the plan participants, giving them an incentive to improve the performance and value of the particular business unit that they directly influence.

A public company can establish an ESOP for a subsidiary unit only if the unit is taken public through an offering of a partial interest. In the absence of such a partial public offering, a public company is required to use parent company stock in an ESOP, a restriction that makes it difficult for a public company to forge a link between pay and performance as strong as that available to employees of private firms.

Index

The Institutional Investor Series in Finance

The Institutional Investor Series in Finance has been developed specifically to bring you—the finance professional—the latest thinking and developments in investments and corporate finance. As new challenges arise in this fast-paced arena, you can count on this series to provide you with the information you need to gain the competitive edge.

Institutional Investor is the leading communications company serving the global financial community and publisher of the magazine of the same name. Institutional Investor has won 36 major awards for distinguished financial journalism—including the prestigious National Magazine Award for the best reporting of any magazine in the United States. More than 560,000 financial executives in 170 countries read Institutional Investor publications each month. Thousands more attend Institutional Investor's worldwide conferences and seminars each year.